Explanation
Cities
Borough Towns
Market Towns
Stages
1755
Isis
Highworth
Wotton Basse
Marlborough
Kennet
R
Savernake Forest
Martensall Hill
Wans Ditch
Downs
Hungerford
to Newbery
BERKS
Great Bedwin
Hypnescomb
Chute Forest
Ludgershall
Everley Warren of Hares
PART OF HAMP SHIRE
Milston
to Andover
Haradon Hill
Amesbury
Avon R.
Bourn R
Stone Henge
Old Sarum
SALISBURY
Wilton
Newton
to Stockbridge
Race
Plain
Downton
Avon R
Lavington
Black Heath
Long: 50 from 40 London 30 20

Andrew + Joanna Taylor
(from mum + dad Rosier)

A BRUISED REED

Anne Steele:
Her Life and Times

Grandfathers, Broughton

Home of Anne Steele 1717-1769

A BRUISED REED

ANNE STEELE:
Her Life and Times

by

J. R. Broome

Together with Anne Steele's Hymns, Psalms and a Selection of her Prose Works

Gospel Standard Trust Publications.
12(b) Roundwood Lane,
Harpenden,
Hertfordshire AL5 3DD

2007

ISBN-10 1 897837 18 6
ISBN-13 978 1 897837 18 4

Cover Picture: Broughton House,
Her brother's house,
the home of Anne Steele
from 1769 to 1778.

Printed and bound in Great Britain by
The Cromwell Press Ltd,
Aintree Avenue,
White Horse Business Park,
Trowbridge,
Wiltshire. BA14 OXB.

Contents

PART I

PART II

PART III

PART IV

APPENDICES

Acknowledgements

Having come to Trowbridge in September 1959, to take up a teaching post at the Trowbridge Boys' High School, I attended the Strict Baptist chapel in The Halve. Among the people there was an old couple whose names were Arthur and Bessie Townsend. Arthur had been to a sale at the Auctioneers, Quartley Son & White, in Trowbridge and purchased a sack of books for a few shillings. Among these books was a first edition of Anne Steele's Hymns, in two volumes, published in 1760. When I visited his home in 1964, Arthur gave me the two volumes.

This occurrence led to an interest in Anne Steele. I took the two volumes to Baynton's, the Antique Bookseller, in Manvers Street, Bath, and they rebound them in leather, keeping the original maroon titles from the spine, milling the edges of the new leather cover and replacing the flyleaves with handmade paper. Now they were usable and I set about researching the life of Anne Steele and her family. I discovered that her grandfather [on her mother's side] was buried in the main nave of Edington Priory, that her stepmother, Anne Steele [née Cator], had grown up on Trowle Common, near Trowbridge and that Anne herself had been at school in Trowbridge in 1729.

In 1967 I reprinted, in paperback, Anne Steele's hymns as published in the 1863 Edition of Daniel Sedgwick together with a brief memoir of her life and family history, as I then knew it. There followed many visits to Broughton, Anne Steele's home village in Hampshire, where I met Ethel Davis, a member of the Particular Baptist Church of which Anne Steele had formerly been a member, and the local historian of the village, who lived to be well over ninety and died in 1999. I also visited *Grandfathers*, Anne Steele's old home and met Nita Bompas, a direct descendant, and Rev. Langdon, another relative living in the village. I was shown the original Church Books, dating back to 1655, by Miss Ayles, treasurer of the Baptist chapel. [These church books are now housed in the Angus Library of Regent's Park Baptist College, Oxford.] I remember finding the date of Anne Steele's baptising recorded in the Church Book as 9th July 1732, and being allowed to examine and copy extracts from these old records.

At the same time I visited the Wiltshire Record Office at Trowbridge and with the help of the County Archivist, Ken Rogers, and his staff, researched the seventeenth and eighteenth-century history of the Particular Baptists in Wiltshire from Sedgehill in the south to Erlestoke and Devizes in the east. In this I was greatly indebted to the late Dr Marjorie Reeves and her research in the chapter on *Protestant Nonconformity in Wiltshire* in Volume III of the Victoria County History. In March 1979 I came into contact, through the publication of my paperback, with the owner of the Steele family archive, Hugh Steele-Smith of Ilkley in Yorkshire. He had inherited a large collection of family records, diaries, wills, letters, manuscript poetry and oil paintings and had researched them extensively. I am indebted to him for his work and generosity in sharing it with me, constantly sending me photocopies of his material. He died on 29th December 1999 and was buried at Bolton Abbey. He bequeathed the larger part of the Steele archive to the Angus Library at Regent's Park Baptist College, Oxford. Other relevant material he deposited with the Hampshire Record Office and the Bristol Record Office. A copy of a selection of the Steele archive at the Angus Library is held on microfilm at the Bodleian Library and also in the Wiltshire Record Office.

About 1975 an archive containing Steele material was discovered at *Yew Trees,* Bratton, Wiltshire, the home of the Whitaker family, connected to the Steeles through Anne Steele's stepmother, Anne Steele [née Cator]. This archive came into the possession of the late Dr Marjorie Reeves, whose mother was a Whitaker. She allowed me to view the material soon after she took possession of it and gave me photocopies of it. Since then she has published her own research in a book entitled *Pursuing the Muses* [Leicester University Press 1997], which deals, among other things, with the poetry and letters of the literary circle of which Anne Steele was the central figure.

I have been grateful for the help of Stephen Pickles of Oxford, who has researched the Steele archive at the Angus Library and spent his dinner hours for many years in copying sermons, diaries etc. for my use. His work has been invaluable. I am grateful also to Mrs S. Mills, Librarian of the Angus Library, for helping him in his researches and granting permission to publish William Steele III's sermons and to quote at length from the Steele archive.

I am indebted to the Steele family descendants, who wish to remain anonymous, for allowing me to photograph and publish five oil paintings in their possession, being those of Anne Steele's brother, William Steele IV; Mary Steele (Polly), daughter of his first wife, Mary Steele (née Bullock); William Steele IV's second wife, Martha Steele, and their two daughters, Anne and Martha. Photography of these was by Neil J. Broome. I am also similarly indebted to the owner of the oil paintings of William Steele IV in his youth, and of *Broughton House and Farm* circa 1820 for permission to reproduce them. Photography was by Sebastiaan Hartman. Finally I acknowledge my gratitude to Caleb Pearce and John Kingham for their work with the illustrations and the text, in preparing the book for publication.

J.R.B.

List of Illustrations

Preface

An extract from the preface to the three-volume edition of Anne Steele's Works, published in Bristol in 1780, written by Dr. Caleb Evans, President of the Bristol Baptist Academy.

As the life of Theodosia [Anne Steele] was for the most part a life of retirement in the peaceful village [Broughton, Hants] where she began and ended her days, it cannot be expected to furnish such a variety of incidents as arise in the history of those who have moved in circles of greater activity. The duties of friendship and religion occupied her time, and the pleasures of both constituted her delight. Her heart was 'apt to feel' too often to a degree too painful for her own felicity [happiness], but always with the most tender and generous sympathies for her friends. Yet united with this exquisite sensibility, she possessed a native cheerfulness of disposition, of which not even the uncommon and agonising pains she endured in the latter part of her life could deprive her. In every short interval of abated suffering, she would in a variety of ways, as well as by her enlivening conversation, give pleasure to all around her. Her life was a life of unaffected humility, warm benevolence, sincere friendship and genuine devotion. A life, which it is not easy truly to describe, or faithfully to imitate.

Bristol, May 12, 1780.

The Advertisement of the American Publishers to the Edition of Anne Steele's Works published in Boston, Massachusetts, U.S.A., in 1808.

The Works of Anne Steele were published in England at different times. Two volumes under the title of *Poems on Subjects Chiefly Devotional*, by Theodosia, appeared in the year 1760, during the life of the author; a third volume, entitled *Miscellaneous Pieces in Prose and Verse* was published in 1780, after her decease, by Rev. Caleb Evans of Bristol, accompanied with a new impression of the preceding volumes. The editor of the posthumous pieces has prefixed to his volume a notice of the life of the author which in this edition precedes the whole work.

Boston, December 1, 1808.

Extract from the Memoir of John Sheppard, which formed the Preface to the single volume Edition of Anne Steele's Works, published in London by Daniel Sedgwick in 1863.

Unlike some other sacred lyricists, Anne Steele has found no biographers. Perhaps the current of her life flowed too smoothly to invite anyone to follow it. She founded no church, built no chapels, went on no foreign mission. She only wrote a few of the sweetest hymns; but in thus using the poetical talent, which she recognised as divine, she did that which exceeds in importance and value the works of many who have filled more conspicuous places in the history of the church and of the world. Her usefulness has far distanced her fame: she exerts an influence where her history is unknown; she ministers by many a sick bed; she furnishes the song in many a night of affliction. Every Sunday hears her hymns in many churches.... Men use her hymns who never heard her name, and many a one has uttered his penitence and desires, in language whose author he never knew, until he joined with her in higher and holier songs before the Throne of God.

The Cottage, Frome, Somerset,
February, 1863.

Postscript

It had been hoped that Hugh Steele-Smith of Ilkley, Yorkshire, the owner of the Steele family archive and a direct descendant of Anne Steele would write this preface. However he died suddenly in December 1999 at the age of seventy-nine. He was a son of Dr. William Steele-Smith whose mother was Sophia Steele-Smith [née Sophia Bompas]. Sophia was a daughter of Charles and Mary Bompas. Mary Bompas [née Mary Tomkins] was a daughter of Anne and Joseph Tomkins. Anne Tomkins, who died in 1859, at the age of ninety, was the eldest daughter of William Steele [Anne Steele's brother] and his second wife Martha [née Goddard].

Abbreviations

ASD	Mrs Steele's Diaries 1730-1736, 1749-1760 (STE 2/1)
BBCB	Broughton Baptist Church Books
BPR	Broughton Parish Registers
EHB	The Early Hampshire Baptists, G. Lyon Turner [1911]
HBBCW	History of Bratton Baptist Church by Dr M.E. Reeves
HBBCH	History of Broughton Baptist Church by E. Compton
HRO	Hampshire Record Office, Winchester, Hants

OBC	The Old Baptist Church, Devizes by R. Cawley
PRO	Public Record Office
ALRPC	Angus Library, Regent's Park College, Oxford (STE 1-14)
TGC	Twenty Golden Candlesticks by W. Doel
VCH	Victoria County History, Wiltshire
WRS	Wiltshire Record Society
WSRO	Wilts & Swindon Record Office, Trowbridge, Wilts
WSRO[BL]	Wilts & Swindon Record Office – Copy of a microfilm of the Bodleian Library, Oxford. WSRO Ref: 4-137039-000

Pen names used by Anne Steele's circle of friends

Caroline Attwater [Whitaker]	Dorinda
Gay Thomas Attwater	Florio
Jane Attwater [Blatch]	Myrtilla
Marianne Attwater [Head]	Maria
Mary Froude	Amanda
Sarah Froude	Sarrissa
Philip Furneaux	Lucius
John Lavington	Lysander
Mary Scott	Myra
Anne Steele	Theodosia, Silvania
Mary Steele [Bullock]	Delia
Mary Steele [Dunscombe]	Silvia
Mary Steele [Wakeford]	Amira
William Steele	Philander
Joseph Wakeford	Portius

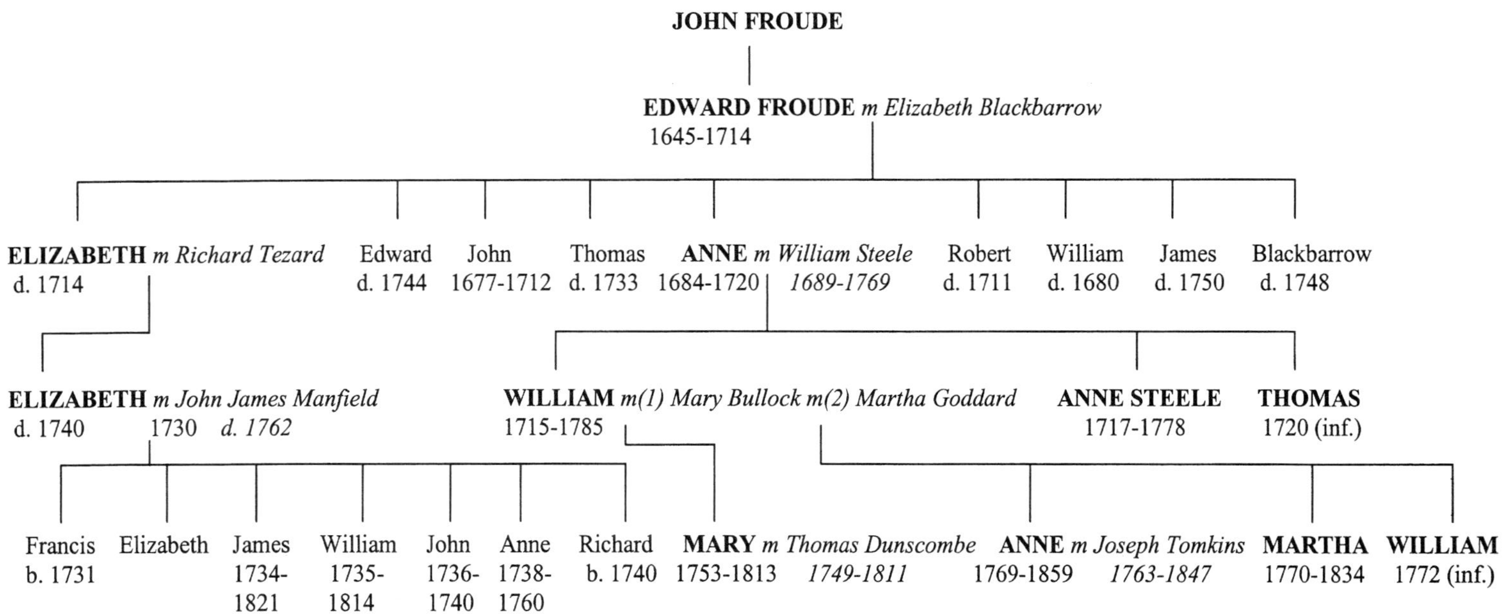

Figure 1: The Froude Family Tree

Chapter 1

An Age of Intolerance [1645-1688]

Anne Steele, the eighteenth-century poet and hymnwriter, was born at Broughton in Hampshire in 1717. Her father, William Steele, was a Particular Baptist minister and her mother, Anne Steele [née Froude], was the daughter of a Particular Baptist minister, Edward Froude. Both her parents had been born into the homes of a persecuted group of Christians, persecuted because they refused to conform to the Anglican Church in a day when the norm was 'one state, one religion' [una civitas, una religio]. The Anabaptists, as the authorities termed them, were a group of Dissenters that believed in freedom of conscience and freedom of worship. They did not agree with the traditions of the Church of England and, like the Brownists at the end of the 16th century in the reign of Elizabeth, they suffered gross intolerance from Church and Government for their views, views which we now accept as normal, but which in their day were regarded as revolutionary. As is well known, many of the Brownists separated from the Church of England, left this country at the beginning of the 17th century and went to the Netherlands, seeking freedom of speech and worship. Many eventually in 1620 crossed the Atlantic to set up the New England Colonies, founding the United States of America as a bastion of liberty.

The Baptists had supported the Cromwellian side in the Great Civil War, when Cromwell's government allowed a greater amount of religious freedom than had ever been known in this country before, though not complete freedom to all religious groups. [Roman Catholics were excluded because of the political involvement of the Roman Catholic Church in the reign of Queen Mary in the burning of the martyrs, in the Armada and the Gunpowder Plot.] This allegiance brought the Baptists no favours when the Stuarts were restored in 1660. As they were a close community and mostly meeting in their own homes [cottage meetings] for worship, the authorities were thoroughly suspicious of them, and regarded them as potential material for conspiracy against the Stuart monarchy and the Anglican Church. Hated by bishops and magistrates, their ministers were regularly imprisoned for preaching and like their well-known minister, John Bunyan, spent long years mercilessly incarcerated in damp jails where some ended their days. The aftermath of the great Civil War had understandably left the Royalist Government in a state of neurotic tension, believing that the country was riddled with groups of revolutionaries just waiting to remove them from power. Revenge was also in the air for the beheading of Charles I. Feelings naturally ran high between the protagonists, and when the defeated Royalist party led by their King, Charles II, regained control in 1660, they did not feel too generous towards the former victors. So in the years from 1660 until 1688 the country witnessed considerable religious persecution, and Anne Steele's ancestors, coming from Particular Baptist stock, found themselves in the midst of it.

The Froude Family

Edward Froude, her maternal grandfather, was born in 1645, during the Civil War, a year after Cromwell's victory at the battle of Marston Moor and the same year as the battle of Naseby. Where he spent his youth is not known, but on 20th March 1673 his father, John Froude, purchased

Figure 2: Sweetwell Farm (now demolished)

Sweetwell Farm [about 102 acres] in Sedgehill, a village between Shaftesbury and East Knoyle in the county of Wiltshire and on his death it passed to his son.[1] It is of interest that Sir Christopher Wren, the architect of St Paul's Cathedral [built between 1675-1710] and founder and President of the Royal Society [1680-82], was born in 1632 at East Knoyle, two miles from Sedgehill, and it seems highly likely that the Froudes and the Wrens must have known each other. It is also of interest

[1] Will of Edward Froude Jnr. 1744 – WSRO.

that in Edward Froude's will of 1714[2] a gift of £20 is left to mistress Anne Clifford, the wife of Samuel Clifford of East Knoyle. Samuel Clifford was the vicar of East Knoyle ejected at the time of the Great Ejection in 1662, when over 2,000 clergymen were forced out of the Church at the time of the Act of Uniformity. It is interesting that a Particular Baptist minister should be helping his widow in her old age.

In 1674 Edward and his wife Elizabeth were named in the Edington presentment at the Quarter Sessions for non-attendance at the Priory Church. He was by now married to Elizabeth Blackborrow whose family lived in Tinhead a hamlet beside the parish of Edington, with its Priory Church, beneath the Westbury White Horse Hill and it would seem that he had left Sedgehill in the charge of one of his brothers [his father John Froude had died in 1674][3] and was living in Tinhead. John Blackborrow [brother of Elizabeth] and his wife Anne were also presented at the same time. In 1683 Edward Froude was presented in the parish of Edington for non-attendance at the Priory and was designated 'Anabaptist preacher'. His wife Elizabeth and Anne Blackborrow were presented at the same time. By this time John Blackborrow was dead and in his will [proved in June 1682] had left his farm at Tinhead to his brother-in-law, including over an hundred sheep, four oxen and fourteen cows. At the age of thirty-eight Edward was a minister among the Particular Baptists and was in possession of two farms, one in Sedgehill and the other in Tinhead. He had come from Sedgehill to join, and later pastor, a group of persecuted Particular Baptists. These presentments usually resulted in heavy fines or imprisonments. Here was a man willing in this era [1662-1688] to suffer for his faith.

Persecution was particularly strong in the Diocese of Salisbury, instigated by Bishop Seth Ward. The 1664 Conventicle Act stated that all above the age of sixteen attending a meeting where there were five present more than the household were subject to a five pound fine or three months' imprisonment for the first offence, ten pounds or six months' imprisonment for the second offence and one hundred pounds or seven years' transportation [in case of escape or return, death] for the third offence. These punishments took effect on conviction before a single JP and without trial by jury. Soldiers were stationed in some areas to enforce these draconian measures and informers were freely used.

The congregation Froude had joined was a group that originally met in the village of Erlestoke, a few miles to the east of Tinhead. It did not have

[2] Will of Edward Froude Snr. 1714 – WSRO.

[3] Will of John Froude 1674 – WSRO.

a church building but met in cottages. The Erlestoke presentment on 3rd November 1662 listed its congregation, two preachers and nine other people, accusing them of non-attendance at the parish church, holding private conventicles in their houses, and refusing to have their children baptised. At that time their ministers were John Axford and William Aldridge.[4] On 8th April 1671 Thomas George of Erlestoke was fined at the Quarter Sessions for having a conventicle in his house on 19th March when about twenty were assembled.. When the Declaration of Indulgence was granted in 1672 and religious freedom came for a short while, licences were granted for a conventicle in the house of Thomas George at Erlestoke and for William Aldridge and John Axford to preach. When Edward Froude and his relations were named in the Edington presentment in 1683 the congregation at Erlestoke was cited in the Erlestoke presentment. John Axford and William Aldridge were still alive and so with Edward Froude there were three Particular Baptist ministers in the area, all watched closely by the authorities in Church and State.

There was also another minister in Erlestoke at this time, a Presbyterian called William Gough. He had been born in 1626 at the rectory at Great Cheverell, the next village to the east along the Salisbury Plain escarpment. He was educated at Queen's College, Cambridge and Christchurch College, Oxford. Cambridge was a great Puritan stronghold and Oliver Cromwell had been elected its MP in 1640 just prior to the time when Gough would have come up as a student. He was educated in Latin, Greek and Hebrew and as his father had been an Anglican minister he was undoubtedly destined for the ministry in the Anglican Church. There seems no question having regard to his future life that he was greatly influenced by the Puritans at Cambridge. After leaving Oxford in 1650, at the age of twenty-four he returned to Wiltshire and taught in a school and preached in his own house at Warminster. In 1655 under Cromwell's government he was appointed rector of Inkpen, a village near Hungerford, Wilts, where he stayed for seven years until 1662. In this year, together with men like Samuel Clifford of East Knoyle, he was ejected from his parish by the Act of Uniformity which required full agreement with the Anglican Prayer Book. He was then thirty-six and returned to his family property at Erlestoke and preached in conventicles in the area. In 1672 his house was licensed as a place for Presbyterian worship. In 1687 Gough was deputed by the local Dissenters to preach an address of thanks to King James II as he passed through Bath. He faithfully told the King that he did not approve of the recent Act of Toleration which gave religious liberty not only to Nonconformists but

[4] HBBCW.

also to Roman Catholics. In the same year he accepted a call to be pastor of the Presbyterian Church at Devizes where he stayed for six years until he went to Marlborough in 1691 where he died in 1693. It would appear that it was his help and influence that was the means of educating a man like Edward Froude, a farmer and a preacher. It is of considerable interest that the inscription on Edward Froude's grave in the main nave of Edington Priory is in Latin, as is also that of his son John who died in 1712 two years before his father. Gough seems to have had an influence on the Particular Baptists as regards education and leadership, with whom he agreed fully in doctrine but not entirely in practice, when it came to baptism.

Five more years of persecution remained in 1683. In 1685 the West Country witnessed the Monmouth Rebellion, when the Duke of Monmouth landed at Lyme Regis from the Netherlands and gathered together a large group of followers from among the local Dissenters, moving as far as Bristol but eventually being defeated at the Battle of Sedgemoor. This was followed by the Bloody Assize of Judge Jeffreys which resulted in the death of three hundred and thirty Nonconformists, being hung, drawn and quartered, and eight hundred and fifty-five being transported to Barbados. Several men were hung at Norton St Philip on the Wiltshire-Somerset border. It must have struck horror into the little congregation at Erlestoke and into the family of Edward Froude. Among those who died at Lyme Regis and Taunton were the two grandsons of a leading London Particular Baptist minister, William Kiffin. The boys' names were William Hewling, aged nineteen at the time of his death and Benjamin, aged twenty-two. But in 1688 a second attempt was made to remove the Catholic monarch, James II, when William of Orange landed with an army at Torbay in Devon and this attempt was successful.

Now religious freedom, on the same lines that Oliver Cromwell had allowed it in the days of the Protectorate Government, was restored. In 1689 the Particular Baptists ministers from all over the country gathered in London. In the days of Cromwell's Protectorate in 1655 there had been two Particular Baptist Churches in Wiltshire at Porton and Southwick. Now, in 1689, there were twelve such churches; Cleychase, Bradford, Calne, Devizes, Erlestoke, Knoyle, Malmesbury, Melksham, Porton, Southwick, Warminster and Westbury.[5] The Erlestoke congregation was represented by Edward Froude and William Aldridge. Knoyle, near Sedgehill, was represented by John Williams. The ministers representing about one hundred Baptist Churches in England and Wales [denying

[5] TGC p.222.

Arminianism] met together from 3rd - 11th July and published the 1689 Baptist Confession of Faith, as well as discussing ways of helping the poor and training the ministers. The 1689 Confession drew its inspiration from the Confession drawn up by the Westminster Assembly of Divines meeting in London from 1643-1647 but differs from it as regards baptism, the Lord's Supper and church government. It also drew some inspiration from the First London Confession of Faith of 1644, produced by seven London Particular Baptist congregations during the Civil War. It was first compiled by 'The Elders and Brethren of many congregations of Christians baptised upon profession of their faith, in London and the country' in 1677. For fear of persecution the compilers of this Confession did not subscribe their names to it. But when the ministers and messengers gathered in London in 1689 thirty-seven of the most eminent Baptist ministers of the day set their names to it, Wiltshire being represented by James Webb of Devizes. Also present at the Assembly was Joseph Houlton of Trowbridge, a wealthy clothier. Edward Froude was forty-four at the time and was undoubtedly in the company of a group of Wiltshire ministers whom he knew well. He would also have met such Particular Baptist leaders as Hanserd Knollys, William Kiffin, Andrew Gifford and Benjamin Keach.

Edward Froude returned to Erlestoke and Tinhead for another twenty-five years of preaching. Now the days of persecution were over. He was living in Tinhead, presumably in the farmhouse of his late brother-in-law John Blackborrow. John's wife Anne Blackborrow made bequests of £5 each in her will[6] to Edward Froude's children [her nephews and nieces]. The residue of her estate she left to Edward Froude's daughter Elizabeth. This reveals that by 1689 Edward Froude had five sons and two daughters. They were in order Elizabeth, Edward, John, Thomas, Anne, Robert and William.

Elizabeth Froude inherited the residue of Anne Blackborrow's will, the family property of her mother, who was John Blackborrow's sister. She married Richard Tezard of Donhead St Andrew near Sedgehill. A letter[7] which William Steele senior wrote to Anne Froude, before they married in 1713, was addressed to Mrs Anne at Mr Richard Tezard's at Donhead, which shows Anne was staying at the home of her sister. Edward Froude in his will in 1714 left 'Elizabeth Tezard, his grandchild £20'. But there is no mention in his will of Elizabeth, the grandchild's mother, which suggests she may have died before her father's death.

---

[6] Will of Anne Blackborrow, proved 1693. WSRO.
[7] Letter of William Steele dated 18 May 1713 – ALRPC. STE 1/2/ii.

By 1700 Edward junior was living at Sedgehill having taken over Sweetwell Farm and the farmhouse was registered as a place of worship for Protestant Dissenters. The Agreement, accepted by the Justices in Quarter Session at Warminster on 16th July in the 12th year of the reign of William III, is signed by, among others, John Williams, who represented this Baptist congregation at the Particular Baptist Assembly in London in 1689. This Certificate[8] is confirmation of what was standard practice, that the Particular Baptists continued to worship in their homes until they built chapels [as they did for the Erlestoke congregation at Bratton in 1734] in the early eighteenth century. Edward farmed at Sweetwell until his death in 1744 at about the age of seventy.

John was born in 1677 and died on 17th November 1712. He is buried in the main nave of Edington Priory. He has a large flat Portland stone memorial and the inscription is in Latin, probably the work of his father. It reads:

> Sub hoc lapide corpus Johannis, Edwardi Froud generosi et Elizabethae uxoris eius filii secundi tumulatum iacet qui obiit die Novembris 17 Anno domini 1712 aetatis suae 35.
>
> [Under this stone lies buried the body of John, the second son of Edward Froude and his wife Elizabeth, who died on 17th November 1712 at the age of 35]

His death must have been a great sadness to his father.

Thomas died in 1733 leaving his wife Sarah his property valued at £600. He had four children, Elizabeth, Edward, Thomas and John. The last son John was born in 1711 and died in 1777. He was twice married. He and his two wives lie buried in the main nave of Edington Priory together with his grandfather and his uncle. It would appear that the family lived in the Edington area but where is not known.

Anne was born in 1684, a year before the Monmouth Rebellion. She married William Steele in 1713/1714, [just a year before her father died] when William was twenty-three and she twenty-nine. They had three children, William junior born in 1715 and Anne, the subject of this biography in 1717. She lived throughout her married life at Broughton in Hampshire where her husband was a Baptist minister and had businesses in timber and farming. She died in childbirth on 22nd May 1720 at the age of thirty-six. The baby boy, Thomas, only lived for three months. His mother is buried in Broughton Parish Churchyard.

---

[8] WSRO – Wilts Meeting House Certificates 1689-1852.

Of Robert little is known except that in his father's will eighteen acres of land at Sedgehill were left in trust to Edward Grant, a clothier of Trowbridge, and William Aldridge of Erlestoke for the use of Robert during his lifetime, then to go to his brother Edward. This would suggest that possibly Robert was either mentally or physically disabled and needed financial support. But the help was not needed for long as he died in 1714 shortly after his father. Of William nothing is known except that his name is mentioned in Anne Blackborrow's will.

Two more sons were born after 1689. James, who lived in Tinhead, was a yeoman farmer. The Steele family often stayed with James. He died in 1750. It would appear from his will[9] that he had one daughter, Mrs Pinock, though she would seem to have been dead at the time he made the will in 1749. A large part of his money was left to his two nephews and a niece, the children of his brother Thomas. The youngest son of Edward Froude was called Blackborrow, after his mother's maiden name. He lived at Steeple Ashton and died in 1748.

So Edward Froude had a large family, seven sons and two daughters, though his two daughters and two of his sons died young. From his will it is clear that one boy and one girl had predeceased him. He himself died on 20th November 1714. In the oldest Minute Book of the Bratton Baptist Church [1737][10] [the church which had originally met at Erlestoke now had two centres, one of which was at Bratton], they looked back over the past to their former minister, speaking of him as 'Edward Froude of Tinhead, a man eminent for piety and preaching'. They recorded that he was a good leader, telling how after his death in 1714 trouble arose in the Erlestoke Church and how they were pastorless until the Lord raised up John Watts, a member of the Westbury Leigh Particular Baptist Church, who though called to the pastorate of the Bratton/Erlestoke Church did not feel able to accept it until 1731. Then in 1734 they built themselves a commodious little Chapel in Bratton, Edward Froude junior of Sedgehill together with others helping toward the financing of the project.

Edward Froude senior was buried in the Priory Church at Edington on 26th November 1714. The Church Burial Register records that he was 'buried without Christian burial'. What lay behind this written record of the vicar is not clear. The animosity between Anglican and Dissenter was still rife twenty-five years after the Glorious Revolution of 1688. No doubt the Dissenters did not wish the vicar to have any part in the burial service of their minister which would have meant use of the Book of

[9] Will of James Froude 1749 – WSRO.
[10] HBBCW.

Common Prayer, which had resulted in the Great Ejection of clergy from the Anglican Church in 1662. How Edward Froude and his family came to have a right to burial in the main nave of the Priory is not altogether clear. His son John had been buried there before him in 1712 and others of his family were to be buried there as late as 1786. It would appear that the one claim to burial within the Church would be that Edward Froude was a churchwarden, which was a type of local government appointment, dependent on income, status and property and did not necessitate that he be a regular attendant at the Priory.

Figure 3: Edington Priory

A large congregation of Dissenters, consisting of his family and all the members of the Erlestoke Church must have entered the Priory that November day, and watched his coffin lowered into the vault in complete silence. Presumably they had the funeral service at his home in Tinhead. His grave was covered with a large Portland stone slab with the inscription in Latin. This inscription is almost completely obliterated today by constant walking over it. But an English translation of it has survived among the Steele family records[11] made in the eighteenth century when it was in near perfect condition. This reads,

> 'Stay traveller and know that what was mortal of that truly reverend man Mr Edward Froud lyes under this stone. If you ask what he was, know that he was famous for his great piety toward God, love and

[11] WSRO[BL].

kindness to his wife and children, a faithful friend, kind and courteous. Go thou and imitate his example.'

A copy was taken in 1821 of the Latin inscription and is recorded in Phillip's *Monumental Inscriptions of Wiltshire*. These two sources have made possible a complete recovery of the Latin inscription which is as follows:

> 'Siste, viator, et sub hoc lapide quid erat mortale habuit depositu dilectus viri, discere reverendi Eduardi Froud: Qualis fuit si quaeras eximius pietate Deum, amore in conjugem, in liberos charitate, in amicos fide, in cunctos benevolentia humanita clarum. Exito et exemplas imitare. Inter vivos esse desiit 10 Calendas Decembris A.D. 1714 aetatis suae 69.'

Figure 4: The Froude Graves at Edington Priory

These then were Anne Steele's grandparents, neither of whom she knew, and these were her mother's brothers and sister. Anne's brother William was born a year after his grandfather's death and Anne herself in

1717. As her mother died in 1720 she can have had only dim recollections of her. But she knew her Uncles Edward of Sedgehill, and Thomas and James of Tinhead. Also she knew her cousin Elizabeth Tezard who married the lawyer John James Manfield of Ringwood on 12th August 1730 and in later life she often went to stay with the Manfield family at Ringwood.

The Steele Family

The earliest mention of the Steele family in Broughton is to be found in the Broughton Parish Register under baptisms dated 5th June 1641; it reads, 'Oliver, son of William and Dionisia Steele'. No more is known of Oliver but his father William is the earliest known relative of Anne Steele. He was her great-great grandfather. Steele family tradition placed his birth in 1600 at the end of the reign of Queen Elizabeth I. He was thought to have been active in the Civil War on the Parliamentary side and built the family home, *Grandfathers*, where generations of Steeles, including Anne herself, have lived. Family tradition links him with the early Baptists in the area, but his name does not appear in the earliest records of Broughton Baptist Church[12] which began in 1653. The earliest record of Baptists meeting in Broughton is at the time of the Declaration of Indulgence [1672] when a licence[13] was granted for worship in 'the house of Henry Abbot for Anabaptists'. In 1669 a conventicle had been reported at Over Wallop with forty members. In 1672 a licence was granted for worship at Over Wallop when John Kent was recorded as the teacher and his house as the place of meeting William Steele I died in 1663 and from his will[14] we learn that he had ten children. He styles himself as a 'carpenter'. The inventory with the will gives a description of the house which fits with what is known of *Grandfathers* today. The total sum of the inventory was £27-7s.

Of the ten children of William Steele I, the eldest was named after his father and through him descended the Steele family line. William Steele II was a carpenter like his father. He had two sons and two daughters who survived infancy. Ellen married James Haytor and had six children one of whom, Charity, born in 1676, was baptised at Broughton in 1701 and died three years later at the age of twenty-eight. Nothing is known about Mary who was born in 1653. Of the two surviving sons little is known about Thomas while Henry was minister at the Broughton Baptist Church for forty years. Henry was baptised on 10th October 1680[15] and Thomas was

[12] ALRPC.

[13] EHB.

[14] HRO.

[15] HBBCH.

baptised on 28th August 1684.[16] Almost certainly these baptisings would have been in the open river. Henry persuaded his brother Thomas to accompany him to his baptism and it was the means of the conversion of Thomas. In a document regarding the lease of a piece of land, on which the Broughton Baptist Chapel later stood, the two brothers are referred to as 'House Carpenters' which suggest they were working together building timber cottages.

Thomas married twice. This is revealed by his will.[17] His first wife was the Mary Steele 'Anabaptist' who died in 1692 and his second wife was Mary Knight. He had three sons and three daughters, one of whom died in infancy. It would seem from his will dated 25th May 1708 [four days before his burial] that he died very suddenly. His daughter Mary and her two brothers Thomas and William were the children of his first marriage and his son Henry and his sister Elizabeth were the children of his second marriage. From the legacies in his will it is possible to estimate the value of his estate at death, which was about £1000, a considerable sum in 1708. No longer did he style himself 'Carpenter' and from the existence of freehold estate bequeathed to his two boys Thomas and William it would seem his estate included land and property. Sadly in just over a year Thomas, the older of the two boys, died and was buried on 9th July 1709. In his will[18] dated 10th June, he styled himself 'Carpenter' and left £100 to his sister Mary, small bequests to his half-sister Elizabeth and half-brother Henry and fifty pounds to a Trust set up by Mr Rede of Devizes, a Colonel in the Parliamentary Army and for many years minister of the Porton/Broughton Baptist Church. The residue of his estate was left to his brother William, who was only twenty at the time.

This William, William Steele III, was Anne Steele's father. He was baptised by his uncle, Henry Steele, on 22nd June 1708, together with his sister Mary, just a few weeks after their father died. He had been born in 1689, the year of the Particular Baptist Assembly in London following the Glorious Revolution of 1688. He started preaching as soon as he was baptised, assisting his uncle Henry Steele in preaching and becoming pastor on his uncle's death on 16th June 1739[19]. He married Anne Froude of Tinhead late 1713 or early 1714. It seems quite probable that he met her in the early days of his ministry when he travelled round the Wiltshire Baptist Churches. He had already been preaching for six years when they married. He had two children, William born in 1715 and Anne in 1717.

[16] BBCB.
[17] HRO.
[18] HRO.
[19] HBBCH.

Sadly his wife died in 1720 in childbirth and the little boy, Thomas, named after his deceased grandfather and his deceased uncle, only lived three months.

The Porton/Broughton Church

The Baptist Church over which Henry Steele had been pastor for forty years [1699-1739] and of which he had been a member for sixty years [1680-1739], traced its beginnings back to 1653, to the days before the Cromwellian Protectorate. It was originally centred at Porton. It is possible that the influence of the ministry of Richard Hooker, writer of the *Laws of Ecclesiastical Polity*, who was vicar at Boscombe just up the road from Porton from 1591-1595, had first brought the Gospel to the area. Remarkably three volumes [Vol. 1 1653-84; Vol. 2 1710-29; Vol. 3 1730-49] of the original Church Books have survived and are now kept at the Angus Library at Regent's Park College, Oxford. The first entry in Volume 1 is dated 3rd April 1653 and contains an account of the gathering of the church, called the church at Porton and Broughton. It reads:

> On the third day of the fourth month the brethren and sisters residing about Wallop, Sarum, Amesbury, Stoford, Chalk, Porton and the parts adjacent, met together as a Church of Jesus Christ, and then with one accord declared their resolution for the future [Christ strengthening them] so to walk as becometh saints, according to the Gospel, in all obedience to His commandments, in love to one another as brethren and sisters, partakers of the same grace through Jesus Christ our Lord; and for their more orderly proceeding and profit they appointed John Rede, Henry Penn and Edward Bundy, orderly and by course to administer the ordinances as often as called for, and for the provision of the Church, and taking care of the poor saints, they have appointed Robert Blake and Thomas Webbe to oversee and take care in their places as their duties in all things that necessarily belong to the care of deacons. The same day were baptised by our brother Bundy, nine disciples.

While in the church at Porton this meeting was taking place, when eighty-five members met and ministers and deacons were being appointed, in London great events were taking place in the House of Commons. On 20th April, just seventeen days after the Porton Church meeting, Oliver Cromwell was to enter the Chamber of the House with his troops, drive out the members, ending the days of the Rump Parliament, and say regarding the Mace, 'What shall we do with this bauble? Take it away.' The Parliament was refusing to sanction funds for the New Model Army and so Army and Parliament were in conflict.

The Porton Church was not so far removed from these events as one might think. Their minister John Rede was not an insignificant figure. He had fought in the Civil War on the Parliamentary side.[20] He had risen to the rank of Lieutenant Colonel. He had served in the regiment of Colonel [later General] Ludlow when there were twenty-five Baptist officers, he being one of them. He had joined the regiment when it was raised in 1643. When Ludlow's regiment was disbanded, Colonel John Rede joined the New Model Army formed in 1645-6. He was mentioned for distinguished service in battle in one of Oliver Cromwell's letters sent to the Speaker, William Lenthall, at the House of Commons after the battle of Preston on 20th August 1648. Cromwell writes of the 'incredible valour and resolution' of his troops and says, 'Lieutenant Colonel Rede and Colonel Ashton had the greatest work, they often coming to push of pike and close firing, and always making the enemy to recoil.' Rede had been entrusted with the sieges of Tenby and Pembroke Castle in Wales in May/June of the same year. In 1649 he became Governor of Poole and Brownsea Castle and later commanded a garrison in Scotland. He was a Member of Parliament for Wiltshire and served on committees dealing with Wiltshire from 1647-1652 and in 1657, 1659 and 1660. In 1653 he was a judge concerning prisons and prisoners It is not clear when he came out of military service, but the Porton records show that he was preaching at Porton as early as 1651. He lived at Birdlimes Farm, Porton, just outside Salisbury. He was a landowner and a Justice of the Peace and an MP. As a JP he conducted several marriages under the Barebones Act [1653], when for a time marriage became a civil matter, conducted by JPs, and his signature appears in the Parish Register of Porton-cum-Idmiston.

Birdlimes Farm exists today, but not the same buildings in which Colonel Rede lived. The early Manor House was demolished in the 19th century. Here it was that the Porton/Broughton Church met. A sheepwash nearby in the River Bourne was probably the site of the baptisings. A burial ground still existed in 1908 with memorial stones to John Rede's wife and his young daughter. It shows that his wife Sarah died in 1708 at the age of forty-nine and that his daughter, Sarah Carteret Rede, died in 1700, a few days short of seven. According to the custom of using the maternal maiden name for children, it would suggest that the maiden name of the girl's mother was Carteret. The Advocate-General of the New Model Army was Philip Carteret, who was a Baptist lawyer. This would suggest that late in life John Rede married into the Carteret family. So here is evidence that John Rede knew leading men in the New Model Army and also knew Oliver Cromwell well and had served under

[20] OBC pp.46-63.

him in battle, equally knowing him on the floor of the House of Commons.

It is clear that John Rede was the founder of the Porton Baptist Church. It seems that as the Parliamentary Army moved about the country with its Baptist officers, many Particular Baptist Churches sprang up in its wake. The officers were obviously evangelists and John Rede was one of them. As with the Steele family who were firstly timber merchants buying standing timber and having contracts with the Admiralty for ship building, and secondly landowners and farmers, so John Rede was a landowner, a soldier, a JP [probably, having regard to this office and being a judge in 1653, a lawyer] and an MP, a man of considerable importance in his locality. The Porton/Broughton Church was led by a well-to-do, able man. This was not only true of Particular Baptists in the Wiltshire/Hampshire area, but also true of the City of London where their leader, William Kiffin, was a wealthy merchant and in 1687 Alderman of the City of London. He had personally met Charles I, Oliver Cromwell, Charles II, James II and William III. In 1688 the Government of James II considered that if there were an election, John Rede would stand as a candidate for the borough of Wilton and be elected a Member of Parliament. If many Particular Baptist ministers were men of the social calibre of John Bunyan, a tinker, a good number of others such as William Kiffin and John Rede were to be numbered among the upper echelons of society. The Broughton/Porton Church was composed of weavers, farmworkers, yeoman farmers, carpenters, house builders and also business and professional men, who would sign their wills as Edward Froude did at Edington, 'Gent', and have gravestones with the inscription in Latin. Knowing a little of this political and cultural background among the Particular Baptists helps us to understand the type of Particular Baptist society into which Anne Steele was born in 1717.

The Porton Church Book shows that its members and leaders in 1653 were scattered along the valleys of the Rivers Wylye, Avon, Bourne and Ebble and came from nearly twenty different towns and villages which included, on the Avon, Salisbury [Sarum], Bodenham, Durnford, Amesbury, Bulford, Durrington, Netheravon and Enford; on the Wylye, Stoford and South Newton; on the Ebble, Broad Chalke and Stoke; on the Bourne, Porton, Idmiston and Allington; and a further group over toward Broughton in Hampshire at Grinstead, Farley and Dean. Of their leaders John Rede lived at Porton, Henry Penn at Broad Chalke and Edward Bundy at Amesbury. This little group was centred at Porton in a circuit of about forty miles. It was about ten miles from Porton to Broad Chalke and the same from Porton to Enford, both villages on the outer edge of the circuit and five miles from Porton to Salisbury.

In 1655 Rede was actively involved in preaching and administering the Lord's Supper and believer's baptism.[21] On March 15th of that year John Penruddock with two hundred cavalry entered Salisbury, arrested the High Sheriff and Assize Judges and set out into Somerset and Dorset to start a Royalist uprising. Troops from the Parliamentary garrison at Exeter confronted the rebels at South Molton in Devon and defeated them. It was in the autumn of this year that Oliver Cromwell instituted the rule of the Major Generals, having himself been appointed Lord Protector in December 1653 and having dismissed the First Protectorate Parliament in January 1655. These senior officers of his army were appointed to govern large areas of the country and watch for any further attempted insurrections by the Royalists. Major General John Desborough was appointed to govern Cornwall, Devon, Somerset, Wiltshire and Gloucestershire. It seems certain that Colonel Rede would have known him. The Porton Church in 1655 must have trembled at the possibility of further conflict on their doorstep.

The first clear record of church business occurs when the Porton church met at Salisbury [Sarum] on 17th November 1657. By this time the church numbered one hundred and six members, there having been about twenty members added to the church in the previous four years. On 27th April 1658 the Church Book records that John Rede baptised brother Plumley and William Boodle at Porton. On 3rd September 1658 Oliver Cromwell died suddenly and unexpectedly. Richard Cromwell, his son was completely unfit to take his place and eventually Charles II was invited back in April 1660 to take the throne. A delegation from England met him at Breda in Holland before he returned, when he promised that on his return he would declare a general pardon, religious toleration and satisfaction to the Army. The Porton Church met at Amesbury on 19th May that year for the last time until 1671. Almost certainly this meeting took place to discuss a plan of action for the days of persecution that inevitably lay ahead with the restoration of the Stuart monarchy. Charles II never kept the promise of toleration. Within two years the Act of Uniformity was passed, which drove over two thousand clergymen out of the Church of England on grounds of conscience. It required ministers to consent wholeheartedly to the revised Book of Common Prayer, to be ordained by a bishop and to renounce the 1643 Solemn League and Covenant. This was followed by the Conventicle Act in 1664 which

[21] OBC p.50.

banned meetings of five or more persons 'not according to the Book of Common Prayer'. In 1665 came the Five Mile Act by which all nonconformist ministers were banned from coming within five miles of a town having a Member of Parliament, or where they had been ministers before.

Within a few years of the Restoration John Rede was arrested and imprisoned in the Tower of London.[22] This was partly for political and religious reasons [he was suspected of being involved in a plot to overthrow the Government] and partly on account of his military service. It is not certain how long he was detained there but on 1st September 1665 he was brought before Lord Arlington, a Secretary of State, for questioning, a record of which survives and is kept in the Public Record Office. The questioning related not only to rebellions and plots against king and government but also contained questions regarding which church he attended, whether he abode by the rules of the Conventicle Act, with which sect he was associated. He eventually satisfied his judges and was released and returned to Porton.

Four days later on 4th September 1665 he wrote a long letter to Lord Arlington in which he pleaded fearlessly for religious toleration.[23] In it he speaks of having 'formerly met with rigidities' referring to his incarceration in the Tower, and says on this account he was surprised that he had been granted his liberty. He says that there is nothing more unwelcome than the restraining of part of that liberty 'which was once indulged to tender consciences by His Majesties Gracious Declaration.' Here he refers openly to the Declaration of Breda and how the promise of the King was being broken. He pointed out that not all conventicles [house meetings] of Nonconformists were seditious and how awful it was to suppress them with 'the terrors of transportation'. Many who worshipped thus were loyal supporters of king and government. He said that there were many 'who yet cannot understand the Lord's mind in Scriptures as to discern it to be their duty to be present at their Popish assemblies in the times of the appointed service of that Church, neither can they be persuaded thereunto, nor will they be compelled, whatsoever they suffer.' He spoke of these persecuting laws [the Conventicle Act 1664 and the Five Mile Act 1655] allowing ungodly men to become informers on the godly, saying that 'the godly render to Caesar the things that are Caesar's and to God the things that are God's'. It was not fit that good men that were quiet subjects of the King should be disturbed in their devotions in their houses. Here he fearlessly pleads for conventicles to be

[22] OBC p.51.

[23] P.R.O. 29/132 *State Papers Domestic,* Vol. 182, 29.

allowed by law. Then he went on to say, 'Let this liberty be indulged at least if not proclaimed, that whilst the severe hand of God is stretched out in judgement over this nation, that no sincere persons that can pray shall be prohibited their assembling together unto that duty in their houses ... this course I am persuaded, effectually performed, will prove the best remedy to assuage the pestilence... Let the Scriptures be the rule of devotion for all Christians'. He went on to plead for Christian liberty to be combined with civil obedience saying that such a policy of the Government would bring about a situation in the country 'far more peaceable and happy than now it is'. He concluded his letter to Lord Arlington by pleading that he might have 'a private protection under His Lordship's hand, desiring all officers forbearance to molest me in my devotions, services and prayers to God, so long as he had no grounds to believe that he [Rede] had done anything to disturb the peace.'

It is a remarkable letter in that it has survived. It is remarkable in that it shows a man as fearless in religion as the Colonel who was mentioned in the House of Commons in 1648 for his bravery in battle. It is equally revealing of the man as being a very able, lucid thinker and writer, probably a lawyer by profession. What a giant he was as a leader of the humble Baptist congregation and poor unlettered members of the Porton/Broughton Church. The forebears of Anne Steele's church were certainly a hardy people made ready, as the Apostle Paul, to endure unto the death for the truth's sake. The Porton Church Book [1653-1684] is silent from 1660-1672. There is no mention of any persecution which must have inevitably taken place. Thomas Crosby in his *History of the English Baptists* [1740] Vol. III p.126 says, 'Peter Coles, a Baptist preacher at Downton in the county of Sarum, Walter Penn, pastor of the Baptist church at Sarum, and John Kingman of Burford near Sarum were all for several years prisoners in the county gaol at Sarum for nonconformity.' Walter Penn was one of the leaders of the Porton Church and later, in 1689, represented it at the Particular Baptist Assembly together with John Andrews. In 1669 Bishop Ward of Salisbury produced a survey of the Particular Baptists in his diocese. He reported groups at Broad Chalke [about 10, very mean, led by Henry Penn, a husbandman], and at Amesbury in the house of Thomas Webb about 30 inconsiderable persons; John Rede from Porton came over to hold a conventicle. The Bishop of Winchester reported an Anabaptist conventicle at Over Wallop in Hampshire numbering about 40. The Quarter Session Rolls showed other conventicles at Rolleston and Stoford in South Newton, also at Allington, Idmiston, Durrington and Farley, all places connected to the Porton Church. Bishop Ward wrote, 'The teachers of the Anabaptists....

are vagabond, run-about, unknown fellows. The authority they all pretend is His Majesty's connivance and that they have some friends that, if occasion be, will interpose between them and the punishment of the laws.' It was not entirely true to say their teachers were 'unknown' but it was true to say that 'they had some friends' who would 'interpose' for them with the authorities. It is of interest to remember that this persecution was countrywide, and that many of the Anabaptist teachers were in prison for preaching the Gospel. The most well known of these was John Bunyan who spent much of the period from 1660-1672 in prison at Bedford.

In 1672 Charles II wanted to give a measure of toleration to Roman Catholics and decided to include in the *Declaration of Indulgence* of 15th March all sects which did not conform to the Anglican Church. The requirement was that all places of worship [mainly houses] and all ministers should be registered. But the Declaration was issued by Charles II without the sanction of Parliament and therefore did not contain the force of law. Between April 1672 and February 1673 over four thousand houses were registered in England and Wales. Two entry books among the State Papers Domestic[24] contain the registrations. The seventy Wiltshire house registrations are printed in the Appendix to Wiltshire Meeting House Certificates (1689-1852) [WRS.40]. For the Porton Church the houses registered included that of Henry Penn at Broad Chalke, that of widow Blake at Stoford in South Newton, that of Thomas Batts in Salisbury, that of Thomas Webb (alias Long) in Amesbury and that of John Rede in Idmiston. The house of Edward Grant, a friend of Edward Froude, was registered in Trowbridge. Two Presbyterian houses registered and relating to Anne Steele's ancestors were that of Samuel Clifford at East Knoyle and that of William Gough at Erlestoke, both ejected ministers of the Church of England in 1662. In Hampshire the house of John Kent at Over Wallop, the house of Henry Abbot at Broughton and the house of John Dozzell at Whitchurch were registered. Ministers registered included John Kent of Over Wallop, Richard Bunney of Whitchurch, John Rede of Birdlimes, Porton, Henry Penn of Broad Chalke, Samuel Clifford of East Knoyle and William Gough of Erlestoke. All these registrations [excepting those of Clifford and Gough] were designated Anabaptist, which was a term of abuse, much like the original use of the name 'Puritan'.

Now for a few brief months the Porton congregation had rest from persecution. But when Parliament was called in 1673 this ended as there was universal hostility to Roman Catholics and therefore to all

[24] PRO SP444/27. SP44(38A).

Nonconformists from the Government and the Church of England. Charles II hated all Protestant Nonconformists because of their hatred of the Roman Catholic Church. John Bunyan, who had received a licence to preach in May 1672, had a warrant issued for his arrest on 4th March 1675, when the Test Act [Feb. 1675] was passed and the Government withdrew all the ministers' licences. Now everyone in the civil and military employment of the state was required to give oaths of allegiance and supremacy, make a declaration against the Roman Catholic doctrine of transubstantiation, and receive communion according to the rites of the Church of England. The King was pro-Catholic and the Parliament anti-Catholic. Intolerance appeared again and the Porton Church was in the midst of it. In fact the Church Book began to be used again. On 14th May there was a meeting of the church at Hoxton and John Rede was there. On 23rd April 1674 a meeting took place at Salisbury and another at Wallop on 12th September 1675.

Particular Baptist Confessions of Faith

In October 1675 a group of London ministers led by William Kiffin, Daniel Dyke and William Collins sent out a circular letter to Particular Baptists throughout the country asking them to meet in London in the following May. In the Porton Church Book is an entry dated 24th January 1676 mentioning a letter received from London and the appointment of John Rede to attend the meeting on the first Wednesday in May. Because of the times of persecution it is not certain whether the meeting ever took place but there seems to have been some sort of meeting for the *Second Particular Baptist Confession* was published in 1677, though it was without any signatories or naming of any printer on account of the dangerous times. In the minute book of the Petty France Particular Baptist Church in the City of London, the authorship of the 1677 *Confession* is ascribed to the two pastors of the Petty France Church, William Collins and Nehemiah Cox [Nehemiah being the son of Benjamin Cox], both educated and scholarly men.

There were several factors which brought the Particular Baptists to feel the need for a new Confession of Faith. The *First London Confession* had been issued in 1644 and revised in 1646 and in 1651 and reprinted in 1652. By 1677 after twelve years of intense persecution copies of it were quite rare. Also by that time the three groups of Nonconformists, the Presbyterians, the Independents and the Particular Baptists were coming much closer to each other, a situation brought about by their common sufferings. The Presbyterians had produced the *Westminster Confession of Faith* between 1644-1647. This had largely been copied by the Independents in their Articles, the *Savoy Declaration*, in 1658. When the

Particular Baptists produced their *Second Confession* in 1677, they used the *Savoy Declaration* as their model, making various additions and alterations, but keeping Article 20 on 'The Extent of the Gospel' which replaced the Article in the *Westminster Confession*, 'On Christian Liberty.' They felt it was best to follow the example of the Independents, making use of the words of the *Westminster Confession*, to show agreement in all fundamental doctrines with the Presbyterians and Independents. So by and large the 1677 *Confession* had its roots in the *Westminster Confession*. Equally it followed some of the alterations made by the Independents in the *Savoy Declaration*. The *Savoy Declaration* had been the work of John Owen, Thomas Goodwin, Joseph Caryl, William Greenhill and others.

It is not entirely clear why the *First Confession* of 1644 with its revisions of 1646 was not republished in 1677. That *Confession* had been the independent work of the Particular Baptists. They had not been allowed to take part in the Westminster Asssembly which met from 1644-47 to produce the *Westminster Confession*, though they knew the Assembly was composed of godly men. It would appear that there was a doctrinal movement among the Particular Baptists between 1644 and 1677. Article 25 of the 1644 edition of the *Confession* reads, 'That the tenders of the Gospel to the conversion of sinners are absolutely free.' The 1646 revision of the same article reads, 'That the *preaching* of the Gospel to the conversion of sinners is absolutely free.' On this point of difference the 1677 *Confession* would appear to blend both the 'tender' [offer] and the 'preaching'. It reads in Article 7.2, 'Wherein He freely *offereth* unto sinners life and salvation by Jesus Christ,' while in Article 20.3 it reads, 'In all ages the *preaching* of the Gospel has been granted to all persons and nations.' The 1644 *Confession* emanated from seven London Particular Baptist Churches. They appear to have been largely influenced by two Church of England clergymen, Hanserd Knollys and Benjamin Cox, who had recently joined them. In the production of the 1644 *Confession* they used as their basis the English *Separatist Confession* of 1596 taking from it twenty-six of their fifty-three Articles. For Articles twenty-one to thirty-two there is no known source, but as they clearly contain the substance of the Articles of the Synod of Dort [1619] on the Five Points, limited atonement, unconditional election, total depravity, irresistible grace, and the final perseverance of the saints, it would seem that the London Particular Baptist Churches had come under the influence of Dutch Calvinistic orthodoxy.

Soon after the publication of the 1646 edition of the *Confession*, Benjamin Cox, who had been a signatory of it, together with such men as

William Kiffin, Thomas Patient, John Spilsbury, Paul Hobson, Hanserd Knollys, published *An Appendix to a Confession of Faith,* 'which was evidently intended not merely to expound his personal views but those of the whole group in answer to certain questions that had been raised by some who had read the 1646 Confession.'[25] In Article 4 of the *Appendix* Cox writes, 'We teach that they only do, or can believe in Jesus Christ, to whom it is given to believe in Him by a special, gracious and powerful work of His Spirit: and that this is [and shall be] given to the elect in the time appointed of God for their effectual calling and to none but the elect. This we hold against those that do maintain a freewill and *sufficient ability in a man to believe*; and do deny election.' In Article 5 he writes, 'We affirm that as Jesus Christ never intended to give remission of sins and eternal life unto any but His sheep, so these sheep only have their sins washed away in the blood of Christ. The vessels of wrath, as they are none of Christ's sheep, nor ever believe in him... have all their sins remaining upon them, and are not saved by Christ from any of them *under any consideration whatsoever*.' And in Article 6 he writes, 'Though some of our opponents do affirm, that by this doctrine we have no Gospel to be preached to sinners for their conversion, yet through the goodness of God we know and preach to sinners this precious Gospel, 'God so loved the world ....' Finally in Article 9 he writes, 'Though we that believe in Christ, be not under the law, but under grace, yet we know that we are not lawless, or are left to live without a rule; not without law to God, but under law to Christ [1 Cor. 9. 21]. *The Gospel of Jesus Christ is a law, or commanding rule unto us*, whereby, and in obedience whereunto, we are taught to live soberly, righteously and godly in this present world; the directions of Christ in His evangelical word guiding us unto, and in this sober, righteous and godly walking.' In the 1646 *Confession* and in these Articles of Cox's *Appendix* there is no mention of 'offers' or 'tenders' of grace and there is an explicit statement of the Gospel as the believer's rule of life, but no mention of the Law as the believer's rule of life in the *Confession* itself, only a reference in Article 8 to the Holy Scriptures, 'which are the only rule of holiness and obedience for all saints.'

When we look at the *Second Particular Baptist Confession* [1677], Article 7, taken word for word from the *Westminster Confession of Faith*, Section 2 states, 'The Lord had made a covenant of grace ... wherein He freely *offereth* unto sinners life and salvation by Jesus Christ.' In Article 19 section 6, the Law is described as '*a rule of life* for true believers', though in Article 20 on the Gospel and the Extent of Grace [copied from *The Savoy Declaration*] 'in the revelation of the Gospel to sinners the

---

[25] *English Baptists of the 17th Century*. B. R. White p.73.

words, *the preaching of the Gospel*' is spoken of as the channel of salvation and no mention is made of the offer. It is of interest that William Kiffin, among others, signed the *Confessions* of 1644, 1646 and 1677 and there can be no doubt, that when the *Confessions* of 1646 and 1677 are compared, they contain good evidence to show that in the years of persecution the Particular Baptists were influenced by the *Westminster Confession of Faith*. What effect this may have had on the ministry of William Kiffin or Colonel Rede is not clear. It would seem that if Colonel Rede went to the London meeting in 1676 then these issues would have been discussed. What is clear is that in the eighteenth century, these issues which separated between the 1646 and 1677 *Confessions* came out into the open again in the writings of John Gill [1697-1771] and John Brine [1703-1795] and there was a reversion to the 1646 Articles as expressed by men like Benjamin Cox. By then the varying interpretations were labelled High Calvinism and Moderate Calvinism. It is hard to tell where the Porton Church stood on these issues. They could hardly have stood aloof from them. There are no copies of sermons preached in the Broughton/Porton Church until the time when Anne Steele's father, William Steele III, was sent out to preach by the church in 1709 and became its pastor in 1739, on the death of his uncle Henry Steele. Some sermon notes, dated as early as 1710, survive, which could be either those of Henry Steele taken down by William Steele III or could be those of William Steele III himself,[26] but they throw no light on the doctrinal situation at that time.

The Final Years of Persecution

After the publication of the 1677 *Confession* there remained another eleven years before the Glorious Revolution of 1688. They were to be years of further intense persecution. The Porton/Broughton Church Book makes no mention of this persecution which is understandable since much of their work had to be done in secret to escape the attention of the many paid informers that the Government was using to stop their services and hinder their activities. Two concerns appear in the Church Book. The first was that of the ministry and whether a minister should be ordained with the laying on of hands. The other concern of the church was regarding discipline.

Many cases are recorded in the Church Book of members of the church who had sinned. Of twenty-four cases, fifteen were men and nine women. Of these, fourteen were excommunicated, eight were admonished and one was restored. It would appear that there was an increase in church

[26] ALRPC. Broughton Church Records.

discipline as a direct result of the persecution. The Porton Church was very conscious that, while it was being constantly watched and persecuted, informers would glory in demonstrating that it was harbouring worldly and licentious people. So for the cohesion and strength of the persecuted body, strong discipline was maintained. It was in fact a spiritual strength for the church.

The other matter that concerned the church was the correct ordination of ministers. From a Particular Baptist Association meeting at Wells, Somerset on 9th September 1653, a letter had been sent which read, 'We judge that the ordination of ministers is an ordinance of Christ in His Church now in force [Titus 1.5, Acts 14.23] and ought to be performed with fasting and prayers and the laying on of hands. [Acts 6.6, and 13.3].' A minute in the Porton Church Book, dated 2nd November 1676, records that the church elected and chose elders of the congregation to perform the work of the ministry. It lists John Rede of Porton, John Kent of Wallop, Henry Penn of Broad Chalke, Walter Penn of Salisbury [Sarum], and Thomas Long of Amesbury; also Stephen Kent of Broughton and John Andrews of Amesbury were chosen as deacons for the congregation. A minute of 1678 says, 'Agreed that assistance shall be called in that the Church may proceed in their duty touching the laying on of hands upon their ministry which they have chosen.' Then on 21st April 1679, Thomas Long and John Andrews were appointed to go as messengers of the Church to Bristol to consult with the ordained ministers there. Following this visit an entry is recorded in the Church Book, 'The 19th day of ye 4th month 1679 at ye church meeting then at Porton [according to their former conclusion and desire] did attend [by desire and advice of ye messengers at Bristol] Brother Andrew Gifford, Brother Thomas Millard ordained ministers by imposition of ye hands, when by imposition of ye hands of ye aforesaid ministers, Brother John Rede, Brother Walter Penn and Thomas Long ministers were ordained.' Andrew Gifford [1641-1721] was pastor of the Pithay Church, Bristol for forty-four years until his death and was a very influential and highly respected minister in the west of England. He had himself been imprisoned four times in the Newgate Gaol, Bristol, and once in Gloucester Gaol.

The Porton Church in the heat of persecution had returned to the scriptural practice and had seen the truth in its simplicity and followed the Apostle's example. These godly men discerned vital doctrine and practice under intense suffering, often heavy fines and imprisonment. John Rede had been imprisoned from 1661-65,[27] Walter Penn had spent time in

[27] *History of English Baptists*, A. C. Underwood p.90.

Fisherton gaol, Salisbury and William Kiffin, the London minister, had been arrested on many occasions. Final entries in the Porton Church Book include the information that on 25th October 1683 Stephen Kent came before the church to exercise his gift as a minister and be chosen an elder. Lastly it is recorded that on 28th August 1684 Walter Penn took a baptising at Porton when the candidates were Thomas Steele and John Sturges of Broughton and Martha Wheble of Horton. This Thomas Steele was Anne Steele's grandfather and a brother of Henry Steele, who himself had been baptised in 1680 and was to be pastor of the Broughton Church from 1699 to 1739.

Now, once again the Church Book is silent as it had been between 1660-1671 and the next Church Book does not commence until 1710. These were momentous years in the Porton/Broughton Church and in the nation. Thomas Long had died in 1681 and so the church carried on with its two pastors John Rede and Walter Penn. The country was in political turmoil as King Charles II ruled without a Parliament from 1681-85 since he feared it would pass an Exclusion Bill which would remove his brother, the Duke of York [a Roman Catholic] from the succession. In 1681 the King sent the Protestant Earl of Shaftesbury to the Tower and ordered the suppression of all conventicles. Heavy fines were imposed on all who did not attend the parish church, juries were packed and spies were everywhere. Daniel Neal says that, 'The liberties of England were delivered up to the Crown.'[28] While the bishops of the Anglican Church feared that Roman Catholicism would be restored if the Duke of York became King, at the same time they set out to destroy the Dissenters and nowhere was persecution stronger than in the Salisbury diocese under Bishop Seth Ward. Daniel Neal[29] says that estimates varied from 5,000-8,000 who died in prison, to over 60,000 who suffered in the reign of Charles II [1660-1685] out of a dissenting population countrywide of possibly one hundred and fifty thousand. But like all persecution this suffering only strengthened the will of the Dissenters and from the prisons came forth such masterpieces as John Bunyan's *Pilgrim's Progress*. Charles II died on 6th February 1685 at the age of fifty-four and was succeeded by his brother James II. Now Dissenters and Anglicans could see a return to Catholicism.

The ill-conceived and ill-planned rebellion, led by the Duke of Monmouth who landed at Lyme Regis on 11th June 1685, only heightened the persecution. After the landing many Baptists joined the ragged army, ill prepared with weapons. After marching round the West

[28] *History of the Puritans*, Daniel Neal [1732] Vol. 4, p.513.
[29] *History of the Puritans*, Daniel Neal [1732] Vol. 4, p.554.

Country to Taunton, Bristol and Bath, they were eventually annihilated by the army of James II near Bridgewater at the battle of Sedgemoor on 6th July 1685, when there followed a fearful retribution at the hands of Judge Jeffreys. There is no record of how many Baptists suffered overall, but at Lyme Regis alone, on 12th September, the pastor of the Lyme Regis Particular Baptist Church, Sampson Larke, together with a leading Baptist and former officer of Cromwell, Abraham Holmes, and William Hewling, the nineteen-year-old grandson of William Kiffin, all lost their lives at the hands of the hangman. William Kiffin, the London minister and Particular Baptist leader would have been well known to John Rede, as almost certainly he would have known Abraham Holmes, since each had been officers in Cromwell's Army. Andrew Gifford, the Particular Baptist leader in the west, had been implicated in procuring weapons for the rebels but managed to avoid detection and so his life was spared.

Now the Anglican leaders and the Court turned on the Particular Baptists as complicit in the rebellion. There was also brutal persecution in Scotland after a failed attempt by the Duke of Argyll and the Campbell clan to wrest Scotland from the control of James II. Both the Earl of Argyll and the Duke of Monmouth [the illegitimate son of Charles II] were hurried to a traitor's death. In response to the persecution Dissenters and Scottish Covenanters met only in small groups, moved constantly from place to place, placed guards on their meetings to warn of danger, while their ministers went about in disguise. Beside imprisonment, many of the victims suffered huge financial losses in fines. Some fled abroad to the New England Colonies. There was great damage to trade in the country as Dissenters, being barred from university education, had turned their hand to business. In the West Country it was largely the Dissenters who owned the west of England cloth trade.

But within a year James II had other ideas. His great wish was to bring Roman Catholics back into office in the State. They had come under the same penal laws as the Dissenters. If he were to halt the persecution of Catholics he must do the same for Dissenters. His object was to reverse the changes made by the Reformation and restore the Anglican Church to the Catholic faith. To do this he would need to pack Parliament and subvert the constitution. Suddenly the Anglican bishops and clergy realised that the King was looking to ease the situation for Catholics and Dissenters and use them against the Anglicans. They had bitterly persecuted Catholics and Dissenters in the past, while trying to force the whole nation into one ecclesiastical and political mould and retain political power in the hands of the Anglican Church.

On 10th March 1686 James issued a royal decree releasing all who had been imprisoned for religious reasons. In November 1686 he set up a Licence Office which offered protection from persecution for a fifty-shilling fee. On 4th April 1687 he issued his First Royal Declaration of Indulgence for Dissenters and Catholics and hoped they would respond with Royal Addresses of support for his Government. While some of the London Particular Baptist ministers, led by Nehemiah Cox, responded positively, most were too wily and could see that once James II had got Catholics into office in the Church and State then persecution would again be their lot. Among those in London who refused to welcome the Declaration were William Kiffin and Joseph Stennett for the Baptists and Richard Baxter for the Presbyterians. The King went so far as to persuade Dissenters in London to take on the office of Alderman of the City of London and William Kiffin was eventually forced to become Alderman, which office he held for only nine months. The Anglicans, seeing the increase of Catholicism, made serious promises to the Dissenters that, if they would support the Anglican Church by opposing James II's unconstitutional measures, then they would offer them toleration at a future date. Sadly they soon forgot their promises when in 1688 the Glorious Revolution took place and James II fled the country. While granting Dissenters freedom to worship under Licensing Laws, they still barred them from the universities and all offices in the State and the Army.

On 2nd April 1688 James II promised to call a Parliament and issued his Second Declaration of Indulgence which would be established by law. All Anglicans and Dissenters were required to read it to their congregations. Most refused and the Archbishop of Canterbury and six bishops signed a protest to the King and were promptly sent to the Tower. After a trial they were all acquitted, but by then all the clergy and the country was in uproar. Now James II had turned the whole population against the monarchy. On Sunday 10th June 1688 the Queen gave birth to a son, James, later called the Old Pretender, [some wondered whether he was in fact a child of the Queen] and now a Catholic Succession was established and it appeared that the work of the Reformation would be lost. The Anglican bishops responded to the threat by secretly sending an invitation to William of Orange and his wife Mary. Mary was a daughter of James II by his first wife Anne Hyde, and together with her sister Anne [who was to become Queen in 1702] was in direct succession to the throne. Here was a strange irony, that Dissenters branded as revolutionaries now saw Anglicans [their accusers] supporting potential rebels, who invited William of Orange to invade their country and remove the legitimate monarch and take the throne. After some time for preparation William of Orange landed at Torbay in Devon with his army on 5th November 1688. He went first to Exeter to consolidate his position and wait to see whether the country would support him. Riots broke out in London and Judge Jeffreys was nearly lynched until troops rescued him and put him in the Tower where he eventually died. James II went at the head of a small army to Salisbury to oppose the invaders. This must have been an anxious moment for the Particular Baptists at Porton, who were only a few miles outside Salisbury, on the east side of the city from which the Royal Army must have approached, eagerly watching events to see who would win in the coming battle. James II realised however that his support in the country was dwindling by the hour, and so suddenly he left his army and fled back to London, from where he eventually left the country for France. 'Thus ended the short and unhappy reign of James II and with him the male line of the Royal House of Stuarts, a race of kings Providence raised up to be the scourge of these nations for they were every one chargeable with tyranny and oppression.'[30] William and Mary entered London in December and on 2nd January 1689, 'William Kiffin himself led a deputation of Baptists to present an address of welcome to the new rulers of England and made a personal contribution of £500 towards the financial needs of their government when it sought to raise a loan to tide it over the first six months.'[31]

---

[30] Ibid, p.601.

[31] *English Baptists of the 17th Century*, B. R. White p.162.

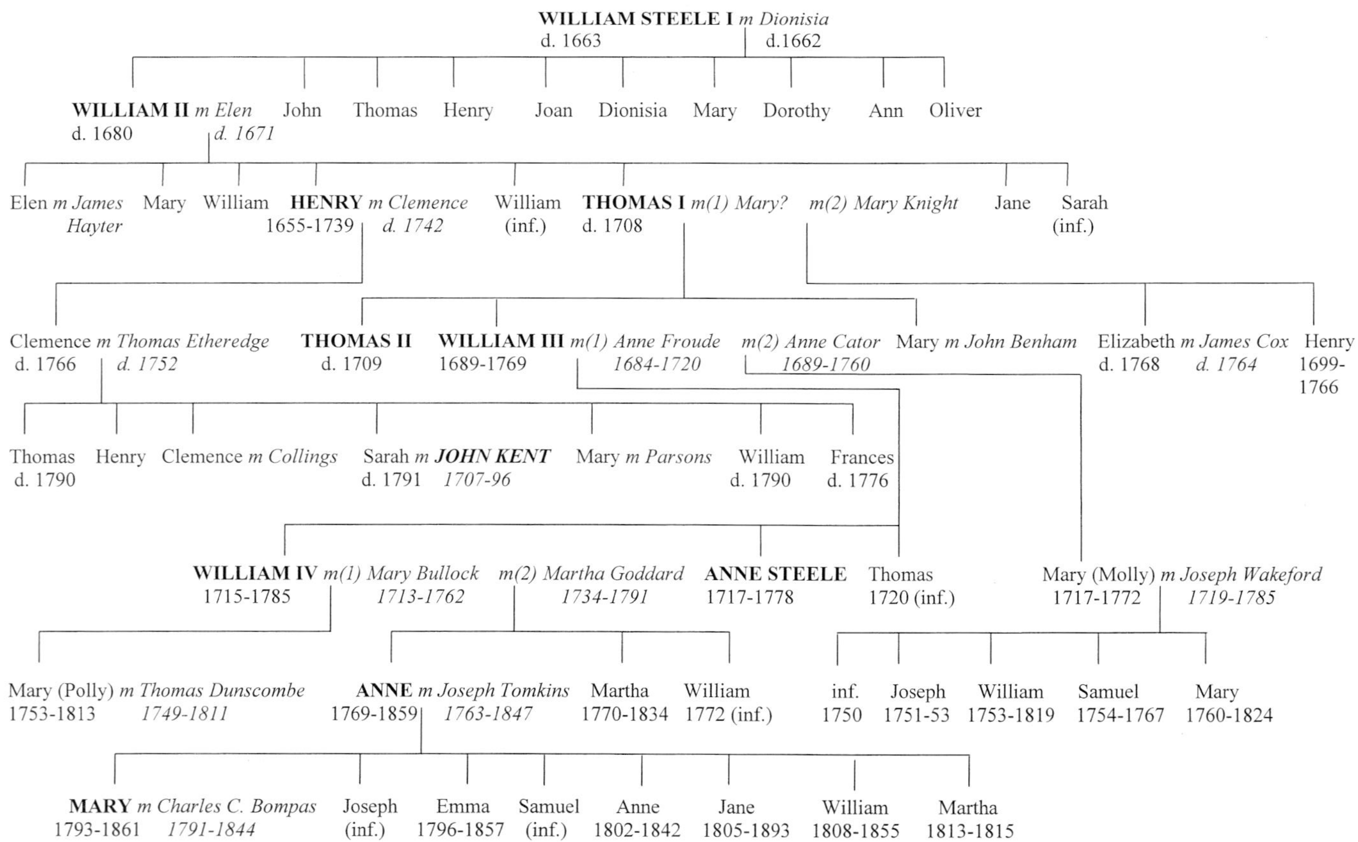

Figure 5: The Steele Family Tree

Chapter 2

A Child of Dissenters [1688-1720]

In the spring of 1689 soon after William and Mary had come to the throne, Parliament passed an Act of Toleration. While it provided protection for Dissenters as its title indicated: 'An Act for Exempting their Majesties' Protestant Subjects dissenting from the Church of England from the Penalties of Certain Laws', it had great limitations. It allowed toleration only for Trinitarian Protestants; dissenting ministers had to subscribe to thirty-six of the Thirty-Nine Articles of the Church of England [Baptists did not have to subscribe to the Article on infant sprinkling]; all Dissenters had to pay tithes and Church rates, and if they wished to take any office of State, or a position in local government, or take a Commission in the Armed Forces, or enter Oxford or Cambridge Universities, then they had to take communion in the Church of England. Also all their meeting places had to be licensed and this could only be done on condition that they took oaths or made declarations of supremacy and allegiance to the new government. These oaths or declarations had to be taken before a Justice of the Peace. Their churches had to be registered in the Court of a Bishop, Archdeacon or a magistrate at a cost of sixpence. The Conventicle Act, the Act of Uniformity and the Test and Corporation Acts were all left unrepealed and no indulgence was granted to Roman Catholics or Anti-Trinitarians, but Parliament allowed that these laws did not apply to Dissenters who had taken the oaths or declarations of allegiance and supremacy. 'After two revolutions, Dissenters had secured a real measure of religious liberty, but they were still disqualified from office, though no longer criminals. The State Church was still privileged but could no longer persecute.'[32]

The 1689 Particular Baptist Assembly

Though they had not been granted full equality of citizenship, yet Dissenters were greatly relieved that persecution had ended. Now William Kiffin, Hanserd Knollys and Benjamin Keach together with four other ministers met in London in July 1689, and on 22nd July sent out a letter inviting all the Particular Baptist Churches throughout the country to send representatives to London for a General Assembly to meet on 3rd September. The letter spoke of the Glorious [bloodless] Revolution and

---

[32] *A History of English Baptists*, A. C. Underwood p.116.

their remarkable deliverance from persecution but also spoke of the condition of the churches and the ministry. The delegates had to be 'one of the ministry and one principal brother of their congregation'. The churches had to reply to either Hanserd Knollys [who was ninety] or William Kiffin [who was seventy-three], ministers who had been leaders in the 1640s and 1650s. Over one hundred churches in England and Wales sent delegates. A list of these men is to be found in *A History of English Baptists* by Joseph Ivimey Vol. 1 pp. 503-511. Those going from the Porton /Broughton church were Walter Penn and John Andrews. It would appear that Colonel Rede was too old to take the journey. William Aldridge and Edward Froude represented Erlestoke Church; Joseph Houlton and John Layes represented the Southwick/Trowbridge Church; John Williams went up from the East Knoyle/Sedgehill Church; James Webb went from Devizes Other churches in Wiltshire represented included Bradford-on-Avon, Malmesbury, Westbury, and Warminster. Andrew Gifford went up from Bristol, Richard Gay from Haycombe, Bath, Richard Kent and Stephen Kent from Whitchurch [Hants] and Richard Ring and John Greenwood from Southampton. The delegates came from all areas of the country, from Durham and Northumberland to Devon and Cornwall, from Cardiganshire and Monmouthshire across to Suffolk and Norfolk, with some of the largest contingents coming from Wiltshire and Hampshire, Somerset and Middlesex.

It must have been an extraordinary gathering as they shared details of their prolonged sufferings and sorrows and remembered their own imprisonments and their brethren who had died in prison. How one would like to have listened to their conversations. In the later publication of the proceedings of their Assembly, they made it clear that they had no jurisdiction whatever over the churches, which were independent. Even their advice was not binding until individual churches had accepted it. They discussed a wide range of subjects including the ministry. It was decided to set up a fund to help poorer churches pay their ministers, to send ministers 'where the Gospel hath or hath not yet been preached and to visit the churches'. It was also agreed to assist ministerial candidates to acquire a knowledge of Latin, Greek and Hebrew, though there was a difference of opinion on this subject and at a later Assembly at Bristol in 1693 they passed a resolution that 'the knowledge of tongues is not essential.... to constitute a minister of the gospel, but they dare not limit the Holy One, who bestows gifts for edification upon the learned as well as upon the unlearned.' They agreed that it would be a good thing for smaller churches who were near each other and could not afford to pay a minister to join together to be able to support one minister. They denounced worldly dress and the wearing of long hair by men, especially ministers. Finally they agreed to republish in its entirety the *Particular Baptist Confession* of 1677 and between thirty to forty ministers signed it, representing churches from all over England and Wales, among whom were leading names such as Hanserd Knollys, William Kiffin, Benjamin Keach, Andrew Gifford, Richard Ring and James Webb. They agreed to meet again at Whitsun 1690, but by then fewer delegates attended through difficulties of travel and because it was easier to meet in local groups or associations. At a later date the Western Association of churches was to bring together churches in Hampshire, Wiltshire, Somerset, Dorset and Devon. The men of 1689 had had high hopes after the persecution ended that there would be a spiritual revival among them, but they were to prove that it was persecution that kept them spiritually most healthy.

The Last Years of John Rede

They returned home to be able to worship in quietness and peace. Now there would be no informers, no ministers in prison and they knew that King William and Queen Mary were Protestant monarchs and the King was a Calvinist. John Rede no doubt listened to what Walter Penn and John Andrews had to relate, but he was now an old man and after 1690 his name appears no more in the Porton Church Book. An old document among the Broughton Church records, marked, 'An extract from an old book [now missing] belonging to the Baptist Church at Sarum', details a decision made on 9th October 1690. It reads:

> 'At a meeting at Sarum[Salisbury] of the brethren formerly bearing the denomination of the Church of Christ at Porton being then and there met together to consult what would be the most effectual method in order to promote the public interest of Christ in converting souls and building up each other in the faith and order of the Gospel, do jointly agree that in order to accomplish this their design it will be most expedient for the time to come to sit down in two distinct congregations, those in and about Sarum to sit down together with Brother Penn to their Pastor, who formerly belonged to the whole in that capacity, and the other part to sit down in the country at what place they think most fit for their conveniency, having Brother Rede for their Pastor formerly in that capacity with Brother Penn. And as we do by this signify our free and unanimous consent to the premises. Witness our hands,
>
> John Rede, Stephen Kent, John Andrews, Andrew Wheble, Henry Abbott, William Knight, John Lane, John Smith. Abraham Froud, Thomas Sturges, Henry Blake, Richard Beaumont, Edward Strugnill, Thomas Steele, John Whit, John Willdren etc.'

This decision reflects the Government's change in policy. No longer were the dissenting ministers barred by the Five-Mile Act from living in or visiting any town. Now they took advantage of their new found freedom and the Porton congregation divided into two congregations, one at Salisbury and another at Porton. Walter Penn who had suffered long imprisonments in Salisbury Gaol now moved to have his own church there. John Rede stayed as pastor at Porton. It is interesting that the first Porton Church Book shows among the accounts payments made regularly from 1657 to 1679 for the renting of accommodation for a meeting place in Salisbury. This possibly may have been the scene of secret meetings in the city. There may also have been other reasons for the division of the congregation. Several minutes in the Church Book for 1681 record a dispute between Walter Penn and John Rede over a loan of money and its repayment. The matter is first mentioned in March 1680 and after other brethren were called in to arbitrate the matter was finally settled in August 1681. It shows that a dual pastorate could have its problems and that these strong-minded men who had suffered so much could in more peaceful days let their warrior instincts gain an upper hand over their gracious hearts. The final minute shows grace uppermost as it reads, 'The Church received full satisfaction in ye matter relating to Brother Penn and Brother Rede and they with each other to their mutual comfort.' But all in all, by 1690 in more peaceful times, it would seem better for these two leaders to each have their own pastorates.

Some time between 1690 and 1699 when Henry Steele was appointed pastor, John Rede moved to Devizes.[33] This may have been as late as 1698. His name appears low on the membership list of the Devizes Particular Baptist Church where James Webb was pastor from 1689-1701. The church records contain two bequests by Rede of £100 each, payable on his death to the Particular Baptist Churches at Devizes and at Southampton. Andrew Gifford who had ordained him at Porton in 1679 was a signatory of both bequests. It is also of interest that Richard Ring of Southampton was one of the ministers that officiated at the ordination of Henry Steele at Porton in 1699. These records show the close contact of all the Particular Baptist Churches and ministers throughout Hampshire, Wiltshire and Somerset. John Rede died at Devizes, January 2nd 1710.[34] Why he moved there is not clear. It is possible that his regiment fought there with Cromwell in 1645, which is the year the Devizes Old Baptist Church is reputed to have been formed. So he may have already had connections with the Particular Baptists in that town. He was an aged

[33] OBC p.31.

[34] WSRO 1215.24.

man in his late eighties or nineties when he died. It is not known where Rede lies buried, but a tomb at a small Baptist cemetery near Birdlimes Farm, Porton records,

> 'Here lieth the body of Sarah the wife of John Rede, gent. late of Birdlimes Farm in the Tything of Porton. She departed this life at Devizes ye 24th of February 1708 aged 49 years.'

In fact Sarah Rede was a member of James Webb's church at Devizes where her husband had his membership. Nearby at Birdlimes Farm graveyard is the tombstone of Sarah Carteret Rede, daughter of John and Sarah Rede who died at Devizes 12th December 1700 aged 6 years 11 months. From this it would appear that Rede married late in life and had one daughter. His end must have been sad, losing both his child and his wife in his old age and being left alone for the last year of his life.

Henry Steele [1655-1739]

The leadership of the Porton/Broughton Church now passed to a new generation, though still one that was not without experience of persecution. Henry Steele had been born in the Protectorate of Oliver Cromwell and was thirty-three at the time of the Glorious Revolution in 1688. He was a lad of seventeen in 1672, at the time of the Declaration of Indulgence, though it probably did not affect him much as he was unconverted at the time. But 'he was a child of the Porton Church, for it was there he heard the word of God and felt its saving power.'[35] It was there he was baptised by William Bunday on 10th October 1680, the same year that his father William Steele II died. Henry was the means of bringing his brother Thomas [Anne Steele's grandfather] to the meeting and he was baptised at Porton by Walter Penn on 27th August 1685. Dr Steadman [pastor at Broughton 1791-96] says in his *Journal* that Henry Steele at the time of the separation [in 1690], if not prior to it, was an occasional preacher, and in the year 1699 was ordained pastor of the church, which office he held for forty years. There is no record of his being sent by the church to preach because the first Church Book ends in 1684 and the next one does not start until 1710. But it is certain that he will have exercised his gift before the Porton Church under the pastorate of Walter Penn and John Rede [whom he will have known well], as did Stephen Kent [in 1683], who later ministered at Whitchurch, Hants. In an entry in the second Church Book [1710-29], which was inserted after 1710, it reads,

> 'On 22nd September 1699 Henry Steele was ordayned pastor of this congregation, by fasting and prayer, and ye laying on of ye hands of ye

[35] HBBCH p.15.

> Eldership, namely, Brother Richard King of East Street Southampton, and Richard Kent of Whitchurch.'

John Rede had resigned the pastorate, but would almost certainly, if able, have attended that ordination service. He was to live on for another ten years at Devizes and, as his bequests show, keep in contact with the Hampshire and Wiltshire churches.

Henry Steele had been a member of the Porton Church for nineteen years and was forty-four at the time he accepted the pastorate. His name first appears in the Porton Church Book in 1680 at the time of his baptising. It next appears on a document dated 1689 relating to the Deeds of the Broughton Meeting House, in which in which he is described as a house carpenter. There is extant[36] a contract between himself and Sarah Rollo of Lockerley near Broughton to build a house and a schoolhouse at Lockerley and in this document he is described as a timber merchant. The house was to have solid oak floors and wainscotting four feet high, and ten chimneys. The total cost of the building was £550. He must have been married before 1699 as in a late undated list in the first Church Book his name appears with Clemence Steele [his wife], Thomas Steele and others. His ordination is recorded in the second Church Book and thereafter his name appears regularly. A letter survives which he wrote to the church at Whitchurch dated 18th February 1698/9 asking for consideration to be given to raising money to help Stephen Kent, their minister. He says,

> 'When I was with you at Whitchurch and since, I have been much concerned in my mind about the state and condition of Brother Stephen Kent and what might be requisite for myself and you to do.'

On the reverse of the letter are various names with certain sums of money beside them, among which is Henry Steele £2, by far the largest sum.

A deed dated 1701 for the Meeting House at Broughton shows that Henry gave the land for the Baptist burying ground and two cottages which his brother Thomas converted into the Meeting House. As pastor of the church meeting at Porton and Broughton [eight miles apart] it is not clear how Henry Steele shared his time. Perhaps he preached in the morning at Porton and the evening at Broughton, or vice versa, or he may have preached alternate Sundays in each place. Equally what the situation was at Porton after John Rede moved to Devizes about 1699 and left Birdlimes Farm, is unknown. Was the farm sold or did the congregation retain a barn as a meeting place? The fact that in 1701 they were building

---

[36] HRO.

a proper Meeting House in Broughton suggests that Broughton was becoming the official centre for the congregation and Porton was becoming an outpost. Since the division of Porton and Salisbury congregations in 1690 one would assume that the members living to the west and north of Salisbury attended Walter Penn's ministry and that there were not so many left at Porton. In an undated list of members in the first Church Book seventy-eight members are listed according to the villages in which they lived. Those within reach of Salisbury, living in Amesbury, Bulford, Durrington, Stoford, Pitton, Winterbourne, Broad Chalke and Salisbury itself numbered thirty-five. There were only six actually living in Porton. But in Hampshire at Broughton, the Wallop villages, a mile or so to the north of Broughton, at Tytherley and Dean close to Broughton there were thirty-four. In fact it would be easy for the remnant left at Porton to go into Salisbury. These figures represent baptised members only, so that as there were no doubt many in the families unbaptised, including children, the congregations could have been quite substantial. From these figures it is clear that to facilitate travel the original Porton/Broughton Church was being divided, not between Porton and Salisbury, but between Broughton and Salisbury, i.e between Wiltshire and Hampshire. Porton had been ideal in the days of persecution when many were willing to travel many miles to meet together in isolated places. In the days of peace and freedom congregations were beginning to meet locally.

The second Church Book records a decision at a church meeting at Broughton held on 24th May 1704. It reads,

> 'Agreed at a Church meeting at Broughton that those Lord's days that the Broughton and Wallop friends meet together at Broughton, it shall be esteemed a Church Meeting and therein they shall have full power to do any church business.'

It is witnessed by Henry Steele and eight other members. It suggests, that not only was there coming a division between Porton and Broughton [which is not mentioned], but also between Wallop and Broughton, though in 1704 they regarded themselves as one congregation. Exactly when Porton and Broughton separated is not clear, but after 1710 the second Church Book ceases to mention Porton and only mentions Broughton. Porton had centred around the home and ministry of John Rede. When Henry took over the pastorate and his home, business and property were in Broughton, this meant that a change of venue for the church was inevitable. It would appear that the separation was natural and amicable, if indeed the little Porton remnant continued to exist as a separate church or joined with Walter Penn's church at Salisbury.

Henry was the last pastor of the Porton/Broughton Church and the first pastor of the Broughton Church. The church records, dating back to 1653 were in his hands and so came to Broughton. [They are now deposited in the Regent's Park Baptist College at Oxford.] A nineteenth-century pastor of Broughton wrote of him in 1878, 'Henry Steele was a man after God's own heart and a preacher of no mean order. His sermons were all very carefully prepared, written and probably read, as reading was then the fashion of the day. His popularity became such that the clergyman of Broughton complained to his bishop, Dr Gilbert Burnett,

> 'that one Henry Steele had set up preaching and had drawn all the people after him; asking the bishop how best he should oppose his rival. The good bishop answered, "Go home and preach better than Henry Steele and the people will return." This would have been no easy task for the bishop, and quite impossible to the Broughton parson; therefore the people continued to flock to hear Henry Steele. Under his ministry the Church enjoyed a long season of peace and prosperity. He was not dependent upon the church for his support, which was an element of no mean power.'[37]

The second Church Book records that on 22nd June 1708 Henry Steele baptised his nephew [William Steele, Anne Steele's father] when William, the son of Henry's brother Thomas, was nineteen. Mention is made of Henry in some letters which his nephew William Steele wrote to his first wife Anne Froude around the time of their marriage. In a letter dated 14th September 1713 we learn that William would have visited Anne except for the fact that Aunt Steele [Clemence] was seriously ill. In a letter dated 14th December 1713 to Anne, he writes, 'Uncle is gone to London and thence to Portsmouth.' In a later letter dated 30th November 1714 he writes, 'Uncle is gone to Portsmouth in order to contract.' These references show that Henry Steele was a timber merchant contracting to the Navy and that Henry and William were working together in the same business. They were also building timber houses. It also shows that they were a rich family. Not only were they selling oak to the Navy but also they were purchasing the broken up parts of old ships and using them in the building of timbered houses. Some of the timbers of their 1701 Meeting House at Broughton were reputed to have come from the scrapped warship, the 'Royal Sovereign'.

William Steele III [1689-1769]

In 1708, the year that William Steele was baptised with his sister Mary Steele by their Uncle Henry, his father Thomas Steele died. Thomas, like his brother Henry, was in the building and timber business in a substantial

[37] HBBCH pp.15-16.

way. His will[38] reveals he had five children by two wives. William III had an older brother Thomas and a younger sister Mary. In the will Mary is given all the wearing apparel and childbed linen of her own mother. The Broughton Parish Burial Register contains an entry for 16th September 1692 for 'Mary Steele Anabaptist', which is probably William, Thomas and Mary's mother, and it would seem possible that she died in childbirth, after the birth of Mary. All the other goods in the home were to go to his daughter Elizabeth on the death of his second wife Mary Steele [née Knight]. Elizabeth had a brother of her own, Henry, who was ten when his father died. William III was nineteen at the time, while his brother Thomas would have been about twenty-one. The will shows that the two girls, Mary and Elizabeth, were in their teens. It would seem that their father died between the ages of forty and fifty. The girls were left £150 each and their young brother Henry £190 at the age of twenty-one. The two older brothers received equal shares in the residue of their father's estate which must have amounted to about £400 each. The will shows that their father's estate was worth over one thousand pounds. Young Thomas died within a year of his father and William received in his brother's will the other half of his father's estate. So at the age of twenty William was left as head of his family to help his stepmother with the young lad Henry, and two sisters both in their teens. At the same time the whole responsibility for his father's business had fallen on his shoulders. It seems likely that at some later date his stepmother and her two children may have left Broughton, as there is no further mention of them in family records and in the Baptist graveyard at Lyndhurst in the New Forest there is a stone with the names of Henry and Elizabeth Steele on it. This left William and his sister Mary in the home at *Grandfathers* in Broughton alone, bereaved of both parents, William just twenty and Mary two or three years younger. No doubt Henry Steele, their uncle, was watching over them and helping William with the business, while his sister Mary kept house for him.

William Steele's Marriage

While there is no entry in the Broughton Baptist Church Book, it seems that William Steele began preaching in 1708 at the early age of nineteen within a few months of being baptised in the River Wallop by his uncle.[39] He assisted his uncle for twenty years as preaching elder until his uncle's death in 1739. But not only would he have preached in the Broughton congregation but would have travelled around other Particular Baptist Churches in the vicinity. It seems likely that it was the ministry

[38] HRO.

[39] HBBCH p.16.

that took him to Wiltshire to the church at Erlestoke, where he met his first wife, Anne Froude. A correspondence started between them and she must have treasured his letters for eleven of them have survived in the family archive. They must also have been valued by her children, William and Anne, who would both have been too young to remember their mother when she died in childbirth in 1720. Only one of her own letters to her future husband has survived. The first of these letters from William is headed 'Broughton Dec. 12 1712',[40] when he was twenty-three and she was twenty-eight. [Anne had just lost her brother who had died at the age of thirty-five on 17th November 1712.] It is in verse and runs to more than seventy lines. It is probably the first communication that he had with her. How William learnt to write poetry is not clear. How or where he was educated is unknown. It is possible that he had attended the Particular Baptist Academy in the Conigre Parsonage in Trowbridge, built in 1700 by the rich Baptist clothier, Joseph Houlton, and run by the learned Baptist minister John Davisson. William had come from an affluent family but as a Dissenter he was barred from all university education. But it is likely that, as with Isaac Watts, William Steele was a born poet and that this ability was inherited by his daughter Anne, the hymnwriter who also came to Trowbridge for her education in 1729. He wrote to Anne Froude:

'Ingenious and beloved friend
Who fills my heart with grief,
The noble temper of your mind
Doth yield me great relief.
Else how should I my trouble bear,
As being quite forlorn?
In what dark shades must I reside
If all my hopes were gone?......

My dearest love, let love attract
And draw to me your love,
And with affection let's unite
Like as the turtle doves.
I'm bound to you with bonds of love
That will last to the grave,
Pray therefore let me have your love;
It's only this I crave.
O could I but your love obtain,
'Twould fill my heart with joy,
But then with longing I would wait
To see the marriage day.

[40] STE1/2/i.

A line of answer, love, I crave,
That I may know your mind,
Earnestly begging that I may,
With you acceptance find.
So I your lover now remain,
'Twixt hope and fear do dwell;
An answer now is looked for by
Your fervent William Steele.'

How quickly the courtship developed is not clear. With William's involvement in the timber business and his preaching engagements little time would have been left to travel frequently from Broughton across Salisbury Plain to Tinhead where Anne lived. The next letter is dated 'Broughton May 18th 1713',[41] and reveals that he had come to see her and that their love for one another was developing and that they were seeking divine guidance as to their future. It reads:

> 'Mrs Anne,
>
> The observation I made when I saw your prudent behaviour hath fully confirmed what I heard before concerning you. So can no longer forbear declaring that you are ye subject of my thoughts, ye object of my love, ye darling of my heart, and one whom I am satisfied upon due consideration is every way (for a bride) most worthy of my choice, and a suitable companion in ye nearest relation, is of all the affairs of this life, of ye greatest moment, because according to our choice, we are not only in a great measure happy, or miserable, with respect to this life, but are helped or hindered in our preparation for Eternity, and being entirely satisfied in you, cannot but earnestly long for you, therefore do make bold by this to tell you my mind, praying you to consider and make due inquiry concerning me that by letter or when I see you (which I hope will be shortly) I may know if there is any reason to hope for my desire, which is due returns of love and ye enjoyment of you my beloved. I shall add nothing by way of argument but desire you (as I also will) to ask the direction of God in this matter and then if by His Providence we are united we shall be undoubtedly happy with ye enjoyment of each other. If you have opportunity pray favour me with a line of answer which will very much oblige one who desires to be yours in ye nearest relation, and am now Madam your sincere lover and humble servant, William Steele.'

The next letter is dated September 14th 1713[42] and refers to 'ye pleasing prospect of future joy, which may possibly be made sweeter by

---

[41]STE 1/2/ii.
[42] STE 1/2.

your present absence'. It is addressed to Mrs Anne at Mr Richard Tezard's House in Donhead. Richard Tezard was married to Anne's sister Elizabeth and was living in the area of Donhead St Andrew and Donhead St Mary, just outside Shaftesbury. This was only about three miles from Sedgehill, the farm of her brother Edward. William apologises for being unable to come and see her and explains that his Aunt Steele [wife of Henry] was dangerously ill and he was busy with the business, presumably because his Uncle Henry could not leave his wife. He asks for news of her journey over the Downs from Tinhead to Donhead because of the bad weather. He signs himself, 'Your ardent lover and humble servant'. Two weeks later on 30th September[43] William writes from Salisbury to say that he cannot come to Tinhead as arranged on the following Saturday because of 'multiplicity of business'. The letter speaks of betrothal arrangements. William says, 'I have not heard from your kinsman and know not how matters stand, but be it how it will, I hope with your concurrence all difficulties may be removed and all things concluded to mutual satisfaction that desire may be turned to enjoyment.' He signs himself, 'Your affectionate lover'. Presumably he and Anne had now agreed to get engaged but they still awaited the formal betrothal contract. The marriage licence was issued on 1st December 1713 and two weeks later on 14th December[44] William wrote to Anne, 'Dear Spouse, These are to acquaint you that I shall not come ye Saturday as designed because my Uncle who comes with me, is gone to London and goes thence to Portsmouth and will not return home until Saturday night so I shall not see you until Monday 21st at which time, God willing you may depend on my coming... I rest your own in affection and as a token of my love, I wish you a good husband.' This letter shows 'the multiplicity of business' which included visits to the Admiralty in London and to the Royal Naval Dockyard at Portsmouth to contract for timber in the building of warships of the same type as HMS Victory. With only one day at Broughton, William and his uncle were coming to Tinhead to complete the marriage contract with Edward Froude and his wife.

It has not been possible at the present time to find out the church where William and Anne were married or the date of the wedding. The wedding may have taken place in December at the time when William came with his Uncle Henry to complete the marriage contract. One thing however is clear. By the time of the next letter of William's, dated 8th February 1714,[45] they were married as the letter was addressed to Mrs

[43] ibid.
[44] ibid.
[45] ibid.

Anne Steele, and was written from Broughton to Anne at her home at Tinhead, so that the actual marriage must have taken place between 21st December 1713 and 8th February 1714. She was there to look after her mother who was suffering with breast cancer. He sends his duty 'to mother and father and love to her brothers' and signs himself 'with great pleasure and satisfaction, your loving husband'. On 30th February[46] Anne replied to this letter hoping that he would soon be able to come over to Tinhead when his business allowed. She sent the love of her parents and signed herself, 'Your constant loving wife'. A letter written in May 1714[47] shows that Anne is still at Tinhead looking after her mother and that William is at Broughton presumably being looked after by his sister Mary. The whole situation shows a rather sad start to their married life, and yet it reveals something of Anne's nature in caring for her mother and William's willingness to spare her to do this – a real Christian sacrifice for both of them. The letter mentions the possibility that his sister Mary may come over to Tinhead, probably to help Anne.

Two more letters follow on 18th and 30th October 1714[48] which both reveal how much he is missing her and counting the days until she comes back to Broughton. In the second he says, 'I don't love to live alone.' He refers to receiving letters from her and tells her how depressed he is at her continued absence. The next letter is dated 30th November 1714[49] and opens with the information, 'I got home very well.' Edward Froude, Anne's father had died on 20th November aged sixty-nine and had been buried in the Priory Church at Edington on 26th November. William was in fact returning a few days after the funeral to Broughton leaving Anne behind to help her mother and her brothers. The brothers at home would have been the three youngest, William, James and Blackbarrow. Robert died in 1714 within a few weeks of his father. Elizabeth, the eldest daughter, was living at Donhead and had children of her own at this time so that everything in the home at Tinhead rested on Anne. Edward the oldest boy was running the farm at Sedgehill and Thomas was married with a family of four children the last of whom was born in 1711. The home in Tinhead, with loss of a father and two brothers in three years and their mother suffering from breast cancer, must have been a very sad place and Anne the youngest daughter was bearing the brunt of it. William in his letter consoled Anne with the words, 'The loss of so tender a father cannot but be grievous and hard to be borne; but if we consider it, though

---

[46] ibid.
[47] ibid.
[48] ibid.
[49] ibid.

one great stream of comfort is cut off, yet the fountain's always full.... The use we make of such dispensations is to breathe forth the desires of our souls to the God of grace; to teach us true submission to Himself by Jesus Christ; to prepare us by a work of sanctification for our great change, that when we are called from hence to the other world we may behold the face of God with joy.' Little did he know when he penned these words of consolation to Anne how soon it would be before she herself would be 'called from hence into the other world and behold the face of her God with joy.'

Figure 6: 'Grandfathers' (Frontispiece of Daniel Sedgwick's 1863 Edition of Anne Steele's Hymns)

The last of these eleven letters was written from Broughton to Anne at her mother's house at Tinhead and is dated 26th May 1716.[50] Anne has taken her young son, William, born in 1715, to show him to her mother. The letter has been carried by John Sutton, one of William Steele's employees who plans 'to be in Tinhead Sunday morning by eight o'clock in order to go to Stoak', i.e to attend the morning service there at the Particular Baptist Meeting at Erlestoke, over which Edward Froude had been pastor for many years. William says, 'Sister [Mary] remembers her love to you and Willy,' and adds, 'Next Tuesday God willing, I hope to

[50] ibid.

see you at Winterbourne.' The Winterbourne villages were just outside Salisbury on the road that led up to Porton, the home of Colonel Rede. It would be interesting to know what route and what form of transport Anne used to travel from Tinhead to Winterbourne with her baby son. William was to meet her with the family carriage [the chaise] and take her the last eight miles to Broughton. The new little family was living in the old family house in Broughton, called *Grandfathers.* Here the Steele family had lived for several generations. Anne, the subject of our memoir, was born in the home by the River Wallop in Broughton, during the second week of May 1717. Another boy, Thomas, was born in May 1720, but he only lived a month and was buried on 1st July. Their mother died suddenly on 22nd May 1720 at the age of thirty-six and was buried in the parish churchyard at Broughton. The large table grave has on the side, 'Anne, the first wife of William Steele died on 22nd May 1720 aged thirty-six.'

Figure 7: The Gravestone of William Steele's Two Wives

William Steele was again in the throes of sorrow. Having lost both parents by the age of nineteen, now he had lost his young wife whom he loved so dearly, almost certainly in childbirth, and was left with William aged five, Anne aged three and Thomas, who was to survive his mother by a matter of weeks, being buried on 1st July. He was only thirty-one at the time, and was travelling to preach at the weekend, as well as conducting, with his Uncle Henry, an extensive timber business which required constant travelling. When Henry Steele died in 1739 at the age of eighty-four he left three farms and when William Steele died in 1769, he also left several farms. It would seem probable that by 1720 the Steeles had begun to invest the profits of their timber business in farms and that they had farm managers in charge of them. This would suggest that in 1720 William Steele was heavily involved in business and preaching. His sister Mary eventually married John Benham of Whitchurch, but when is not known. It is probable that in 1720 she was still at home at *Grandfathers* and could help William in the care of his little family. One thing is certain, namely that sanctified sorrow would deepen the work of grace in William Steele's heart and make his ministry more profitable to his hearers. He was still young, yet his life had been full of sorrows and bereavements, not only in his own family but also in that of his wife Anne.

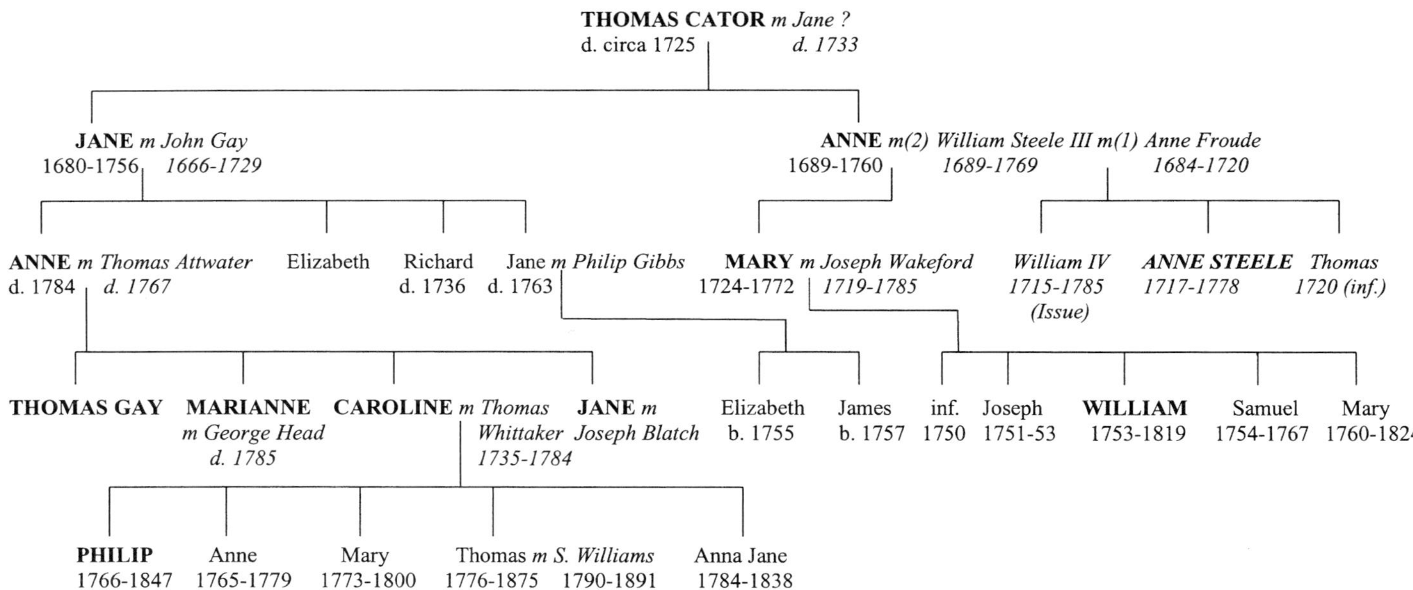

Figure 8: The Cator Family Tree

Chapter 3

A Daughter of Broughton [1720-32]

William Steele's Second Marriage [1723]

William Steele managed in the home at Broughton with his two children for over two years before he sought a second wife. A series of his letters has been preserved in the family collection written to Anne Cator at Trowle Common near Trowbridge. Her father Thomas Cator was a farmer who had two daughters, Jane and Anne. Jane was already married [pre 1710] when the correspondence began and Anne was living at home looking after her parents. The Cators were Particular Baptists. Anne refers in her Diary [28th July 1733] to having heard Andrew Gifford, the Bristol Particular Baptist minister, preach in 1707, when she was eighteen, from Matthew 11.12. 'The kingdom of heaven suffereth violence and the violent take it by force.' She says regarding that sermon over twenty-five years later, 'I hope it was to my advantage.'

The first letter from Broughton to Trowle was dated 18th September 1722.[51] The letter shows that William Steele and Anne Cator had met at least once. William refers to her 'way of conversation', and speaks of 'the captivating power of love which unites my heart to you'. But he also refers to his fears that he would never have his desire, so that it would seem that their friendship was in its infancy. It is not altogether surprising that his two wives should come from the same area of Wiltshire. He himself was travelling, preaching in various meetings in the area. The Meeting at Erlestoke was known to him, as were probably the Particular Baptist Meetings at Trowbridge and Bradford. Trowle Common lay between Trowbridge and Bradford-on-Avon so it was possible for Thomas Cator and his family to have attended either Meeting. It was certain the Particular Baptists, especially in the days of persecution, would have been very close to each other, and it would seem that William Steele came into contact with Anne Cator through his connections with the Froude family at Tinhead and Erlestoke. In the letter William Steele goes on to say,

[51] STE 1/3.

> 'I am well-satisfied, we both desire to be directed by the providence of God in this very weighty matter and there seemeth to me to be a concurrence of providence that leads to the union I so much desire, as being directed and advised to you above all others, though at so great a distance from you [and whether you have not had the same advice to me by indifferent and judicious persons is best known to yourself] that sweet satisfaction and delight that I found in communion and converse with you and as I hope in some measure you with me. The ardency of my affections, which I do assure you runs out in full streams toward you [and should be glad if I knew of suitable returns, but this is best known to you] the ready consent of all my relations and friends and doubt not also of some of yours, these with many others, I conclude are providences that direct us to the union and I cannot see but 'tis our duty to be directed by it.'

But there was one great obstacle to which he alludes as he writes,

> 'The unwillingness of your parents to consent unto it on account of distance of the place do not seem to be a weighty argument, because it is mutually agreed on all hands that we have satisfaction in the great things.... The backwardness of your parents must proceed from their nature of affections to their daughter exceeding their due bounds, which should not be suffered to prevail against the spiritual advantage of the child... 'Tis our duty to obey God rather than man... If you have any inclination to grant my request pray don't conceal it from me.'

He adds a footnote to the effect that he hopes to come to see her the following Tuesday, unless his mother Froude should meet him at Salisbury, when he would not then be able to get to Trowle Common until 5th October. This shows us that he was still in close contact with his first wife's family and that they were coming to stay at Broughton. Presumably Mrs Froude's breast cancer had gone into remission. He asks for a letter from Anne and says, 'You may send by Hayward the carrier, who cometh to Sarum [Salisbury] every Monday and direct to me to be left at the Three Lions by the Council House in Sarum.'

At the time of this letter both William and Anne were thirty-three. It seems rather injudicious and selfish of Thomas Cator and his wife to put their own interests before their daughter's. Anne was torn in two directions. It brought her into great distress and obviously brought her to prayer. In her Diary[52] many years later she remembers especially 'a promise [God] sent me in my distress on 3rd October 1722', but she does not say what the promise was, but it obviously relates to this time of sorrow and anxiety brought about by her parents' attitude. It is clear that

[52] ASD 6th February 1732 STE 2/1/1.

Figure 9: The Salisbury Coach Road at Tinhead

this date was significant in their courtship. The next two letters are dated 26th November and 3rd December.[53] In the first William writes of his journey home from Trowle and shows that his base in visiting the area was at Tinhead with the Froude family. He tells Anne that on his return to Broughton he waited at Tinhead 'for my brother Froude [one of his late wife's brothers] to go with me and the rain coming on very bad, we went no further than the top of Tinhead Hill, but returned and stayed at Tinhead till the next day and so had very good weather and through mercy got home well.' The road they travelled across Salisbury Plain was the coach road which crossed the Plain from Tinhead to Stapleford and then to Salisbury. It was signposted by milestones and it was unsafe to travel in bad weather when it was not possible to follow these. He goes on to say

[53] STE 1/3.

that he had had some conversation with a friend of his and sends the substancc of it to Anne. It is obviously an outline of himself as his friend saw it. It throws an interesting light on William Steele's temperament and make-up. It reads, 'As to temporal concerns, honest and industrious; as to common behaviour somewhat light and merry and as to religion a constant hearer [listener] is the most that can be said.' It is a very frank assessment of himself, and he tells Anne, 'It is better to be well-informed,' so that if they married she would have no surprises. He ends his letter, 'With sincere desires to be enabled to subscribe, Your loving husband William Steele.' In the second letter[54] in December he asks for an interest in her prayers, 'that I may not only have that necessary grace but have it in due and proper exercise that [as I profess to believe in the providence of God] I may arrive to true contentment of mind and cheerfully submit to God's wise disposal who orders all things as it is most for His glory and His people's good, and if it tends to this end, I doubt not but my desire may be yet obtained.' This shows that he still did not have the full consent of Anne who was a woman who was of a very anxious disposition and did not find it easy to make decisions, especially leaving her own environment, in which she had lived for over thirty years and move to a completely new one. One wonders also whether a deep affection for her parents, who were not young, [her father died in 1725 aged sixty-three and her mother in 1733] may have been influencing her to hesitate. In this letter he goes on to make a very revealing statement about himself. He speaks of an occurrence in which he was at fault and says,

> 'It was for want of due consideration that I was guilty of that fault respecting our friend [which was in some measure made up by you and brother Froude]. He had a bad journey but arrived safe. I heard him both parts of the day. He seemed at first under some surprise, but soon recovered it and went through the work very well, and I doubt not but as God has bestowed a gift on him, he will make him useful for His glory and the good of souls.'

This incident shows a true Christian spirit in William Steele, a willingness to openly confess a fault and seek to put matters rights. It obviously concerns a young minister. Who it was we shall never know. William Steele had been preaching for at least fifteen years. These letters reveal the true man who was Anne Steele's father; he was cheerful, hardworking, conscientious, a good listener and had a forgiving spirit. He was open, sincere and honest; not proud, though a man of some wealth and station in life.

---

[54] ibid.

His next letter to her is dated 18th February 1723.[55] He tells her that he had reached home safely and says, 'The love I have to you makes me long to see your face.... I am now in good measure freed from my former thoughts of fear [having better ground to hope God will give me the desire of my heart in His own due time].' He speaks of the pleasing reflections of 'your endearing conversation, particularly when I was last with you', and goes on to speak of 'desire being turned into enjoyment'. He concludes, 'My duty to Father and Mother, and love to brother Gay's family if you see any of them.' 'Brother Gay' was John Gay, the husband of Anne's sister Jane. The Gays were living at Haycombe, south of Bath, on the opposite side of a most beautiful valley to the village of Englishcombe. The Gays were people of some wealth, farmers. They were also Particular Baptists and had a meeting in their home at Haycombe. On 23rd March[56] Anne sent a brief letter to William to tell him, 'My father has been that designed journey and has a promise of a Rough Draft to be ready by Tuesday 2nd April, and my father thinks it most advisable for you with him to go thither and see it, if you shall think fit. The gentleman will be at home on Tuesday or Wednesday 2nd or 3rd of the next month, and after that not certain to be spoke with unless it be on a Saturday.' She sends her services to William's uncle and aunt [Henry Steele and his wife] and to your mother Froude [his mother-in-law]. William replied on 26th March[57] to say, 'I am very willing to come at the time proposed and go with your father.' He also tells her that there is a remote possibility that he may not be able to come as he has two parcels of timber he expects to buy which may prevent his coming. On 1st April[58] he wrote to say that on the previous Saturday he had bought £700 worth of timber 'and was well pleased'. He did this hoping to come to Trowle the following Tuesday. But now he had heard of another parcel of timber which he wants to buy and must go to see it on Wednesday 3rd so he cannot come to Trowle until Friday. He adds, 'Affection must give place to reason.' He says, 'I desire nothing but our mutual interest and therefore doubt not that you will put the best construction, this being the only time to buy and lay the foundation for my business for the rest of the year.' He asks her to pray for him for divine direction and a blessing in all his affairs and promises he will not forget her in like season. This exchange of letters shows that a marriage contract was in process of being drawn up and it would appear that 'the designed journey' to which Anne refers was a visit of her father to a lawyer at Bath. In fact the actual

[55] ibid.
[56] STE 2/2/2.
[57] STE 1/3.
[58] ibid.

marriage was within a month of taking place.

In his next letter dated 15th April[59] he says that 'the satisfaction of that union does give him a foretaste of it, which yields that calmness and serenity of mind', that in some time past he was too much a stranger to. 'I now rest satisfied in the providence of God,' he writes, 'though I am sensible that the thought of removing from your parents, may sometimes oppress your mind.' But he knows she has a desire for guidance and can clearly see the wise direction of providence in answer to her prayers. He tells her that the second timber deal with Squire Harris fell through and goes on to say that after doing his bidding at Redbridge [at the head of Southampton Water] on Wednesday, he went on Thursday to Ringwood, then to a wood near Christchurch on Friday, on to Wimborne Fair that same afternoon after which he returned to Sir John Webb's house 'and made a good fasting supper with the papists [Roman Catholics], it being Lent and Good Friday, and returned home Saturday, a long and tedious journey to no purpose'. He had not clinched the deal but only brought it a little nearer and deferred it until another time. He says that he passed through all without any considerable disturbance of mind... 'having resigned the matter to the wise providence of God, who orders all things for His people's good'. Now he proposes to come to Trowle on Saturday and stay until Tuesday. He signs himself, 'Your intended loving husband'. Anne replied to this letter on 20th April[60] and was glad that he enjoyed such a cheerful frame of mind. She had had severe toothache, had the tooth taken out, but it broke and made the pain worse. It took several days to calm down. She confesses to apprehensions with respect to leaving her dear parents and changing her native place for a strange one. She hopes following God's guidance as to the future, 'she will be in a capacity better to improve the talent that God has entrusted her with.' She says such thoughts give her some intervals of peace in the midst of her self-accusing thoughts and adds, 'I know you are not insensible of the contrary winds of unbelief, distrust, discontent that a poor creature is liable to through the depravity of a corrupt nature.' She goes on, 'My ardent desire is to be a humble, submissive, close walker with God. This I have formerly found a means to screen me from those gusts of temptation which otherwise would shake the roots of my faith.' She says that her father was trying to purchase some land but had met with no better success than William had done with Squire Harris. She signs herself, 'Your obliged friend', and adds a most interesting footnote which reads, 'Yesterday my Aunt Bush made us a visit to enquire for her scholar and

---

[59] ibid.
[60]STE 2/2/2.

make her apology for not knowing you when there. Leaving a deal of service for you when you come.'

The Trowbridge Particular Baptist Academy

There is no surviving information on William Steele's education. The construction of his letters and the way he writes in long sections without a break, moving from one thought to another, suggests that he was a Latin scholar. His father-in-law, the minister Edward Froude at Tinhead, certainly was. The inscriptions on the Froude graves in Edington Priory show an excellent command of Latin. We have suggested earlier that

Figure 10: Conigre Parsonage in Trowbridge

Edward Froude was taught by William Gough, the Presbyterian minister and scholar from Oxford and Cambridge Universities. But there is another possible source of classical education for Dissenters and that was the Trowbridge Particular Baptist Academy. This had been built up by the Particular Baptist minister, John Davisson.[61] He was the minister of the Particular Baptist Church in Southwick to the west of Trowbridge and

[61] VCH Vol. III *Protestant Nonconformity,* M. Reeves.
Birth of Modern Education, J. W. Ashley-Smith.

later, when the congregation divided, of the Conigre Particular Baptist Church in Trowbridge. He was a learned man, a good preacher and a writer of several books, one in Latin on the subject of ordination. On the succession of Queen Anne in 1702 he preached and published a sermon [1703] which demonstrated the loyalty of the Particular Baptists towards the monarchy and their gratitude for the Act of Toleration. Joseph Houlton, a wealthy Trowbridge clothier and Particular Baptist, had in 1700 built a beautiful house, which later, in 1731, became known as the Conigre Parsonage, when it was used by the Conigre ministers. It was probably in the Conigre Parsonage building that the Trowbridge Particular Baptist Academy was situated.

John Davisson was a scholarly man and the Academy was principally for the training of young ministers. He preached a sermon at Taunton in 1720 on the subject of the ordination of ministers. The emphasis of his teaching lay in the study of the classical languages and the Scriptures. He felt that truth must be revealed by the Holy Spirit to his students. He was wary of too much use of commentaries. On the other hand he recommended elocution for his students and there is evidence that such subjects as mathematics, French and English Literature were taught in the Academy. Ken Rogers in his *Book of Trowbridge* [p.65] tells us that one of the rich Trowbridge clothiers, William Temple, who was a deacon and a member of the Conigre Church and died in 1736, had a taste for poetry and mathematics and that his son who died in 1773, had a good knowledge of Latin, French and Classics, none of which could have been gained at a university.

As William Steele first began preaching in 1709 at the age of twenty, there is a distinct possibility that his education was under John Davisson. This would explain the reference of 'Aunt Bush' to 'her scholar…' It might also help to explain, as we shall see later, how Anne Steele [our poet and hymnwriter] was at school in Trowbridge in 1729, at the age of twelve. She was following in the steps of her father. If William Steele did spend several years in Trowbridge in his teens [between 1700-1709], then it might explain how he came to enter the ministry in 1709 and also explain his connection with the Froudes and the Cators, so that when he sought Anne Cator for his second wife, it may be he already knew her as a girl of his own age in Trowbridge, for they were both born in 1689. It would also explain Aunt Bush's failure to recognise him, since he was now [1723] thirty-four and she last knew him as a student in his teens. There seems an unexplained ring of familiarity about Aunt Bush's reference to 'her scholar'. There is no doubt that William Steele was an educated man. It is quite clear in his letters that he had an ability to write well and think clearly which one would not normally expect from a housebuilder and timber merchant. Equally in buying timber he seemed able to mix easily with gentry. He was, in fact, an educated Dissenter, educated among his own people.

The Wedding Day

Marriage Bonds show that William Steele considered two churches as possible places for his marriage to Anne Cator. One was the parish church at Steeple Ashton, and the other was St John's, the Norman Church beside the castle at Devizes. The St John's Church marriage register[62] shows that William Steele and Anne Cator were married there on 7th May 1723. Why they chose Devizes to get married rather than the

Figure 11: St John's Church, Devizes

church at Steeple Ashton, just outside Trowbridge, is not clear. Mrs Steele's [née Cator] diary entry for 18th September 1731, refers to a visit of Anne [then aged fourteen] to Devizes and how she had returned to Broughton with 'cousin Collings'. A later reference on 8th May 1732 refers to the marriage that day of Mr Collings and Cousin Clemence Etheredge. Clemence was a granddaughter of old Henry Steele. This

---

[62] WSRO.

would suggest that the Steeles were in some way related to the Collings in Devizes and this was the reason for the marriage taking place there. In the first membership roll [8th January 1704 - 29th September 1705] of baptised members at the Old Baptist Church at Devizes are listed John Collings and Katerina Collings.[63]

John Gay of Haycombe, Bath

William Steele now had a new brother-in-law, John Gay, married to Jane, the sister of his second wife. Jane and Anne, the only two children of Thomas and Jane Cator, were particularly close. On 8th February 1718 Thomas Cator made his will. He left Anne as her portion five hundred pounds. 'Three hundred pounds to be paid to her in three months after my decease and one hundred pounds part thereof to be paid to her at the birth of her first live child in marriage and the other hundred pounds residue thereof to be paid to my daughter after she is married if living...' The will goes on, 'As to the rest and residue of my personal Estate, lands, tenements and hereditaments not before bequeathed... the same shall be in TRUST for my said daughters Jane Gay and Anne Cator and to be equally divided between them...' What was the extent of Thomas Cator's property is not certain. There was land on Trowle Common and a farmhouse and there were also houses in Bradford-on-Avon. A Deed[64] dated 1761 relates to several cottages in Woolley Street in Bradford-on-Avon owned by William Steele, and two of Jane's daughters and their husbands. This was part of the residue divided between the two daughters and kept in the family. Jane Gay who had originally held them had died in 1756 and so they were being sold. A letter from John Gay to William Steele dated 27th March 1725 shows that Thomas Cator had died. John Gay was in process of selling all the ricks of hay on the farm at Trowle Common which had belonged to his father-in-law and says, 'Mother has been at Trowle this fortnight to clear the house for the farmer who is in the possession of it and I suppose we may now take mother to Haycombe.' The farm had been sold, the home cleared and Mrs Cator was going to live with her daughter Jane. How old she was is not known but she lived about eight years at Haycombe, dying in 1733.

John Gay did not live very long after this. He died in 1729 at the age of sixty-three. He had married late in life when he was about forty-three. His wife was fourteen years younger than he. They had four children living at the time of his death, Anna aged nineteen [she married Thomas Attwater of Bodenham, near Salisbury], Elizabeth aged fourteen [she

---

[63] WSRO.

[64] WSRO.

Figure 12: Sermon Notes of Richard Gay

married Mr Phipps of Westbury, dying in 1743 when she was only twenty-eight], Richard aged twelve [he died suddenly of a fever in 1736 at the age of nineteen] and Jane aged six [she married Philip James Gibbs of Trowbridge, a very rich clothier, dying in 1763 at the age of forty].

John Gay was the son of Richard Gay, an influential Particular Baptist minister in the days of persecution. Richard Gay was a lover of the works of John Bunyan. This is shown in a book plate which reads, 'Is presented to my Honoured Christian Brother, Mr Richard Gay, Minister of the

Glorious Gospel, at Haycombe in Somersetshire, by Charles Doe, because of his good will in subscribing to the Printing of the Folio in 1692.'[65] This volume was published posthumously after Bunyan's death in 1688. Richard Gay had been in prison in the Newgate Prison in London in 1662.

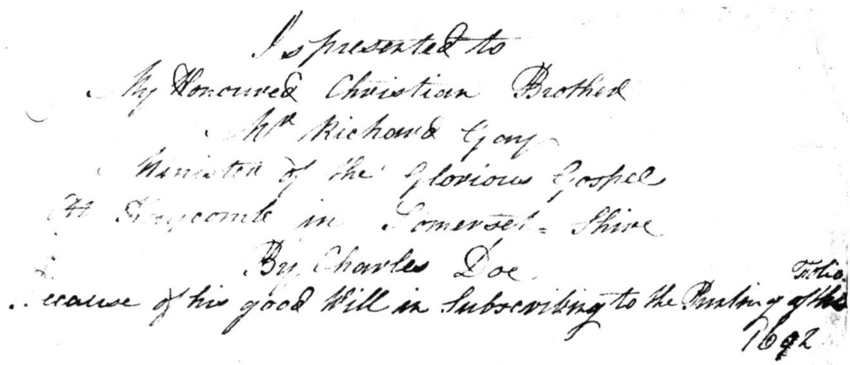
Is presented to
My Honoured Christian Brother
Mr Richard Gay
Minister of the Glorious Gospel
At Haycombe in Somerset-Shire
By Charles Doe
because of his good Will in Subscribing to the Printing of the Folio
1692

Figure 13: Inscription in a Book of Bunyan's Works, presented to Richard Gay

He had also spent three years in prison in Ilchester Gaol in Somerset for the sake of the Gospel and according to his great-granddaughter Jane Blatch, who wrote about him at Bratton, Wiltshire in 1802, he had had a wife and several children at the time. She says that her mother Anna Attwater [the daughter of John Gay] told her how Richard used to recount the great goodness of God to him during his imprisonment with tears of gratitude running down his face and one text which her mother mentioned which was blessed to him was, 'But now thus saith the Lord that created thee O Jacob, and he that formed thee O Israel, Fear not: for I have redeemed thee, I have called thee by thy name; thou art mine. When thou passest through the waters, I will be with thee; and through the rivers, they shall not overflow thee; when thou walkest through the fire, thou shalt not be burned; neither shall the flame kindle upon thee. For I am the Lord thy God. [Isaiah 43. 1-3]'

The Episcopal Returns of 1669 show that Richard Gay had a congregation of about fifty at the Haycombe Meeting, which almost certainly was in his own house. He had inherited the Haycombe estate through a great-uncle and was a man of property. In the days of persecution he paid the fines for his congregation, continually levied on them for non-attendance at the parish church at Englishcombe on the opposite side of the Combe. Haycombe and Englishcombe lie on each side of a beautiful deep, south-facing valley on the southern outskirts of Bath.

[65] The late Dr. Marjorie Reeves' Collection.

In the days when Dissenters were not allowed to have meetings, it was an ideal site for worship and to have guards to spot anyone trying to watch their meetings and report them to the authorities. In 1667 Richard Gay is reported in Southwick, near Trowbridge, with William Kiffin and Nehemiah Cox, London ministers, who had come down to Wiltshire to deal with a case of a minister [Thomas Collier] charged with heresy. Later, on 3rd August 1667 Richard Gay was present at the ordination of Andrew Gifford. [Andrew Gifford who became the leading Particular Baptist minister in the west of England, died in 1721 at the age of eighty.] In 1689, 1690 and 1691 Richard Gay represented the congregation at the Particular Baptist Assemblies in London. He also attended the Western

Figure 14: Haycombe from Englishcombe Churchyard

Association Meetings of ministers at Westbury in 1692 and at Bristol in 1694 and 1697. Some of his sermon notes are preserved, which, though very difficult to read, show that he preached from his text dividing his discourse under various headings.[66] He pastored the Meeting at Haycombe from at least 1670 - 1700. Jane Blatch says he lived to be an hundred. The last information about him is found in a legal document which he signed, with very shaky handwriting, in 1704. This then was John Gay's father and Jane Gay's father-in-law. When Jane Gay was

[66] ibid.

widowed in 1729 at the age of forty-nine, being left with her aged mother Jane Cator and her four children, it was to her sister Anne Steele and her brother-in-law that she turned for help and we shall see as the years go by constant visits of the Steele family, including our hymnwriter Anne Steele and her brother William to Haycombe to stay with their cousins.

Grandfathers 1723 Onwards

After the wedding on 7th May 1723 William Steele returned to Broughton with his new wife to run the home for him and care for his two children, William aged eight and Anne aged six. It must have been strange for their stepmother, and for the children, who had been cared for by their father's sister Mary, since the death of their mother three years before on 22nd May. They had been dependent on their Aunt Mary day and night in the last three years, while their father was away on long journeys in connection with his timber business and his preaching. They cannot have seen much of him, nor he of them, in these vital growing years. Yet the home at *Grandfathers* would have provided them with a sense of security and they could roam in the countryside around the house which was only a few yards away from the River Wallop, which flowed across a stretch of marshy willow ground on its way from the Wallop villages, where it had its source, down to the River Test just south of the village of Houghton. Their father was one day to own the mill on the river downstream from their home. No doubt they played together being close in age. The beauty of their Queen Anne house [*Grandfathers*] just to the south of the village of Broughton, standing in a lane, with a few other cottages around it, in the river valley, with the Hampshire downland stretching away to the east and the west, made a great impression on them both and brought them to love the beauties of nature and the countryside. Such beauties we shall see reflected in the poetry and letters of Anne Steele in later life.

In 1724, just over a year after Mrs Steele came to Broughton there arrived a little new life in the home. On 29th June a little girl was born. She was named Mary, but was always called Molly. Anne was known in the family as Nanny. No doubt Anne, at the age of seven, was delighted to have a sister. William was now nine and probably was spending much of his time outside. The Steeles had invested the profits of their timber business in real estate. When Henry Steele died in 1739, he left three farms to his grandchildren, one at Nether Wallop, one in Broughton and one near Whitchurch. When Anne's brother William died in 1785 he left three farms in Broughton [a total of about 500 acres] as well as other estate at Nether Wallop, at Roydon near Lymington, at Sedgehill and at Halstock in Somerset. Exactly when all these farms were acquired is not

Figure 15: 'Grandfathers'

known. William farmed some himself but the rest were let out to tenant farmers. What his father possessed in 1724 is not clear, but it seems probable that there was at least one farm in the family, when young William was a boy of ten and would be spending a large part of his time in the fields.

Anne's Education

When, or where, William went to school is unknown, but if he had done the same as his sister he was at least at school before the age of twelve. As we have previously suggested it is possible like his father he was sent to Trowbridge Academy under John Davisson. What we do know from one early letter of Anne Steele is that she was at school in

Trowbridge in 1729. On 26th September of that year she wrote to her stepmother:[67]

> 'I received your acceptable letter ['tis good to hear from you] but am sorry to hear of my brother's illness and Aunt's death and doubt not but my cousins are in a great deal of trouble for the death of their mother, but I hope the same God that no doubt for wise ends took her from them, will enable them to bear their affliction with patience. As to my liking the place, I suppose you know my mistress is an odd tempered woman, but she is as kind to me as to the rest. Our work is most on headcloths and I hope I shall learn very well. I think your acquaintance here are all very well at present. I also am through mercy in good health. Cousin Betty is sent for home, which makes me a little dull to be without her. I long to see you all and hope I shall see my father in a little time. Cousin Cottles and Mrs Hurn give their services to you, this with my duty to my father and to yourself and love to sister Molly is from your dutifull and obedient daughter, Anne Steele.
>
> P.S. I desire you would excuse my bad writing being by candle, because we work till it's dark now. Trowbridge Sept 26th 1729.'

This letter is written in neat, regular handwriting. The spelling is excellent. Later in life Anne's handwriting became quite small, though still neat and regular. It shows that Anne had obviously had some previous education before she came to Trowbridge. One wonders whether there was a school attached to the Particular Baptist Meeting in Broughton, or whether her stepmother, who was herself quite literate, had taught her. Her brother was not with her but was at home. He was now fourteen. Molly was five. The references to Cousin Cottles and Mrs Hurn tell us that Anne was worshipping at the Particular Baptist Meeting on the Conigre in Trowbridge, where Thomas Lucas was the pastor and also in charge of the Trowbridge Academy. The membership of the church numbered two hundred and thirty and the congregation about six hundred. There were four deacons, one of whom was John Hurn. Kathern Hurn and Kathern Hurn Junior are listed among the baptised lady members of the church. It is probable that it was Kathern Hurn senior that is referred to in the letter. Also among the members were Richard Cottles, Elizabeth Cottles and Elizabeth junior. It would appear that the Cottles family were related either to Anne's stepmother or to her father. It is probable that Anne was staying in the Cottles household. The family lived in Fore Street, Trowbridge, at the top end on the right, just where Fore Street joined with Silver Street.

---

[67] STE 3/7/i.

Cousin Betty was the second daughter of John and Jane Gay from Haycombe. She had been born in 1715 and was the same age as Anne's brother William. She had gone back to Haycombe almost certainly because her father was ill. He was fourteen years older than his wife and died in 1729 at the age of sixty-three. It would not appear that at the time of this letter he had died, but Cousin Betty had been called away from school to her home in term time to see him. Betty had a brother, Richard, who was the same age as Anne, but there is no mention of his being in Trowbridge. As part of her education Anne was working in the evenings and was learning to do elegant sewing to make headcloths. Presumably her 'mistress' was in fact her teacher in the day, when she did the more academic part of her education. Trowbridge and the area around was in the heart of the west of England cloth trade. Joseph Houlton, who heads the list of Conigre church members, and William Temple who was one of the deacons, were both wealthy clothiers. We have already referred to William Temple as having a liking for poetry and mathematics. Joseph Houlton owned and lived at Farleigh Hungerford Castle where he bought the Manor in 1702 for £6,500 and the Castle itself in 1731. He also owned Grittleton Manor estate, where he built himself a small Baptist Chapel in the grounds in 1720. This chapel is still in use today. It is possible that Joseph Houlton and William Temple were financially supporting both the Trowbridge Particular Baptist Academy and the Particular Baptist School for girls, which would be under the control of the Conigre Church.

So Anne was doing sewing and learning something about the cloth trade, which was the most important industry in England at the time. Much of the cloth was exported to Europe. It would be interesting to know where the school was that Anne was attending. Equally whether boys and girls were taught together or whether there were separate schools for each. The fact that Cousin Betty had come from Haycombe and she had come from Broughton suggest that they were attending some type of Particular Baptist school for girls, which was complementary to the Trowbridge Academy, which was for training young men for the ministry, but also others like William Temple and his son William Temple junior, who acquired a good education, though not training for the ministry. John Davisson died in 1721, a few weeks after preaching at the graveside of Andrew Gifford and was buried in the Conigre Chapel. The Academy was continued by Thomas Lucas, who was pastor of the Conigre Church until his death in 1742. How long Anne stayed in Trowbridge for her education is not known. Writing in her diary for 25th July 1730, Mrs Steele says, 'Willy Steele was brought home in safety. I beg of the Lord sincerely that he would make us a blessing and comfort to each other – he being to continue at home.' This seems to suggest that William, who was now fifteen, had been away at school, but now his education was over, he would work with his father in the timber and farming businesses. It is significant that Cousin Betty's brother Richard was not at school with her in Trowbridge. He was twelve in 1729. It is possible that he too was at the Trowbridge Academy with William. On 26th August 1730 Mrs Steele wrote in her diary, 'Nanny Steele is now to come home to abide with us.' Another entry for 25th March 1731 records, 'Our girls are gone to school.' Anne was within a few weeks of her fourteenth birthday and Mary was coming seven in June. If Anne were sent to school at the same age as her stepsister Mary, then it would suggest that she started school in Trowbridge in 1724, but as her stepmother's diary for the period 1720-30 period has been lost, it is not possible to confirm this.

Anne's Health

In November 1730 Anne had had measles, which one would expect, being at school. In January 1731 Mrs Steele was taken seriously ill and there were fears that she might die. She had severe pains in her stomach and on Sunday 10th January Mr Steele gave up his preaching engagements to stay with her. The severe pain continued for over a week and it seems possible that she either had appendicitis or a stomach ulcer. It is clear that both he and his wife feared that the illness might prove fatal. In February Anne was ill again with what Mrs Steele called 'the ague'. As we shall see, this fever type illness recurred all her life. It seems clear now that she was suffering from tertian malaria [marsh fever], an illness common in England in the eighteenth century, especially in marshy valleys in the south of the country. Her sister Molly also had been suffering from it. Mrs Steele in her diary for 5th January says, 'Molly had something of the ague every third day.' The girls were away from school for another two months, not returning until 29th March. By August Anne was home again from school and went on holiday on 2nd August to stay with the Collings family at Devizes. She did not return until 18th September. During the summer months the Steeles had travelled far. William Steele junior, now aged sixteen, had been staying at Haycombe and returned on 7th May. His father had also been to Haycombe and came back on 1st June with Richard Gay, a lad of fourteen. Two weeks later he took Richard with him to Portsmouth when he went on business to the Naval Dockyard. On 11th August Mr & Mrs Steele set out for Lavington and Trowbridge on their way to Haycombe. Mr Steele went on to Bristol to preach and they returned eventually on 17th August via Trowbridge, bringing Elizabeth Gay with them.

In October and November both Anne and Elizabeth were taken ill and Anne appeared to be 'going into a consumption'. Her stepmother's diary refers to her 'declining', and being 'at a poor weak rate'. But considering the fact that she lived on to be sixty-one, it would seem that she was not a victim of tuberculosis. A consultant pathologist has examined her symptoms and says, 'There is no doubt that Anne Steele suffered from malaria for most of her life... Chronic malaria would have had a progressively debilitating effect on Anne, the major consequences of which would have been anaemia, weakness, lassitude and a proneness to other infections. This liability to complicating infections is well known and underlies such statements of her step-mother as "Anne is likely to go into consumption."' The pathologist could find no clear indication that Anne ever developed consumption, though she suffered frequent coughs and colds, only to be expected in a debilitated girl living in damp surroundings by the River Wallop. In later life she suffered from stomach troubles and shortness of breath. The pathologist suggests that the stomach trouble was either caused by peptic ulceration or irritable bowel syndrome, and the breathlessness by coronary insufficiency or by repeated respiratory tract infections, chronic bronchitis or recurrent attacks of pleurisy. She also suffered in later life from very bad toothache and dental abscesses. Sadly her troubles began early in life, but there is no indication that she was naturally depressive from a child, though obviously her recurrent illnesses would have had an effect on her.[68]

Anne's Baptism

Anne's malaria had started on 10th October and continued intermittently until at least 30th November 1731. It is not until 21st December that Mrs Steele records, 'All our family is in health.' But Anne's schooling had ceased for the time being. On Sunday 7th November her stepmother stayed in with her, since she was particularly weak, and had a talk with her about 'the concerns of her soul'. Her stepmother says that that conversation stirred her up 'to cry earnestly on Anne's account that as God has been pleased to make her sensible of the want and worth of a Saviour, so he would also give her a well-grounded hope that she have an interest in that Saviour that so she might be happy here and forever.' On 30th November when Anne was still poorly her stepmother wrote, 'I beg the affliction may be sanctified to her and that her life may be spared.' But by January the next year Mrs Steele is still recording, 'Nanny have had an ague.' On 2nd March Mrs Steele wrote, 'I have great hope that God have indeed begun to work upon the souls of

---

[68] Baptist Quarterly Vol. XXXII No. 7. July 1988. pp.351-6, *Anne Steele's Health,* M. F. Dixon and H. F. Steele-Smith.

our children.' Her prayers for her three children were beginning to be answered in regard to the oldest two, William and Anne. On 8th May Clemence Etheredge [granddaughter of Henry Steele] married Mr Collings of Devizes. On 27th May Clemence's sister Sarah Etheredge and Anne's brother William went to see Henry Steele to give in their spiritual experience.

This was normal practice. Those who felt led to be baptised first went to see the pastor, and if he were satisfied then they came before the baptised members of the Church who listened to their experience and voted whether to receive them into church membership or not. If this were agreed by pastor and church then the candidates were baptised by immersion and could then attend communion at the Lord's Table. Mrs Steele says in her diary for 27th May, 'Cousin Sarah Etheredge, being under a great deal of trouble last night, William was hindered in his design of talking to Uncle this day. She manifested her desire and this evening they both talked with him in order to give in their experience and he was willing both of them should do it on the ensuing day. Nanny was troubled and seemed very much cast down. I cried to the Lord on her account... I desired to know if God would subject her will and bring her in to His house, and that came, "Him that overcometh will I make a pillar in the temple of my God." I had many thoughts on the eminency of a pillar, hoping God had designed her for some great work, he having given her a good capacity. I beg she may have love to God and a zeal for His glory agreeable thereto.' Anne was affected by her brother's coming forward for baptism.

It was Saturday evening and William and Sarah were due to come before the church on the following Sunday. Mrs Steele was carrying a confidence. Clemence Etheredge, who had recently been married, had confided in her that she also desired to join the church at Broughton. After some concern Mrs Steele told Clemence about her sister and William, and she also came forward for baptism. Henry Steele preached the next day in the morning and after the service William, Sarah and one of Mrs Steele's maids all gave in their experience and were received by the church. In the afternoon Mr Steele preached and after the service Mrs Tailor and Clemence Etheredge gave in their experience and were received. On the following Monday evening all the Steele family went to Henry Steele's for dinner and Mrs Steele says that they had 'some agreeable discourse'. There was much to discuss. There was great joy for Henry Steele who was now seventy-seven and had been pastor of the Porton/Broughton Church for well over thirty years. Five young people had felt constrained to be baptised and three of them were from his own family. He had only had one child, a daughter Clemence, and now here were two of his grandchildren blessed and brought forward as well as his great-nephew William. The first baptising took place on the following Thursday [8th June] when William, the Steeles' maid, and Mrs Tailor made their open profession of the name of Christ.

On the Saturday evening, 10th June, Mrs Steele wrote in her diary, 'I have been drawn out earnestly to desire assistance and direction for Nanny, she thinking she is willing, God assisting and directing her, to give in her experience tomorrow. I have had very encouraging Scriptures and have talked with her and find God has been very gracious to her in that way also. That was on my mind, "Happy art thou, O Israel, who is like unto thee, O people saved by the Lord," and "Who is a rock like our God." I went with Nanny to Uncle Steele, where I had great cause to rejoice in beholding the goodness of God to her.' Now it was apparent, that Anne's long illness in the previous autumn had been used for her soul's good and that the great issues of eternity had weighed in her soul as her strength appeared to be ebbing away. Being a victim of tertian malaria, it was a venture of faith to be baptised. But faith can overcome mountains and it did for Anne at the age of fifteen.

That Saturday night Mrs Steele hardly slept being 'kept awake through a sense of God's goodness to this child, and His late mercy in His thus reviving our Church... and His mercies to our family'. On the following Sunday [11th] Mr How, a minister from Kent, preached and Clemence Collings and her sister Sarah Etheredge were baptised. Also on that same Sunday Anne Steele, together with Betty Green and John Parsons, gave in their experience before the church and were received. In the evening the family went to Henry Steele's home and Mr How and a friend of his were there and had much profitable conversation. Mrs Steele says, 'This day was one of the days of the Son of Man to my soul.' For some unexplained reason Anne's baptising did not take place until Sunday 9th July. Mr Steele preached from, 'He that believeth and is baptised shall be saved,' and afterward Anne was baptised with two others. The same evening John Kent preached before the church members with a view to being sent into the ministry. His text was, 'Him hath God exalted with His right hand to be a Prince and a Saviour.' It seems that the church agreed to send him, since Mrs Steele says in her diary, 'I hope he is like to be a useful man.' John Kent was twenty-seven at the time and lived to preach for sixty-four years, dying when he was eighty-nine in 1796. He married Sarah Etheredge on 9th May 1734 and they eventually had eleven children.

What Henry Steele heard of the work of God in Anne's heart is not reported. How interesting it would have been to listen to the testimonies of William and Anne and the six others that came forward, and to hear the first sermon of John Kent. But when we come to examine the hymns that Anne later wrote, we shall see that much of her spiritual experience lies embedded in them. It was a time of true revival for the Broughton Church and a great encouragement to their pastor in his old age; eight baptised and one sent into the ministry. Since his own baptising by William Bunday in the River Bourne on 10th October 1680, and the baptising of his brother, [William and Anne's grandfather], Thomas Steele, by Walter Penn on 27th August 1685, half a century had passed, persecution had ceased and old Henry Steele was now in the thirty-third year of his pastorate. He had good cause to rejoice in the revival of his church, and the fruits of his ministry, and that of his nephew, William Steele, who was assistant pastor at this time and would later take over the pastorate from him in 1739; also for the blessing among his own grandchildren and the grandchildren of his brother Thomas.

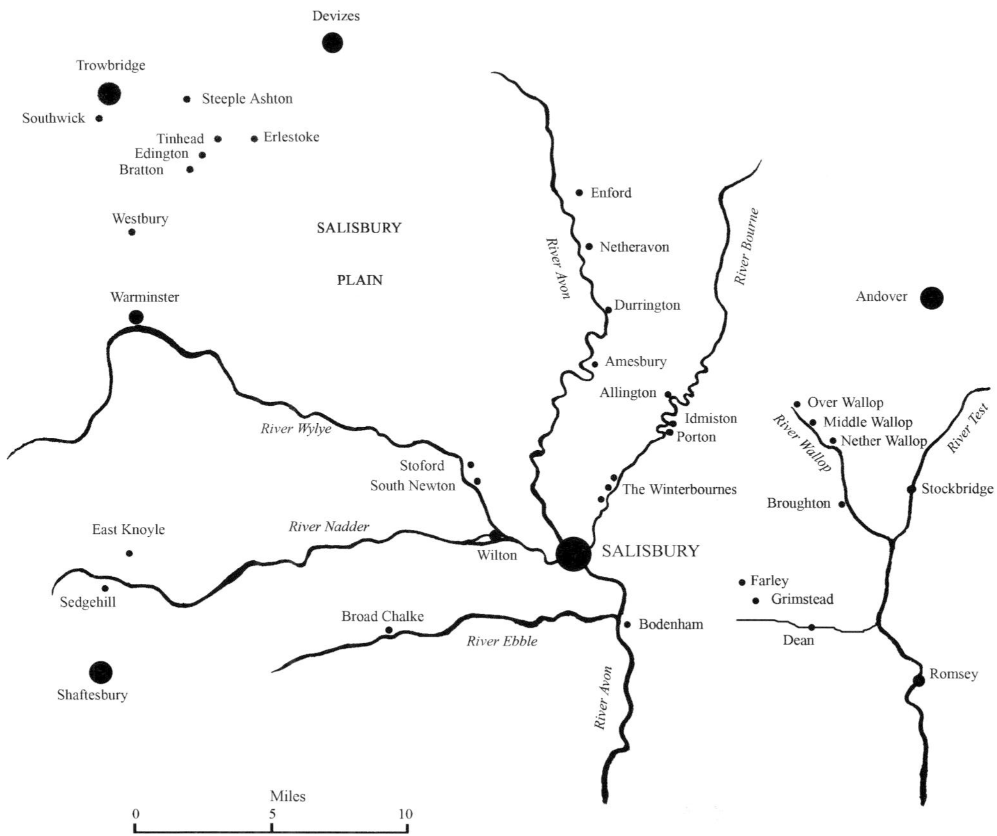

Figure 16: Map of the Hampshire/Wiltshire Area

Chapter 4

In the Spring of Life [1733-48]

Anne's Education

In the autumn of 1732 Anne was far from well and caused her stepmother a good deal of anxiety. She was almost certainly suffering from anaemia associated with her tertian malaria. Her stepmother describes her has looking 'very pale and bad'. She appears to have had no schooling since her illness in October to November 1731. But on January 23rd 1733 she went to Salisbury with her father and did not come back to Broughton until 31st January. It would appear that she had gone with her father to look at a school or be interviewed for entrance to it. A few weeks later [20th February] Mrs Steele speaks of 'putting our daughters out to a boarding school'. She had many doubts about it, knowing that they must be exposed to 'airy vain company'. She says that she talked to the school mistress in order to send them there. Later references in her diary [2nd April] show that she was talking to Mrs Connor, head of a boarding school in the Salisbury Cathedral Close. This would almost certainly have been an Anglican School. At the end of March Anne had a recurrence of malaria [the ague] but by 2nd April the decision had been taken after much anxiety. On that day Mrs Steele wrote in her diary, 'My desires being drawn out concerning the children going to a school, desiring it may be prevented if the Lord saw it best, yet I have often thought the providence of God did direct it... I now think, as I have before, whether God has not designed some work for this, His young servant, but presently thoughts would rise, how can that be, and then that came, "Out of the mouths of babes and sucklings hast thou ordained strength."'[69] Mrs Steele recognised that Anne had ability, though she could not have realised that her poetry and hymns would still be in print and in use in the twenty-first century. The Lord had designed some work for her. Her hymns have been blessed to untold numbers in the years since they were written.

Anne had lost over a year's education as a result of her ague. At this moment she was within a month of her sixteenth birthday. What was

---

[69] ASD 2nd April 1733. STE 2/1/1.

being proposed was a type of finishing school. It is clear that the Trowbridge School had been a Particular Baptist School as there had been no anxiety about sending the girls there, but the Trowbridge School was too far from Broughton and was not up to the educational level of Mrs Connor's school. On 3rd April Anne and Molly were taken to the boarding school in the Cathedral Close. They came home at Whitsun for a week and returned on 15th May. They came home again for a few days in June and then returned until 1st August, when they stayed at home for a week and returned to school until 2nd October. At that point they stayed at home for the winter. One wonders what they learnt by this intermittent education from April to October. Henry Steele did not approve of the girls going to such a school and on Sunday 9th June Mrs Steele says, 'He reproved me concerning our girls going to school, charging it upon me as sin. I defended myself as well as I could in such a doubtful case, but my thoughts were pretty much ruffled about it.' William Steele was away preaching in Salisbury that day and did not return until the following Tuesday when she related her grievance to him 'and was entirely freed from it'. It is clear that William Steele could afford to pay for this high-class education for his girls and felt it would be to their advantage. But it was at some risk, which involved a sharp division between the aged pastor and his assistant minister. Obviously Henry Steele saw a worldly element in it and certain dangers, whereas Mr and Mrs Steele wanted to do the best for their daughters. But after October 1733 when Anne was sixteen she does not appear to have had any further education.

While Anne and Molly were at school in Salisbury, Mrs Steele took the opportunity to go to Haycombe to visit her mother, old Mrs Cator who was coming near her end. On Friday 18th May she set out from Broughton, riding with William to Tinhead, to the home of James and Anne Froude. On Saturday and Sunday they stopped off in Trowbridge to see friends and eventually reached Haycombe on Monday where they stayed for ten days returning home via Tinhead and Salisbury where they visited Anne and Molly at their school. Mrs Steele went again on 10th August with Sarah Etheredge and one of their workmen and stopped with the Collings family at Devizes, before, accompanied by one of the Collings family, they came to Trowbridge and eventually to Haycombe. Now her mother was dying of dropsy and she stayed with her sister Jane until old Mrs Cator passed away on Sunday 26th August. She was buried in Englishcombe Parish Churchyard at one o'clock on Monday night, the funeral being lighted by torches and taken by the vicar. Mrs Steele was saddened by the situation of her sister, who was struggling to keep the farm business going and at the same time bring up her four children without a husband. She returned to Broughton via Trowbridge and Devizes on 31st August, bringing Richard [sixteen] and Jenny [eleven] with her, leaving the two older girls Anne and Elizabeth with their mother.

Broughton Hymnology

1733 is the year when we first begin to hear about hymns being composed in the Steele family. Mrs Steele records in her diary for Sunday 24th June, 'I was very much affected with the hymn, it being one of Mr Steele's composition.' It would seem that the roots of Anne Steele's ability to compose hymns originated with her father. But this is not the only evidence that she had grown up in a family which had a tradition of writing poetry. As already seen, her father's first approach to her mother had been with a lengthy poem. In Mrs Steele's diary for the period 1730-36,[70] there is inserted a hymn of eleven stanzas signed W.S. Jun. and dated 24th June 1734. This shows that Anne's brother William at the age of nineteen was composing hymns like his father. The hymn is written, as many of Anne's hymns were, on the basis of a text. The one William gives is Colossians 3.2, 'Set your affections on things above.'

In the era of the Particular Baptist Meeting at Porton from 1653 to 1710 the Psalms would have been sung, the ones available being the work of Thomas Sternhold and John Hopkins, usually bound with the Authorised Version of the Bible. Towards the end of the seventeenth century John Bunyan and Benjamin Keach pioneered hymn singing in their own churches among the Particular Baptists, but there was a serious division of opinion, many maintaining that only psalms should be sung in divine worship. Isaac Watts felt he would like to express gospel truths in verse. It is said of him that he is the first Englishman to set the gospel to music. He can in many ways be described as the Father of English hymn singing. He published his *Hymns and Spiritual Songs* in 1707 and his *Psalms of David* in 1719. Within a short while these were printed as the *Psalms and Hymns of Isaac Watts*. When these *Psalms and Hymns* were first used at Broughton is not known. Eventually in the eighteenth century hymns became accepted and many appeared from the pens of such men as Doddridge, Cowper, Newton, Toplady, Berridge, Cennick, Hart, Charles Wesley and Haweis. There were two hymnwriters among the Broughton Particular Baptists in the eighteenth century, Anne Steele and Charles Cole of Whitchurch. Other Particular Baptist hymnwriters of the eighteenth century included Joseph Stennett, Benjamin Beddome, Samuel Medley, Joseph Swain, Richard Burnham and John Lacey of Portsmouth.

---

[70] ibid.

While the hymns of Anne have been published in several editions [1760, 1780, 1810 (Boston, USA), 1863, 1967] those of her brother and father have been lost and forgotten. But the hymn that William, her brother, wrote in 1734 is worth reprinting.

'What hidden sweets or tempting joys,
Mistaken soul, attract thy choice;
That earth with her delusive charms,
Detains the prisoner in her arms?

Celestial joys invite my taste,
And Jesus spreads the heavenly feast,
With pleasures permanent and true
Forever sweet, forever new.

From thee alone, dear Saviour, flows
The sovereign balm for all my woes;
In thee alone the craving mind
Substantial happiness can find.

From earth and all her transient scene
Of hopes and pleasures, cares and pains,
On wings of love, my soul, ascend
To joys that never, never end.

Let faith with heavenly-minded eyes
Explore the regions of the skies,
Through boundless realms of glory rove,
Prepared by everlasting love.

Those realms where happy spirits find
Delights immortal as the mind,
Where pleasure flows in living springs,
And peace expands her balmy wings.'

The influence of Isaac Watts is apparent in these verses, as also is the resemblance to his sister's hymns, she also being influenced by Watts. It would seem possible that Anne who was seventeen in 1734 may have seen these verses and suggested improvements. A manuscript tune book has survived among the Steele papers. It contains about forty tunes arranged for part-singing in the order alto, tenor, soprano, base. The index allocates individual tunes to psalms and hymns. The index is divided under psalms, and hymns, Book 1 and Book 2, and is clearly designed as a companion tune book to Isaac Watts' *Psalms and Hymns* which is divided in exactly this order. There is no indication as to the date of the tune book, but it contains such well-known tunes as Stroudwater, Old Hundredth and Bedford, and is beautifully produced in the form of a small book for use in the church services. How many of the congregation could read music is unknown. How many could read at all is not clear, though wills often reveal an inability to read and write, where they are signed with a cross and it says, 'His mark.' On 8th April 1734, Mr and Mrs Steele paid a visit to Salisbury Cathedral and were present at Evensong. Mrs Steele's curt comment on the service was, 'The organ and singing makes such a confused noise that I cannot help admiring how any pretending to sense can think that to be the right way of worshipping God.'[71] It is of course a matter of every man to his own opinion, and Mrs Steele did not like Anglican church music. But the tunes used in the Cathedral were those usually set to the Psalms and bound with the current versions of the Bible. Most Bibles, whether the Bishops' Bible, the Geneva Bible or the Authorised Bible, contained at the back the Psalms set to music. Strangely it is these tunes such as the Old Hundredth, Stroudwater and others that were sung in the Anglican Church, that were also sung in the Church of Scotland and among Dissenters. It is clear from Mrs Steele's remarks that there was no organ at Broughton though, no doubt, the Steeles were rich enough to afford one. It would appear from the settings of the Broughton tune book that singing was led by a precentor, as in the Church of Scotland. It is possible that some musical instruments were also used such as a violin, viola, flute or oboe, but this is speculation based on nineteenth-century practices among Particular Baptist Churches in Wiltshire. Also it is possible at Broughton that each verse of the hymns was read and then sung, in order to help those who were not literate. Again this was a practice used in the nineteenth century. This would have enabled Mr Steele's hymn to be sung without it being printed as a single copy for each member of the congregation. It is likely that those members of the congregation who could not read or write, and yet possessed an ear for music, could play an instrument, and thus take part in the worship.

The Cousins at Haycombe

1734 was a year of much travelling on horseback for Anne. Now she had finished her education and was better in her health, she took advantage of the warm weather and began to travel. On 10th May she and Molly went to stay at Whitchurch for a fortnight with their uncle John Benham, partner in the Steele timber business, and brother-in-law to William Steele, having married his sister Mary Steele. Anne would have known her aunt well, as she looked after her as a child when she was

[71] ASD 8th April 1734. ibid.

motherless. Jenny Gay, Mrs Steele's niece, had come over from Haycombe for a summer holiday at Broughton and on 31st May she and Anne rode to Lyndhurst with Mr Steele, who was on business in the New Forest. It was to Lyndhurst that Mr Steele's stepmother had gone with her two children, Elizabeth and Henry, when his father had died in 1708. It was probably to the home of his half-brother, Henry Steele, that he took the girls. Anne was seventeen and Jenny eleven at the time. On 18th June Anne and Jenny went with Mr Steele to Salisbury and on 3rd July the girls accompanied Mr Steele and Cousin Collings to Portsmouth, where the Knight family lived. William Knight was a cousin of William Steele and was agent for the Steele timber business in its trade with the Royal Naval Dockyard. On 30th July Anne's brother William and Richard Gay, who was staying at Broughton with his sister Jenny, went to Oxford for three days to see the University, which they were unable to attend because they were Dissenters.

On the 6th August, Anne, Molly, William, Richard and Jenny set out together on horseback from Broughton for Haycombe. Mrs Steele records in her diary that it was 'fine harvest weather'. William was the oldest, aged nineteen, Richard and Anne were seventeen, Molly eleven and Jenny ten. Running the home at Haycombe were the two elder sisters, Anna and Elizabeth, helping Mrs Gay with the farm business. Anna was twenty-four and Elizabeth nineteen. Elizabeth had been baptised at Haycombe eight months before on 5th January and joined the church there. The journey to Haycombe was about fifty miles and took the youngsters two days. They probably stayed with the Collings at Devizes for one night and passed through Trowbridge and then across the steep sides of the Avon valley to Combe Down and eventually to Haycombe. Anne and Molly stayed eleven weeks until Mr Steele came down to Haycombe and brought them home on 22nd October. The farmhouse at Haycombe was high up on the west side of the south-facing valley. The Particular Baptist Meeting was in a building on the farm, where old Richard Gay had been pastor for many years. Across the opposite side of the valley was the village of Englishcombe. The views to the south were splendid and over to the north the road dropped down into Bath, where the River Avon ran on the east side of the old city on its way to Bristol. In the week the young people could ride in the hilly countryside round Haycombe or go down into Bath and see the city that was in process of development.

Richard [Beau] Nash had come to Bath in 1705 and as Master of Ceremonies was working to make the old medieval city into a clean, respectable, civilised place. He persuaded the Corporation to set about cleaning the streets and repairing the main roads as they entered the city.

He began to bring order to Bath, setting standards of dress, banning the carrying of swords and duelling, bringing gambling under control, licensing sedan chairs, the main source of local transport, and having wider pavements. Then he planned Assembly Rooms and had the Assembly House and the Harrison Rooms built in 1708 as a centre of social life in the city.

In 1712 Ralph Allen came to Bath at the age of eighteen as Deputy-Postmaster. He found the whole system corrupt, local postmasters pocketing much of the revenue. By 1715 he was appointed chief Postmaster at Bath. He borrowed £6000 and bought the right to operate the Bye-way and Cross-road postal services, that is the delivery routes to places not served by the main routes. With great efficiency he set about reorganising the postal system in all the area around and removing many corrupt practices of the postal staff, making the business profitable. Having made a large amount of money, he invested it in the purchase of the stone quarries on Combe Down to the south-east of Bath. He could see the possibility of Bath stone being used in extensive development in the city, and also being shipped to London and elsewhere. The River Avon had recently been made commercially navigable as far as Bath, and so the stone could be shipped out through Bristol. The map of Bath, drawn by William Stukely in 1723, shows the city exactly as it was before the new developments began.[72]

In 1727 a twenty-year-old builder and surveyor, John Wood, came to Bath with plans to turn the city back to its former Roman roots and make it into the Rome of Britain. The aim was to build in Bath stone using classical Palladian designs. In 1727 he built himself a town house in classical design to give the inhabitants of Bath a taste of what his plans were to build a new city in the Palladian style. In 1728 Wood built the Pump Rooms where patients could come to the watering spa and drink the waters in comfort under the supervision of Dr William Oliver. By 1729 he was ready for the first grand scheme of Palladian architecture when he began to build Queen Square in honour of Queen Caroline, wife of George II. He entered into negotiations with Robert Gay, a London surgeon, for the lease of land just to the north of the city walls. It is possible that this man was some distant connection of the Gays of Haycombe. Queen Square took seven years to build and was completed in 1736. By 1735 John Wood was working on his next scheme, a great mansion in Palladian style for Ralph Allen, situated at the head of the Lyncombe Vale, looking down on the village of Widcombe, which lay

[72] *Bath in the Eighteenth Century*, E. J. Sheppard, 1971 p.49.

beside the bridge across the River Avon that led to the medieval South Gate of Bath. This mansion was sited right beside Ralph Allen's stone quarries on Combe Down from which he had built a tramway to take the quarry stone down to Bath and to the river. It was on the same line of hills as Haycombe and just three miles to the east.

Anne Steele's stay at Haycombe in 1734 came at the very early stages of the building of the new city of Bath. The old medieval walls of the city would still have been in existence with their four gates. The access to Bath for the Gays would have been across the river to Southgate Street and through the old gate which lay at the junction of Southgate Street and Stall Street. Queen Square, built on land to the north of the old city, was just outside the walls. It would have been largely completed in 1734 with the splendid palace front on the north side of the Square. Up in Lyncombe Vale the foundations of Ralph Allen's new home were being laid, which was to become a cultural centre for Bath with leading artists such as Gainsborough and Hoare, the Bath portrait painter, Alexander Pope, the poet, and other well-known writers being entertained there. The Gay family, who had for several generations owned the Haycombe estate and had had many relations in old Bath itself, while as Dissenters they would have been completely separate from the godless and worldly atmosphere of Bath, yet they were to be influenced by its culture in architecture, furniture, painting and poetry. Anne's brother William had beautiful oil paintings of himself and his family, which possibly are the work of Hoare or Gainsborough. Anne shows in her writings that she had read the poetry of Alexander Pope. But now at the age of seventeen, coming from the little village of Broughton and staying at the estate at Haycombe she would have been a sightseer, while she may have bought a few books in Bath for herself. She could have visited the Abbey surrounded by new and old buildings. One thing was certain: the bracing air up at Haycombe was far better for her health than her home at *Grandfathers* beside the marshy valley of the River Wallop. Her brother and Richard Gay had just visited Oxford. Now she and William could see the beginnings of beautiful eighteenth-century Bath. It is just possible that when Anne was at school in Trowbridge in 1729 she had stayed at Haycombe with her cousin Betty and been taken to see Bath before John Wood began to develop it.

On 13th August Mrs Steele in her diary refers to 'a certain affair relating to my eldest niece'. William had returned alone after a week at Haycombe bringing news that Anne and Molly had settled in and some other news about Anna Gay, who was now twenty-four. On 13th September, a month later, Anna Gay came to Broughton and what was happening became clear. On 17th September Mr and Mrs Steele took her to Bodenham, just south of Salisbury, in the Avon Valley to have dinner at the home of Mr Thomas Attwater. He was a gentleman farmer, attending the Particular Baptist Meeting in Salisbury. As such Mr Steele would have known him well. He was forty-three, had lost his first wife in 1732 and now wished Anna to be his second wife. On 27th September Anne Steele wrote to her stepmother at Broughton to say that her aunt was a little uneasy at not having heard from Cousin Anna. She says that Molly would like to stay at Haycombe for the whole winter, but says she herself would rather come home to Broughton. She reveals Cousin Grace Cottle had come over to see them from Trowbridge and that there was smallpox in the town.[73] She says, 'Mrs Shrapnel has lost two children, Mr Truman his apprentice and Betty Culverhouse her son.' In the entry to her diary for 22nd October, Mrs Steele says, 'This morning Mr Steele is gone towards my sister's [Haycombe] in order to settle the matter between Mr Attwater and my niece Anna Gay, and also to bring home our two daughters.' A note among the Steele papers appears to have come from Anna Gay to her mother and was possibly inserted in a letter from Mrs Steele to Anne. It reads, 'I hope you will promise £1000, or considering Mr Attwater's proposal is so large and I am satisfied of his ability, if you talk of less you will make me look very little. I hope you will consider it and consult with my uncle and remember your former promise.' This was, in fact, the arrangement of the marriage contract between the two families and Mr Steele was negotiating the dowry. The figures reveal something of the financial situation of the Gay family at Haycombe. Four days later, on 30th October, Mr Steele reached Broughton with the two girls. On 16th December Richard and Elizabeth Gay arrived in Broughton and on the 17th Mrs Steele writes, 'This day appointed for Mr Attwater to be married to my eldest niece.' The wedding breakfast did not take place until 19th when Mrs Steele records, 'This morning Squire Jarvis came with his coach to take us to Barford; also my sister's children with our whole family and other company... there was great feasting and ado...' Andrews & Drury's Map of Wiltshire [1773] shows two large houses in the Avon Valley, between Bodenham and Downton, just south of Salisbury. One was Standlynch House which in the early nineteenth century was presented to Nelson after the Battle of Trafalgar [in 1805] and was renamed Trafalgar House, and lying between Standlynch and Downton was a sizeable estate house at Barford, presumably the property of Squire Jarvis. Here the Steele and Gay families gathered with other guests. Mr and Mrs Steele came home on 20th but left their three children

[73] STE 3/7/ii.

at Bodenham. They did not return to Broughton until New Year's Eve. Now Mrs Steele had a close relation in the area. It was about ten miles cross-country from Broughton to Bodenham. As the years went by and a family was born there was to be close contact between the Steeles and the Attwaters.

In the New Year after coming home from Bodenham, Anne was constantly ill with her tertian malaria. Mrs Steele records for four months, 'Anne in a poor weak state.' She also mentions trouble with Molly. Her health was not good and she too was probably a victim of malaria. But Molly was also difficult and bad tempered. In the previous year Mrs Steele had mentioned in her diary that there were constant feuds between Anne and Molly and she had reasoned with them. She also said, 'If I am partial I desire the Lord to make me sensible of it.' In April of 1735 she

Figure 17: The Attwaters' House at Bodenham

said, "I observed the stubbornness and crossness of my child [aged eleven]... the child is often thrown into anger... which grieved me.' All this shows that Anne's life was not easy. She was now ill over long periods with weakness and the ague and was plagued by this young half-sister. Also her father was constantly away from home, either preaching or going out to value timber.

On 6th February Mrs Steele makes a rare complaint, 'I found myself pensive [depressed] on account of my husband being so long and so often away from home...I have but little of his company.' Mr Steele had got up on 3rd February at 3 a.m. to go to Alresford Fair. Alresford was about six miles to the east of Winchester and about sixteen miles from Broughton. He had returned home but gone again to Alresford on 6th February. Mrs Steele was having to bring up the family alone. William was now twenty and often travelled for his father, Anne had reached eighteen, Molly was still a child. Mrs Steele was carrying the worry of the health of Anne and Molly and having to get them to the doctor at Stockbridge. In April Mr Steele and William were away for three days to Redbridge to value timber. The day after they went Molly was playing with some young people in the barn, when she was hit hard on the chin and quite badly injured. Mrs Steele in her diary begs pardon for her 'unbecoming behaviour'. She had obviously lost her temper, having to manage alone. Molly was 'venturesome and took risks'. Mrs Steele feared the worst and no husband in sight.

The Western Association

On Tuesday 27th May 1735 William went to Bratton, where the Erlestoke congregation of his late grandfather, Edward Froude, had just

Figure 18: Bratton Particular Baptist Chapel 1734

built themselves their first chapel. High on the wall of this beautifully designed building, carved in stone is the date 1734. This was a very similar move to that of the Porton Church when it divided and moved to Salisbury and Broughton. It must have meant that most of the congregation had either died or moved from Erlestoke, and the great majority were now living in the Bratton, Edington, Tinhead area. The reason for the journey was that the Western Association of Particular Baptist Churches had decided to hold their annual gathering in the newly erected chapel. Barring extensions on either side of the chapel, the building is the same as when erected in 1734, both inside and out. The old pews and pulpit have been preserved. Here about twenty ministers and elders gathered for a three-day meeting, to discuss the condition of their churches. The meetings would have heard letters read from all the churches in the west, reporting on blessings and problems. Discussion would have followed. A sermon would have been preached by one of the elder ministers at the close of the assembly. William, now twenty, went to represent the Broughton Church. A similar meeting of the Western Association was held at Bratton in 1752 when William went with his father and his uncle John Benham. The closing sermon that year was preached by Joseph Stennett II from Romans 10.16, 'But they have not all obeyed the Gospel...' It was later printed and a copy survives.[74]

Here in Bratton William would have met with his mother's family. His uncle Thomas Froude had only died in the previous year, but his uncle James was living in Tinhead in the old family home, and his uncle Blackborrow was living in Steeple Ashton. Almost certainly he stayed with James at Tinhead and visited the graves of his grandfather and uncle John in the main nave of Edington Priory. In his stepmother's diary for the period 1730-36 is a scrap of paper which contains an English translation of the Latin inscription on his grandfather's grave. It is possible that this translation is the work of William, which he brought back to Broughton for the benefit of his sister Anne on that occasion. He returned to Broughton on Saturday 31st, with Bernard Foskett [1685-1758] Principal of the Bristol Particular Baptist Academy [1720-54] and pastor of the Broadmead Particular Baptist Church, Bristol [1724-58]. Later several other ministers came to stay at *Grandfathers*. Mrs Steele records in her diary for Monday 2nd June, 'Here were four ministers to lodge. The evening was spent conversing of diverse things.' Foskett would have been a man able to teach Greek, Latin and Hebrew. He was the first Principal of the Academy and was to be followed by Hugh Evans in 1754, who was succeeded by Caleb Evans in 1781. Anne must have met Bernard Foskett that evening. She was now eighteen. These events reveal something of the home life of the Steele family, and their

[74] ALRPC.

connections within the Particular Baptist churches. Much later when a second edition of Anne's Hymns and Poems was published [after her death] in 1780, it was Caleb Evans who wrote the preface. One of the ministers, who was tutored by Foskett, was Benjamin Beddome [1717-95]. Bernard Foskett, a single man, had lived with the Beddome family in Bristol and had given the charge and offered the ordination prayer when Benjamin Beddome was ordained pastor of the Particular Baptist Church at Bourton-on-the-Water on 23rd September 1743. No doubt old Henry Steele, who was now over eighty, would have been present to meet Bernard Foskett and the other ministers.

Mr Steele's Accident 1735

Two weeks later, on Sunday morning, 15th June, whilst riding to Wallop to preach at the meeting there, Mr Steele was thrown from his horse and sustained very serious injuries. He was due back for lunch to preach at Broughton in the afternoon. But when he was due home John Kent came to fetch Mrs Steele to the home of Stephen Kent at Wallop where Mr Steele had been taken after the accident. His horse had trampled on him and he had a badly bruised and injured right leg; his left hip was broken and his left leg had a compound fracture. He had lain on the road for half an hour before he had been found. Three surgeons and a doctor came to treat him. They set his hip but could do very little with his left leg. He developed a high temperature and the doctor feared he would develop gangrene. His temperature did not go down for two weeks and he had to stay at the home of Stephen Kent for six weeks. The doctor got him up for the first time on 23rd July and on 28th July eighteen men came with a specially constructed stretcher to carry him in relays of six from Wallop back to Broughton. He walked for a few yards on 12th August, gradually recovered and preached again for the first time on Sunday 12th October. Many people came to visit him as he lay at Wallop, including the Attwaters from Bodenham, the Knights from Portsmouth, the Gays from Haycombe. John Sharpe, the pastor of the church at Frome from 1690-1740, now an old man, came to see him on 24th July to tell him how concerned they were in the West Country for him. When he got back to *Grandfathers*, Mr Sharpe returned thanks in prayer with great warmth. Sunday 9th November was set apart by the Broughton Church as a thanksgiving day for his recovery. By December the use of his left leg returned though it was fully an inch shorter than his right leg. He went out on timber business for the first time on 20th December to Andover in the family chaise with Mrs Steele. It would seem by now he was riding his horse again and returning to his normal work. He was forty-six at the time of the accident.

The effect on the family can only be imagined. Mrs Steele, who had grieved over his long absences, now had him at home for six months. It appears to have had an effect on his soul. Mrs Steele describes the sweetness of his prayer when he was first able to pray at Wallop and the savour of the first sermon he preached at Broughton on 12th October. He had suffered excruciating pain and been at the gates of death, but it is clear that the suffering had been for his spiritual profit and for that of his wife. His life had seen other tragedies in the death of his first wife, followed by the death of his baby Thomas. Anne and William no doubt prayed much for their father. Mrs Steele speaks on one occasions of being greatly moved by William's prayer in the home. By October Mr Steele was sufficiently recovered for Anne and Molly to spend two weeks at Whitchurch at the Benhams. By the spring of 1736 Mr Steele was returning to the normal frequency of his travels in search of timber.

The last days of Richard Gay

On 14th January 1736 Mr Steele went with William and John Benham to value a great quantity of timber at Whiteparish, just to the south-east of Salisbury. On 19th January he negotiated with the owner at Salisbury and eventually paid £3,200 for it.[75] At the end of February and beginning of March Elizabeth Gay was ill at Salisbury for ten days and Mr & Mrs Steele went over to visit her on 8th March and stayed with the Attwaters at Bodenham for the night. That same day Richard Gay came from Haycombe to see his sister and stayed at Broughton for ten days. On 17th March Mr and Mrs Steele went to Romsey and the next day Richard Gay went home. Mr Steele went to Romsey on business on Saturday 3rd April and stayed the night so he could preach there on the following Sunday. On 17th April Mr Steele went to Winchester and Elizabeth Gay returned to Haycombe. It would seem that Elizabeth Gay had come down to visit her sister at Bodenham and had been taken ill at Salisbury. In a letter dated 29th November 1736,[76] Anne tells her brother William that the smallpox is increasing at Salisbury. It would seem possible that this is what Elizabeth Gay had. Early in March Mrs Gay wrote from Haycombe to her sister at Broughton asking her to visit Elizabeth again at Salisbury. Mrs Steele says in her diary that she had not the courage to undertake the journey, but one wonders if she were also concerned about catching the disease.

During the summer Anne accompanied her sister Molly to Trowbridge to school. They stayed with Joseph Cottles' family, in the same home

---

[75] ASD.
[76] STE 3/8/iv.

where Anne had stayed in 1729 when she was at school there. On 27th June Anne wrote to her brother William at Broughton.[77] She refers to having received a letter from her father and says she had waited for a long time for a letter from her brother. She tells him of the 'continual noisy din of the town' and longs for the quiet enjoyment of the 'solitary fields where there is no clamorous noise or hurry'. She mourns her carnal state of mind and 'dead, inactive frame', feels incapable of doing anything acceptable in the sight of God, acknowledges her own impotence and flies to the blood of the Redeemer where alone relief is to be found. She was nineteen at the time that she wrote this letter and Mary [Molly] was twelve. She adds in a footnote that she was suffering from toothache, and her sister was 'going to school as mother ordered; also that they had been to Haycombe for a week and that the weather was very hot...' William replied to this letter on 28th June.[78] He writes in a beautiful script [it seems clear that he had had a good education] telling his sister of the summer scene at Broughton in the river valley with the surrounding hills and ends by speaking of the illness of a relative and the accident of Thomas Attwater who had been thrown from his horse near Winchester onto new gravel and adds, 'His lips were cut almost to pieces; he is a dismal spectacle to behold.' The diaries of Mrs Steele reveal a constant series of accidents among horse riders in the family. Both Anne and her brother William were thrown from their horses on more than one occasion and Mrs Steele records an accident outside *Grandfathers* at Broughton when their chaise was turned over and three of them were thrown out. William appears to be far too busy to write on a regular basis to his sister but when she complains, he writes at once. While Anne sat at her desk writing letters, as she did all her life to a large group of friends, William was riding the countryside valuing timber. But it would appear nevertheless that they were very close to each other, as well as to their cousins at Haycombe.

In the autumn of 1736 Anne and William exchanged another couple of letters, but in very sad circumstances. Richard Gay, the heir to the Haycombe estate, died suddenly in early October at the age of nineteen. He had last been at Broughton when he came to Salisbury to see his sister Betty [Elizabeth] when she was ill in the spring. He had stayed ten days and left Broughton, almost certainly for the last time, on 18th March. William had been staying at Haycombe when Richard was taken ill and was present when he died. On Sunday 5th October he wrote to his sister at Broughton to tell her what had happened. He said,[79]

[77] STE 3/8/ii.
[78] STE 3/8/ii.
[79] STE 3/8/iii.

"Dear Sister,

Nothing could be more welcome than your moving letter, (which I yesterday received) to revive those tender sentiments of grief and compassion which seemed to languish in my breast. I have indeed, as you observe, been witness, and not only so but have been partaker of the most affecting scene of sorrow and distress. What did I behold, what did I feel, when first, pale and trembling, I entered the melancholy room; instead of that friendly embrace, which was usual to our first meeting, I saw the poor unhappy youth (a dismal image of death) stretched on his bed and panting for breath amid his tortures. He bore his afflictions with the greatest patience, nor once murmured or repined at Almighty Providence, while death gradually approached and stretched his gloomy sceptre over his brows. 'Twas enough to have melted a heart of stone or made even a statue to weep to have heard him, while he drew every breath shorter and shorter and his heart throbbed violently in a higher station. I say to have heard him call on his Lord, his Saviour and his Judge; which was all we could distinguish, his voice was so very low; I was forced to retire to hide my rising grief and give vent to my passion. But how shall I paint the awful hour, how shall I describe the fatal minute when the wandering soul took her flight from her earthly mansion and sought a dwelling in a strange unknown region? I was with him in the last moments, I heard his speech falter, I saw his breath fail and his every motion cease; when the gloomy tyrant did his message and took away his soul into eternity, which he resigned without a groan or a struggle, which he resigned into the hands of his Almighty donor, fetching only a deep sigh and everlasting silence ensued... How great, how momentous is a preparation for a future state; it should certainly be the chief concern of life since thereon depends eternal happiness. May my dear sister seek the true means of salvation, which is surely an interest in our dear Redeemer, and never give over until we have finished our race with Glory. My Aunt is [blessed be God] pretty well recovered from her distemper, though she is yet very low spirited, and talks very much of dying and complains of her head. Cousins are pretty well and are gone to Mr Crabbs at Rode for a little time... I am, thank God, very well now, though I have been pretty much disordered for two or three days past. My hand is almost well. I design to return home sometime this week (though Aunt is very unwilling) but I believe not till near the latter end... I remain dear sister,

Your loving brother and faithful friend,

Wm Steele Jun.

Mrs Gay had been widowed at the age of forty-nine. Her husband had been fourteen years older than she. Richard had been twelve when his father died and was nineteen when he himself died. He was the only son and heir. His sister Anna was married and living at Bodenham; Elizabeth, baptised two years before her brother's death, was to marry Mr Phipps of Westbury and die, probably in childbirth, in 1743 at the age of twenty-eight. Jane, who was six when her father died and thirteen when her brother died, was to marry Philip Gibbs, a clothier, and live at *Rosefield House* in Trowbridge. The tragedy for Mrs Gay was very great. A letter[80] of Anne's, dated 29th November, has survived in which she speaks of the long period her brother has been away and how she longs to see him again. She mentions the death of Richard and refers to 'the agonising tortures of a cruel disease, which baffled the utmost skill of physicians'. She considers the distracting sorrows of her aunt in the loss of her only son, and the fact that her aunt was a victim of the 'same distemper', also the 'loss of the hopes of an ancient family'. Her heart is touched by the great distress of Richard's sisters. She mentions 'the fatal accident which threatened you', which suggests that something had happened to endanger William's life and the possibility that she also might have lost her brother. She says, 'Forever blessed be that almighty power that preserved you from the gates of death.' She hopes her cousins might escape the infection and wonders whether her brother is perfectly recovered. She adds in a postscript, 'The smallpox increasing at Salisbury and John Kent not thinking it proper to go any longer, makes your presence at home necessary and my father bids me tell you he would have you be at home if possible to go next week.'

It had been a long time from 5th October until 29th November. Mrs Gay had obviously needed William and he had stayed to help her with the farm for nearly two months. All the evidence points to an outbreak of smallpox in the family. Elizabeth [Cousin Betty in Mrs Steele's diary] had been ill at Salisbury a few months before. Richard and his mother had the same infection and it appeared to be a lethal disease. The tragedy lay in the close connection of the two families. William was the same age as Cousin Betty, Anne was the same age as Richard, and Jane was thirteen, one year older than Anne's half-sister Molly]. Anna, the oldest Gay girl, had been born in 1710 and married in 1734. William and Anne had no blood ties with the Gay 'cousins', but Molly did. Anne had stayed for long periods with the Gay family at Haycombe and one wonders if there were any friendship between Anne and Richard. What a sad change it was from the happy day in July 1734 when William and Richard visited Oxford together, and all the cousins rode out from Broughton on that lovely August morning in 1734 to travel over Salisbury Plain in the 'harvest weather' on their way to Haycombe via Trowbridge. There was

[80] STE 3/8/iv.

one ray of light in their sorrow and this was in the fact that Richard was a believer. Mrs Steele in her diary entry for 7th November 1733 writes, 'Being to go to Wallop... my nephew walked with me and we had very agreeable discourse. I hope the Lord has made him sensible in some measure of the evil of sin and the need of a Saviour and his own insufficiency to do any good thing. My desires went out earnestly to God for him and that came, "To God the Lord belong the issues from death."' [Psalm 68. 20]. The whole verse reads, 'He that is our God is the God of salvation; and unto God the Lord belong the issues from death.' For Mrs Steele the record in her diary three years previous to his death must have taken on a new significance in October 1736. Sad as it was, there was hope in his end. The religion of the Gays, Cators, Steeles and Froudes is clearly revealed in the hymns and poetry of Anne and never more so than in their deaths.

James Elcomb of Ringwood 1737

In 1830 Joseph Ivimey wrote an account of a sad event which took place in the life of Anne Steele in 1737 in his *History of the English Baptists,* Vol. IV p.312. Referring to Dr Caleb Evans' preface to the second edition of Anne Steele's hymns [1780] he says, 'Dr Evans has not mentioned an incident in the life of the "pious Theodosia" [Anne's pen name] which must have been most painful to her heart. She had consented to give her hand in marriage to a young gentleman, James Elcomb, who resided in Ringwood, and the day of the marriage was fixed. The day preceding it he went to bathe in the river [the Avon] below the town at a place called South-Mead, and was drowned. A tradition which the writer, who is a native, recollects, was that his shrieks were heard in the town, and the place is still called, on account of the circumstance, "Elcomb's Hole."' A footnote adds, 'The following inscription is taken from the headstone in Ringwood Churchyard:

Here lieth the body
of James Elcomb
who departed this life
May 23 1737
Aged 21 years.

Stand still and see how frail we are,
Who walk with life and vigour here.
He with one breath sucked in his death
Though danger seemed not to be near.'

Though Caleb Evans made no mention of this sad event in 1780, Ivimey's account has generally been repeated by later biographers of

Anne Steele. But in recent years a letter dated May 25th 1737[81] was discovered among the Steele family papers written by John James Manfield, a lawyer who lived in Ringwood. It was directed to William Steele, Anne's father and reads,

> 'I heartily wish the subsequent part of my letter may not be an unseasonable surprise to any of your family and therefore it is with very great concern I acquaint you that this evening our dear friend Mr Elcomb was unfortunately drowned in the river in washing himself; where he went in it was shallow, but going a little too far the rapidity of the current drew him out of his depth where he finished his life. He had only one person with him who could not swim, and who dared not venture to assist him.
>
> I submit to your prudence to communicate this unhappy accident to the rest of your family in suitable manner and not knowing how far he may have prevailed on the affections of Miss Steele, I send my man on purpose to prevent any shock that may attend her hearing it in too sudden a manner. I wish I could say he did not deserve her esteem, but am as heartily sorry to say [as his loss is generally lamented here] that nobody deserved the general esteem of mankind more, and I heartily condole him. My wife joins with me in due regrets.'
>
> John James Manfield.

It is quite clear from this letter that the drowning did not take place the day before their marriage. It is equally clear that Mr Manfield knew something about their feelings one for another. He did not know how far they had gone. John James Manfield was the husband of Elizabeth Tezard, a first cousin of Anne. Anne's mother and Elizabeth's mother had been sisters, children of Edward Froude. Anne Froude had stayed with Elizabeth her sister at Richard Tezard's home at Donhead in September 1713, prior to her marriage to Anne's father. Their daughter, Elizabeth Tezard, had been married in 1730. In the years after 1737 Anne Steele was to be a frequent visitor to their home at the Manor House at Ringwood in Hampshire. John James was a lawyer of some repute and was at one time Sheriff of South Hampshire. His son James went to Eton and Cambridge University, was called to the Bar in 1752, became King's Counsel in 1772, was Member of Parliament for Cambridge 1779-1784, Solicitor General 1780-1782, Chief Justice of Common Pleas 1804, in which year he was knighted, and High Steward of the New Forest in 1811. In April 1749, when James was fifteen, he had stayed at Broughton with the Steeles.[82]

---

[81] STE 1/5/i.

[82] ASD. STE 2/1/1.

The diary of Mrs Steele records visits from Ringwood to Broughton prior to 1737. On 5th November 1733 'Strangers came from Ringwood.' Was this possibly James Elcomb? On 8th April 1735, 'William [Anne's brother] went to Ringwood,' but no explanation is given as to the reason for his visit. Ten days later on 18th April, 'Mr Manfield of Ringwood came to Broughton.' Again there is no explanation for this visit. But these visits are reminiscent of the part played by Mr Steele in introducing Anna Gay and Thomas Attwater at Bodenham. Was John James Manfield acting for James Elcomb with regard to a marriage contract? It would appear from his letter to Mr Steele that if something was being discussed it was far from settled, but it is possible that Anne and James were engaged. It would seem probable that the Manfield family and the Elcomb family were attendants at the Particular Baptist Church at Ringwood, though John James Manfield and his son James must have been occasional conformants at the Church of England to have taken the offices they did in County and State.

In 1760 Anne Steele published the first edition of her hymns and poems. Among them is a hymn entitled 'Desiring resignation and thankfulness'. Verses eight and nine read:

'And O, whate'er of earthly bliss
Thy sovereign hand denies,
Accepted at thy throne of grace,
Let this petition rise:

Give me a calm, a thankful heart,
From every murmur free;
The blessings of thy grace impart,
And let me live to thee.'[83]

It has been suggested that these verses relate to the death of James Elcomb, but there is no evidence to confirm this as the hymn concerned is completely undated and was not published until over twenty years after the event. It is possible that this event was in her mind when she wrote these verses, but it could equally refer to her constant poor health through malaria, or to the death of any other of her friends. It is equally unsafe to use this event in her life to explain [as some writers have done] her poor state of health and alleged melancholy. Her hymns do manifest a sombre tone but this is connected with her spiritual experience and natural temperament. One thing is clear that between James Elcomb and Anne there was a friendship, but it is equally clear that she never wrote any special poem in his memory, as she did for others of her friends and

[83] Hymn 74.

family when they died, and that there is no mention of him in her stepmother's diary.

The Death of Henry Steele

On 19th June 1739[84] a major event took place in the Particular Baptist Church at Broughton. Henry Steele passed away to his eternal rest at the ripe old age of eighty-five after a pastorate of forty years and a membership of fifty-nine years. His preaching and pastoral care had been the backbone of the church in which Anne Steele had grown up. It was to him that she had given her testimony in 1732, as had her brother William. Their father had assisted 'Uncle Henry' [as he was known in Anne's family] for many years. Some time in the last few years of Henry's pastorate Anne's father received a call from the church to become assistant pastor. The letter read:[85]

> "The Church of Christ baptised upon profession of faith in Broughton, and every member of the same. To our Honoured minister and well-beloved brother in the Lord, Mr William Steele, send Christian salutation, wishing the continuance and increase of all spiritual gifts, Grace, Mercy and Peace be multiplied.
>
> Dear and well-beloved Brother. We taking into consideration the great age of our much honoured, worthy and beloved pastor, Mr Henry Steele, whose name and service for this church we hope will always be precious and had in thankful remembrance amongst us, and which we do heartily desire may continue and be lengthened out if it be the will of God further amongst us; but as we find the decays of nature are upon him, whereby he has been for some time past disabled from preaching the word, and with great difficulty and labour has been able to administer the Lord's Supper amongst us to this time;
>
> And as God of His infinite mercy and goodness has been pleased to raise you up amongst us, granting and bestowing on you ministerial gifts, and given great success and blessings to your labours for the conversion of sinners and the edification of saints, whereby our Church has been of late greatly increased and built up; and as we judge and are well satisfied, that besides your ministerial gifts for preaching the word, God of His great mercy has endowed and furnished you with every other gift and qualification to enable you to, and fit you for the work of a pastor, to administer and dispense all other ordinances and duties belonging to that office; and as we have seen the good hand of providence to this Church in raising up from time to time persons among ourselves who have been gifted and qualified and called to this work and office, so now we cannot but judge and conclude that you are

[84] HBBCH p.16.

[85] STE 1/6.

the person designed and appointed by the same good hand of providence for that work and service, and we should be wanting to ourselves as well as ungrateful to divine goodness if we should not give you a call and an invitation to it.

We therefore in obedience to divine providence and goodness [and having had the advice and approbation of our ancient and worthy pastor], do hereby solemnly, sincerely and heartily and with unanimity, call and intreat you to take upon you the work and office of a pastor jointly with our ancient pastor, to watch over us, and go before us in the administration of the Word, prayer, sacraments, according to gospel constitution, beseeching the Divine Majesty from whom every good and perfect gift comes to engage your heart with all willingness and readiness to accept of and take upon you the same, also humbly intreating He will guide, strengthen and support you in the work and office, that so the issue and consequence thereof may be the honour and glory of His great Name, the poor lambs of Christ be watched over, fed and nourished, and you with all faithful shepherds receive a crown of glory when the head Shepherd and Bishop of our souls shall appear, is and shall be the constant prayers of your unworthy brethren in the bonds of the everlasting Gospel of our dear Lord Jesus Christ.

Henry Steele	Jno Sharp	Frank Wade
Stephen Kent Snr	William Steele Jnr	Thomas Etheredge
George Barton	Stephen Kent Jnr	X the mark of Jos Dewy
John Kent	Tho Taylor	Benjamin Strong
X The mark of Ed Dugoe	Nicholas Parsons	John Parsons
George Tanner	Samuel Hatcher	William Futcher
Henry Sturges	Samuel Loach	Henry Gibbons
William Browning	William Knight	

It was a most tender-hearted and affectionate call from the aged pastor and the unanimous male membership of the church for William Steele to take the first step to becoming their pastor. William Steele was finally to assume the full office in 1739 on Henry's death and hold it until his own death in 1769. The Porton/Broughton Church was to be supplied with pastors from their own midst for one hundred and fifteen years. The letter was signed by his own son, William Steele junior, and as he was not baptised until 1732, this establishes the fact that William Steele senior assumed the joint pastoral office after that year.

Henry Steele's will is dated 4th June 1739.[86] He left his wife Clemence the family home, his farm in Broughton to his grandson Thomas Etheredge, his farm at Freefolk Priors, Whitchurch to his

[86] HRO.

grandson Henry Etheredge, and his farm at Over Wallop to his grandson William Etheredge when he became twenty-one. He left his granddaughter Frances Etheredge £400 when she became twenty-one. Thomas and William had to pay their grandmother £15 a year and William £10 a year. Henry was a man of some means, his farms being investments made from the profits of his house building and timber trade businesses. He was never dependent on the Broughton Church for financial support; in fact he gave the burying ground [which was solely for the use of the church] and the two cottages which his brother Thomas fitted up as a Meeting House and which remained in use until the present chapel was built in 1816. The inscription on his flat tombstone in Broughton Churchyard is now obliterated. He was a preacher of no mean order. The church prospered during his long pastorate. When he died, Anne, who was now twenty-two, was staying with the Manfields at Ringwood with her half-sister Molly, aged fifteen. Three letters survive written during this visit to her stepmother at Broughton dated 21st May, 1st June and 29th June. In a footnote to the last letter she writes, 'The news of my uncle's death, though it was no more than I expected, was very mournful. I am concerned for my aunt and want sadly to hear how she does.' It does not appear that Anne and Molly returned to Broughton for his funeral, though their father would have taken it and there would have been a large congregation present to witness it.

The Manfields

In the Manor House at Ringwood staying with her cousin Elizabeth Manfield, Anne was living with a young family. By 1739 there were six children and Elizabeth was expecting another the following year. Francis was eight, Elizabeth six, James five, William four, John three, and Anne one. It must have been a fairly noisy household. No doubt Anne and Molly were helping their mother as she waited for the next arrival. Sadly little John died the following year [1740] just as his brother Richard was born. But sadder than anything Elizabeth Manfield also died, probably as a direct result of the birth of Richard. This visit in May, June and July 1739 must have been a very memorable time for Anne. She obviously was deeply attached to Elizabeth her cousin, who was probably ten years older than she, since she had married John James Manfield in 1730. But Elizabeth cannot have been much over thirty when she died. Anne reveals some of her thoughts in the letter dated 21st May[87] when she writes, 'We have neither of us clothes to be fine enough for the Ringwood ladies. I want a new suit and sister a new gown, but I think it's a matter of no great consequence.' This reveals a more sophisticated society in the lawyer's

[87] STE 3/7/iii.

home, and the Ringwood Particular Baptist Church, than that of rural Broughton and its farms and timber business.

Anne says in the letter of 21st May and again on 1st June[88] that Molly was learning dancing and was being taught the Minuet and had had lessons for nine weeks. She herself had considered learning to play the spinet but the teacher had asked a crown a week and she considered this too dear. She says Mrs Manfield has advised her to work a Brussels handkerchief and Miss Goss is to teach her to do one like hers, which she thinks is the prettiest she has ever seen. Anne is dependent on her family for more money, though she is not sure how much she and her sister will need but asks her stepmother for more. We hear of Thomas Attwater coming to do business with John James Manfield, and of a very busy home. Anne writes, 'We are treated with a vast deal of kindness and affection by Mr Manfield and his wife, and indeed by everybody in general, but there is one circumstance which I cannot but call a misfortune. Our time has been so much taken up that I have not had the pleasure of Mrs Manfield's company, free from visitors and ceremony, I think hardly a day.' It would appear also that Anna Attwater had come down from Bodenham as Anne refers to her opinion of a minister, called Mr Wheeler, whom she did not like and Anne agrees with this and says she preferred the minister at the 'other Meeting'. The minister at the 'other Meeting' was Mr Miller whom they had heard once and she hoped that her brother William would be coming down to Ringwood for a weekend, as he was eager to hear Mr Miller preach. This reveals another church in Ringwood beside the Particular Baptist Church in St Thomas Lane, probably an Independent Church. In her last letter[89] she asks her stepmother for permission to stay at Ringwood for another three weeks. She writes, 'My cousin asks that you will give us leave to stay with her till Mr Manfield returns from London. He sets out next Monday with both his clerks and stays three weeks.' It would appear from this correspondence that Anne and Molly stayed at Ringwood for the best part of three months in 1739. They were in the most beautiful country of the Avon Valley and right on the edge of the New Forest and no doubt this was beneficial for Anne's health.

1740-1742

In 1740 Anne stayed with her sister at Devizes, at the home of Clemence Collings, a granddaughter of old Henry Steele. She had previously stayed there in 1731. She wrote home to her stepmother on 4th

[88] STE 3/7/iv.

[89] STE 3/7/v.

September[90] of the pleasant situation of the town. She had made very few friends, but her sister Molly had become friendly with six or seven girls of her own age [sixteen] and was taking dancing classes in the New Town Hall. They had been to the prehistoric camp at Oliver's Battery on Roundway Down, the scene of a battle in the Civil War. As a postscript she mentions that Molly was deeply saddened for poor Jacky Manfield. This was the Manfields' boy John, who died at the age of four and was buried at Ringwood on 17th August 1740. In the second letter dated 22nd September[91] she speaks of her anxiety for her parents and her brother because of the 'fatal distemper near you', and goes on to say that 'the smallpox is very hot in Trowbridge and Mr Truman has died from it.' There is no mention of the Particular Baptist Church in Devizes where the Collings family worshipped. It seems that Anne, in caring for her teenage sister, had a problem. Molly was more sociable and was becoming involved in a society life, different from that of Broughton and her godly forebears there. Anne, a baptised member of the Broughton Church, was standing separate from it.

In March 1741 Mrs Steele wrote to Anna Attwater at Bodenham, inviting her to come to Broughton to stay for a fortnight. Anna who had been married in 1739 may well have had her first child, Thomas, by then. The reason for the invitation was as Mrs Steele said, 'Here was three spoke lately, and we expect two or three more on the same occasion next Sabbath day and believing it will be very agreeable to you to hear them, we desire [God willing] to send for you next Saturday.' So five or six were coming before the Broughton Church to give in their testimonies and this at the outset of William Steele's pastorate. The fact that Anna was going to hear their testimony shows that she had already been baptised and was a member of the Broughton Church. The testimonies were always heard at a meeting of the baptised members of the church and not of the congregation.

In September 1741 Anne and Molly were at Ringwood again. But by then Elizabeth Manfield had died leaving six children, the oldest aged nine and the youngest born in May 1740. Anne wrote to her stepmother,[92] 'We are here in a pleasant situation, but alas the chief ornament of this agreeable place is wanting. Her loved idea presents itself to my thoughts and every pleasing amusement is mixed with pain at the mournful remembrance. We are treated here with a great deal of kindness and respect. Miss Martin's behaviour is very agreeable and engaging and we

---

[90] STE 3/7/vi.

[91] STE 3/7/vii.

[92] STE 3/7/viii.

seem equally pleased with each other.' She adds in a footnote that there have been lights in the night sky which have alarmed her but says, 'I am quite low-spirited.... so far as it is a weakness I wish to overcome it.' Anne obviously had a very nervous temperament. Miss Martin and Mr Manfield sent their regards to Mr & Mrs Steele and it would appear that Miss Martin was looking after the children.

The year 1742 opens with a reference in the Broughton Church Book for 20th February, 'Mary Steele baptised.' Mrs Steele in her diary for 1731 [when Molly was six or seven] speaks on 5th January of Molly talking about her soul's concerns that evening. The next day she writes, 'That my child might be truly converted in God's own time.'

A book[93] of Mary Steele's has survived entitled *A Looking Glass for Children*, written by Henry Jessey and Abraham Cheare. It is a second edition published in 1673. Inside the front cover there is written, 'Mary Steele. Her book bought at London June the 5 in 1730.' Underneath is an acrostic which reads,

'**M**y God, my refuge and delight,
Attend my humble cry;
Remember I'm a sinner great,
Yet Thou canst me supply.

So shall I love and live Thy praise,
Till I resign my breath;
Eternally adore Thy name,
Ev'n now and after death.
Lord, lead me by Thy Spirit still,
Ev'n guide me to Thy holy hill.'

As Mary's birthday was 29th June and she was approaching her sixth birthday in 1730, this acrostic was undoubtedly written by her father in what would appear to be an early birthday present.

In February 1731 Molly was taken seriously ill and it appeared that they might lose her. The maid asked at that time whether she was ready to die, and with tears in her eyes she responded, 'No.' Sadly the maid herself must have caught the disease [probably smallpox] for she herself died two days later on 6th March. She asked on her deathbed for Mr Steele to bury her and preach from the text, 'Therefore be ye also ready: for in such an hour as ye think not the Son of man cometh.' [Matthew 24. 44]. What impression this made on Molly is not clear. It would appear that afterwards she went through a period of worldliness when she was at

[93] ALRPC.

Devizes and Ringwood, but now at the age of eighteen a change had been wrought in the heart of the worldly 'adventurous' girl, her mother's and father's prayers had been answered and she had come before her father and the church with her testimony and had been baptised. Blessed and sobered in her soul she was now a companion for Anne, a fellowship that was to deepen as the years went by. Molly was to marry Joseph Wakeford of Andover, a widower, in May 1749 and suffer ill-health and bereavement in her married life. Anne and Molly wrote to each other under the pennames of Silviana and Amira. Ten of Anne's letters and four of Molly's have survived in the family archives. Anne followed this practice with a whole group of friends and later we hope to refer to this extensive correspondence which also included writing poetry to each, an eighteenth-century Particular Baptist literary circle, of which Anne [Silviana] was the centre.

In the summer of 1742 Anne's brother William went to Lewes, probably on timber business and wrote to Anne in a letter from Morley, dated 7th August.[94] He was staying at a country house outside Lewes 'entirely at leisure, without company, in one of the most delightful places I have ever seen... Mr Pope's *Letters* have agreeably entertained me all morning in the garden, which being rising ground, adjoining to a fine valley, enriched by a noble river [The Ouse] is by nature the finest terrace you can imagine, from whence is a beautiful prospect of the town of Lewes, on an eminence at half-a-mile distance across the valley; an old ruined castle on a high hill almost in the middle of the town which seems with its nodding walls to threaten the inhabitants, and the lofty mountains which surround the country give it a very romantic air; it is I think on the whole, though not the most extensive, yet one of the most charming landscapes I have seen.' While William was involved together with his father in farming and the timber trade, yet there was an educated and romantic side to him. He appreciated the historic old town surrounded by the South Downs with the River Ouse flowing beside it, though he makes no mention of the burning of the Protestant Martyrs there in the reign of Bloody Mary. There is every reason to expect that he was well acquainted with Foxe's *Book of Martyrs*. It is clear that he knew what would appeal to his sister, with her great love of the Hampshire Downs and the Wallop Valley.

Benjamin Beddome

In December 1742 Anne received a letter[95] from Benjamin Beddome the hymnwriter and pastor of the Particular Baptist Church at Bourton-on-the-Water in Gloucestershire. It read:

---

[94] STE 3/8/v.

[95] STE 3/13.

Dear Miss,

Pardon the boldness which prompts me to lay these few lines at your feet. If continued thoughts of you and a disrelish to every thing besides may be considered as arguments of love, surely I experience the passion and if the greatness of a person's love will make up for the want of wit, wealth and beauty, then may I humbly lay claim to your favour. Since I had the happiness of seeing you, how often have I thought of Milton's beautiful description of Eve, Book 8 line 471 Paradise Lost;

So lovely fair!
That what seemed fair in all the world seemed now,
Mean, or in her summed up, in her contained,
And in her looks, which from that time infused
Sweetness into my heart, unfelt before: &c-------

Madam give me leave to tell you that these words speak the very experience of my soul, nor do I find it possible to forbear loving you. Would you but suffer me to come and lay before you those dictates of a confused mind, which cannot be represented by a trembling hand and pen. Would you but suffer me to cast myself at your feet and tell you how much I love you, oh what an easement might you thereby afford to a burdened spirit and at the same time give me an opportunity of declaring more fully that I am in sincerity,

Your devoted servant,

Bourton, Dec. 23 1742 Benjamin Beddome

Benjamin Beddome had been born at Henley-in-Arden just to the north of Stratford-on-Avon and to the west of Warwick on 23rd January 1717. He was the same age as Anne. His father, John Beddome, had been a Particular Baptist minister like Anne's father, becoming co-pastor at the Pithary Church, Bristol, in 1724. In 1739 Benjamin had been apprenticed to a surgeon, but had moved to London and joined the Baptist Church in Prescott Street. At the call of this church he was sent into the ministry. For a time he had attended the Bristol Baptist Academy under the direction of Bernard Foskett. In 1743 he had taken the pastorate at the Particular Baptist Church at Bourton-on-the-Water in Gloucestershire, not so far from his home.[96]

When or where he saw Anne is not known, but it was probably travelling in the country preaching at various churches, either at Devizes, Broughton or Ringwood. Beddome was a biblical scholar and a hymnwriter. Over one hundred of his hymns were in common use in England and America in the eighteenth and nineteenth centuries. His

[96] *Dictionary of Hymnology* J. Julian D.D. 1908.

habit was to write a hymn each week on the subject of the Sunday morning text, which was sung after the sermon. Thirteen of his hymns appeared in 1769 in the hymnbook of Ash and Evans, and thirty-six were included in Rippon's Baptist hymnbook in 1787. After his death eight hundred and thirty were published in a single volume with an introduction by Robert Hall. Hall spoke of the beauty of Beddome's language and its original turn of thought. He added, 'The experimental Christian will often perceive the most secret movements of his soul strikingly delineated and sentiments portrayed which will find their echo in every heart.' A volume of his sermons was published after his death with a brief memoir. In the memoir are a couple of verses which are attributed to the year 1742. They are of considerable interest in connection with his letter of December 1742 to Anne. They would appear to be his prayerful concern prior to writing to Anne and show spiritual exercises which do not appear in his letter. They show that he had thought deeply about the sort of wife he was seeking, and Anne, who was twenty-five at the time, was his choice. He wrote:

'Lord, in my soul implant thy fear,
Let faith, and hope, and love be there;
Preserve me from prevailing vice,
When Satan tempts,or lusts entice.
Of friendship's sweets may I partake,
Nor be forsaken, or forsake.
Let moderate plenty crown my board;
And God for all be still adored.

Let the companion of my youth
Be one of innocence and truth;
Let modest charms adorn her face,
And give her thy superior grace.
By heavenly art first make her thine,
Then make her willing to be mine;
My dwelling-place let Bourton be,
There let me live and live to thee.'

Sadly, Beddome's prayers were not answered in the way he desired. Anne did not respond favourably. Many years later in an undated letter[97] to her sister Molly, who obviously had pointed to the blessings of marriage she replied, 'No indeed my sister, I have no mind to climb the stile you point to. It is true a gentle swain offered his hand to help me over, but I made a curtsie and declined his officious civility, for I looked over and saw no flowers but observed a great many thorns. Beside I think

[97] STE 3/10/xiv.

the path is much smoother on this side of the hedge than the other, and I am too staid to ramble for the sake of novelty.' Whether this refers to Beddome's letter is uncertain, but it does show her attitude to marriage. It is noteworthy that her own mother died in childbirth after only six years of married life. Also Anne was a constant sufferer from tertian ague [malaria] and had a very nervous temperament. If it does apply to Beddome's approach, then his approach does not deserve to be called 'officious civility'. Anne preferred the quiet life of Broughton, rather than being a pastor's wife among a big congregation and having a large family of children. She was essentially a private person who liked a small group of close friends. But it is interesting that Anne kept his letter and that among her unpublished material is a sheet of paper with three short hymns on it marked 'Mr Beddome Jnr.'

Figure 19: Benjamin Beddome's Manse at Bourton-on-the-Water (now a hotel)

Benjamin Beddome did not marry for another seven years. In 1749 he married Elizabeth Boswell and had several sons by her. Tragically, on Sunday 14th January 1778, when the congregation at Bourton first sang Beddome's hymn,

> "My times of sorrow and of joy,
> Great God, are in thy hand;
> My choicest comforts come from thee,
> And go at thy command."

one of his sons died unexpectedly in Edinburgh at the age of twenty-four or five. Another son also predeceased him. Beddome was awarded, later in life, an M.A. by Providence College, Rhode Island, U.S.A, for his hymnology and biblical scholarship. He was noted for his generosity and for his courtesy. Anne and he seemed very suited for one another, but one wonders whether Anne would have written so many hymns, the fruit of much weakness and illness, had she married and had a family. It is certain that the air of the Cotswolds at Bourton would have been a much healthier environment for Anne than the damp valley of the Wallop. Some of the best known of Beddome's hymns include, 'God's ways are just, his counsels wise,' 'Great God! to thee I'll make, My griefs and sorrows known,' and, 'So fair a face bedewed with tears; What beauty e'en in grief appears! He wept, He bled, He died for you; What more, ye saints, could Jesus do?' There is a distinct similarity in the tone and character of Beddome's hymns and those of Anne Steele. They are both distinct from Isaac Watts, in revealing more of the feelings of the heart, but equally in versification they were influenced by the first great hymnwriter of the eighteenth century. Benjamin Beddome died on 3rd September 1795 at the age of seventy-eight, having been pastor at Bourton-on-the-Water for fifty-two years.

On October 6th 1743[98] Anne penned a poem to 'A Friend on his Marriage'. She obviously thought marriage a blessing, but not for her. She wrote:

'May the kind providence whose gracious smiles
Form all our present bliss and future hopes,
On you and on the partner of your joys
Shine with distinguished ray and crown your life
With every blessing, every valued good.
May blooming health and calm content be yours,
And love and friendship blend their sweetest charms
To soften care; for cares will rise
To cloud the fairest scenes of earthly bliss....'

Ringwood

No information survives about Anne for the year 1744, but in December 1745 a letter[99] to her stepmother shows that she was once again at Ringwood with the Manfields. During this year John James had remarried. His new wife was Grace Fitch, a rich widow, from Wimborne in Dorset. Anne says that in some respects she has great reason to be

[98] Unpublished poem. STE 3/3.

[99] STE 3/7/ix.

satisfied with her present situation, but she complains of headaches and stomach disorders and says she is terrified with apprehensions of 'an invasion', and adds, 'If the danger approaches near us, I shall desire to be with my dear parents.' The danger of invasion was in fact the Jacobite Rebellion of 1745. The Young Stuart Pretender, Prince Charles Edward, had landed in Scotland and as G. M. Trevelyan says in his *History of England*, [pp. 536-7]

> 'He found an island almost denuded of troops, utterly unaccustomed to war or self-defence, so selfishly indifferent to the issue between the Stuarts and the Hanoverians, that the inhabitants let five thousand Highlanders with targe and broadsword march from Edinburgh to Derby, gaped at, but equally unassisted and unopposed.... The consequence of a coup d'état by wild Highlanders in London must have in any case been tragic and absurd. Britain was saved from them by her small, but excellent Army summoned home in haste from fields of fame abroad.'

Turning from Derby on 6th December 1745, the rebels were eventually defeated at Culloden Moor near Inverness on April 16th 1746 by an army led by the Duke of Cumberland, who went on to stain a good military reputation by cruelties against the Highland population. A medallion was struck at Carlisle in December 1745 marked 'William, Duke of Cumberland British hero, born April 1723,' and on the reverse 'Rebellion justly rewarded'. The danger which disturbed Anne Steele's holiday at Ringwood in December 1745 was in fact a very real threat to the hard won civil liberties of 1688. Anne's fears at Ringwood were well grounded. It would be interesting to know just how well-informed John James Manfield was and how he came by his information, and how long it took to get up-to-date news from Scotland to Hampshire.

In August 1746 Anne was again invited to go to Ringwood, but she declined, saying, 'We are all obliged by your kind invitation but believe we cannot have the pleasure of complying with it; my brother and sister have been ill and are not yet quite well and I have a sort of agueish disorder. If you are at leisure and can think it agreeable, should be glad if you would come and see us and bring the dear little prattler with you.' Mr Manfield had been married the second time for two years and there was already a new addition to the family – another son, John James, one year old in August 1746. This was the little 'prattler', probably just learning to walk. The youngest boy of the previous marriage, Richard, was six by this time and his eldest sister, Frances, was fifteen. Anne had been going to this home for many years and had seen the children grow up. But for her it could never be quite the same after the death of her cousin Elizabeth six years before. In her letter dated 12th August Anne thanked Mr Manfield for buying and sending her a hoop. She says, 'I like it exceeding well and think it is large enough for me, whom you know, am not very modish.' The letter gives us a brief picture of Anne with her eighteenth-century hooped dress; though as she says, 'not very modish', yet for all her rustic surroundings at Broughton, keeping up with the fashions of the times.

Isaac Watts

On 12th December 1748 Isaac Watts died. Whilst he was not a Particular Baptist, but an Independent and pastored the church in Mark Lane, London [over which John Owen had been pastor until 1683], from 1702-1748, his *Psalms and Hymns* had become widely used in Dissenting Meeting Houses of all kinds in the eighteenth century. Anne Steele had grown up with them at Broughton and her hymns and poetry had been greatly influenced by them. Now at the age of thirty-one on the death of this great spiritual mentor she penned two poems in his memory. In the first she wrote:[100]

'True I have raised the vocal shell,
And bid lamenting echo dwell
In praises o'er the bier,
Oft brought some hidden grace to light
And poured its blaze upon the sight
While passing crowds revere.

But when these awful virtues rise,
That dazzle fancy's ardent eyes,
And scorn my boasted lays;
Expressive silence must declare
At once my grief and my despair
To form a Watts' praise.'

The second memorial poem[101] Anne wrote was considerably longer running to nearly fifty lines. In it she shows her love for his hymns.

'O could I write like Watts whose charming strain
Could heighten pleasure and alleviate pain,
Then should the sacred verse harmonious flow,
And waken joy amid the shades of woe.
Then should my heart suppress the rising sigh,
And trace the shining journey to the sky.
Some gentle seraph, lend your soaring wing,

---

[100] Unpublished poem. STE 3/3.
[101] ibid.

Teach me the notes that warbled on his string;
Such notes as Heaven inspires and Angels join
All breathing harmony and love divine;
While almost to the gates of Paradise
His powerful numbers raised our hearts and eyes,
Heaven smiled approving, earth's low scenes retired,
And Jesus' lovely Name, each pleasing passion fired.
  Such were his songs in this dark world confined;
Thus beamed through mortal clouds the heaven-borne mind.
But now removed to mansions in the skies,
What unknown glories meet his wondering eyes;
All his ideas now enlarged and bright
Expatiate free in worlds of perfect light,
The shades of human error purged away,
And knowledge shines with pure unclouded ray......
  O lost to Earth. No – in his works he lives,
And pleasure still and sweet instruction gives.
Here let me read and cheer my gloomy hours,
And warm and animate my languid powers.'

Her eulogy does not exclude a reference to the fact that Watts had been constantly involved in controversial writings on the doctrine of the Trinity. He published his first treatise on the subject in 1722 followed by ten others the last two being written in 1746, two years before his death. It would appear that Anne had read some of these dissertations and knew that his views were unorthodox and not in accord with the Athanasian Creed, which prompted her in her poem to refer to 'the shades of human error'. Watts was influenced by the Puritan writers of the seventeenth century, but he was also influenced by the rationalistic spirit of the eighteenth century. In trying to provide a rational explanation of the doctrine of the Trinity, Watts was accused of Arianism [denying the true and proper Godhead of Christ] and claimed by Unitarians as one of their number. Some felt that Watts had become confused through old age, but he had stated his belief in the pre-existence of the soul of Christ as early as 1725 when he was fifty-one. Anne would have known that his home town was Southampton and that born in 1674, he had grown up in the days of persecution. His father was a deacon of an Independent Church and suffered imprisonment for his beliefs when Watts was a baby. She would also have known that his *Hymns* were published in 1707 and his *Psalms* in 1719, both prior to the start of the Trinitarian controversy. She greatly valued his hymns and felt that in eternity his knowledge of the Trinity would 'shine with pure unclouded ray.'

Anne was now moving into the next decade of her life and to the publication of her hymns, poems and versification of the Book of Psalms in 1760. She was 'too staid' to marry and leave her home. Her health was a continual cause of concern to her family, but her writings and especially her hymns show that suffering was sanctified to her and used to enable her to write hymns which manifest feeling and compassion.

Chapter 5

In the Prime of Life [1749-60]

1749

A major event occurred in Anne's life with the marriage of her half-sister on 16th May 1749. Her brother William was already married by this time to Mary Bullock of Yeovil in Somerset. He was living at *Pigeon House*, just along the lane from *Grandfathers* towards Broughton village. Here on 17th May Molly's wedding breakfast took place. She had married Joseph Wakeford, a widower, who had a prosperous drapery business in Andover. He was five years older than she and had one girl named Hannah, aged four, by his first marriage. Anne penned a poem to Amira, as Molly was known in their literary circle,[102] on her marriage.

While round you hourly gratulations rise,
And joy and happiness [gay soothing sounds]
Salute your ear; accept the artless wish
That friendship dictates, breathing from the heart.

May gracious heaven the happy union crown,
Propitious still and kind, with all the bliss
Which mortals can enjoy; may health and peace,
And love and friendship guide the circling hours....

But earthly bliss is ever mixed with pain,
And thorns among its flowery pleasures grow.
May all the joys, the nobler, purer joys
Religion yields be yours; to fairer scenes
And brighter prospects, may your hopes ascend....

The early part of the year had seen a long period of illness for Anne. Taken suddenly ill on 2nd January, she had only recovered a few weeks before her half-sister's wedding. Almost immediately after the wedding she had a relapse. She went to the Attwaters at Bodenham for a day in June, and spent two weeks at Andover at the end of June and beginning of July, but by 14th July her stepmother described her as being 'weak and low'. She spent another two weeks at Andover in August with her half-sister and at the end of September managed to go to Weyhill Fair with all the family. But in November she was ill again with 'bad pains in her

[102] *Poems of Anne Steele*, 1760. Vol. 1, p.222.

stomach'. As has already been suggested Anne, in 1749, could have been suffering either from a stomach ulcer, or irritable bowel syndrome.

But while she spent much of the year ill, her father and brother were leading a very active life. On 19th January Mrs Steele says in her diary, 'We had a letter from William that he cannot yet accomplish the business he went to London about, and that the great storehouse at Deptford was burnt, the loss of which is computed at £200,000.... a great loss to the Nation.' The Steeles were contracting with the Admiralty in London for the sale of their timber and a huge storehouse of timber had been burnt. William went to Petworth in Sussex in March and purchased £6,000 worth of timber. He was now thirty-four, strong and active and able to conduct big business on his own. Her father went to hear George Whitefield preach at Salisbury on the evening of his daughter's wedding breakfast [17th May]. The hearers numbered about three thousand and Mrs Steele says in her diary, 'Mr Steele came home at midnight having heard Mr Whitefield on "Dost thou believe in the Son of God?" a very good stirring sermon but the mob treated him rudely.... I praise God who delivered Mr Steele from danger.' A few days later on 22nd May Mr Steele and William went to Taunton in Somerset for eight days, and Molly's husband, Joseph Wakeford went to London in connection with his drapery business. By 9th June William had set out for a second visit to Petworth to see how the felling of the trees, which he had purchased in March, was progressing and on 14th June Molly came to Broughton for the day with her husband and stepdaughter. In August William went to Plymouth returning on 22nd, and on 28th he went to Portsmouth. His business on both occasions was at the Naval Dockyards, selling the timber he had purchased at Petworth for the construction of warships. On the same day he left for Portsmouth, his half-sister and her husband went to Exeter. In the midst of all this activity, Anne who was now thirty-two, was suffering constant ill-health and staying at *Grandfathers* with her step-mother who had reached her sixtieth birthday on 19th April. Her half-sister kindly wrote to her on 23rd September and in her letter[103] she said, 'Are not even true Christians generally more secure and careless about heavenly things, when their earthly circumstances are most prosperous? Surely every Christian may say, "It is good for me that I have been afflicted."' Anne's recurrent illnesses were to last all her life.

1750

In January 1750 Anne spent two or three weeks with Molly at Andover. On 14th March William's wife Mary was baptised at

[103] STE 3/10/i.

Broughton. Since coming to *Pigeon House* she had become a companion to Anne, though she was four years older than she. On 1st April 1750 Molly gave birth to a son but sadly he died seven months later on 10th November. Such deaths were a constant occurrence in the eighteenth century when the infant mortality rate was very high; but for all its frequency the heart-sorrow was no less than it is today, and the parents and the whole Steele family, including Anne, must have been deeply grieved. On 29th April Anne's uncle, James Froude, died at Tinhead. He was the brother of the mother Anne could never remember, and as he was able to tell her about her own mother, she must have been very close to him. He had taken over his father's farm in Tinhead. A few weeks later on 2nd June James' wife Elizabeth also died. William and his father represented the Steele family at the funeral of Elizabeth. In his will[104] James left Anne and William a mourning ring each. The Steeles in their journeys to Trowbridge and Haycombe had often stayed with the Froudes at Tinhead, as no doubt Anne did when she was at school in Trowbridge in 1729.

A letter survives written by Anne dated 7th May 1750.[105] It is addressed to William's wife who was staying at her own home at Yeovil in Somerset. It is an answer to an invitation to stay at Yeovil. Anne writes, 'Your kind solicitude for seeing me at Yeovil is very obliging, but no time can be yet fixed for my journey.' Anne goes on to describe the lovely garden at *Pigeon House* at Broughton and hopes that the flowers may survive for Mary to see when she returns. She describes her own room at *Grandfathers* and says, 'My cell too has its charms. The honeysuckle at my window is in full bloom and I am sometimes entertained with the soft warbling of a neighbouring nightingale... The rural scenes are in their perfection.' At this time Anne's health was considerably better, enabling her to enjoy the summer beauties of Broughton's lovely countryside. By 28th May the date had been fixed for Anne to go to Yeovil with William to stay at his wife's home and they set out together probably on horseback, possibly in the family coach, or perhaps by stagecoach on a journey of fifty miles, via Salisbury, Shaftesbury, Milbourne Port and Sherbourne. Anne stayed at Yeovil until her return on 7th July, five weeks later.

In late August Anne's father and stepmother set out in their carriage on the long journey of over fifty miles to Haycombe near Bath to visit Mrs Steele's sister, Mrs Gay. They went via Tinhead, where they stayed at the George Inn, having no relatives with which to stay since the death of

[104] WSRO.
[105] STE 3/9/i.

Figure 20: The George Inn, Tinhead

James Froude and his wife. They reached Trowbridge on 29th August and the same day arrived in Haycombe. They stayed four days and returned by the same route on 3rd September. On 12th September William and Mary went to London. An interesting light on all this travelling, and the dangers entailed in it, is revealed in an entry in Mrs Steele's diary[106] for 6th November 1750, it reads, 'Cousin Anna Attwater and her children returned home to Bodenham in their chaise and our servant went with them, but three miles this side of Salisbury, they were stopped by a highwayman, well-mounted, and robbed of rings and one guinea. Cousin was not so much surprised [shocked] as might be expected.' When Molly's little boy died four days after this, Anne wrote a poem 'To Amira on the death of her child.' She wrote[107],

> 'So fades the lovely, blooming flower
> Frail, smiling solace of an hour!
> So soon our transient comforts fly,
> And pleasure only blooms to die!
> To certain trouble we are born,
> Hope to rejoice but sure to mourn....
>
> O let religion then be nigh,
> Her comforts were not made to die;

---

[106] STE 2/2/2.

[107] *Poems of Anne Steele*, 1760. Vol 2. pp.33-34.

Her powerful aid supports the soul,
And nature owns her kind control....
Hope wipes the tear from sorrow's eye,
And faith points upward to the sky.'

She had already written a previous poem to her half-sister Molly, [Amira] on her recovery from ill health following the birth of this child. The year ended with the marriage of Jenny Gay, her stepmother's niece and youngest sister of Richard Gay who had died in 1736. Jenny the youngest of the Haycombe cousins married Mr Gibbs, a wealthy Trowbridge clothier. They were to live at *Rosefield House* in Polebarn Road, Trowbridge and in later years the Steele family would often stay there with them.

Figure 21: North Parade, Bath

Bath 1751

The year 1751 was marked by a long stay in Bath. Anne went there with her sister-in-law Mary on 30th April and did not return to Broughton until 26th June. She wrote several letters to her stepmother which reveal that they drank the waters and bathed in the Roman Baths. Both suffered from recurrent illness and it is clear that they had come to try and improve their health. They stayed at the North Parade, which had just been completed in 1748, and was the work of John Wood the elder. He had been the architect of Ralph Allen's great house, built at Prior Park between 1735 and 1748. This house, set in a beautiful valley looking down on Bath city, was not far from Haycombe and must have been seen by Anne and Mary in all its classical beauty within a few years of being built. Allen was the owner of the stone quarries on Combe Down to the south of Bath, from which came the stone to build eighteenth-century Bath in all its beauty. Mrs Steele had written in her diary for 29th April, 'Tis agreed for both our daughters, Mrs Steele and Nanny, to set out toward Bath for the spring season for their better health.' But Anne was far from happy there and longed for her rural life in Broughton. In a poem entitled, 'On walks in Bath',[108] two separate lines show her feelings regarding Bath,

> Dear native rural scenes for you I sigh,

and

> And fly the laughing crowds and gay parade.

Her brother visited them early in June and Mrs Gay came over from Haycombe to see them. This was not the first time that William had been in Bath that year. Mrs Steele's diary records, 2nd April, 'Our son now gone to Bath in order to buy a great quantity of timber which he has viewed at Horndean [north of Portsmouth in the Forest of Bere] from the Duke of Beaufort. [His seat was at Badminton, just to the north of Bath.] On 6th April she wrote, 'Our son is returned having bought about £10,000 worth of timber, the property of the Duke of Beaufort.' Bath at the time was mostly within the city walls. The big development of Bath in the eighteenth century was progressive. So in 1751, neither the Circus nor the Royal Crescent had yet been built. Building of the Circus to the north of Queen Square commenced in 1754 and the Royal Crescent in 1767. The construction of Poultney Bridge over the River Avon began in 1769. The Royal Mineral Hospital was on Upper Borough Walls and had been built between 1738-42. No doubt Anne and Mary would have visited it. They would have seen the Great House at Prior Park, where Alexander Pope, the poet, and Thomas Gainsborough, the portrait painter, were frequent visitors. Anne and her brother were both acquainted with Pope's poetry and letters. The Palladian Bridge in Prior Park was not constructed till 1755. So in 1751 Bath consisted of the old city with the developments outside the walls of Queen Square to the north, and the North Parade to the east. North Parade had an excellent view of the River Avon and the weir across the river with its two mills, Monk's Mill to the left and Bathwick Mill to the right. Here also was the pool in front of the weir

[108] Unpublished poem. STE 3/3.

where boats came up from Bristol and turned round to take the Bath stone for use elsewhere.

Anne wrote three letters from Bath, on 11th, 18th and 25th May,[109] to her stepmother at Broughton. Both Mary and Anne had drunk the waters and been bathing. Both had been ill and Anne had stayed indoors for a week. Anne had had a pain in her side and was not allowed to bathe until it stopped. She said, 'I have such ill success in the first attempts at bathing that I am quite afraid to venture again, but cannot be easy without it because you thought it would be of service to me.' She also wrote of Mary as having a bad foot but she was afraid of 'Bath surgery!' and said that Mary was worried that 'the trouble and expense of this journey would be lost'. One would guess that William was funding the whole trip for the good of his wife and sister, both having poor health. When they both finally returned to Broughton on 26th June, though they might not have gained much healthwise, yet they had had experience of one of the great cultural centres of eighteenth-century England.

William Hoare, the portrait painter, had come to Bath from London in 1740 and worked there for fifty years. He frequented Prior Park and painted many of the celebrities that came to Bath. Thomas Gainsborough came to Bath from Ipswich in 1759 at the age of thirty-two and his success as a portrait painter was immediate. He was in Bath until he went to London in 1778. In London Joshua Reynolds had set up as a portrait painter in 1753 and by 1760 had established himself, charging £25 for a head, £50 for half length and £100 for whole length.[110] The present day descendants of the Steeles have in their possession half-portraits of William Steele junior, of his second wife, Martha [nee Goddard], of his daughter Polly, child of his first wife Mary [née Bullock] and of his two daughters, Anne and Martha, children of his second wife. None of them are signed but they are of a very high quality and could possibly be the work of either Hoare, Reynolds or Gainsborough. As long as *Grandfathers* at Broughton was in the hands of the Steele family and their descendants, these paintings were housed there. When the family finally sold the house about 1970 the portraits were dispersed, though still kept by the family. Anne and Mary would also have seen some of the beautiful furniture being produced for the Bath houses. Thomas Chippendale [1718-1779] published *The Director,* a pattern book, in 1754. Up till this time cabinet makers in England had developed their own styles. Chippendale presented three styles of furniture in his book: *The Modern Style*, based on the rococo style of the 1740s, *The Chinese Style* which evolved from the

[109] STE 3/7/x, xi, xii.

[110] *The Reign of George III*, OUP, 1960, S. Steven Watson. p.342.

publication in 1741 of *Travel in the Chinese Empire* by du Halde, and lastly *The Gothic Style* a revival of the style of Jacobean furniture. Chippendale thus set a fashion for beautiful furniture and no doubt some of this would have found its way into *Pigeon House* at Broughton. It would seem highly likely that Mary and Anne spent their weekends at Haycombe with Mrs Gay and worshipped in the Particular Baptist Meeting there.

Mary and Anne returned to Broughton on 26th June and ten days later Jenny Gibbs came to Broughton from her home in Trowbridge and was baptised into membership of the Broughton Church. On Sunday 14th July at the Lord's Supper, Mrs Steele records that all her family except her sister at Haycombe, sat down to the Table. William Steele senior took the Communion and present were his wife, his son William and his wife Mary, Anne Steele and Molly Wakeford, Jenny Gibbs and her sister Anna Attwater. Later in July William went again to London with 'a prospect of contracting at the Navy Board'. Clearly he was there to sell some of the timber he had bought from the Duke of Beaufort, which would be used at Portsmouth to build ships for the Fleet. In mid-September 1751 Anne went to stay with Molly at Andover and on 18th September her half-sister gave birth to a son, calling him Joseph. Anne returned to Broughton to manage the home, while Mrs Steele went to help her daughter at Andover for a month. Anne was unwell throughout most of the rest of the year. On 30th November her father purchased about £4,000 worth of timber from the Eyers family, who had woods lying between Downton and Landford in the south-east corner of Wiltshire. The Steele business was prospering as they bought £14,000 worth of timber in one year, and as we shall see later, much of the profit was being invested in farms in and around Broughton, Wallop and Tytherley, with something like five hundred acres being in their possession. Mrs Steele in her diary often refers to the harvest, or the sheep, or how the weather was affecting the farming. Anne, in the midst of all this activity, while her brother William was in London, Portsmouth or Bath, was quietly writing her poetry and hymns and feeling as she expressed in a letter to him written in May 1755,[111] 'Can you not my dear brother unbend a little from your business.' If the Steeles were barred by the Test Act from going to Oxford or Cambridge Universities, or from taking office under the Crown or in the municipalities, yet they were able to direct their energies toward self-education and business and were quite as rich and cultured as many of their aristocratic contemporaries.

---

[111] STE 3/8/vi.

The Evangelical Awakening

But of more concern to them were their contacts among the Particular Baptists and the men of the Evangelical Awakening. In May 1752 Mr Steele and William went to Bratton in Wiltshire, to the Western Association Meetings of the Particular Baptist Churches. Mrs Steele records in her diary for 22nd May, 'Mr Steele came [home] in the afternoon. Mr Stennett and Mr Evence preached and he found the opportunity much to his satisfaction, there being associated together more than twenty Baptist ministers.' Dr Joseph Stennett [1692-1758] had been awarded his doctorate by Edinburgh University. He was pastor of the London Particular Baptist Church in Little Wild Street, and was highly esteemed by George II and was a friend of some of the leading men of his day. The sermon that May at Bratton was preached from Isaiah 53. 1, 'Lord, who hath believed our report?' It was published the same year and a copy is to be found at Regent's Park College, Oxford.

Figure 22: George Whitefield

Four weeks after the Bratton Meetings, Mr Steele went to Whitchurch, just beyond Andover, to hear George Whitefield preach. Mrs Steele records in her diary for 22nd June,[112]

> 'Mr Whitefield being to preach at Whitchurch this evening, I went with Mr Steele in the chaise and we took Andover in the way to see the child [Joseph], but no sign of teeth yet. May a gracious God preserve his life if it be His pleasure. Mr Whitefield preached to about four hundred people on, "I am come that they might have life and that they might have it more abundantly." He proposed a method and in some measure kept to it, but made frequent and large digressions. He was very active and loud and endeavoured to strike the passions. Some part of it was very affecting and experimental. I desire it may be made useful to many souls. Mr Steele spent the evening with him. As I had long wanted to hear him preach, I attended with diligence and liked some parts of it better than I expected

[112] STE 2/1/2.

> and some parts worse, yet as God has been pleased to make him wonderfully useful in the world as an instrument in His hand for the conversion of sinners, so I desire his life may be continued to that end for the glory of God.'

Anne would have had a first-hand account of George Whitefield from her parents. It is interesting to see in the diary entry how these Broughton Particular Baptists were no separatists, but in their slightly reserved way were outward looking, evangelical and warmed toward the men of the Evangelical Awakening, who were largely clergymen of the Anglican Church. George Whitefield had been in America on his fourth visit there from September 1751 to May 1752, so he was only back in the country by a few weeks when the Steeles heard him at Whitchurch.[113] Whitefield was thirty-eight at the time and William Steele was sixty-three. It would seem that at least part of the evening conversation concerned the progress of the Revival in America and Whitefield's experiences in crossing the Atlantic. They might also have discussed the doctrinal controversy that was taking place at the time between John Wesley and Whitefield, for Mr Steele and Whitefield were at one, being Calvinists, and John Wesley was an Arminian. George Whitefield was chaplain to Selina, Countess of Huntingdon [1707-1791], who was a lady-in-waiting at Court. She supported many Anglican clergymen during the Evangelical Revival in the eighteenth century and spent much of her time at Bath where she had a house in Edgar Buildings. She built a group of chapels, known as 'the Countess of Huntingdon's Connexion', one of which was built in 1765 in The Vineyards, at Bath. Anne would have been aware of this Connexion, and also the fact that these churches had their own hymnbook, of which two editions were published in Bath in 1765 and 1770. This last edition was sold at the Circulating Library in King's Mead Square, Bath.[114]

1753

In Broughton the year 1753 opened with the formation of a new Meeting at Lockerley, a small village about half way between Broughton and Romsey. This was followed in 1754 by a house being licensed for worship at Winterslow lying between Broughton and Salisbury. Mr Steele preached there for the first time on 30th June. In her diary for 26th November 1754[115] Mrs Steele records, 'Mr Steele often at Wallop where he is altering a malthouse of our son's into a Meeting House.' On 20th May Mrs Steele lamented in her diary, 'Our little flock decays – no increase.' But there seemed to be a reason for it, with the development of

---

[113] *George Whitefield*, Arnold Dallimore, BOT, 1980, Vol. 2, p.343.

[114] *Dictionary of Hymnology*. J. Julian, 1908, p.543.

[115] STE 2/1/3.

these new Meetings in the surrounding villages. The days when, as at Porton, the people had been willing to walk miles to worship were gone. Now they were dispersing to their own neighbourhoods and the Meeting at Broughton was not as large as it once had been.

1753 was marked in the Steele family by the birth of a new generation of nieces and nephews. On 1st March Mary Wakeford gave birth to her third son. She had lost the first boy in 1750 at seven months old, and had had Joseph in September 1751. Joseph was seventeen months old when his brother William was born. Within four weeks tragedy struck again in the Wakeford family, when little Joseph succumbed to a fever on 2nd April. What sorrows the Steele family were living through, though life was full of such sorrows in the eighteenth century. William was to survive childhood and grow up to take over his father's draper's business at Andover and eventually prosper until he owned his own estate and country house at Lockerley and his own bank in Andover until his death in 1819. On 24th June Anna Attwater gave birth to a little girl at Bodenham whom they called Jane. She was a late arrival, having an elder brother Thomas aged eighteen, and two sisters Marianne and Caroline. Her father was sixty-two at the time of her birth and her mother forty-three. Caroline stayed with Anne at *Grandfathers* from May to October around the time of her sister's birth. Both Jane and Caroline grew up to be close companions of Anne Steele and often stayed at Broughton with her. Jane wrote a diary[116] which has survived and describes the last days and hours of the life of Anne Steele at the time of her death in 1778. On 22nd July 1753 William and Mary Steele had their first child, born at *Pigeon House*. They named her Mary, but she was always known in the family as Polly. She was to become Anne's best loved niece, principally because her mother died suddenly at Yeovil in 1762 when she was only nine and Anne acted as a surrogate mother for her until her father remarried in 1768. She grew up to be a poet and author like her aunt, and in her aunt's last years at the *Pigeon House* she nursed her. After her father married Martha Goddard she had two half-sisters, Anne born in 1769 and Martha in 1770. A little brother, William, born in 1772, only lived for a month. Thus the year 1753 marked in Anne's life the arrival about her of a group of children for whom she was later to write a volume of poems which were to be published in 1788, after her death.

Another major event in the family calendar for 1753 was the launching at Redbridge, at the head of Southampton Water, of a ship called 'The

[116] The late Dr. Marjorie Reeves' Collection.

Willing Mind', built for Anne's brother William. This merchant ship was launched on 31st August. Mrs Steele's diary records, 'Our son and his guest are gone to Redbridge to see his vessel launched and desire to go from there to Portsmouth.' They thus sailed down Southampton Water, past the old town walls, from under which the Pilgrim Fathers had sailed to America in 1620, past the beautiful shoreline of the New Forest to the west and eventually through the Solent to Portsmouth, among the great ships of the Fleet. This ship must have been several hundred tons in weight, and as the Steeles were in the timber business trading with the Admiralty, it would seem safe to presume that its principal cargo would be timber for the Navy. It eventually was lost in the Channel in January 1758 during the Seven Years' War with France [1756-1763], at a time when Admiral Hawke was blockading the French Fleet in Brest. Possibly at that time 'The Willing Mind' was carrying supplies to the British Fleet that was lying off the coast of Brittany. Mrs Steele's diary for 6th January 1758 says, 'Mr West sent William the unwelcome news of his vessel, "The Willing Mind" is supposed lost on the coast. May a prepared mind meet every disappointment.' One can gather the interest for the Steele family in August 1753 at the ship's launching, though Anne did not write any poem to record the event. For her it was very much part of her brother's business. While the ladies commented in their diaries on the Steeles' business of timber, farming and now merchant shipping, they did not have anything to do with the men's business activities. Another significant event in 1753 was the preaching of one of the Methodist ministers of the Evangelical Awakening, Mr Smith, in the Particular Baptist Meeting at Broughton. He preached morning, afternoon and evening, his texts being Ephesians 1. 2-3, Ephesians 2. 19 and John 3. 16. Mrs Steele says, 'We had pretty much Church people.' It is interesting to reflect on Mr Steele senior's attitude to the eighteenth-century Revival. Mrs Steele says, 'I begged that I might attend to the word preached without indifference or prejudice, which I hope I did.' The Baptists were obviously a little uncertain about some aspects of the Revival but did not cut themselves off from it and the Anglicans were willing to mix with the Particular Baptists. No doubt the Broughton vicar and his congregation had a measure of respect for the Steele family who owned a large part of the village and the local mill on the Wallop, and had a large estate which they were farming.

1754

In 1754 Mary Wakeford had another son Samuel, born on 21st April. Mrs Steele reports that his brother William was already walking. Jenny Gibbs had had a boy at Trowbridge in February but it had only lived a few days. In May Mr and Mrs Steele senior went to Trowbridge to stay with Jenny at her home, *Rosefield House*. They went on to Haycombe to see Mrs Steele's sister and Mr Steele preached at the meeting there on Sunday 2nd June. On the following Wednesday Mr Steele went on to the Particular Baptist Western Association Meetings which were being held that year at Frome. He returned to Haycombe having met many ministers and left for Trowbridge on Friday 7th where he preached in the evening at the Particular Baptist Chapel in Back Street, returning to Broughton on Saturday. Mr Steele was sixty-four at the time and he must have travelled at least one hundred and fifty miles, and that with his crippled leg. Anne stayed at home for most of the year but went for nine days to the home of Mr Eyers at Landford, a village on the main road between Salisbury and Southampton and on the edge of the New Forest. The Steeles had often done business with Mr Eyers who had a large estate containing much woodland. An entry in Mrs Steele's diary for December 1757 says, 'Mr Eyers came for our son to go to Landford to value timber... Our son bought nine hundred oaks.' The Eyers had a beautiful house at Landford and it seems probable that Anne went out riding in the forest around Nomansland, Fritham and Eyeworth. At the time Britain was heading toward a major conflict with France, and the Government was strengthening the Royal Navy and building new ships for the Fleet. Mrs Steele had recorded in January, 'The newspapers speak as though we shall soon be involved in a war with France.' In March Mr Steele and William had been in Somerset, staying at Taunton and viewing a great quantity of timber. In October Mr Steele had been to Devizes, Trowbridge and Haycombe, and in the last three months of the year William had been to Yeovil, Portsmouth and Arundel.

1755

By the beginning of 1755 a major world conflict was developing, first in Europe and then in India and America. There were fears of a French invasion along the Sussex coast and the country was full of rumours. While war was as yet undeclared, the French claimed right in America over the river basins of the Mississippi and the St Lawrence and built Fort Duquesne to establish their hold. A British force under General Braddock set out to destroy this fort but was wiped out by a force of Indians supporting the French. Mrs Steele records in her diary for 27th August, 'In the evening the papers brought the melancholy news of the defeat of General Braddock's Army.' In October, when William junior was at Redbridge, he heard rumours of 50,000 French troops having landed in Romney Marshes but this proved to be false. Then on 28th November came the dreadful news of a major earthquake in Portugal. Mrs Steele wrote, 'Lisbon, the capital city, is said to be half swallowed up by the earthquake – the other half in flames; 'tis a very shocking account.' On 11th December the danger of war and the devastating earthquake in Portugal had its effect on the Particular Baptists in Broughton and that day was set apart for prayer for the nation. This was to be the first of many such prayer meetings for the nation to be held at Broughton in the coming years, and Anne was to compose hymns which were sung on these occasions. The year was also marked by several sadnesses, Molly Wakeford and Mary Steele both losing babies through miscarriages, while Jane Gibbs at Trowbridge had a little girl, Elizabeth Theodosia born on 25th April. In April Mr Mansfield came to Broughton with his daughter Nancy [Anne's cousin] who was now seventeen and Anne went to stay with them at Ringwood in June. The year closed with the death of old Henry Sturges at the age of eighty-five. His first wife, Joan Knight, had been sister to Mr Steele senior's mother, and he was the last of the older relations. He had been a stalwart of the Broughton Church being first mentioned in the Church Book in 1719. His father Thomas Sturges was a member in the old days at Porton. He was buried on the last day of 1755, Mr Steele preaching his funeral sermon from the text, 'To die is gain.'

The Seven Years' War [1756-1763]

As the new year opened in 1756 the nation waited for the official declaration of war which eventually came in May. Prior to that declaration King George II called the nation to prayer on 6th February 'for a day of public fasting, humiliation and prayer to God on account of the dangers we are in from our encroaching enemies, the French, and the judgments that are abroad in the earth.' Anne, though too poorly to attend the prayer meeting at Broughton, composed a hymn which was sung at the service. The hymn reads,[117]

'See gracious God, before thy Throne
Thy mourning people bend !
'Tis on thy sovereign grace alone,
Our humble hopes depend.

Tremendous judgments[118] from thy hand,
Thy dreadful power display;
Yet mercy spares this guilty land,
And yet we live to pray.

Great God, and why is Britain spared,
Ungrateful as we are?

[117] *Anne Steele's Hymns*, 1760, Vol. 1, p.248.

[118] The Lisbon earthquake.

O be these awful warnings heard,
    While mercy cries forbear.

What numerous crimes increasing rise,
    O'er all this wretched isle!
What land so favoured of the skies,
    And yet what land so vile!

How changed, alas! are truths divine,
    For error guilt and shame!
What impious numbers, bold in sin,
    Disgrace the Christian name!

O bid us turn, almighty Lord,
    By thy resistless grace,
Then shall our hearts obey thy word
    And humbly seek thy face.

Then should insulting foes invade,
    We shall not sink in fear;
Secure of never failing aid,
    If God, our God is near."

Following this prayer meeting the nations of Europe aligned for war. The issues were a major conflict between Britain and France, involving supremacy of the seas and of their interests in India and North America, and the jealousy between Prussia and Austria regarding the control of Germany [then divided into numerous small states] – would the capital of a united Germany be Vienna or Berlin? The remaining great Power of Europe, Russia, instead of remaining neutral, in a dispute in which it was not directly involved, sided with France and Austria. Prussia in fear of isolation signed a treaty with Britain, whose monarch was also Elector of Hanover, a province of North Germany. Thus Europe divided into two armed camps in what amounted to something approaching 'a World War' with Britain and Prussia against France, Russia and Austria. In April the London ministers of the Particular Baptist Assembly sent to all their churches in the country setting aside 22nd March as a day of prayer on account of national dangers. The Broughton Church began their service at 4pm and Mrs Steele says, 'Several prayed very affectionately.' The following day William Steele junior set out to Wales to cross the Severn Estuary at Bristol to buy timber, and though this deal fell through it shows the great demand there was for timber to build more warships and reveals the distances the Steeles were prepared to travel to procure timber for the War effort. On 19th May over a thousand French troops landed on the

British island of Minorca in the Mediterranean and about 7,000 Prussian troops landed at Southampton and were stationed at Romsey. War was declared with France within a few days.

The Death of Mrs Gay

Then came news in the Steele family on 26th May that Mrs Steele's sister was dying at her home in Haycombe. William Steele senior set out to see her on 27th May and she died on 12th June and was buried on 17th in the parish churchyard at Englishcombe, just across the valley from her home, where her son Richard had been buried twenty years before. On 21st June Thomas Gay Attwater, brother of Caroline, Marianne and Jane, a young man now of twenty-one, came over from Bodenham to ask William Steele junior to go to Haycombe 'to assist with the parting of the Gay family estate there'. He was sent to represent his father. The estate now came into the hands of Anna Attwater at Bodenham and Jane Gibbs at Trowbridge and would be dealt with by old Mrs Gay's brother-in-law and her two sons-in-law, Thomas Attwater and Philip Gibbs. It appears in the Particular Baptist circles that all real estate was retained in the families and never sold. Wills in the family show that Mr Steele, Philip Gibbs and Thomas Attwater were now dealing with houses in Bradford-on-Avon, which had originally been owned by old Farmer Cator of Trowle, Mrs Steele's and Mrs Gay's father. Mr Steele was still, late in his life, in possession of fields at the old Sweetwell Farm at Sedgehill, property of his first wife's family, the Froudes. Exactly how extensive the Haycombe property was is not known, but the fact that it is always referred to as 'the estate' suggests it was bigger than a single farm. It had come down from old Richard Gay and had been in the family for at least one hundred years. There were several members of the Gay family living in Bath in the 17th and 18th centuries and how they were related is not clear. Some of the family owned land in the Bath city area which was later used for development by John Wood and his son. There still exists a street in Bath named after the family,[119] leading from Queen Square to the Circus.

The Seven Years' War [cont.]

As the Gay family estate was being divided among the family, the first events of the Seven Years' War were taking place. At Port Mahon, on the island of Minorca, the French under the Duc de Richelieu besieged the British garrison. A fleet under Admiral Byng, sent to relieve it, eventually gave up and sailed away, leaving the garrison to the mercy of the French. For this Admiral Byng was later court-martialled and shot. On 19th

---

[119] *Baptist Quarterly* article based on B.A. dissertation, Bristol University, by Kerry J. Birch 1997.

August the Duke of Beaufort sent half a buck [venison] to William Steele junior, who invited all the Steele family to dinner at *Pigeon House* to enjoy it. This gift was no doubt in appreciation of the good business deals that were going on between the two, especially the Duke's timber at Horndean north of Portsmouth. On 4th September the family dined again at *Pigeon House* and Mrs Steele records, 'We saw the wonders of nature through the microscope.' She mentions the presence of the grandchildren William and Samuel Wakeford, aged three and two, and Polly Steele, William's little girl, aged three. One would gather that Anne was deeply involved with the children, as well as with the national events and the viewing of nature through the microscope. Within the secluded village at Broughton the Steeles were fully acquainted with national events via their newspapers which seemed to arrive with regularity, as did their letters. In October Mrs Steele records a great battle between the Austrians and the Prussians, and how Frederick the Great had seized Dresden and forced the army of Saxony to surrender. On 20th October William junior went to Devizes Fair and met Philip and Jane Gibbs. Mrs Steele records that due to the war prices were high, food in short supply and the poor were badly hit. The Steeles had had a very good harvest in August and September and it would seem that the poor inhabitants of Broughton and those of the Baptist Chapels in the area did not lack through the goodness of the Steeles. In December the Government in London issued a proclamation 'about the selling of corn designed for the benefit of the poor'. William Pitt, famous as a war leader, was Secretary of State for War for a brief period from November 1756 to February 1757.

As the year 1757 opened William junior was again in contact with the Duke of Beaufort to buy more timber and visited him at his seat at Badminton on 1st February. The 11th February was appointed by the King as a day of humiliation and fasting, when the annual prayer meeting took place at Broughton and Mr Steele preached from Hosea 14. 3, 'Asshur shall not save us etc.,' and called on six members of the church to pray. Anne wrote two hymns for this occasion. The first was entitled, 'National Judgments Deprecated, on the fast 11th February 1757.'[120] She writes in the first,

'Pale famine now, and wasting war,
With threatening frown thy wrath declare;
But war and famine are thy slaves,
Nor can destroy when mercy saves.

[120] *Anne Steele's Poems*, 1760, Vol. 1 pp.250-253.

Our arms, O God of armies, bless,
[Thy hand alone can give success],
And make our haughty neighbours own
That heaven protects the British Throne.'

In a second hymn 'Pleading for Mercy' Anne wrote,

'In armies, fleets and strong allies,
No more we place our trust;
On God alone, our hope relies,
Kind, potent, wise and just.

Though justice near Thy awful throne,
Attends Thy dread command,
Lord, hear Thy servants, hear the Son,
And save a guilty land.'

On 23rd March a sergeant came to Broughton to enlist young men for the army and one wonders whether the infamous press gangs also came to enlist men for the Navy. On 11th April Mr Steele senior went with Mr Benham, his nephew, to the Western Association Meetings of Particular Baptist Churches at Bradford-on-Avon, Wilts and returned home on 15th.

On 3rd May Mrs Steele records that the price of corn was high, wheat 6-8 pence a bushel and barley 3-4 pence in Broughton, though much dearer elsewhere. She hoped corn supplies would hold out till the harvest. One can understand Anne's reference in her hymn of 11th February to 'pale famine'. On 23rd May news reached Broughton that Frederick the Great had captured Prague, capital of Bohemia, defeating the Austrians, but shortly afterwards suffered a defeat at their hands. At the same time a British Army of 50,000 troops was defeated by the French and forced to sign a treaty and disband. Mrs Steele wrote, 'Melancholy news from Germany and Prussia.' The battles of the War and the names of the generals were household words in the Steele homes.

In July Jane Gibbs gave birth to a boy, James, who later became an officer in the Army, but sadly died at the age of twenty-two as a result of a fall from a horse. In September there was a riot at Andover Market when seven sacks of wheat were taken from the jobbers and rapidly distributed among the poor. Anne had been staying in Andover with her sister and only returned home about a week before the riot. In mid-October Anne went to live with her brother at *Pigeon House* and stayed there until May 1758. The reason seems to be that with his help she was preparing a manuscript of her hymns and poems for publication. On 29th November she sent part of the manuscript to Andover to her brother-in-law Joseph

Wakeford, for him to take to London on one of his frequent visits to the City. By November 1757 William Pitt had succeeded the Duke of Newcastle in the direction of the War. In the same month came news to Broughton that part of the Fleet had been badly damaged in a storm, but this was followed on 24th November by the news of a great Prussian victory over the French at Rossbach. Mrs Steele wrote, 'News gives account of a complete victory obtained by the King of Prussia over the French and combined armies – for this my heart was thankful.' This battle marked a major turning point in the Seven Years' War and in the future history of Europe. Prussia would dominate Germany rather than Austria. Five days later Anne's hymns went to London for printing and the last hymn in Volume I of the 1760 Edition was entitled, 'National Judgment and Mercies – a Call to Repentance – November 1757.' It must have gone to the printers fresh from Anne's pen. Its opening verses read,

'Long has divine compassion strove
With this rebellious land;

O justice, long has pleading love
Withheld thy dreadful hand.

At length, ye Britons, lift your eyes,
Your crimes no more pursue;
Behold the gathering tempests rise,
And tremble at the view.'

And verse 4 reads,

'Late raging storm,[121] 'twas mercy spared,
Her voice destruction heard,
The impetuous winds her voice obeyed,
And awful justice spared.'

Thus Anne revealed her awareness of the policy of William Pitt in sending a Fleet under Admiral Holbourne to blockade Louisbourg, a French fortified town, guarding the mouth of the St Lawrence, near Cape Breton and protecting Quebec. This Fleet had been hit by hurricane winds in September, two ships had been lost and many damaged, being forced to return to England for repairs. News of the 'late raging storm' had reached Broughton where there was more than a casual interest in the Royal Navy. In December Mr Steele and William bought 900 oaks from Mr Eyres of Landford and on 22nd December news reached Broughton of the victory of Frederick the Great over the Austrians at the Battle of Leuthen.

[121] Off Louisbourg.

William Pitt and the British Government were sending large subsidies from England to help finance the army of Frederick, while keeping a British army in Europe on the River Elbe, and concentrating the main British War effort at sea and in America and India. On 23rd June 1757 at the Battle of Plassey Robert Clive had won a great victory over the French and Indians, capturing Bengal and opening the way to the building of British influence in India.

But while the year 1758 opened with good news from India for William Steele junior it had opened with the sad news of the loss of his merchant ship 'The Willing Mind' in the Channel, almost certainly captured by the French. In mid-February news reached Broughton of the death at Bath on 7th of Dr Joseph Stennett [1692-1758]. William Steele had heard him preach at Bratton at the Western Association Meetings in 1752 and had gone to Bath to see him when he was ill there in October 1757. They were great friends. Dr Stennett had pastored his congregation in Little Wild Street for twenty years and was highly respected by many leading men in the City. It is clear that William Steele and his son would have known him well as one of the leaders of the Particular Baptists.

On 17th February King George II called for another Day of Humiliation and Prayer for the Nation and the Church at Broughton met again for the fifth such prayer meeting. Mr Steele began with prayer and preached from 2 Chronicles 20. 3, 'And Jehoshaphat feared and set himself to seek the Lord and proclaimed a fast throughout all Judah.' Five of the male members of the church prayed.' Mrs Steele wrote, 'Oh that God may hear and answer those earnest prayers for our poor kingdom and our Allies.' The day following the prayer meeting, the news of Plassey reached Broughton. The cause of the conflict had centred on the imprisonment of one hundred and fifty English traders at Fort William in the Province of Bengal in a small underground prison later called 'The Black Hole of Calcutta'. There in the heat of the Indian summer all but twenty-three of them had died of thirst and hunger. Robert Clive went with an army of 3-4,000 troops to fight against an Indian host of sixty thousand. He obtained a complete victory. In America the French had expanded up the valleys of the Mississippi and the Ohio and down the valley of the St Lawrence, and had set up a chain of fortified settlements which cut off the New England Colonies from any expansion westwards. General Braddock had attempted to break this chain in his attack on Fort Duquesne in 1755 and had failed. Now William Pitt masterminded a large and comprehensive plan of attack to drive the French out of North America. 'The St Lawrence valley was best approached and conquered by a land force conveyed and covered by the Fleet. The perfect cooperation of the two services led first to the capture of Louisbourg and Cape Breton Island commanding entry to the great river [St Lawrence] in 1758 and the following year to Wolfe's daring ascent of the Heights of Abraham and the capture of Quebec. Both Wolfe and his magnanimous rival Montcalm [leader of the French] were mortally wounded on that memorable day which decided the future of Canada.'[122] In the same year that Louisbourg was captured a force from Philadelphia captured Fort Duquesne and renamed it Pittsburg. The name commemorates for the New England colonists the great minister who first opened the West to them. G. M. Trevelyan comments, 'The unexplored West was the Great Commoner's [Wm Pitt] present to the English speaking race.'[123] News of these events reached Broughton in August 1758. Mrs Steele wrote, 'The news of Cape Breton being taken brings great rejoicing.' On 4th September she refers to the good news that the King of Prussia had defeated the Russians. This was a reference to the Battle of Zorndorf when Frederick drove the Russians back into Poland. But this victory was soon followed by a series of defeats against the Austrians. Mrs Steele kept abreast of it all in her diary.

1758

Back in Broughton, so far removed from the world scene and yet in such close contact with it, the Particular Baptist Church saw nine new members join and be baptised, six women and three men, this all within five weeks in March and April 1758, together with one more woman in October. Spiritually it was a year of great prosperity for the church which only recently Mrs Steele had felt was declining as members moved away and formed other Meetings. Mrs Steele refers to hearing some 'deride and scoff at our way of administering the sacred ordinance of baptism'. There was obviously reproach to be borne in the village for the Lord Jesus Christ and taking His name in a public profession of it. Mrs Steele herself was declining in health during the year. In March she complained of a numbness that had taken her on her right side and her eyesight and memory were beginning to fail and on occasions she had periods of dizziness. She was approaching seventy. In September she wrote, 'I am now cast down by reason of the decay of natural faculties.' Anne was continually ill with shortness of breath and was unable to walk to the Chapel and had to be taken with Mrs Steele in the chaise. Mr Steele and William were travelling constantly to select and buy timber. Mr Steele's preaching engagements took him to Whitchurch, Romsey and Downton. On 15th May a young minister named Charles Cole came to preach for the

---

[122] *History of England*, G. M. Trevelyan, 1926, p.545.
[123] ibid.

first time at Broughton in Mr Steele's absence. He had recently been sent to preach by the church at Bradford-on-Avon. Anne had come back to *Grandfathers* in May and except for ten days in June and ten days at the end of September and the beginning of October, when she had been in Andover with Molly, she spent the whole of the year in Broughton. On 12th July William junior had to go to the Assizes at Winchester to serve on the jury. In November one of William junior's men went to London to be inoculated against smallpox. Throughout the eighteenth century about eight per cent of each generation died of smallpox. The vaccination which William junior's man had was not the vaccination of Jenner, first performed from cowpox in 1796, but was the inoculation introduced by the traveller, Lady Mary Wortley Montague from Turkey, at the beginning of the eighteenth century and carried out at the Inoculation Hospital set up in London.[124] Mrs Steele's diary often records the presence of smallpox in Trowbridge, Salisbury, Romsey and on occasions in Broughton itself. In December William's wife Mary was very ill for about two weeks with a miscarriage. On 15th December Frank Wade, a deacon of the Broughton Church and one of the managers for the Steele timber trade, died suddenly at Horndean. It is possible that he was the man who had recently been inoculated against smallpox and died from the after effects of the inoculation.

James Hervey

On 25th December 1758, James Hervey died at Weston Favell, near Northampton at the age of forty-five. He had been a close friend of George Whitefield, had been at Oxford University with him and had taken over Whitefield's curacy at Dummer in Hampshire for one year in 1737. Dummer was eight miles to the east of Whitchurch, where many of Anne Steele's relatives lived, including the Benhams and the Etheridges. Benjamin Britton had become the pastor of the Particular Baptist Church there in 1732 and had a congregation of about fifty. Whether there was any contact between James Hervey and the Whitchurch Particular Baptists is not known. Anne Steele was twenty-one at the time he was at Dummer. Later in life, Hervey was to publish works which would come into the hands of Anne. In 1745-6 he wrote his

Figure 23: James Hervey

[124] *English Social History*, G. M. Trevelyan, 1942, p 344.

Meditations, and in 1755 his work entitled *Theron and Aspasio* which was a defence of the doctrine of the imputed righteousness of Christ. Both of these works came into the hands of Anne Steele and she wrote poems in appreciation of them. Her poem on the *Meditations in the Tombs* ran to ninety lines and opened with the words,

> 'Happy the man whom grace divine has taught
> To raise to nobler scenes the flying thought;
> Beyond the bounds of time and sense to soar,
> And awful immortality explore...'

and included,

> 'Thus Hervey mourns; his kind instructive page,
> Full of compassion for a thoughtless age,
> In all the charms of eloquence appears,
> And wakes our pleasure, while it steals our tears.'[125]

On reading his work *Theron and Aspasio* [1755] she penned the following lines, in a poem of seven stanzas; the last stanza reads,

> 'O Hervey, be thy labours crowned
> With bliss beyond the low rewards of fame !
> Such joy be thine, as thy Aspasio found,
> While many a Theron owns the Saviour's name.'[126]

When Hervey died Anne wrote a poem of nine stanzas in his memory. We quote three of the verses;

> 'O Hervey, honoured name, forgive the tear,
> That mourns thy exit from a world like this;
> Forgive the wish that would have kept thee here,
> Fond wish! have kept thee from the seats of bliss.
>
> Yet its own loss must every heart deplore,
> That feels the power of Hervey's moving page,
> That wished [but ah, that wish avails no more,]
> His life prolonged to bless the rising age.
>
> O lost to earth! No, in his works, he lives,
> Here shall the rising age his portrait view;
> Here, his own pen, the mind's bright image gives,
> In fairer tints than painting ever knew.'[127]

---

[125] *Hymns of Anne Steele*, 1760, Vol. 1, p.211.
[126] ibid. Vol. 2, p.50.
[127] ibid. Vol. 2, p.50.

THERON and *ASPASIO*:

OR, A

SERIES

OF

DIALOGUES

AND

LETTERS,

UPON THE

Moſt *Important* and *Intereſting* Subjects.

IN THREE VOLUMES.

By JAMES HERVEY, A.M.

Late Rector of *Weſton-Favell*, in *Northamptonſhire*.

The Memorial of thine abundant Kindneſs *ſhall be ſhewed, and Men ſhall ſing of thy* Righteouſneſs. *Pſal.* cxlv. 7.

VOL. I.

THE FIFTH EDITION.

LONDON:

Printed by Charles Rivington,

For John and Francis Rivington, at the *Bible* and *Crown*, in *St. Paul's Church-yard.*

MDCCLXVII.

Figure 24: Title Page of 'Theron and Aspasio'

It is interesting that when Anne's father spent an evening in June 1752 at Whitchurch with George Whitefield, Whitefield was only eight miles from Dummer where he had been a young curate. One wonders if at that evening meeting there was any mention of James Hervey, also if in fact Whitefield already knew the Particular Baptists at Whitchurch through his previous stay in the area, and was returning to preach among friends. Anne obviously was well read in James Hervey's works and had a great love and affection for them, but there is no mention, either among her letters or in her stepmother's diary, that she had ever met him.

1759

1759 was a momentous year for Britain and her Allies in the Seven Years' War. France was planning an invasion across the Channel. In the previous year a British Naval Force had attacked St Malo on the French coast and destroyed an hundred vessels, probably the flat-bottomed boats intended to transport a French Army across the Channel. The British Fleet had blockaded the French Navy in Brest on the coast of Brittany and in Toulon on the French Mediterranean coast, thus keeping it from opening up the Channel for an army to cross. On 11th January young Charles Cole [1733-1813] came again to preach, this time to the meeting in Ben Street, Nether Wallop. Neither Mrs Steele nor Anne was well enough to go to hear him. He was only twenty-six at the time, but within a few months, in June, he was to become pastor of the Particular Baptist Church at Whitchurch where Mrs Benham, William Steele senior's sister, and her family attended. Charles Cole was a hymnwriter and published a volume of over an hundred hymns in 1789, entitled *A Threefold Alphabet of New Hymns*, on the ministry of the Word, Baptism and the Lord's Supper. He was to remain as pastor at Whitchurch for fifty-four years, dying at the age of eighty in 1813. His hymns include,

> 'Hark! how the gospel trumpet sounds!
> Christ and free grace therein abounds;
> Free grace to such as sinners be;
> And if free grace, why not for me?'

and,

> 'Show me some token, Lord, for good,
> Some token of thy special love;
> Show me that I am born of God,
> And that my treasure is above.'

It would be interesting to know what influence Anne Steele had in the development of this hymnwriter. They must have known each other very well and no doubt he visited *Grandfathers* and *Broughton House*.[128]

The annual prayer meeting for the nation on the day set apart by the King and Government was held at Broughton on Friday 16th February. In January news had come that Louisbourg and Fort Duquesne had been captured from the French. In June ships arrived at Portsmouth with the news of the capture of Guadaloupe in the West Indies. On 10th August Prince Ferdinand of Brunswick defeated the French at the Battle of Minden though before the end of August the Prussians had suffered two defeats at the hands of the Russians and Austrians. On the same day as Minden, a major naval battle took place at Lagos, off Cape St Vincent, Portugal, after part of the French Fleet broke out of Toulon and came through the Straits of Gibraltar, heading for the Channel. Admiral Boscawen, commanding the British Fleet won a major victory over the French, sinking several of their capital ships. On 12th September General Wolfe was ready to storm the Heights of Abraham and capture Quebec from the French. The French assembled an army of eighteen thousand troops at Brest ready to cross the Channel. Admiral Hawke, aware of the imminent danger, though the seas were running high, and the coast dangerously rocky, moved in to the attack on 20th November and with the loss of only two British warships, destroyed the French Fleet at the Battle of Quiberon Bay on the Brittany coast. The news of the victory at Lagos reached Broughton on 10th September, and rumours of the naval victory at Quiberon Bay were in Broughton on 22nd November, only two days after the victory, probably via Portsmouth. The full details came via Mr Nyke, one of their ministers, on 1st December.

In the midst of these momentous national events, Broughton had been hit in July and August by an outbreak of smallpox. Many died from it and on 20th July the church had a special prayer meeting on account of it. Anne was ill at the time and greatly feared catching it in her weak condition. On 19th October the two volumes of her *Hymns* and *Poems* reached Broughton in an unbound copy, and on 20th November the bound volumes arrived in a beautiful leather binding. Mary Wakeford wrote in her diary for 25th November that she had spent the evening reading her sister's hymns.[129] While Anne penned her hymns, around her was being shaped future world history.

---

[128] *Broughton House* – William Steele Jnr. rented the property until he bought it in 1758 and changed its name from *Pigeon House* to *Broughton House*.

[129] The original diaries have been lost. Extracts exist, copied by Selina Anne Bompas.

King George II appointed 29th November as 'a day to be kept for thanksgiving for the great mercies of our God'. Anne penned a hymn entitled 'On a Day of Prayer for Success in War'.[130] Part of it reads,

'With all the boasted pomp of war
In vain we dare the hostile field;
In vain, unless the Lord be there;
Thy arm alone is Britain's shield.

Our arms succeed, our councils guide,
Let thy right hand our cause maintain
Till war's destructive rage subside,
And peace resume her gentle reign.'

In her entry in her diary for 3rd January 1760[131] Mrs Steele writes, 'I read the last three months of my diary for the past year where I see, admire and have cause to praise God for quite dispelling all our fears of a French invasion with which we have so long been threatened.' 'With the victory of Rossbach, began the re-creation of Germany, the revival of its political and intellectual life, the long process of its union under the leadership of Prussia and Prussia's kings. With that of Plassey the influence of Europe told for the first time since the days of Alexander on the nations of the East. The world in Burke's phrase, "saw one of the races of the north-west cast into the heart of Asia new manners, new doctrines, new institutions." With the triumph of Wolfe on the Heights of Abraham, began the history of the United States.'[132] Little could the Broughton Baptists have understood the full answer to their prayers. One may have stood out clearly in later generations of Baptists as William Carey from Leicestershire and Joshua Marshman from Westbury, Wiltshire led the vanguard of world missionary work to India, founding the Baptist Missionary Society, the great sub-continent now opened under British rule to the Gospel.

Anne visited Andover several times in 1759, went to Devizes Fair with her father in May and in August stayed for ten days at Yeovil with her brother and sister-in-law Mary, at Mary's home. Her stepmother, who was now seventy, was failing fast, though her mind and sight were reasonably good as she had recorded in June 1758 that she was enjoying reading through the *Divine Attributes* by Stephen Charnock and that over a long period. She was beginning to feel her days were numbered and on

[130] *Hymns and Poems*, Anne Steele, 1780, Vol. 3, p.123.
[131] STE 2/1/3.
[132] *Short History of the English People*, J. R. Green, 1902, p.757.

26th June 1758 in her diary had gone back to her early days when having heard John Kent preach she wrote, 'Mr Kent brought that for a proof, namely, "I have no greater joy than to know that my children walk in the truth." 3 John 4; the same that my father mentioned to my sister and me just as we were going to speak our experience, and this caused it to come to my mind, through which I was much affected. The glory is due alone to God for it is His mercy that I can look back on my father's pious [God-fearing] example. What I mentioned was in the year 1706 and God has preserved me in life in that same walk to this time. Blessed be His Holy Name. My thoughts often turn to my deceased parents.' Her father had died in 1725, her mother in 1733 and her sister in 1756. She was the last of her family. She had been a member of the Particular Baptist Church in Trowbridge under the ministry of John Davisson and had been blessed under the ministry of Andrew Gifford when he preached there in 1707, when she was eighteen. She had grown up on the family farm on Trowle Common outside Trowbridge, had married William Steele in 1723 and lived in Broughton ever since at *Grandfathers*. In November 1759 she wrote in her diary, 'My thoughts have been employed in admiring the distinguishing love and care of my God not only in my infancy and childhood, but ever since, and I often admire and praise God for peace in my days, having been born at the restoration by King William.'[133]

1760 – The Last Days of Mrs Steele

As the year turned and 1760 came, Mrs Steele had but six months to live. It was a sick household at *Grandfathers* and must have presented Mr Steele and his son with considerable worry. It would appear that the household was kept going by servants. In January Mrs Steele recorded that 'Nanny is very ill the greatest part of her time.' She herself was 'carried to the meeting' on the second Sunday in January, presumably in a sedan chair. On 31st January Anne was well enough to go to the meeting herself and heard young Charles Cole preach from Psalm 81.10, 'I am the Lord thy God which brought thee out of the land of Egypt: open thy mouth wide, and I will fill it.' Intermittently the two of them were able to get to the meeting; sometimes they stayed at home together. It must have been hard for Mr Steele to leave them to go to preach. On 21st April William junior went to Roydon, between Brockenhurst and Lymington in the New Forest, to look at some property he had purchased there. There were meetings of Particular Baptists in Lymington and Brockenhurst and this purchase may have been in some way connected with some of these congregations. Otherwise it is hard to understand why he should be interested in a property so far from Broughton. He sold it again in 1771.

[133] STE 2/1/3.

On Sunday 15th June Mrs Steele described herself as 'very ill.' On Sunday 22nd June she was at the meeting at Broughton in the afternoon when her husband preached from Luke 4. 10, 'The Spirit of the Lord is upon me, because he has anointed me to preach the Gospel to the poor.' She wrote in her diary of this sermon, 'It was delightful to me, but I shall soon forget it.' On 25th she wrote, 'Nanny is very ill and I am thoughtful about her. I want to be in a more spiritual frame, but I can make no progress in the ways and things of God and yet sometimes I can hope I am a child of God.' On 26th June she wrote, 'We sheared our sheep the day past, yet I have very little concern with worldly business.' Her final entry was on 27th June when she wrote, 'My weakness and depravity is exceeding great and my whole dependence is on the merits and righteousness of the Lord Jesus Christ.' What a solid foundation on which 'to finish her course'. Of her it could truly be said, 'I have fought a good fight, I have finished my course, I have kept the faith.' 2 Timothy 4. 7. The inscription on her grave in Broughton Parish Churchyard reads, 'Anne, the second wife of William Steele, died June 28th 1760, aged 71 years.' She had been a baptised member of Trowbridge[134] and Broughton Particular Baptist Churches for fifty-four years, husband of William Steele for thirty-seven years and a pastor's wife for twenty-seven years. She took a great interest in the prosperity of the Broughton Church and recorded in her diary for 13th June, 'I have earnest desires for some increase in our Church and this evening one came here to speak with Mr Steele that she might give her experience and she talks very well.' On Sunday 15th June, Martha Tub spoke her experience to the satisfaction of the church and was baptised.

Anne penned two poems to Mary Wakeford [Amira] on the illness and death of her mother. In the first 'To Amira on the Illness of her Mother,' she wrote,[135]

> 'The blessings God hath lent, when he recalls,
> Faith bids the heart with full consent resign,
> Low at his feet the heart adoring falls!
> Lord, 'tis enough, I'm blest while thou art mine.'

In the second poem of ninety lines 'To Amira on the Sudden Death of Her Mother,' she wrote,[136]

> 'Though nature, friendship, filial love awake
> The springs of grief, and though the sudden shock

---

[134] ASD. 30 May 1754. STE 2/1/3.
[135] *Miscellaneous Works*, Vol. III. Anne Steele, 1780, pp.28-30.
[136] ibid. pp.91-94.

O'erpowered the mind [too weak to meet surprise],
At length my dear Amira, be our griefs
Restrained, obedient to the voice divine
Which calms the winds and seas, that sovereign voice
Which bids the tempest of the mind – 'Be Still.'

Look up, Amira, see the Father's hand,
Indulgent, tender, in the stroke we mourn!
Say, could the awful messenger appear
In a more gentle form? how soft the touch
That loosened nature's bands, dissolved the tie
That held the weary spirit, prison'd long
In a frail ruined tenement below,
And bade her rise to liberty and joy!
Say do we mourn the friend, the parent lost?
Ah no, retract the word, she is but called,
Before us, called to her celestial home,
The blissful home, so long, so much desired;
And hope soft whispers we shall meet her there.
Meet her – but how? enfeebled, bent with years,
Worn out with pains, her mental powers decayed
And lost to social joys? though hope, and trust,
And patient resignation shone serene,
The Christian's pattern, and the friend's support;
Their work fulfilled, those graces have resigned
Their seat to perfect joy and endless praise.'

In a third poem Anne wrote to Amira after the death of Mrs Steele she spoke of her new place in the home at *Grandfathers*,[137]

'To me hath providence assigned a part
Which claims the tenderest passions of the heart,
No less than yours: to soothe a parent's care
In life's decline, his every grief to share,
By every act of cheerful duty prove,
Sincerest gratitude and filial love.
O long, [propitious to my ardent prayer,]
To me, to you may heaven indulgent spare
His valued life! and when we must, must part,
Sustain the sad survivor's fainting heart!
Before the mental eye may he display
A blissful prospect of the realms of day,
Whose presence cheers affliction's deepest gloom,
And sheds a ray of glory on the tomb!'

[137] ibid. pp.91-94.

From these verses it appears that Mrs Steele's end was sudden. While she had been declining, 'enfeebled', 'bent', 'worn out with pains', 'her mental powers decayed and lost to social joys', yet still her death came as a 'sudden shock to her family'. By the way Anne speaks of her end, death coming in a 'gentle form' and 'How soft the touch that loosened nature's bands', one would gather that Mrs Steele died in her sleep, or possibly was unconscious after a stroke. With her death life changed completely at *Grandfathers* and the burden of running the home now fell on Anne's shoulders, a burden she was to carry until the death of her father in 1769.

King George III

In October 1760 King George II died at the age of seventy-seven. He had reigned since 1727 when Anne was a girl of ten. His heir, Frederick Prince of Wales, had died at the early age of forty-four in 1751, leaving his young son, aged thirteen, as heir to the throne. He now succeeded his grandfather at the age of twenty-two, as King George III, marrying Princess Charlotte Sophia, a German princess, in September the following year. Anne penned some verses entitled a 'Hymn to Jesus', to commemorate his coronation.[138]

'Shall loyal nations hail the day,
That crowns their King with loud acclaim?
And shall not saints their homage pay
To their beloved Saviour's name?
Ye saints, resound in joyful strains,
Jesus, the King of glory reigns.

Jesus who vanquished all your foes,
Who came to save, who reigns to bless,
From him your every comfort flows,
Life, liberty, and joy and peace
Resound, resound in joyful strains,
Jesus, the King of glory reigns.

How mean the tribute mortals pay,
How cold the heart, how faint the tongue;
But Lord, thy coronation day
Shall tune a more exalted song:
Resounding in immortal strains,
Jesus, the King of glory reigns.

He comes, he comes, with triumph crowned,
In dazzling robes of light arrayed,

[138] ibid. pp.134-138.

Faith views the splendour dawning round,
Earth's fairest lustre sinks in shade.
Resound, resound in joyful strains,
Jesus, the King of glory reigns.'

At the time Anne wrote this she had reached the age of forty-three in a life that had seen much sorrow and suffering. She had published a two-volume set of poetry entitled *Poems on Subjects Chiefly Devotional* by Theodosia. This included a large selection of spiritual verses, many described as hymns, a selection of paraphrases of the Psalms, and a selection of her more secular verse. She undoubtedly had a natural talent.

Chapter 6

A Natural Talent [1743-60]

Anne Steele and her Contemporaries

Anne Steele wrote in an age of great hymnwriters, in the century of the Great Evangelical Revival. While there was undoubtedly a tradition of writing poetry and hymns in her family [her own father and brother were poets] yet it would appear that the very fact and existence of the revival must have had a bearing and influence on the production of her spiritual verse. As we have seen, her people, including her father, were in direct contact with the leaders of that revival and had heard them preach. While the ministers in that revival were largely Church of England ministers, the life history of Anne Steele and the Particular Baptists shows that they were not casual, disinterested onlookers, but were prayerfully concerned for the salvation of the souls of their compatriots. They shared a part in the vision of the godly ministers of the revival such as George Whitefield, probably its most powerful and eminent leader, who stood firmly in the orthodox faith of the Thirty-Nine Articles, the reformed doctrinal basis of the National Church. The Particular Baptists stood in that stream of orthodoxy side by side with their Anglican brethren, differing only on the question of baptism of infants and adults. They were one with truly converted people in the Anglican Church, ministers such as John Newton, John Berridge, Augustus Toplady, Charles Wesley, Thomas Haweis, and the poet William Cowper, and others outside the Baptist and Anglican orbit such as Philip Doddridge, John Cennick, and Joseph Hart. Numbered among Particular Baptist hymnwriters, with Anne Steele, were Daniel Turner, James Fanch, Benjamin Wallin, Benjamin Beddome, Samuel Stennett and Charles Cole.

It was a century of great names, whose verse has stood the test of time and whose hymns are still sung two hundred and fifty years later and are nationally known, such as Isaac Watts' 'O God our help in ages past,' and John Newton's 'Amazing grace.' Anne Steele therefore found herself among giants in hymnology and it is important to understand where she is to be placed in that hierarchy of gifted men, for she was in fact the only woman of that period whose hymns have stood the test of time. Anne

Dutton, wife of the Particular Baptist minister Benjamin Dutton, pastor of a church at Great Gransden in Huntingdonshire, published about sixty hymns in 1734 but none have passed into common use. Most modern hymnbooks contain Anne Steele's hymn beginning, 'Father of mercies, in thy Word' and in others can be found 'When sins and fears prevailing rise', 'And did the Holy and the Just.' Since the republication of a volume of her hymns in 1967, there has been in recent years a revival of interest in her work. In *The British Particular Baptists* edited by Michael. G. Haykin and published in the United States in three volumes between 1998-2003, there is an up-to-date analysis of her work by Sharon James. [Vol 3. pp.1-21, 2003].

Though she may be seen as a minor contributor to the hymnology of the eighteenth century, yet John Julian D.D. in his *Dictionary of Hymnology* [1892] considered that seventy-five of her hymns deserved to be listed in the entry that related to her as being in common use. W.R. Stevenson M.A. [Editor of the *Baptist Hymnal*, who wrote the entry on Anne Steele in *The Dictionary of Hymnology*] states that within nine years of the publication of the first edition of her hymns in 1760, sixty-two of them were included in the *Bristol Baptist Collection of Hymns* of Ash and Evans and thus became available for the first time outside the Broughton Church for congregational use. In 1780 Dr Caleb Evans, Principal of the Bristol Baptist Academy and a friend of the Steele family, published a new edition of Anne Steele's hymns, poetry and writings in a three volume edition, including a preface of his own on the life of Anne Steele. In 1787 in Dr Rippon's *Selection of Hymns* forty-seven of her hymns were included, and in 1812 Dr W.B. Collyer published his *Collection of Hymns* which included twenty-six of her hymns.[139] In Boston, U.S.A, a two volume edition of her hymns was published in 1808, being a reprint of the English 1780 edition and thus her hymns became widely used in America. Anne Steele wrote under the pen-name of 'Theodosia,' 'Gift of God,' attributing her undoubted 'natural talent,' to her Creator. The entry of W.R. Stevenson says, 'Among Baptist hymnwriters Anne Steele stands at the head, if we regard either the number of her hymns [144 Hymns and 34 Psalms in verse] which have found a place in the hymnals of the last one hundred and twenty years, or the frequency with which they have been sung. Although few of them can be placed in the first rank of lyrical compositions, they are almost uniformly simple in language, natural and pleasant in imagery and full of genuine Christian feeling.'

---

[139] *Dictionary of Hymnology*. J. Julian, 1908, p.1089.

It is difficult to ascertain how much Anne Steele was influenced by hymnwriters that preceded her. It is clear that Watts' *Psalms and Hymns*, published in two parts, as *Hymns and Spiritual Songs* [1707] and as *Psalms of David* [1719] was the primary influence in her hymns and paraphrases of the Psalms. Watts' hymnbook was used in the Particular Baptist congregation at Broughton and Anne had grown up from childhood with these Psalms and hymns. They were written in three metres, long, common, and short. Most of Anne's hymns were composed in these three metres. But there were other collections of hymns that had been published prior to 1760. Joseph Stennett [1663-1713] the Particular Baptist pastor at Pinner's Hall, London had published a set of hymns for the Lord's Supper in 1697. These had been reprinted and added to in 1703 and 1709 when they numbered fifty hymns. In 1712 Joseph Stennett had composed twelve hymns for the ordinance of Baptism. Anne Dutton, the wife of Benjamin Dutton, Baptist minister at Great Gransden in Huntingdonshire had published a poem on *The Wonders of Grace* in 1734, to which she had appended about sixty hymns. Charles Wesley had published his *Psalms and Hymns* in 1738 and a further volume *Hymns and Sacred Poems* in 1749. In 1750 Benjamin Wallin [1711-1782], a Particular Baptist minister in Southwark, London, published *Evangelical Hymns and Songs*, which included the hymn which begins, 'Hail, mighty Jesus! how divine is thy victorious sword.' Daniel Turner [1710-1798], the Particular Baptist pastor at Abingdon, published *Divine Songs, Hymns and other Poems* in 1747. Turner's brother-in-law, James Fanch, [1704-1767] was also a Baptist poet and hymnwriter. He had preached at Whitchurch in 1744/5 and then became pastor at Romsey in 1745. He published *Paraphrases of a Select Number of Psalms* in 1764. As Anne Steele's father often preached at Romsey for him, it is possible that Anne had seen some of these *Psalms* before they were in print. These *Psalms* were translated from the Latin version of George Buchanan [1506-1582] and show that Fanch was a Latin scholar like Anne's grandfather Edward Froude. He also translated the *Odes of Horace*. Fanch found a place in Julian's Dictionary of Hymnology where he is recorded as the joint author with Turner of the hymn, 'Beyond the glittering starry skies,' which ran to twenty-three stanzas and was published in 1791 after his death by his brother-in-law.[140]

Benjamin Beddome had become pastor at Bourton-on-the-Water in 1743 and had composed a hymn every Sunday, based on the text of the morning sermon and sung at the conclusion of the service. How far these hymns were distributed beyond Bourton is not known, but certainly, as we

[140] See Appendix III.

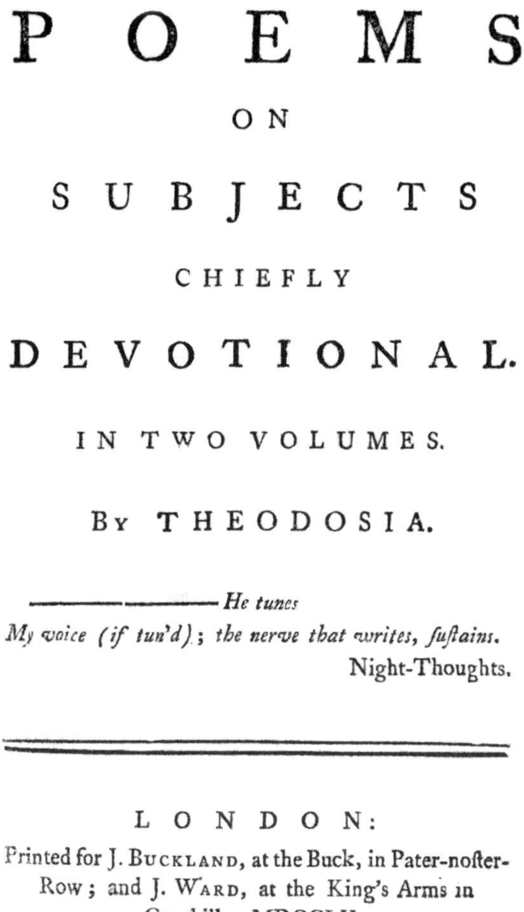

POEMS

ON

SUBJECTS

CHIEFLY

DEVOTIONAL.

IN TWO VOLUMES.

By THEODOSIA.

——————He tunes
My voice (if tun'd); the nerve that writes, sustains.
Night-Thoughts.

LONDON:
Printed for J. Buckland, at the Buck, in Pater-noster-Row; and J. Ward, at the King's Arms in Cornhill. MDCCLX.

Figure 25: Title Page of the First Edition of Anne Steele's Hymns

have shown, Beddome had some sort of contact with Broughton, having probably preached there in his early ministry and had proposed to Anne in 1742. The hymns of Philip Doddridge [1702-1751] were published in 1755 after his death. In the same year [1759] as Anne's two volumes of hymns came from the printing press, Joseph Hart [1712-1768] published a volume of hymns in London. Dr Samuel Stennett [1727-1795] the son of Dr Joseph Stennett [the younger 1692-1758] was a well-known hymnwriter. He was assistant pastor to his father at Little Wild Street, London in 1748 at the age of twenty-one and became pastor on his father's death in 1758. He was a leading London Particular Baptist minister and contributed thirty-eight hymns to Rippon's Collection in 1787. Anne's father had heard his father [Dr Joseph Stennett the younger] preach at the Western Association Meetings at Bratton in 1752. It is not clear exactly when Dr Samuel Stennett began composing hymns, but considering that the Stennetts and the Steeles were in close contact, it is feasible that before 1760 Anne may have seen some of Dr Samuel Stennett's hymns in manuscript form. As Anne was interested in writing hymns and poems, it would seem reasonable to suppose that she had handled at least some of these volumes or manuscripts of hymns, especially those of her own Particular Baptist hymnwriters.

Helpers and Advisers

Help with the production of the two-volume edition of her hymns in 1760 came from a number of quarters. Anne's father was in close contact with James Fanch [1704-1767]. They frequently preached in each other's pulpits. Anne would have known Mr Fanch well and through him his brother-in-law, Daniel Turner. James Fanch's verse is of a high order, as is apparent in his paraphrase of the twenty-third Psalm. He wrote,

'The Lord, my Shepherd, safely guides,
And constantly for me provides.
I cannot want a sure defence,
Or suffer through his negligence.
To flowery meads, in sweetest air,
He leads me with indulgent care.
How blest am I, who always find
Pastures so sweet! Shepherd so kind.

On mossy banks, by crystal streams
Gilt with the sun's refreshing beams,
I oft my weary head recline,
And sleep in arms of love divine.
His heavenly favours daily shed
The choicest blessings on my head.
How blest am I who always find
Pastures so sweet! Shepherd so kind.

When like a simple sheep I stray,
Neglect my guide and lose my way,

His gentle care conducts again
My steps to his delightful plain;
A willing captive, now I own
That rest remains with him alone.
How blest am I who always find
Pastures so sweet! Shepherd so kind.

My foes disarmed, all standing round,
Behold my board with plenty crowned;
The generous vine my cup supplies
With wine like that of Paradise;
While heavenly bounty cheerful smiles,
And every anxious care beguiles.
How blest am I, who always find
Pastures so sweet! Shepherd so kind.

But what's to come? Suppose the worst;
A dying bed: – Nay, die I must.
What room have I for anxious fear
When my Protector is so near,
Whose crook and staff long since have proved
Dear evidence how much he loved.
How blest am I, who always find
Pastures so sweet! Shepherd so kind.'[141]

James Fanch had opened a new Particular Baptist Meeting at Lockerley near Broughton in 1753.[142] Mrs Steele recorded in her diary for 17th February 1753, 'Mr Steele came and told us of some remarkable things, in particular as last Thursday was the time for Mr Fanch to preach at Broughton. There was a great many of the Lockerley people of which there was ten men and six women baptised [by Mr Steele and Mr Fanch] who designs to form them into a Church at Lockerley.' As Daniel Turner went to Abingdon as pastor in 1748 and James Fanch went to Whitchurch and Romsey in 1744/5, it would appear that Anne was being advised by them on the quality of her verse and which of them to publish in the early 1750s. Daniel Turner had published his own book of hymns and poems in 1747, while he was pastor of the Baptist Church in Reading. He was the author of many hymns one of which was,

'Jesus, full of all compassion,
Hear thy humble suppliant's cry;
Let me know thy great salvation;
See, I languish faint and die.

[141] *Paraphrases of a Select Number of Psalms*, James Fanch, 1764.
[142] *History of English Baptists*, Joseph Ivimey, pp.501-504.

Guilty, but with heart relenting,
Overwhelmed with helpless grief,
Prostrate at thy feet repenting,
Send, O send me quick relief.

Whither should a wretch be flying,
But to him who comfort gives?
Whither, from the dread of dying,
But to him who ever lives?

Hear, then, blessed Saviour, hear me!
My soul cleaveth to the dust;
Send the Comforter to cheer me,
Lo! in thee I put my trust.

On the word thy blood has sealed
Hangs my everlasting all;
Let thy arm be now revealed;
Stay, O stay me, lest I fall.

In the world of endless ruin,
Let it never, Lord, be said,
"Here's a soul that perished suing
For the boasted Saviour's aid."'

Mrs Steele's diary shows that Daniel Turner came to Broughton on 17th November 1756 and stayed with the Steeles for two nights and afterwards he and Anne had an exchange of letters regarding this visit. There seems little doubt that this visit concerned the preparation of Anne's hymns and poems for publication. Thus to these two ministers Anne went for advice on which of her verses to publish. James Fanch was her immediate adviser, an able scholarly, gifted man who was well able to suggest variations and improvements to her verse, and Daniel Turner added his suggestions. It is interesting to see that Anne sought the advice of others in this venture into print.

But these were not the only advisers Anne had. Mrs Steele's diary shows that on 11th June 1751 James Fanch had been at Broughton together with Philip Furneaux [1726-1783] and John Lavington [1690-1759]. Furneaux had studied at Dr Jennings' Academy in London between 1743-1749. He was a Hebrew scholar, editing Jennings' *Hebrew Antiquities* in 1766. When he left the Academy he was ordained as assistant minister at the Presbyterian congregation at St Mark's, Southwark, where he stayed until he was appointed minister at The

Independent Church in Clapham in 1753. He was awarded the degree of D.D. by the Marischal College, Aberdeen in 1767.[143] John Lavington was a Presbyterian divine, probably educated for the ministry in London, who became assistant minister of a Presbyterian Meeting in Exeter in 1715. In the Arian Controversy in Exeter he was the one Presbyterian minister that held to the orthodox view of the Trinity. He founded the Western Academy at Ottery St Mary in Devon in 1752 for the training of an orthodox ministry.[144] When they came to Broughton in 1751, Furneaux was a young minister of twenty-five and Lavington a minister of the same generation as William Steele senior. Joseph and Mary Wakeford had brought them over to Broughton from Andover. The Wakefords attended an Independent Church in Andover and almost certainly one of the ministers had been preaching there. They were not Particular Baptists. No more is heard of John Lavington's coming to Broughton, but in a letter of Anne to her brother William, dated 16th May 1755,[145] we hear that Philip Furneaux had been there again. She writes, 'Mr Furneaux came yesterday a little before noon, preached in the evening and returned to Andover this morning. We had agreeable deal of chat intermingled with reading my papers and canvassing the printing affair in which his opinion corresponds with yours. I wish you were here. He says he will call on us again, if he can, on his return from the West about a fortnight hence. I hope you will be at home. Brother and sister Wakeford were with him. We walked in your garden, which is now in its gayest dress.'

Here was a London Independent minister preaching at the Broughton Baptist Meeting and helping Anne in the printing of her hymns and poems. He had come to Andover as a friend of the Wakefords, probably having met Joseph Wakeford in London, which he visited frequently in connection with his large drapery business in Andover. Furneaux was in Broughton again in 1757. Anne went to live at her brother's house in October 1757 and on 29th November Joseph Wakeford took part of her hymns and poems to London to be printed. It would appear that the cost of publication was being borne by her brother and that Philip Furneaux was watching over the publication from the London end. The title of the books was *Poems on Subjects Chiefly Devotional* in two volumes by Theodosia. It is probable that the first volume was taken to London by Joseph Wakeford in 1757 and the second volume in 1758. It is probable when Anne stayed at *Broughton House* from October 1757 to May 1758 that she was writing out the verses of volume II. Unbound copies of the

143 *Dictionary of National Biography*.
144 ibid.
145 STE 3/8/vi.

two volumes did not reach Broughton until 19th October 1759, with the bound volumes coming on 20th November. The title page tells us that the books were printed in London for J. Buckland, at the Buck, in Paternoster-Row; and J. Ward, at the King's Arms in Cornhill. They were dated MDCCLX.

Here then lies the history behind the production of Anne's hymns and poems.

The Influence of Isaac Watts

In the writing of her hymns, Anne Steele was shaped in the school of Watts. He was a pioneer in hymn singing, writing hymns that were paraphrases of Old and New Testament subjects, hymns on divine subjects but not based on any particular Scripture, and hymns for the Lord's Supper [1707]. It would seem as Joseph Stennett's hymns [1697] were only for the Lord's Supper and in 1712 only for the ordinance of Baptism, that hymns among the Baptists were first used in these two services. Benjamin Keach, pastor of Horsleydown, Southwark, introduced hymns for the Lord's Supper in 1673 and then for general worship in 1691.[146] Watts, while producing hymns for the Lord's Supper had gone the next step and introduced hymns for general worship, while at the same time retaining the Psalms, which he paraphrased twelve years after publishing his hymns. From the foundation of the Porton/Broughton Church in the mid-seventeeth century, only the Psalms, collected in English metre by Thomas Sternhold and John Hopkins, attached to the Geneva and Authorised Bibles, would have been available for singing by the congregation. Watts had been brought up in the seventeenth century to sing these Psalms, and being a natural poet had realised their limitations. The language of the seventeenth century [witness the writings of men like John Owen] was not the most easy to understand. The twenty-third Psalm

Figure 26: Isaac Watts

[146] *The Excellent Benjamin Keach.* A. Walker, 2004, p.289.

from the Sternhold and Hopkins' collection, though beautiful in its own right, reveals some of the limitations:

'The Lord is only my support,
And he that doth me feed;
How can I then lack anything
Whereof I stand in need.

He doth me fold in cote most safe,
And tender grass fast by,
And after leads me to the streams,
Which run most pleasantly

And when I feel myself near lost,
Then doth he me home take;
Conducting me in his right paths,
Even for his own name's sake.

And though I were even at death's door,
Yet would I fear none ill;
For by thy rod and sheep herd's crook,
I am comforted still.

Thou hast my table richly decked
In despite of my foes;
Thou hast my head with balm refreshed
My cup doth overflow.

And finally while breath doth last,
Thy grace shall me defend;
And in the house of God will I,
My life for ever spend.'

Watts set out to improve on this poetry of the seventeenth-century Psalms. One of his three versions of the twenty-third Psalm reads,

'My Shepherd will supply my need,
Jehovah is his name;
In pastures fresh he makes me feed
Beside the living stream.

He brings my wandering spirit back,
When I forsake his ways;
And leads me, for his mercy's sake,
In paths of truth and grace.

When I walk through the shades of death,
 Thy presence is my stay,
A word of thy supporting breath
 Drives all my fears away.

Thy hand, in sight of all my foes,
 Doth still my table spread,
My cup with blessings overflows,
 Thine oil anoints my head.

The sure provisions of my God,
 Attend me all my days;
O may thy house be my abode,
 And all my work be praise!"

There would I find a settled rest,
 While others go and come;
No more a stranger or a guest,
 But like a child at home.'

He used his abilities as a poet to bring the standard to a completely different level. He had been educated at a Nonconformist Academy in London, where his subjects would have included, Greek, Latin, history, modern languages, natural science and philosophy. He was thirty-three when he published his hymns, forty-four when he published his Psalms and fifty-four when the Universities of Edinburgh and Glasgow awarded him his doctorate. As an able, scholarly, mature man, a born poet, he can claim the credit for introducing hymns in the eighteenth century into the worship of all denominations and putting the Psalms into more simple and polished verse. As the congregations were often ignorant and illiterate he limited his hymns and Psalms to only a few well-known metres.

In his hymns he was concerned with God and the soul of man, while, as he thought on eternity, his mind constantly turned to the vastness of the universe. This is clearly seen in his hymn beginning 'Great God! how infinite art thou,' which has the verses,

'Thy throne eternal ages stood,
Ere seas or stars were made;
Thou art the ever-living God,
Were all the nations dead.

Nature and time quite naked lie
To thy immense survey,
From the formation of the sky,
To the great burning day.'

In his hymn 'When I survey the wondrous cross,' the last stanza is,

> 'Were the whole realm of nature mine,
> That were a present far too small,
> Love so amazing, so divine,
> Demands my soul, my life, my all.'

Watts surveys 'the whole realm of nature' and views its Creator, the Word made flesh, by whom all things were created both in heaven and in earth.

He wrote in another hymn,

> 'Ere the blue heavens were stretched abroad,
> From everlasting was the Word;
> With God he was; the Word was God,
> And must divinely be adored.'

In some of his verses he reaches great heights of grandeur, such as,

> 'God of the seas! Thy thundering voice
> Makes all the roaring waves rejoice,
> And one soft word of thy command,
> Can sink them silent in the sand.'

In others he touches the essence of simplicity and sweetness in his hymn which begins, 'How sad our state by nature is,' and has as its last verse, [which incidentally William Carey asked to be put on his grave in Serampore, India],

> 'A guilty, weak, and helpless worm,
> On thy kind arms I fall,
> Be thou my strength and righteousness,
> My Jesus and my all.'

As a product of the seventeenth century there is a dominance in his verse of the same Anglo-Saxon language that Bunyan used. He was very gifted at the use of repetition, especially the pairing of lines two and three as appears in his hymn 'When I survey the wondrous cross:'

> 'See! from his head, his hands, his feet,
> Sorrow and love flow mingled down;
> Did e'er such love and sorrow meet,
> Or thorns compose so rich a crown?'

He is also gifted in the accumulation of words as appears in line one of the above verse. In his hymn 'There is a land of pure delight,' he shows both his love of nature and his ability to make use of proper names. He writes as he looked across Southampton Water to the New Forest;

'Sweet fields beyond the swelling flood,
Stand dressed in living green;
So to the Jews old Canaan stood,
While Jordan rolled between.'

Watts took an interest in current events and past history, writing verse on the Gunpowder Plot, the Glorious Revolution and the accession of King George I. But his hymns contain no local references and like John Bunyan, nothing denominational. Bunyan's *Pilgrim's Progress* makes no reference to baptism, a subject which has divided Christians for centuries. Watts wrote on hope, fear, doubt, the frailty and transience of human life, when seen in the light of eternity, yet without any sentimentality for the hope of the Christian was centred in the birth, life and death of Christ and in His present intercession at the right hand of His Father. In the hymn beginning, 'Dearest of all the names above,' the last stanza reads;

'While Jews on their own law rely,
And Greeks of wisdom boast,
I love the incarnate mystery
And there I place my trust.'

He was reared in the reformed tradition and this appears in such hymns as 'Keep silence all created things,' where he writes;

'Life, death, and hell, and worlds unknown,
Hang on his firm decree;
He sits on no precarious throne,
Nor borrows leave TO BE.

Here he exalts neglected worms
To sceptres and a crown,
And there the following page he turns,
And treads the monarch down.'

Here was the pattern which Anne Steele had as she grew up and began to write her hymns. Her poems at the time of his death in 1748 show how much she valued his example and longed that she could write like him, 'O could I write like Watts,' she wrote, and,

'Expressive silence must declare,
At once my grief and my despair,
To form a Watts's praise.'

Anne Steele's Hymns

In composing her hymns and psalms, Anne followed Isaac Watts closely. She wrote fifty paraphrases of Old and New Testament Scriptures. Twenty-five were taken from the Old Testament [which included ten from the Psalms] and a similar number from the New Testament. She wrote a series of just under one hundred hymns on divine

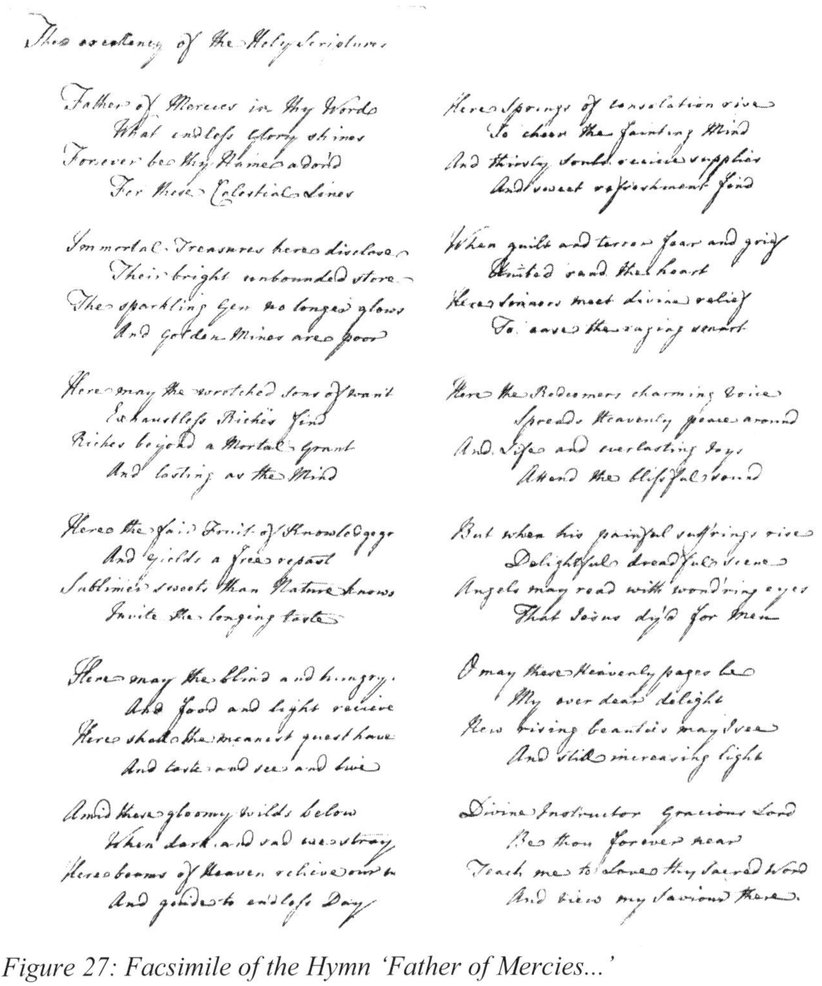

The excellency of the Holy Scriptures

Father of Mercies in thy Word
What endless Glory shines
Forever be thy Name ador'd
For these Celestial Lines

Immortal Treasures here disclose
Their bright unbounded store
The sparkling Gem no longer glows
And golden Mines are poor

Here may the wretched Sons of want
Exhaustless Riches find
Riches beyond a Mortal grant
And lasting as the Mind

Here the fair Fruit of Knowledge grows
And yields a free repast
Sublimer sweets than Nature knows
Invite the longing taste

Here may the blind and hungry
And food and light receive
Here shall the meanest guest have
And taste and see and live

Amid these gloomy wilds below
When dark and sad we stray
Here beams of Heaven relieve our
And guide to endless Day

Here Springs of consolation rise
To cheer the fainting Mind
And thirsty Souls receive supplies
And sweet refreshment find

When guilt and terror fear and grief
United rend the heart
Here sinners meet divine relief
To ease the raging smart

Here the Redeemers charming Voice
Spreads Heavenly peace around
And Life and everlasting Joys
Attend the blissful sound

But when his painful sufferings rise
Delightful dreadful Scene
Angels may read with wond'ring eyes
That Jesus dy'd for Men

O may these Heavenly pages be
My ever dear delight
New rising beauties may I see
And still increasing light

Divine Instructor Gracious Lord
Be thou forever near
Teach me to love thy sacred Word
And view my Saviour there.

Figure 27: Facsimile of the Hymn 'Father of Mercies...'

subjects, but without immediate reference to Scripture. She produced four hymns especially for the Lord's Supper and paraphrases of just under fifty Psalms. Her standard of English followed Watts. Her poetry, though not brilliant, was consistent. She clearly spent time on writing drafts and improving her verse, sending copies for comment to such people as James

Fanch the classical scholar, Baptist minister and poet. One could describe her work as polished and carefully worked out. Her primary object was spiritual and her instrument was poetry. When Fanch and Turner looked at her verses they would have been looking first at the Scripture truths and secondly at the poetry. Like Watts she was orthodox, having been brought up in the Reformed, Calvinistic tradition.

But her ability and her performance was very different from that of Watts. They both had afflicted bodies, both never married. But Watts was a highly educated, able, scholarly man, whereas Anne by comparison had had much less education. Yet Anne's mother came from an educated family as her father's grave in Edington Priory showed, with its inscription in Latin. Also Anne's father composed hymns which were sung in the Broughton Church. Whereas Watts, considering God and the human soul, thought in terms of the vastness of eternity and of the universe writing such lines as,

'Long ere the lofty skies were spread,
  Jehovah filled his throne,
Or Adam formed, or angels made,
  The Maker lived alone.'

and Anne followed him with similar lines as,

'Great Ruler of the earth and skies
A word of thy almighty breath
Can sink the world, or bid it rise,
Thy smile is life, thy frown is death.'[147]

yet they were but a dim reflection of his verse. Watts had a far greater realisation of the majesty and glory of God as he wrote,

'Great God! how infinite art thou,
What worthless worms are we!'

When however it came to matters of the soul, then Anne equalled him. Her ill-health over many years had been sanctified to her and out of it she had learnt that faith in the Son of God was the only source of help, happiness and hope. She did not wallow in self-pity but sought in her hymns to outline the vanity and transience of this life in comparison with the life hereafter. Her hymns carry a vein of experience [sometimes wrongly called introspection], often beginning with a confession such as,

'What death-like lethargy detains
My captive powers with fatal art,

[147] Hymn 18 v. 1.

And spreads its unrelenting chains
Heavy and cold around my heart!'

but then turning to prayer and a desire for the reality of the Saviour's presence to be known ,

'O let thy love shine forth and raise
My captive powers from sin and death;
And fill my heart and life with praise,
And tune my last expiring breath.'[148]

In this context she knew from experience that faith was the gift of God, something to be pleaded for at the mercy seat of Christ and to be obtained in answer to prayer, when a fallen creature could say, 'I know that my Redeemer lives.' Watts walked in an identical path as he wrote,

'O God of mercy, hear my call,
My load of guilt remove;
Break down the separating wall,
That bars me from thy love.'

Anne knew the reality of the 'trial of faith'. Her hymns are pervaded from beginning to end with a desire for assurance. Prayer was for her the breath of her life. To walk in the light of God's countenance was her one desire. Her whole life manifested the language of the Apostle Paul, 'Not as though I had already attained, either were already perfect; but I follow after, if I may apprehend that for which also I am apprehended of Christ Jesus.' As we shall see later, her dying utterance was 'I know that my Redeemer liveth.' But in the interval until she came to that sweet assurance on her death-bed she wrote,

'My God, my Father, blissful name,
O may I call thee mine;
May I with sweet assurance claim
A portion so divine?'[149]

This expression 'call Thee mine' comes out in at least ten of her hymns and is beautifully seen in hymn 134,

'And can my heart aspire so high,
To say, my Father God !
Lord, at thy feet I fain would lie,
And learn to kiss the rod.'

to be followed by the verse,

---

[148] Hymn 66 v.7.
[149] Hymn 62 v.1.

'My Father – O permit my heart,
To plead her humble claim,
And ask the bliss those words impart,
In my Redeemer's name.'

This leads on to another aspect of her hymns, namely the desire for total submission to the Lord's will in her life. She had been brought to realise the blessing of taking up her cross and following her Saviour, and 'having fellowship with Him in His sufferings.' [Philippians 3. 10.] Reminiscent of Watts' lovely hymn, 'When I survey the wondrous Cross,' she wrote,

'When I survey life's varied scene,
Amidst the darkest hours,
Sweet rays of comfort shine between,
And thorns are mixed with flowers.

Lord, teach me to adore thy hand,
From whence my comforts flow,
And let me in this desert land
A glimpse of Canaan know.'[150]

Like the prophet Jeremiah her lot was to know much sorrow, yet as with him, the rays of light and comfort which shone in her path came from heaven in answer to prayer. Here in her poetry we see her making use of proper names in Scripture. Watts was very gifted in this respect, but Anne, while she made use of them sometimes, was not so gifted.

One aspect of her poetry, in which she closely followed Watts, was in the use of repetition, sometimes within a line such as

'*Increase* my faith, *increase* my hope,'[151]

sometimes within a verse,

'*Why sinks* my weak desponding mind?
Why heaves my heart the anxious sigh?'[152]

sometimes between verses,

'My God! O could I make the claim,
My father and my friend,
And call thee mine, *by every name*,
On which thy saints depend!

By every name of power and love,
I would thy grace entreat;

[150] Hymn 74 v.2.
[151] Hymn 39 v.4.
[152] Hymn 42 v.1.

Nor should my humble hopes remove,
  Nor leave thy sacred feet."[153]

Another aspect of Watts' art is the accumulation of words. Anne wrote,

'Jesus in thy dear name I trust,
My light, my life, my Saviour God;
When this frail house dissolves in dust,
O raise me to thy bright abode.'[154]

'*My hope, my trust, my life, my Lord*,
  Assure me of thy love:
O speak the kind transporting word,
  And bid my fears remove.'[155]

'A kingdom of immense delight,
Where health, and peace, and joy unite;
Where undeclining pleasures rise,
And every wish hath full supplies.'[156]

The art of the hymnwriter is to use such poetic devices in such a way that the congregation is entirely unaware of them, and in this Anne Steele succeeded, as did Watts. Yet such devices are very powerful in reiterating truth and act as repetition does in the teaching of children. They drive the truth home with force, gentle and yet powerful.

Anne had a great love for nature as much of her more secular poetry shows. But only on a few occasions does she bring it into her hymns. She wrote;

'The fruitful tree, the blooming flower,
  In varied charms appear;
Their varied charms display thy power,
  Thy goodness all declare.'[157]

'He holds all nature in his hand,
That gracious hand by which I live;
Does life, and time, and death command,
And has immortal joys to give.'[158]

---

[153] Hymn 75 v.3.
[154] Hymn 56 v.6.
[155] Hymn 41 v.4.
[156] Hymn 140 v.4.
[157] Hymn 3 v.6.
[158] Hymn 42 v.2.

She lived in a most beautiful village, with a combination of eighteenth-century houses and thatch cottages, surrounded by the Hampshire Downs, her room looking out to the River Wallop, a trout stream that flowed on its way to the River Test, and hence through the chalk downs to Southampton Water. Her brother had a lovely garden and terrace at *Broughton House*, which was her delight, especially in the summer months. Her father, besides being a timber merchant, also farmed and owned several hundred acres of meadow and downland, with cattle, sheep and corn. Yet surrounding her were all the signs of the transience of life, as the mortality rate among babies and children was very high, epidemics of smallpox and tuberculosis broke out and her own health was constantly in a precarious state. While she appreciated the hand of God in creation, much more she appreciated His hand in salvation, and this occupied her thoughts far more than her surroundings.

While she never speaks of any particular blessing in her own soul, or any sermon that had been made powerful in her heart, or of any revelation of Christ to her own heart, yet her hymns reveal that since her conversion, when she had joined the church at Broughton at the age of fourteen, she had 'grown in grace and in the knowledge of Christ Jesus her Lord'. It would appear that in the sanctification of her life of suffering and weakness, she had often been led to meditate on the suffering sorrows of her Redeemer. In no way does this imply that she was of a melancholy disposition; far from it. Dr Caleb Evans, writing in the preface to the 1780 edition of her hymns, published two years after her death [and he knew her personally] says, 'With an exquisite sensibility, she possessed a native cheerfulness of disposition, which not even the uncommon and agonizing pains she endured in the latter part of her life could deprive her of.... Her life was a life of unaffected humility, warm benevolence, sincere friendship and genuine devotion.'

Her best hymns, therefore are those which testify of her love for Christ. She knew something of true fellowship with Him, ['Truly our fellowship is with the Father and with His Son Jesus Christ.' 1 John 1. 3], and it is many of these hymns that endeared her to her contemporaries and to future generations. There is a sacred grandeur in such hymns as;

> 'Stretched on the cross the Saviour dies;
> Hark ! his expiring groans arise !
> See, from his hands, his feet, his side,
> Runs down the sacred crimson tide.'[159]

which equals anything that Watts wrote. Or

[159] Hymn 102 v.1.

'See, crowned with thorns that sacred head,
With beams of glory once adorned!
That voice, which heaven and earth obeyed,
Is now by traitors mocked and scorned.'[160]

Or,

'He took the dying traitor's place,
  And suffered in his stead;
For man, [O miracle of grace!]
  For man the Saviour bled.'[161]

Or again,

'Was it for sin, for mortal guilt,
The Saviour gave his vital blood?
For sin amazing anguish felt,
The wrath of an offended God?'[162]

It is clear that on such themes as this, very dear and sacred to her heart, she is at her very best, while the truth of the Gospel is foremost and the poetry beautifully suited to present it.

Besides a deep knowledge of Christ Anne had that deep knowledge of sin, which must precede it. This is made clear in many of her hymns. On several occasions in her verse she uses the expression 'vile, ungrateful heart.'[163] In a hymn based on Jeremiah 8. 22, 'Is there no balm in Gilead? is there no physician there?' she writes,

'Deep are the wounds which sin has made,
Where shall the sinner find a cure?
In vain, alas, is nature's aid,
The work exceeds all nature's power.

Sin like a raging fever, reigns
With fatal strength in every part;
The dire contagion fills the veins,
And spreads its poison to the heart.'[164]

In another hymn based on John 14. 19, she wrote,

'When sins and fears prevailing rise,
And fainting hope almost expires;

---

[160] Hymn 103 v.2.
[161] Hymn 99 v.3.
[162] Hymn 104 v.1.
[163] Hymns 65, 81, 125.
[164] Hymn 28 v.2.

Jesus, to thee I lift my eyes,
To thee I breathe my soul's desires.'[165]

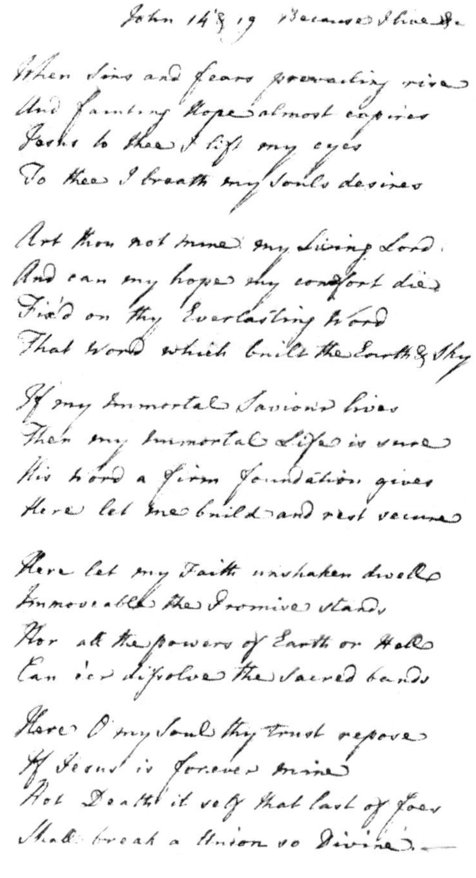
John 14 & 19 Because I live &c

When sins and fears prevailing rise
And fainting Hope almost expires
Jesus to thee I lift my eyes
To thee I breath my Souls desires

Art thou not mine my Living Lord
And can my hope thy comfort die
Fix'd on thy Everlasting Word
That Word which built the Earth & Sky

If my Immortal Saviour lives
Then my Immortal Life is sure
His Word a firm foundation gives
Here let me build and rest secure

Here let my Faith unshaken dwell
Immoveable the Promise stands
Nor all the powers of Earth or Hell
Can e'er dissolve the sacred bands

Here O my Soul thy trust repose
If Jesus is forever mine
Not Death it self that last of foes
Shall break a Union so Divine

Figure 28: Facsimile of the Hymn 'When sins and fears...'

In another hymn based on Matthew 11. 28, 'Come unto me, all ye that labour and are heavy laden,' she wrote,

'Come, weary souls, with sin distrest,
The Saviour says, I'll give thee rest;
The kind, the gracious call obey,
And cast your gloomy fears away.

Oppressed with guilt, a painful load,
O come, and spread your woes abroad;

[165] Hymn 76 v.1.

Divine compassion, mighty love,
Will all the painful load remove.'[166]

Anne has some beautiful things to say about time and its use. She writes,

'Eternity is just at hand;
And shall I waste my ebbing sand,
And careless view departing day,
And throw my inch of time away?'[167]

In another hymn she writes,

'Think, O my soul, how much depends,
On the short period of a day;
Shall time, which heaven in mercy lends,
Be negligently thrown away?'[168]

And again,

'Yes, dearest Lord, my heart is thine,
Sacred to thee be all its powers !
O bid me give to love divine
The little remnant of my hours.'[169]

Though Anne never speaks directly of her spiritual experience, yet her hymns reveal some things about it. Many couplets of her verse show the inner experience of her heart. She writes [hymn 7],

'Twas thy dear hand redeemed the slave,
And set the prisoner free.'[170]

Then she says,

'When blessed with some transporting view,
That Jesus died for me.'[171]

and,

'Sure the blest Comforter is nigh,
'Tis he sustains my fainting heart.'[172]

'When some kind promise glads my soul,
Do I not find his healing voice?'

---

[166] Hymn 12 v. 1,2.
[167] Hymn 68.
[168] Hymn 84 v.5.
[169] Hymn 126 v.2.
[170] Hymn 7 v.6.
[171] Hymn 22 v.11.
[172] Hymn 27 v.3,4.

and,

> 'Oft in the temples of his grace
> His saints behold his smiling face,
> And oft have seen his glory shine,
> With power and majesty divine.'[173]

and in her well-known hymn, 'My God, my Father, blissful name! O may I call Thee mine?' [Hymn 62], she writes,

> 'Whate'er thy providence denies,
> I calmly would resign.
>
> Whate'er thy sacred will ordains,
> O give me strength to bear;
>
> If pain and sickness rend this frame,
> And life almost depart.'

In hymn 81 she writes,

> 'My thoughts recall thy favours past,
> In many a dark, distressing hour.'

When added together these verses tell us that Anne knew what spiritual deliverance was, what it was to have a sacred view of Christ, something of the divine office of the Holy Spirit as the Comforter, the application in her soul of the 'exceeding great and precious promises', the power of the preached word in the ministry of the Gospel reaching into her heart, what resignation was to the Lord's will in giving and withholding such as Job knew, rest to her heart in pain and sickness and finally a sight of divine favours past and an ability to look back over 'all the way the Lord her God had led her'. While no written record survives of her spiritual experience, yet in her open frank way she reveals much of it indirectly in her hymns, which gives to them a peculiar relevance to succeeding generations of Christians who walk in the same spiritual paths as she did.

Like Isaac Watts Anne wrote hymns on matters of national importance. She wrote four hymns for singing on fast days and days of national prayer called by George II in connection with the Seven Years' War [1756-1763], and two hymns of thanksgiving for the peace that followed that war. Other than these she penned a hymn [like Isaac Watts] concerning

---

[173] Hymn 59 v.3.

John 14. – 16&17.

The Influences of the Spirit of God in

Dear Lord, and shall thy Spirit rest
In such a wretched heart as mine?
Unworthy dwelling! Glorious Guest!
Surprizing favour! Grace Divine!

When sin prevails, and gloomy fear,
And hope almost expires in night;
Lord, can thy Spirit then be here?
Great Spring of Comfort, Life and Light.

Sure the blest Comforter is nigh:
'Tis he sustains my fainting heart;
Else would my hopes forever die,
And every cheerfull ing ray depart.

When some kind promise cheers my soul
Do I not find his healing voice
The tempest of my fears controul,
And bid my drooping powers rejoice?

When e'er to call the Saviour mine,
With ardent wish my heart aspires;
Can it be less than power divine,
Which animates these strong desires?

What less than thy Almighty Word
Can raise my heart from Earth and dust?
And bid me cleave to thee, my Lord,
My Life, my Treasure, and my Trust?

And when my cheerful hope can say,
I love my God, and taste his Grace;
Lord, is it not thy blissful ray,
Which brings this dawn of sacred peace.

Let thy kind Spirit in my heart,
Forever dwell, O God of Love;
And Light, and Heavenly peace impart,
Sweet earnest of the Joys Above.

Figure 29: Facsimile of the Hymn 'Dear Lord, and shall...'

the great deliverance from the Gunpowder Plot, remembered every year on 5th November, and a hymn for the coronation of George III in 1760.

Anne had an educated mind, humbled by grace. Hers was not a natural religion, but a religion of the heart. Her hymns reflected things which she had 'heard, seen with her eyes, looked upon, and her hands had handled of the Word of life'. [1 John 1. 1] These were the doctrine of the Trinity, the incarnation, redemption, the sufferings and resurrection of Christ. Simply to state doctrine in her hymns was a source of pleasure to Anne, for she wrote with an authority of an inward experience and could say with Paul, 'The gospel which was preached of me is not after man, for I neither received it of man, neither was I taught it, but by the revelation of Jesus Christ.' [Galatians 1. 11,12] She spoke unaffectedly and with feeling. Her hymns contain truth, experience and worship. They will never grow old while Christians continue to experience the grace of God. They contain a timeless quality, entering into the sufferings, temptations and sorrows of Christians in every generation. She is at her best when writing on the sufferings of Christ. Isaac Watts was a great natural poet and put truth, doctrine and experience into his poetry. Anne Steele had a life of weakness, ill health and suffering and put her prayers, desires, fears, temptations and sorrows into verse. For Watts poetry was engrained in him. For Anne Steele her heart's experience was paramount. No one could excel Watts as a hymnwriter. He influenced a whole century of hymnwriters, one of whom was Anne Steele. No one has excelled Anne Steele in her tender, memorable, sensitive expression of the heart feelings of a tempted, exercised, tried Christian. No one has excelled Watts in his poetic expression of the Psalms, truth and doctrine. Anne would not have been what she was as a hymnwriter without the influence of Isaac Watts.

Figure 30: Facsimile of a Page from Mrs Steele's Diary

Chapter 7

A Father's Need [1760-69]

Mrs Steele's Diary

With the death of Anne's stepmother in 1760, a major source of information on the Steele household dried up. Mrs Steele had kept a diary at Broughton since her marriage to Anne's father in 1723. It was mostly a spiritual record, but constantly she interspersed it with a mass of detailed information regarding the family businesses, the weather, journeys, politics, wars, births and deaths, besides comments on Sunday services at the Broughton Meeting, ministers who preached and the texts from which they preached. The diary ran for thirty-seven years on a regular daily basis. It has provided much of the detailed information of the Steele family in this biography. It comprised six volumes, covering the years 1723-30, 1730-36, 1736-48 (2 vols), 1749-52 and 1753-60. Mrs Steele often went back and read the volumes which speak of all the spiritual blessings under the ministry and in reading her Bible, also profitable, spiritual conversations she had had with many who had visited *Grandfathers*, and she often found this re-reading very encouraging. Before she died she marked volumes one, three and four to be bequeathed to her own daughter Mary Wakeford at Andover. The remaining three volumes [two, five and six] were left to her husband. The Wakeford volumes comprised twenty years and the Steele volumes seventeen years. The sad facts are that the Steele collection has survived, but the Wakeford volumes have disappeared. Direct descendants of both families still survive and it is yet possible that in some family archive the lost volumes still exist. The Steele diaries have been deposited in recent years in the Angus Library at Regent's Park College, Oxford, and microfilm copies are available in the Bodleian Library at Oxford and the Wiltshire and Swindon Record Office at Trowbridge. If the complete set could ever be found and published, they would make a unique document on eighteenth century village life and the history of the Particular Baptists in the West Country in the period. There can be few eighteenth-century diaries to equal them in content, duration and spirituality.

Post 1760

Old William Steele survived his wife by nine years and during this time Anne, with the help of servants, took charge of the home at *Grandfathers*. As she wrote in her poem to Amira [Mary Wakeford] on the death of her mother, Anne's work in these nine years was 'to soothe a parent's care in life's decline, his every grief to share'. The records that survive, to give us a picture of these nine years, are a series of Anne's letters, some of her poetry written in the period, dates of births and deaths, dates of baptisings and other church business in the Broughton Church Book. Also, Mary Wakeford kept a diary like her mother from which, though it is now lost, extracts were copied and the copies have survived.

In 1760, the same year as her mother died, Mary Wakeford gave birth to a little daughter Mary a sister for Samuel aged eight and William aged seven. A letter of 1761 survives of Anne addressed to these two boys, who were at a boarding school, probably at Warminster, Wilts, for it was there, five years later that Samuel died suddenly at the age of thirteen. A letter dated 20th November 1761[174] was written by Polly Steele, Anne's niece, to her mother at Yeovil. Polly told her mother, 'I go to school to my Aunt and learn to read and spell and write of her, and also to walk upright. My Pappa was so kind as to buy me a fine blue satin hat and cardinal [a short hooded cloak] at London, and a medal of the King and Queen... I long greatly to see my Mamma and hope you will come home in a little while and my Uncle with you.' This letter shows that Polly [aged eight] was being educated by Anne and that the girl's mother was staying at her home in Yeovil with her brother. Further letters[175] from Anne to her brother in the first three months of 1762 show that Mary Steele was ill at Yeovil and her husband was staying there with her. Anne tells William that his father is well and 'will do what he can in the care of your affairs'. Gradually it became clear that Mary Steele, who was forty-nine, was in fact dangerously ill and Mary Wakeford's diary records that she died suddenly at Yeovil [her family home] on 13th May 1762 and was buried there. Anne wrote a poem to her brother [Philander] regarding his wife [Delia],[176]

> 'While in the arms of death your Delia sleeps
> And o'er her ashes fond remembrance weeps;
> In tender grief let friendship claim a share,
> Friendship, that fain would ease Philander's care....

---

[174] STE 5/10.

[175] STE 3/8/vii, viii, ix, x.

[176] *Anne Steele's Hymns*. 1780, Vol. 3, pp.32-33.

See my Philander o'er your Delia's tomb,
Hope smiles and dissipates the gloom......

There lives your once-loved Delia's nobler part,
Can you regret that from the scenes of woe,
The long affliction she sustained below,
Heaven called her spirit from its dark abode
To the bright mansions of her Saviour God?'

Mary left behind an only child, Polly. Anne stepped in at once to mother the bereaved girl. William did not marry again until 1768 and during these six years Anne became Polly's second mother. Anne lost in Mary Steele's death a great companion. Mary was about four years older than Anne. As Anne taught Polly from the age of eight to fourteen, Polly learnt the art of writing poetry, and though she was not as gifted as her aunt, yet she penned some beautiful verses. After Anne's death in 1778, Polly wrote of these years from 1762 to 1768,

'Aunt and friend in one, whose anxious care
Watched o'er my helpless childhood...

Ah where is now that friend, to whom my heart
In every past distress was wont to fly,
While the dear sufferer, her own pains forgot,
Would gently sooth my passions into peace?
Where that maternal friend, whose watchful care,
Whose fond, assiduous tenderness sustained
My helpless childhood? ...

My dearest pleasures, my most loved employments,
She taught me first to relish, first awaked
The wish for knowledge...'[177]

Later Polly published a long poem on 'Danebury Hill,'[178] a beauty spot to the north of Broughton. During the last years of Anne Steele, when she lived at *Broughton House* with her brother and his wife, Polly, a girl in her early twenties, lovingly nursed her aunt. Anne, though far from well, now carried the responsibility of two homes, *Grandfathers* and *Broughton House*, both her father and her brother having been widowed.

In January 1763 William went down to Yeovil and took Polly with him, presumably to visit her mother's grave and clear up the family

[177] Miscellaneous Pieces, Vol. III, 1780, pp.xii-xvii.
[178] STE 14/2.

affairs. Anne wrote to him on the 5th[179] from Broughton, showing her care for Polly and her doubts regarding William's ability to look after Polly, 'I hope you will take care that Polly is as little as possible in the kitchen, I fear the cold will hurt her feet.' Anne added a separate part for Polly and wrote to the child,

> 'It is a common compliment at this season of the year to wish a Happy New Year, but my wishes for you reach further that a year, beyond the short revolutions of time which will soon pass away. I wish you, my dear, a happy eternity! The only way to it is by the saving knowledge of Jesus Christ as you read in your Bible, "Whom to know is life eternal." O that your mind might be early impressed by divine grace with a sense of your need of this Almighty Saviour, and that you may be enabled to believe in him and obey him and devote your blooming days [youth] to his service! Does not your mind, my dear, join in this wish while you are reading it? Endeavour then to think often of it, for it is of infinite importance: and do not go to bed one night, or come down one morning without praying to God for his grace. This advice I have given you before, but I fear you do not think of it constantly, and wish that this letter may help you to remember it.
>
> Your truly affectionate Aunt.'

Anne shows here that she had a concern for the child's well-being in more ways than one, following Solomon's advice in Proverbs 22. 6, 'Train up a child in the way he should go: and when he is old he will not depart from it.' There is no doubt that Anne had consistently followed this line with all the young ones in her family, and though she had had no children of her own, yet she desired spiritual children, her wishes being revealed in her letters to them. She also wrote to them in verse.

Verses for Children

A selection of these poems was published in 1788 and in 1806, after her death. Printed at Salisbury by E. Easton, they were entitled, *Verses for Children* by Theodosia. They were not only addressed to Polly, but also to the two girls, Anne and Martha, children of William Steele's second marriage, and to William, Samuel and Mary Wakeford. A typical example of these verses is seen in the following line addressed to the two Wakeford brothers,

> 'Let each little brother be fond of the other,
> Nor quarrel on any pretence;
> When children fall out and argue and pout,
> 'Tis only for want of more sense.

[179] STE 3/8/xi.

How pleasing the sound if the little boys round
Were told by their friends, 'Children, see
There's a pattern for you, behave as they do;
How Billy and Sammy agree!'

But I must not forget, tho' not mentioned yet,
The principal part of my letter;
God only can grant the grace that you want
To make you grow wiser and better.

Then remember each day, that you seriously pray
For His grace to direct and defend;
So shall each little boy to his parents give joy,
And to their affectionate friend.'

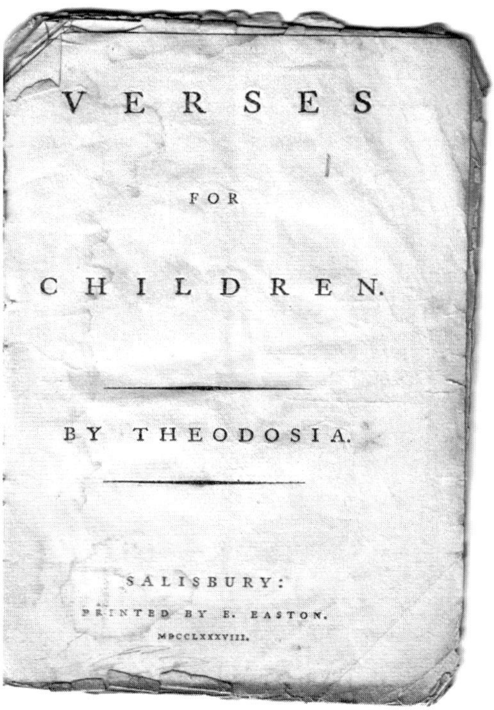

Figure 31: Title Page of 'Verses for Children'

Another poem is written in the form of a letter from William Wakeford to his father at Andover when he was on holiday at *Grandfathers* staying with his Aunt Anne. He says,

> 'I humbly write in borrowed rhyme,
> To tell you how I spend my time…'

He speaks of doing reading, writing and arithmetic with his aunt and then being allowed to go out and enjoy himself,

> 'And oft, the little scene to vary,
> I go with Grandpapa or Sary
> To Pigeon House, or yard, or so,
> For walks are healthful, Sir, you know.'

This poem in his best handwriting and dictated by his aunt went no doubt by post to his father at Andover. Anne was following Isaac Watts, her mentor in verse. In 1715, he had published a similar series of poems for children entitled *Divine Songs for the Use of Children*. [These have been reprinted many times since then, the last being in 1966.] Watts had stayed at the home of Sir Thomas Abney between 1712-15 and his verses were originally written for the Abney children. Writing to a member of his London congregation when he sent a copy of these verses he said, 'I now desire your acceptance of a few Divine Songs for your young children, for whom they are written... and may God, even your God, cause your families to flourish in grace and build the church in the next generation.' The conversion of the young was something that was never forgotten by the Nonconformists.

Caleb Ashworth

Mary Wakeford's diary records a visit to Andover on Tuesday 14th July 1763 of Caleb Ashworth and his wife. Caleb Ashworth had succeeded Dr Doddridge, as Principal of Doddridge's Ministerial Academy at Northampton in 1751, at the time when Doddridge had been stricken down with tuberculosis. He later moved the Academy to Daventry where he remained as its Principal until his death in 1775. He had come to stay with the Wakefords at Andover and possibly preach at the Independent Church, where the Wakefords attended. Then on the following Wednesday they had taken him to Broughton because he wanted to meet Anne on account of 'his high appreciation of her verse'. No record survives of what transpired, but there exists an exchange of letters between Anne and Caleb Ashworth which followed this visit. Caleb Ashworth wrote to Anne,[180] 'I esteem it a peculiar favour of divine providence that I have been brought acquainted with your family,' and goes on to say how he had re-read her poems and they had given him great pleasure. In her reply dated 9th September Anne writes,[181]

---

[180] STE 3/13/x.
[181] STE 2/13/ix.

> 'The pleasure you gave at Broughton amply compensated for all you could receive... I esteem myself highly honoured by your friendship... Continue your prayers for me and mine, especially for spiritual blessing. I desire ever to count a share in the prayers of my friends among my peculiar privileges; but if this is a desirable advantage, how delightful, how animating, the hope of an interest in the prevalent intercession of our Almighty and glorious Advocate on high! I cannot better express the pleasure I find in your approbation of my verses than by saying that I look on it as a confirmation of the hope that my wishes in the publication are in some degree answered.'

She speaks of her health being better than when he met her, but desires resignation to the divine will. She goes on,

> 'I hope I have reason to bless God for the sweet consolations I have sometimes enjoyed in seasons of affliction, that all the dispensations of providence are not only just and wise but good and kind... The thoughts which occasioned those expressions of doubt which you observed, frequently occur, but also frequently lead me to examine the foundation of the evidences of my hope; and think [if I am not deceived] it is generally more confirmed by the trial. I hope I can sometimes experience the happy effects that you mention of renewed application to the precious blood of of Jesus and desires for the sanctifying comforting influences of his Spirit. O may I ever keep in view my own weakness, my utter unworthiness and the perfect righteousness and all sufficiency of grace of the Great Redeemer!'

She concludes by thanking him for the friendly visit of himself and his wife. The letter shows that the conversation that Wednesday at *Grandfathers* was, in fact, true fellowship in the Gospel. It would seem that Caleb Ashworth may have commented on her hymn beginning, 'My God, my Father, blissful name! O may I call thee mine?' But he also had spoken of the sweetness of a renewing of the blood of Christ to the soul in times of doubt. It is clear that they had openly conversed on the deep things of God as known in their own hearts and that they felt a great union of heart one with another. Anne's publication of her hymns and poems was indeed bringing her into contact with a wider group of Christian people. Caleb Ashworth was not the only principal of a Nonconformist Academy that was to become a life-long friend. There was also Caleb Evans of the Bristol Baptist Academy, who republished her hymns and poems in 1780.

Death of Jane Gibbs

In October1763, just after this visit, Jane Gibbs died at Trowbridge at the young age of forty. Jane was sister of Anna Attwater and youngest niece of old Mrs Steele. Anne had known her well, having often stayed at

Figure 32: Gibbs Family Memorial Stone, Englishcombe

Haycombe with her, and had her to stay at Broughton. Known as Jenny in the family, she had married Philip Gibbs at Trowbridge in 1750. Old Mrs Steele in her diary [4th May 1751] records her as having been dangerously ill for three weeks, probably with a miscarriage. Her first child Elizabeth had been born on 25th April 1755, and a boy James in July 1757. She was a member of the Broughton Church, having been baptised by Mr Steele in the first week of July 1751. In her diary Mrs Steele records the Communion Service of Sunday 14th July, when those present included Anne, Molly Wakeford, William and Mary Steele and Anna Attwater and Jenny Gibbs. At the time of her death, possibly in childbirth, she left

Elizabeth aged eight and James aged six. Their father married again in about three years and had another daughter, Sarah, born in 1767. A letter survives,[182] written by Anne in the winter of 1766 to Jenny's niece, Marianne Attwater, some time before Mr Gibbs' second marriage. She describes the season as severe and says that it makes her 'unfit for anything but to hover over the fire'. She sympathises with Marianne's tender concern for the 'dear little orphans'. She adds, 'I fear your uncle's heart is indeed hard not to have discovered any impressions from so near a prospect of eternity, but there is still room for prayer.' She refers to a visit of Marianne to Bratton under the Westbury White Horse Hill, where her sister Caroline was now living as the wife of the farmer, Thomas Whitaker. She says that Polly Steele was longing to see Marianne's sister Jane. They had been born within a month of each other in 1753.

Then in the same letter to Marianne, Anne goes on to say,

> 'I was more than half disappointed in the expected visit of the American ministers, as only Mr Occom came, nor could I go to hear him; however I had a little conversation with him. Is there not, my dear, something very cheering in the prospect that seems to be opening of the blessed Gospel being preached among the poor, unenlightened savages,
>
> "When shall the Gospel's healing ray,
> Kind source of amity divine,
> Spread o'er the world celestial day?
> When shall the nations, Lord, be thine?"
>
> Oh the glorious blessing of the Gospel being imparted to the poor unenlightened savages. Happy period! when the knowledge of the Lord shall cover the earth as the waters cover the sea [Isa. 11. 9].'

Samson Occom

This Mr Occom,[183] who preached in Broughton Chapel, was in fact an American Indian. He had almost certainly come to Broughton through the Steeles' contact with George Whitefield. When in America in 1743 George Whitefield had financially assisted the Rev. Eleazar Wheelock who had started a school for boys at Lebanon [now Columbia] in Connecticut. In that year Wheelock had received as a student a young Mohegan Indian named Samson Occom and the boy had proved so promising that Wheelock proposed to take in further Indians to train them as missionaries to their own people. Very soon he had twenty Indian boys in his school. Whitefield soon realised the potential for such missionaries

[182] STE 3/12/iii.

[183] *George Whitefield*, Arnold Dallimore, 1980, pp.430, 459.

and when in Scotland persuaded the Marquis of Lothian and later the Society for the Propagation of Christian Knowledge to financially support the school. Soon he was taking collections for it at his meetings and encouraging his friends in England, such as Lord Dartmouth, to help. During his last visit to America Whitefield suggested that in order to raise money for the school the young Indian preacher Samson Occom should come to England on a preaching tour. He eventually arrived in England with the Rev. Nathaniel Whitaker, landing at Brixham on 3rd February 1766 and by July he had preached more than three hundred times in a variety of churches and chapels in England and Scotland. He was an excellent speaker and gave vivid descriptions of life among the Indians in America. He himself was a wonderful example of the converting power of sovereign grace. His appeal extended throughout the land even to the royal household. King George III gave two hundred pounds, Lord Dartmouth fifty guineas and many more made generous donations. The immense sum of £12,500 was eventually collected. No doubt among this was a liberal contribution from the Steele family including Anne herself, and also from the Broughton Baptist Church and Broughton villagers. The result was that the money enabled Wheelock to move the school from Lebanon in Connecticut to Hanover in New Hampshire where it greatly prospered. Three years later an institution of higher learning was added to it which was named in honour of its early benefactor, Dartmouth College. It was under the ministry of Whitefield and others that Occom had been converted and it was through his influence and suggestions that eventually Dartmouth College had been brought into being. It is fascinating to see that Anne had actually sat down and talked with Samson, who must have been about thirty-five at the time; also to see how Anne's heart had been moved by the visit to express such desires from little Broughton for world-wide evangelisation. The Steele family were truly in contact with the eighteenth-century Evangelical Awakening. These associations of the Broughton pastor with George Whitefield, having a Methodist minister to preach in his chapel and having Samson Occom, which no doubt filled his chapel with all the villagers, including the Anglicans, even possibly the local vicar, gives an entirely new light on the generally perceived attitude of Particular Baptists to the Great Awakening.

1767

In January 1767 Mary Wakeford remarks in her diary, 'I had a little agreeable chat with my sister about Polly Steele's dawning genius which is remarkable, and her hopefully serious turn.'[184] The girl was now fourteen and since the death of her mother five years before she had spent

[184] Diary now lost. Extract copied by S. A. Bompas.

most of her time in Anne's company, being educated privately by her and much prayed over. In later years she was to become a minister's wife. On 10th April Anne wrote to Caroline Whitaker, addressing the letter to her old home at Bodenham, after she heard that Caroline was coming from Bratton to Bodenham with her first little boy, Philip, to show him to her relatives. Anne wrote of the 'pleasing expectation of seeing you and your little boy'. Caroline was only just in time with the little boy, for

Figure 33: 'Yew Trees', Bratton

within a few months Thomas Attwater died at the age of seventy-six. But the saddest death of the year was to come, when Sammy Wakeford, aged only thirteen, died suddenly at boarding school at Warminster. An affecting letter survives,[185] written by his father Joseph Wakeford to his father-in-law, William Steele senior, who was now coming up to eighty. It reads,

> 'Hon'd Sir,
>
> This morning a messenger from Mr Fisher informed us that our dear Sammy was very dangerously ill, with a fever, and sore throat. I with the doctor, immediately set out for Warminster. We found him extremely bad without much or indeed any hope of his recovery... However he continued till this morning about two o'clock, when it pleased God to remove him from us, and I would hope through the

[185] STE 10/3.

merit and righteousness of the dear Redeemer, he is a partaker of that great salvation, purchased for his people. From his first seizure he was delirious and continued so to the end, except now and then for a minute or two, he often in his lightness and rambling, talked of going home and once Mrs Fisher [who never left him] said, "My dear I hope you are going home... going to heaven and that is the best home..." "Yes," said the dear boy, "that is the best home," and repeated it several times... with some degree of warmth and satisfaction.

'Tis a very heavy affliction; I hope we endeavour to submit with some degree of resignation to the awful providence... my dear wife is greatly afflicted, yet bears better than I feared. My Hanny is terribly overcome with her grief. Poor Billy's grief is great but inward. I bless God he is pretty well... Oh 'tis a heavy trial! I know not how to support under it... Poor Polly Steele sympathises with the melancholy around her, and feels greatly for her poor cousin Sammy. I feel for Sister [Anne] 'twill affect her sadly, do not let her know it too hastily... We both intreat your prayers that God would be our support and stay in this day of deep distress and trial. May we be enabled to submit.'

This would have been heart-rending news for Polly, and Anne who had often been to Andover to stay at the Wakeford home and frequently had Sammy and Billy staying at *Grandfathers*. It would appear that Polly had been staying at Andover at the time when Sammy died. But Anne in all her sufferings would have had the consolation that she had often pointed these children in their youth toward prayer, toward their Bibles and toward their need of a Saviour, even when so young, and no doubt prayed for their conversion daily. She was a God-fearing, exercised, praying woman, and though having no children of her own, yet she was surrounded with these growing teenagers, who obviously enjoyed her company, loved her and valued her interest and advice, knowing she had their real welfare at heart. Anne was just fifty at the time Sammy died.

William Steele Junior's Second Marriage 1768

The next major event on the Steele family calendar was the second marriage of William Steele junior, early in 1768, to Martha Goddard of Pershore in Worcestershire. A letter[186] dated 25th April 1768 from William to his new wife, signed, 'Your truly affectionate husband', shows they were married, though the exact date and place of the wedding is unknown. The letter reads,

'My Dear,

As I doubt not but the earliest intelligence will be most acceptable, I take the first opportunity to inform you that the good providence of God

[186] STE 4/4/ii.

conducted me home in safety and health Saturday evening, when I had the pleasure to find my friends well.

I communicated our union to my father and sister who cordially joined to felicitate me on the occasion, but my poor dear girl [Polly] on my acquainting her with it, burst into a flood of tears and was forced to retire. She has too much sensibility, but I am satisfied that the tender and affectionate friendship she will find from her new relation will in a little time conciliate her mind to it, and if I am not greatly mistaken, totally win her heart.

I cannot help regretting so long an absence, but I hope it will be the last of long continuance, 'till the lamp of life shall expire and dissolve that union in which we have so lately engaged. And O may that kind providence which has joined our hands; join our hearts in the most endearing ties of love and friendship... My Polly makes no objection to going to Bristol and seems now better satisfied, and I have not the least doubt but we shall be all happy together. I hope Mr Evans and you have a pleasant journey. I suppose you are now, whilst I am writing at 6 o'clock, just arrived at Pershore and entertaining Mr & Mrs Ash with an account of your late expedition to the land of matrimony. Methinks I hear their congratulations on it and wish myself there to partake of it. Pray make my best wishes acceptable to them and theirs and accept my dear of the tender devotion of,

Your truly affectionate Husband,

P.S. I hope to hear from you soon... My Polly has been talking with her Aunt on the subject, seems quite cheerful and talks of a bridecake and favours when you come.'

Any child, who has lost a parent and seen a new mother come into the home, will well understand the feelings of Polly. She was fifteen at the time and had been without a mother for six years. She had been old enough to remember her own mother well. William Steele will have well understood her feelings. He lost his own mother at the age of five and was cared for by his Aunt Mary until his father remarried in 1723, when he was eight. Polly had loved and lost her own mother and the blood tie is very strong. At a later date Polly went with her father to Bristol to a wedding celebration and Mary Wakeford's diary records that they returned to Broughton together with the new wife on 3rd June. They also brought with them Dr and Mrs Ash. Dr Ash preached at Broughton on the following Sunday. Martha Goddard was the daughter of Mark Goddard junior of Bristol, whose father had been a merchant, who had died when Martha was a baby. She had had one brother, Samuel, of Banbury, Oxon., and a sister Elizabeth who married Dr Ash the pastor of Pershore Baptist Church. Dr Ash was a close friend of Caleb Evans and produced a selection of hymns with him in 1769 known as the *Bristol Baptist Collection* of Ash and Evans. At the time of her marriage Martha, having no other home, had been living with her sister at Pershore. She was thirty-four and was a baptised member of the Pershore Church. A document exists among the Broughton Church Records,[187] dated 20th August 1768, granting her an honourable dismissal from the Baptist Church at Pershore to the sister Church at Broughton. It reads,

> 'The Baptised Church of Jesus Christ, Meeting at Pershore, and holding the Particular Doctrines of the Gospel. To the Church at Broughton of the same Faith and Order, send Christian Salutation.
>
> Dear Brethren.
>
> As our sister Martha Steele is, we hope, happily settled among you, and is desirous of being admitted to the fellowship of your Church: This is to inform you that for many years she has been a worthy member of our Society, that her conversation has been suitable to her profession, and that she has endeared herself to many of us. We can therefore do no less than very affectionately recommend her to your communion, wishing both her and you much of the divine presence of our common Master and Lord, in whom we subscribe ourselves,
>
> Your affectionate but unworthy,
>
> Brethren.'

The letter was signed by Dr Ash and five other male members of Pershore Church. This method of transfer from one church to another was a standard practice among the Particular Baptists in the eighteenth century and is still in use among many churches today. It shows that Martha had been a member for many years, possibly having been baptised in her teens. Dr John Ash, her brother-in-law, had been born in Dorset in 1724 and studied for the ministry under Bernard Foskett, pastor of Broadmead Baptist Church, Bristol. He was pastor at Pershore from 1751 to his death in 1779, a life devoted like Benjamin Beddome at Bourton to faithful preaching in a rural community.[188] At the time of his second marriage William was fifty-three and Martha thirty-four. Their first child, a girl named Anne, but called Nancy, was born at *Broughton House* on 24th February 1769. Polly spent some time in May with the Attwater family at Bodenham, a sad home now with the absence of their father.

---

[187] ALRPC Broughton Church Records.

[188] *Dictionary of Hymnology*, J. Julian, p.86.

Death of William Steele Senior

But the chief event of the year 1769 was the death of old Mr William Steele on 10th September. Extracts taken from Mary Wakeford's diary show that he was taken ill on 2nd September and died in just over a week. Extracts from the Journal of Dr William Steadman [a later pastor at Broughton] referring to his Uncle Henry Steele says, 'Henry Steele was succeeded by his nephew Mr William Steele, who in ministerial qualifications was his superior and by no means his inferior in other respects.' This reference to 'ministerial qualifications', and the fact that William Steele started preaching at the age of nineteen, also the reference by his second wife's relative to 'my scholar', lends weight to the possibility that he had trained at the Trowbridge Academy under John Davisson. John Sheppard, writing in the Memoir to the 1863 Edition of Anne Steele's Hymns, Psalms and Poems says,

> 'Mr William Steele, senior, was for many years the faithful and affectionate pastor of an affectionate and harmonious Baptist congregation at Broughton, where the family had long resided and where his memory is still held in the highest veneration. The church over which he presided may be traced back to the times of the Commonwealth. The tolerant spirit of Cromwell brought out of obscurity, and into visible fellowship, in various parts of the country, great numbers who were dissatisfied with the point to which the Sovereigns of England had permitted the Reformation to be carried. William Steele was a man of primitive piety, the strictest integrity, and the most amiable simplicity of manners. The powers of his mind were vigorous, his ministerial abilities great and peculiarly his own; but they were accompanied by the most unaffected humility. He was an uncommon instance of how much may be done by regularity and diligent improvement of time. Without infringing on the duties of his pastoral office [though he wrote his sermons at length, and did not use shorthand], he carried on an extensive business as a timber merchant, like his uncle; and as, by the blessing of providence, he possessed a comfortable independence, his labours in the ministry were all gratuitous. He died 10th Sept. 1769, when only a month less than eighty; after having preached to one congregation sixty years, half that time occasionally as a deacon [supply], the remaining half as their pastor. On the day, a fortnight preceding his death, he preached with his usual propriety and animation.'

This account repeats almost verbatim a manuscript written by Polly Steele in 1791 on the occasion of the death of her stepmother, Martha Steele [née

Goddard].[189] Polly was writing about her own grandfather which gives a strong element of authenticity to John Sheppard's account.

Figure 34: Old Baptist Chapel, Broughton, 1813

Sermons of William Steele Senior

The sermon notes of William Steele, [of which there are several hundred] are now in the Angus Library at Oxford and have yet to be fully transcribed. They range over a period from 1710 to the last decade of his life in the 1760s. They were written out fully in detail and are systematically planned and subdivided. This of itself would suggest that William Steele had received some early training in their preparation. The earliest notes of 1710 are written in a small notebook which contains three sermons on the texts Revelation 2. 4, 1 John 4. 19 and John 14. 3. There is an element of doubt as to whether these three sermons may in fact be those of Henry Steele, but as no other sermon notes of his have survived, and many of William Steele's have, it would suggest these are some of the first sermons of William Steele, preached within the first years of his ministry, he having commenced at the age of nineteen in 1708. He kept the notes filed away and used them over the years in various places. The sermon notes are very extensive and when copied on A4 size paper range

[189] STE 5/9.

from twenty pages to eighty pages. How William Steele used them is not clear. They are written in very small handwriting and it would seem that they could not have been read in the pulpit, especially on winter nights when the only means of illumination would have been candlelight. It is equally clear that they could not have been used on one occasion, as they are far too long. In the margins are dates and places where they were preached, and this would suggest that they were used consecutively. One sermon from Luke 14. 23, 'Go out into the highways and hedges, and compel them to come in,' is marked Broughton, 18th October, 6th November, 13th November, 26th November 1726, showing that William Steele preached from the same text for four consecutive Sundays. The same sermon is also marked Broughton, 22nd October and 5th November 1758. It would seem likely that William Steele read them at home in going over his text in the previous week and that he possibly took the basic headings of his subject into the pulpit with him. In a sermon, marked Broughton and Wallop, 11th April 1762 on the text in Matthew 5. 7, 'Blessed are the merciful, for they shall obtain mercy,' [which runs to twenty-one pages], he opens with the words, 'As I have in several discourses spoken something from the 3rd, 4th, 5th and 6th verses, so I would endeavour to speak something from the 7th verse and endeavour to explain it that we may see something of the wonders of grace contained therein.' Clearly here he was preaching systematically through the Beatitudes, and would probably have gone on to preach on verses 8-11.

The notes reveal that he preached mostly locally, at Broughton, the Wallops, Whitchurch, Romsey, Winterslow, Lockerley and Downton. Mrs Steele's diary also shows him preaching on occasions at Haycombe and Trowbridge. He seems to have frequently attended the annual meetings of the Western Association of Particular Baptist Churches but there is no indication that he ever preached at these meetings. It would seem that Henry Steele, his uncle, was a popular preacher, a gifted speaker, though he appears to have had little education. Henry Steele was a farmer and a timber merchant and almost certainly preached extempore without using notes. It would seem that the power of the Holy Spirit rested on his ministry and accounted for the gathering of the villagers to his church. When William Steele became pastor in 1739, his preaching was different. He systematically opened up his text. One would gather he was well acquainted with the Puritans. He followed their example in exegesis and was faithful in expounding the whole text, never shunning any of its difficulties. His material was solid and weighty. It reveals a profound knowledge of the Scriptures. Like John Bunyan he was versatile in apt quotations of the Scripture. He obviously had a clear mind and a good memory. His preaching was experimental but also practical. He laid great weight in a sincere walking out of the precepts of the Gospel. He was humble and sincere and preached as one that had authority, based on truths that he himself had 'handled of the Word of life'. [1 John 1. 1] He did not give something to his people over which he had not laboured in prayerful study. He had an evangelical zeal for the conversion of souls in the villages around him and it is not surprising that he made a point of hearing and meeting George Whitefield.

Doctrinally, in his preaching he followed the 1689 Confession of Faith. In sermon notes [running to eighty-one pages A4] of a sermon on the text from Revelation 22. 17, 'And the Spirit and the bride say, Come. And let him that heareth say, Come. And let him that is athirst come. And whosoever will, let him come and take of the water of life freely,' he opens up his text with five points, followed by his conclusion. He asks the questions, 'What is intended by the water of life and why is it so called? In what respect and how is it free for every thirsty soul? What is it to thirst and be made willing to partake, for the thirsty are bid to come? Who are the inviters and how do they say, Come? And finally, what is it to come and partake?' In speaking of the water of life and a thirst for it he asks,

> 'Have we thirsted after it and have we been made to truly come unto it? ... if we are come to the enjoyment of it, let us enquire if we have an experimental knowledge and acquaintance with the excellency thereof... which is Christ and all His benefits.'

He goes on,

> 'I told you that like water it is of a refreshing and reviving nature and has it been so to our soul? When we have been sometime ready to faint as it were under the weight and burden of sin, the sense of corruption and hiding of God's face, has then the grace in the promises of the Gospel revived and cheered our drooping soul?'

In speaking in the section regarding what it is to thirst, he says,

> 'In natural thirsting there is a longing, an unsatisfied desire, after water... and so it is respecting this spiritual thirsting... it is a longing desire after salvation which the Gospel reveals and when it is so in truth, O how full is the invitation, how plain is the call to that soul to come unto the water...'

He says,

> 'antecedent to a work of grace upon the heart, there are no desires after the blessings which the Gospel reveals and it is God alone in the implantation of grace who is the author of these desires.'

He says,

> 'The will is made capable by the implantation of grace to choose that which is truly good.'

Again he says,

> 'Unless persons are sensible of the desert of their sins, they will never desire salvation from it... unless persons are sensible of their own nakedness and want of righteousness... they will not desire the righteousness of Christ... unless persons are sensible of the pollution and vileness of their own nature, they will never desire cleansing and purifying grace, but when thoroughly convinced thereof then they will earnestly desire it. David sensible of it, earnestly cried out, "Create in me a clean heart, O God, and renew a right spirit within me." Psalm 51.10... This thirsting desire after it and being truly willing to come unto these waters does suppose and imply a real sight and sense of the worth and excellency thereof... The instrumentality of the word and the use of arguments is not inconsistent with the doctrine of efficacious grace but does well agree therewith for we find that it is God that does create longing in the soul and yet those who have thirsting desires are persuaded both by the Spirit and the Bride to come unto the waters and are given an inward capacity of discerning and choosing.... The real happiness of all those who thirst for and are made willing to come unto the waters and their happiness appears 1] in that it does suppose a real, gracious change of heart, 2] in that they are the very persons that are thus kindly invited.'

In answering the question, How do the inviters say, Come? William Steele says,

> 'The Spirit says, Come, 1] by inspiring the prophets and apostles to reveal the blessing of the Gospel and make known the mind and will of God concerning the great work of redemption and salvation by Jesus Christ. 2] by many express and kind and gracious invitations and encouragements and by the guidance of the Spirit, as for instance such as those in Proverbs 8 4-5, "Unto you O men, I call; and my voice is to the sons of men. O ye simple, understand wisdom, and ye fools, be ye of an understanding heart." 3] by gifting and qualifying and assisting the ministers of the Gospel to open and explain the blessing of the Gospel to poor sinners and persuade them to embrace it... the preaching of the word is the ordinary means for bringing souls savingly to close with Christ. 4] by accompanying the preaching of the word with its powerful operations on the heart to make it effectual to the soul

> hearkening to the invitations of the Gospel so as to embrace it and in this sense it is peculiar to some, though in the former sense the Gospel is to be preached to all, and the Spirit does assist in the doing of it and ministers are to persuade all to embrace it, but there is a peculiar gracious word of the Spirit that does cause them to attend to it. Of Lydia it is noted that the Lord opened her heart that she attended the things that were spoken by Paul and concerning everyone that has been converted we may say, It is the Lord the Spirit that has opened their hearts and caused them effectually to attend unto and embrace the word... The Spirit 1] enlightens the understanding. 2] Efficaciously changes the will. 3] Changes the affections to embrace the good things of the Gospel and causes the soul to delight in them... man can speak only to the ear, but God in this efficacious sense can and does sometimes speak into the hearts of sinners... the Church says, Come, by her ministers whose immediate business is to persuade sinners to come to the waters... as they are sent by the Lord it is their indispensable duty to do their utmost to invite and persuade sinners to embrace the blessing revealed in the Gospel... 1] they endeavour from the word of God, with all that ability that God hath given them to open and unfold the lost and deplorable, miserable state that poor sinners are in... 2] they endeavour to open and explain the way of salvation by the Lord Jesus Christ and hold Him up in the preaching of the Gospel as a suitable almighty and only Saviour... 3] they call them by entreaties, as if they should say, As regards the welfare of your precious and immortal souls, as you would escape a hell of misery and enjoy a heaven of happiness, let me entreat to come as the apostle says, "Now then we are ambassadors for Christ, as though God did beseech you by us; we pray you in Christ's stead be ye reconciled to God." 2 Cor. 5. 20. 4] they will direct them to cry to God for His grace to enable them to come. 5] with all this they will join their own with the Church's earnest prayers and cries to God that their labours to persuade them to come may be blessed to the good of their souls.'

Speaking of how the Bride [the Church] says, 'Come,' William Steele says that she speaks in the ordinances of baptism and the Lord's Supper, in the voice of her converts, by a prudent declaration of her spiritual experience, by the example of her converts, by her self-denying life, and her walk before God, by her spiritual life, by a life of faith, love, peace, joy and satisfaction. Speaking of what is to be understood by the words 'Him that heareth'. he says, it refers 1] to the sound of the preached Gospel 2] to those who hear in a spiritual and saving manner 3] to hear aright is to hear with understanding 4] to hear aright is to hear believingly. He goes on to say that it is 'the indispensable duty and concern of all to embrace the blessing revealed in the Gospel', and that those who live under the Gospel and 'hear the gracious invitations thereof and yet finally reject it, will be left inexcusable'. He speaks about the danger of neglecting the use of the invitations by ministers and then goes on to say,

> 'We should be cautioned against drawing conclusions from hence that man by nature has power to come, for this would run counter to the Scripture account of the state of man which declares his impotency as a fallen creature; and my text speaketh nothing of the power of man, it only reveals the excellency and freeness of the blessing for all that will come or that are willing to come unto the waters and kindly invites them to it and so desires that it is their duty to hearken to it; but speaks not of the power to embrace it... From other parts of the Scripture it is plain that it is from the Lord that any have power to embrace it here. It is said, "To as many as received Him to them gave He the power to become the sons of God." John 1. 12... Christ says, "No man can come unto me except the Father which sent me draw him." John 6. 44. From these and many Scriptures besides it is plain that it is not in man's power but that it is by the grace of God that any can come... From the invitation we must not draw conclusions of power in man to hearken.'

Answering his final point, 'What is it to come and partake?' he says,

> '1] it is a spiritual coming. 2] it is a believing the truth. 3] a coming to the waters by faith. 4] a coming with a real dependence and trust. 5] such a coming supposes an experimental taste of the excellency thereof. It will result in true worship, humility, love to God, a heart filled with joy and praise to God, a changed life, a weaning from the world and earnest, longing and submissive desires... as with the Apostle when he desired "to depart to be with Christ, which is far better." Phil. 1. 23.'

He says,

> 'When the soul is come by faith unto the waters and has some delightful taste thereof in the streams of grace below, he cannot but desire to dwell with Christ at the fountain head of happiness above.'

He concludes by saying that men by nature are destitute of the power to come to these waters, though they are invited. He adds:

> 'Men cannot possibly change their hearts to have desires after these blessings... The sum of all is ascribed to the love of God, where it is said, "God so loved the world that He gave His only begotten Son, that whosoever believeth in Him should not perish, but have everlasting life." John 3. 16. It is from hence that He hath ordained to the enjoyment of it, for this ordination must flow from His own love or the sovereign pleasure of His will, and those he hath chosen and ordained for it, these are the persons that do in time come unto the water. Hence it is said, "As many as were ordained to eternal life believed." Acts 13. 48. and "According as He hath chosen us in Him before the foundation

of the world, that we should be holy and without blame before Him in love." Eph. 1.4.'

His final conclusion regarding coming to the waters is,

> 'It is from the everlasting love of God as the moving cause, from the blood of Christ as the meritorious cause, from the Spirit as the effectual cause, and from the Word as the instrumental cause that any do rightly come unto the waters. Then from here we may infer that a sinner's salvation is all of grace and the God of grace must have all the glory and man who deserves nothing of it nor could do nothing for it, must have no part of the praise, and for men to ascribe their salvation to their own doing does as much as in their eyes rob God of His glory.'

He concludes with such questions as, Do we believe the report? Have we by faith embraced the Gospel? Do we place all our hope in the Gospel? Have we had an experimental taste of the sweetness of the Gospel?

Figure 35: Ben Street and Cottage

We have included this sermon in some detail because it gives an accurate indication of the type and content of the ministry at Broughton in the first seventy years of the eighteenth century. It combined solid exposition in depth of the text, an experimental character which revealed William Steele's own personal knowledge of salvation, with a great emphasis on the precepts of the Gospel. The ministry was experimental and practical. William Steele's godly life was as much a voice in Broughton as his preaching, and this he emphasised to his congregation, that they should let their light shine before men. In his time as pastor he was favoured with many who came forward for baptism as a result of his ministry. Not only did he have the oversight as pastor of Broughton Particular Baptist Church and the Ben Street Meeting in Nether Wallop, but he also had the oversight at Downton where he went frequently to administer the Lord's Supper. Prior to 1734 Particular Baptists in Downton had joined in membership at Broughton under Henry Steele, Broughton being their nearest Particular Baptist Church. But in 1738 Jacob Taunton came to preach at Downton, though he was never ordained pastor. He stayed there for eleven years until sadly he was killed in 1749 by a fall from his horse when returning from preaching at Chalke. In these years and afterwards William Steele watched over the Downton Church. William Steele's sermon notes often have in the margin a reference to their being preached at Downton.[190] William Steele also took an interest in the Particular Baptist Church which was founded at Lockerley by James Fanch, which was in fact a daughter Church of the Romsey Church. While William Steele pastored Broughton from 1739-69 James Fanch pastored Romsey, Daniel Turner Abingdon, Benjamin Beddome Bourton-on-the-Water, Dr Ash Pershore and Caleb Evans Bristol, all men who were his friends.

When William Steele eventually passed away on 10th September 1769, his end was sudden. Two weeks previously he had preached at Broughton as usual. He was ill for about eight days which would suggest that either he suffered a heart attack or a stroke. He had been a strong man, travelling constantly in preaching and business many hundreds of miles on horseback, even after his serious accident, which resulted in one leg being left much shorter than the other. His business journeys alone took him to Bath, Bristol, Portsmouth, Yeovil, Taunton, Devizes and Trowbridge and that on many more than one occasion, often returning in snow and darkness. His wife's diary catalogues these journeys. One imagines that to a degree he was handicapped by his accident all his life, probably having one boot made up and walking with a limp. In his will, dated 27th August 1767 and proved at the London Prerogative Court of Canterbury 23 October 1769, he described himself as a timber merchant, though in the family business much of the profit from the sale of timber had been invested in farms and property in and around Broughton. Evidence of this appears in his son's will proved in 1786 where there is reference to land purchased by him and his father. It would appear that

[190] Rippon's *Baptist Register1794*, Ordination at Downton.

toward the end of his life William Steele had passed the management of the timber business and the farms over to William junior. By her father's will Anne inherited *Grandfathers* and its grounds, a garden, orchard and close, together with the next door property, for her natural life, and if she had no children of her own, it was to go to her half-sister, Mary Wakeford. He also left her an estate called Pewseys and in addition £1,000. He left her another £400 for her natural life, after which it was to go to her step-sister Mary Wakeford. He also left her all the books and household goods that belonged to her own mother, and the rest of his books and household goods for her lifetime. To Mary his second daughter he left £500, the rights of property on Trowle Common, Trowbridge, which belonged to her grandfather, and £200 in her lifetime. He left property in Broughton to his grandson William Wakeford and £100 to his granddaughter Mary Wakeford. Land in Sedgehill and all the remaining property in Broughton, which will have included farms, he left to his son William.

Caleb Evans, writing in the preface to Volume III of the 1780 edition of Anne Steele's hymns says, 'The death of her honoured father gave such a shock to her feeble frame that she never entirely recovered from it.' She never was able to live alone at *Grandfathers* and immediately went to live with her brother and his wife and Polly at *Broughton House*. Anne had obviously leant on her father all her life. In an extensive poetic eulogy in his memory published in the Preface to Volume III [1780 edition], she writes,

> 'Ah ! now one tender, one endearing tie
> That held me down to earth, death has torn off,
> And with it rent my heart strings; bid me come
> To thee my refuge; prostrate at thy feet
> O bid me say, with faith and humble hope,
> Heal, gracious Father, heal my bleeding heart!
> Thy healing hand alone can bring relief
> For woes like mine; can bring what most I want,
> A humble resignation to thy will.
> How hard the lesson! [yet it must be learnt]
> With full consent to say, "Thy will be done."'

This poem reflects the weak state of her health and the dependence that she had felt on her father and her home. Her one close, confidential friend now was her brother's daughter, Polly, who was sixteen at the time of her grandfather's death. Polly was devoted to her aunt who had been a surrogate mother to her from the time of the death of her mother in 1762 until her father remarried in 1768. Obviously the girl would still feel closer to her aunt than to her stepmother, who was not a blood relation. The girl was to devote the next nine years of her life to the care of her sick aunt in her own home at *Broughton House*. For her father's grave Anne penned the lovely verse, to be engraved on its side panel,

> 'Who knew him loved, who loved him must deplore,
> But parting pangs shall rend the heart no more,
> When Jesus comes to wake the sleeping dust,
> And to immortal glory raise the just.'

Edward Compton, writing of him in 1878, says,[191]

> 'William Steele, if he had not all the popular talents of his uncle, at least possessed his piety and solid worth. He was a diligent student of God's Word, and his sermons were sound and eminently practical, if not brilliant. Like his uncle[192] he carefully prepared his sermons, and some of his manuscripts that are preserved show no great amount of originality and imagination, but are of that useful character which, with God's blessing, must be fruitful. Under his ministry the Church continued to flourish.'

With the death of William Steele, a remarkable chapter ended in the Broughton/Porton Church. It had from its own midst been provided with its ministers since its formation in the middle of the seventeenth century. For eighty years Henry and William had guided, nourished and cherished the Broughton Church and its various sister churches in Wallop, Winterslow, Lockerley and Downton, as well as helping churches at Whitchurch, Romsey and Lymington. The labours of these two stalwarts of truth had indeed been 'owned of God' as were the hymns of Anne, which were first used widely in public worship in 1769, when Dr Ash and Caleb Evans included sixty-two of them in their *Bristol Baptist Collection of Hymns*. The Broughton Particular Baptist Church, though nestling away in the Hampshire Downs, off the beaten track, and far from the Metropolis, yet took a significant part among Particular Baptist Churches in preaching the Gospel and spreading the truth at the time of the Great Awakening in the eighteenth century.

---

191 HBBCH.

192 No sermon notes of Henry Steele survive.

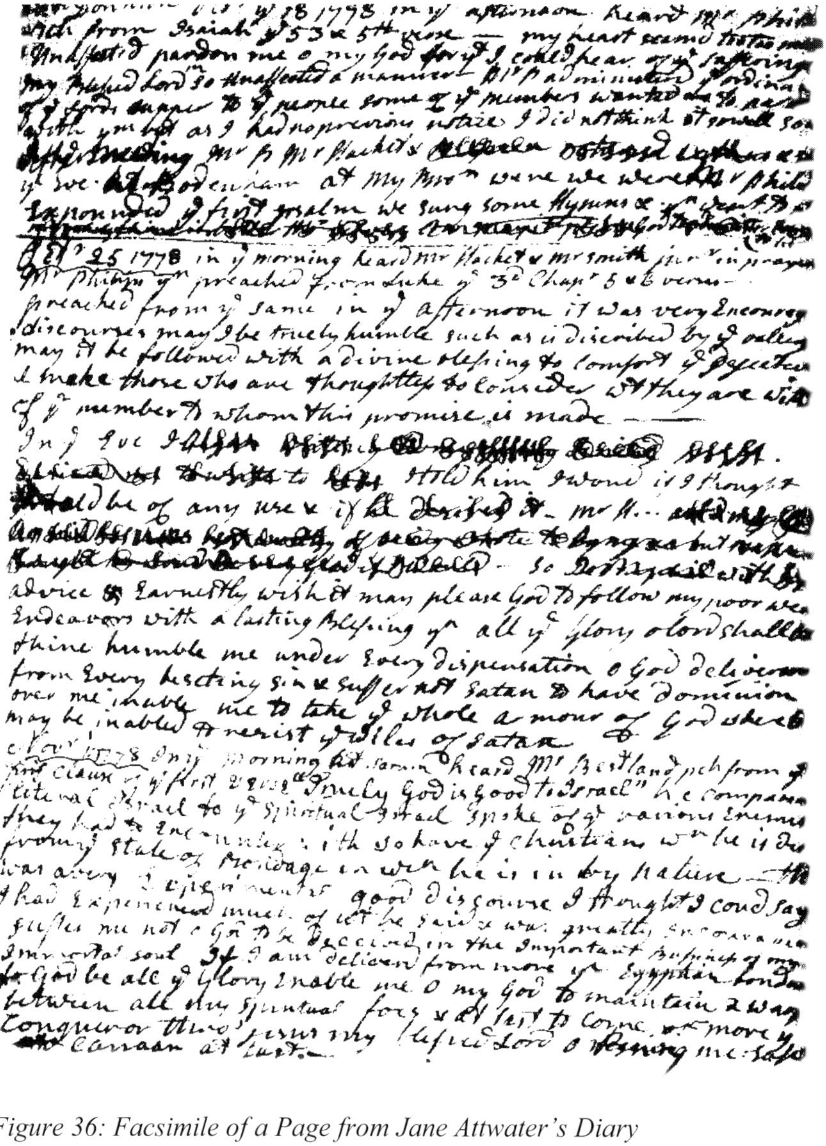

Figure 36: Facsimile of a Page from Jane Attwater's Diary

Chapter 8

Sorrow and Suffering [1769-78]

1769 Onwards

Anne outlived her father by nine years and as her sister Mary tells us in her Journal, she lived the whole of that time at *Broughton House.* Our main source of information for this period comes from about forty letters[193] which William Steele wrote to Polly, the child of his first marriage and a few which her stepmother wrote to her, all of which Polly kept. These letters give us a picture of Anne's health in the years from 1770 to 1778, the year in which she died. They reveal a very sick woman. Just after the death of old William Steele in 1769, on 17th September, Marianne Attwater had been baptised and joined the Broughton Church and at this time though Anne was unwell, as she had suffered with malaria fevers all her life since her teenage years, yet she was still able to get around and travel. She was at this time fifty-three and was often in pain from colic, induced by either 'irritable bowel syndrome', or 'peptic ulceration' of the stomach. Added to this she suffered from bad toothache. Eighteenth-century medical practice was unable either to understand or alleviate her sufferings. The effect of malaria was debilitating, leading to constant infections and anaemia. Also her stepmother's diary reveals that from the age of thirty-nine she had constantly suffered from shortness of breath. In March 1770 she was improved in health but not out of pain. On 11th July she went to Bodenham with Marianne Attwater for a week and when she returned on 21st July she walked for two miles and on Sunday 23rd July walked from *Broughton House* to the Meeting. But the letters show that by the following year her health had seriously declined and by 27th June 1771 she was confined to her room and dangerously ill and the family were prepared for her death. She was suffering from pains in her heart and a tooth abscess which eventually burst on 28th. She was at death's door for about a week and seemed to be out of danger by the first week of July.

[193] STE 4/5.

But after this she never seemed to make much of a recovery. This crisis in her health in 1771 marked a turning point in her life. She became virtually bedridden, except for rare occasions when she came downstairs.

In September 1772 she again became very ill and developed 'fits'. These were not necessarily epileptic fits as the term was often used in the eighteenth century to describe any symptoms resulting from a severe feverish condition. The trembling and shaking which she suffered almost certainly was connected with her malaria. One letter of 12th September records, 'Anne had no fits tonight.' On 19th September she came downstairs, but by 25th September she was having more fits. References in the letters mention recurring fits until February 1773. Throughout this year she showed signs of improvement and came downstairs again and 'was more cheerful'. Her brother William in his letters to Polly reveals that he was very sceptical about the various remedies suggested by her doctor, who came out from Stockbridge. By November Anne did not need a 'night watcher', though there is still mention of 'fits'. In August 1774 William Steele and his wife were planning to visit the relatives at Pershore, but delayed their visit because Anne was so ill. They eventually left on 10th September leaving Nathaniel Rawlings and his wife in charge at *Broughton House*. Nathaniel Rawlings was the new pastor at Broughton. He had come to Broughton on 11th November 1772 from Trowbridge. A letter to Polly from her stepmother speaks of the conflict she felt over wanting to see her sister and relatives at Pershore and her anxiety at leaving Anne. Anne had said to William that if he went away to Pershore it might be the last time he would see her. Anne survived the visit and improved in October, but by May 1775 a letter said that 'her affliction is very great'. But she rallied in the summer weather and on 3rd June went out in the sedan chair carried by some of William Steele's men. She appears to have held her own until the following September [1776] when she again was seriously ill and refused to follow the doctor's orders to have bloodletting. In August 1777 she was described as in great pain and by December the same year her sufferings were described as 'much the same'. At this time she began to suffer from deafness. She lasted another eleven months until her death on 11th November 1778. She had, for the most part, been confined to her room since her illness in June 1771. It is virtually impossible from the brief records to tell exactly what had happened to her. It might seem that the loss of her father had brought on a nervous breakdown. Dr Caleb Evans in his preface to the 1780 edition of her hymns says, 'Her health was never firm, but the death of her honoured father, to whom she was united by the strongest ties of affectionate duty and gratitude, gave such a shock to her feeble frame, that she never entirely recovered from it.' She wrote at the time, recorded in the above preface,

> 'Still bleeds the deep, deep wound! Where is the friend,
> To pour with tender, kind indulgent hand,
> The lenient balm of comfort on my heart?
> Alas that friend is gone! Ye angels say
> (Who bore him raptured to your blessed abodes)
> Can ought on earth compensate for my loss!
> Ah, no! The world is poor, and what am I?
> A helpless solitary worm, that creeps
> Complaining on the earth! Yet ev'n to worms
> The care of heaven extends...'

Anne's Carer

Polly cared for her aunt, except for the weeks in the year when she left for a break. The letters of her father sent to her on these occasions told her about events in Broughton and the condition of her aunt. In 1770 Polly spent June at Exeter and Yeovil with her Uncle George Bullock and July at Milbourne Port with Mary Scott. She was seventeen at the time. She returned to Yeovil in the following year in June to stay with her uncle and went in July to stay at East Knoyle with the Russ family. Mr Russ was a minister and had married one of Polly's Froude cousins from Sedgehill. When Anne was so ill that year, Polly considered returning to Broughton. In 1772 she spent September at Yeovil with her uncle. In 1773 she spent several weeks in the first three months of the year at Bradford-on-Avon with Marianne [Attwater] who had recently married George Head and come to live there. She spent several weeks in the last three months of the year at Yeovil, Motcombe and East Knoyle. Her holiday in 1774 was again at Yeovil with her uncle, this time in the month of September. This was the last of her holidays with her mother's brother, in the town where her mother lay buried, for no doubt she visited her mother's grave each time she came to Yeovil. On 4th March 1775 her uncle died. The inscription on the gravestone at Yeovil reads,

> 'In Memory of George Bullock gent:
> who died March 4th 1775 aged 73
> and of
> Mary Steele, wife of William Steele gent:
> and Sister of George Bullock gent:
> who died May 13th 1762 aged 49
>
> Still o'er the dear remains which slumber here,
> Tho' anguish sheds the unavailing tear,

> Tho' grateful memory swells the tide of grief,
> Yet hope celestial points a kind relief:
> She views these friends, so loved, so mourned below,
> So long divided in this vale of woe.
> United views them – in that blest abode
> Where joys full-beaming speak a present God.'

This verse, undoubtedly from Polly's pen, beautifully composed, shows the sense of loss that she felt regarding the death of her mother when she was only eight and the way her affections had taken her to Yeovil every year from 1770 onwards to be with her uncle until his death in 1775. Poignant, when one considers that she was only twenty-two at the time, and that her aunt, whom she so much loved, was lying at Broughton in great affliction, unlikely to live long. At the close of the year, Polly wrote 'Stanzas written at the close of the Year 1775', showing that her father had been seriously ill himself, soon after her uncle's death. Referring to her uncle's death she says,

> 'Scarce had the Grave received the destined prey
> Again disease assumed its tyrant sway,
> When o'er a parent hung Death's threatening Dart
> Think whose kind Hand withheld the dread Decree...
>
> And lent him yet to bless the World and me....
>
> Still lives the Friend endeared by every Tie
> Which Duty, Friendship, Gratitude can frame,
> Still Heaven permits her Absence from the Sky
> Though Sickness long has dimmed her vital flame.'

In these stanzas, her uncle, her father and her aunt are all mentioned. Polly was surrounded with sadness. In 1776 she spent three weeks at Bradford-on-Avon with Marianne. While there she received a letter from her father telling her that he had received a letter from William Wilkins of Cirencester, asking for his agreement to approach his daughter with a view to marriage. Her father told her that the decision was hers and she must seek divine guidance in the matter. In fact Polly did not take the matter further, but it is interesting to know [as Ivimey tells us in his *History of the English Baptists,* Vol. IV, p.467] that William Wilkins was in fact a minister, who trained at Bristol Baptist Academy, finished his education in Scotland and in 1777 became assistant minister to Benjamin Beddome at Bourton-on-the-Water. The church at Bourton in their letter to the Association Meeting held at Warwick in 1778 wrote, 'The assistant we have procured for our pastor is every way acceptable both to him and us, and we hope the Lord has blessed his labours.' No doubt when Polly returned to Broughton from Bradford-on-Avon, she talked the matter over with her aunt, who must have looked back to 1742 when she herself had received a similar letter from Benjamin Beddome. Whatever Anne said may well have influenced Polly in the decision she took.

Polly did not marry till 1790 when she married a minister, by which time she was thirty-seven. The last break Polly had before Anne died was at East Knoyle with the Russ family when she stayed for two weeks in December 1777.

Joys and Sorrows

While Anne was virtually confined to her room and Polly cared for her except for an annual break, events moved on in the Steele household at *Broughton House*. On 26th August 1770 Mrs Steele gave birth to another daughter, a sister for Nancy, and called her Martha. In 1772 she gave birth to a son, but he only survived a few weeks. This must have been a sad blow for the family as this lad would have been heir to the Steele family business and estate, and would have carried on the family name. At the same time the Steele family suffered another tragedy. On 13th October Mary Wakeford died suddenly at the age of forty-eight. She left a husband Joseph and three children, Hannah, her stepdaughter, aged twenty-five, William her own son, aged twenty-one, and Mary her daughter aged twelve. Born on 29th June 1724, Molly was seven years younger than Anne. In their childhood days, they had not got on too well together, but as they grew older they became close companions, especially spiritually. They kept up a regular correspondence and often wrote in poetry to each other. Molly was not nearly such an accomplished poet as Anne, but she had a keen sense of the ridiculous and often gently mocked Anne's polished verse, well aware that she was unable to compete with it. Much of her verse written to her stepsister has survived in the family archives.[194] Her death must have been a heavy blow and a great shock to Anne in her weak state, and also to the whole Steele household, especially to her stepbrother William. Thus within three years Anne had lost her father and her halfsister as well as a baby nephew.

Nathaniel Rawlings

On 11th November 1772 another event occurred at Broughton. The Broughton Church Book[195] records that Nathaniel Rawlings and his wife Mary were admitted to membership of the church, as Nathaniel Rawlings had become their new pastor. He had come from Trowbridge where he

---

[194] STE 3/10/i-xv.
[195] ALRPC.

had been pastor since 1765. Born at Moreton-in-Marsh in 1733, he had grown up to attend the Baptist Meeting at Bourton-on-the-Water where his parents were long-standing members. He was baptised there at the age of eighteen by Benjamin Beddome. The church soon called him to the ministry and he went to the Bristol Academy for four years under the training of Hugh Evans and Bernard Foskett. During the period of his training he supplied the pulpit at Back Street Particular Baptist Church at Trowbridge and eventually after ten years in the ministry was called to be their pastor, being ordained on 10th October 1765 at the age of thirty-two.[196] Some trouble in the church there caused him to resign in 1771, after which he was called to Broughton, probably recommended to them by Caleb Evans. Just before he left Trowbridge he married a godly woman, Mary Webb. At the time he came to Broughton he was thirty-nine and had been a minister for seventeen years. Sadly he only stayed until 21st November 1777, when he returned to be pastor at Trowbridge where he remained until his death in October 1809. In a letter addressed to Polly from Bristol written in September 1777 William Steele wrote, 'Since our arrival here I have heard news that I had not the least idea of, though I find it to be generally talked of, that Mr Rawlings is about to leave Broughton and return to Trowbridge, the place he so much execrated, O tempora O mores[197] [O the times; O the behaviour]. But he is to join the clothing trade with his, or rather her, relations [the Webb family] and to preach to the people as usual... If it be so [true] I shall not ask him to stay nor in any way endeavour to prevent his going.' When William Steele and his wife returned to Broughton in mid-September there must have been some tension between them and Nathaniel Rawlings. Why he left so suddenly without giving William Steele any indication of his intentions is unknown, but the Church Book of Back Street Church, Trowbridge records significantly that at the time of his death in 1809 'the last thirty-two years of his pastorate had been happy with his people and they united to him'. As the Rawlings had stayed at *Broughton House* in 1774 when the Steeles went to Pershore, Anne would have known them well and been conversant with the whole situation, though owing to her health she hardly ever can have heard Nathaniel Rawlings preach.

William Steele's Journeys

In the years from 1770 to 1777 William Steele travelled long distances and sometimes took his wife and children with him. In June 1770 he went to Bristol and stayed at the home of Caleb Evans. In July 1771 he took his wife with him and called at Bristol at the Evans family on his way to

---

[196] *Baptist Magazine* 1810 pp 27-8.

[197] Cicero. 1st speech against Catiline.

Pershore [his wife's family], returning again via Bristol. In 1773 in February he did jury service at Winchester and in October took Polly to Yeovil. In November he went to Bodenham to the Attwaters. In August 1774 he again took Polly to Yeovil and in September went with his wife and children to Pershore. They went first to Abingdon where they stayed at the home of the minister Daniel Turner, then to Banbury and finally to Pershore. They returned via Bristol and Bradford-on-Avon on their way home to Broughton, staying at Bradford with the Heads. In 1775 William Steele went to Exeter in June and twice to Yeovil in May and November. 1777 saw the biggest excursion of all from Broughton. Mr and Mrs Steele and Martha [known in the family as Patty] set out for London and were away from Broughton for six weeks. In a series of ten letters to Polly, William Steele records all the events of the visit. They called at Basingstoke on the way to visit friends and arrived in London in Newgate Street at 1pm on 5th August. In London they stayed with the Townsend family. William Steele records that the City was hot, noisy and smoky. They spent an afternoon at Richmond Hill and visited Kew Gardens. They visited a Mr Dun in his 'elegant villa' at Dulwich, who sent his personal coach to bring them to his home. They went to Muswell Hill just beyond Highgate, to dine with Dr Samuel Stennett. William Steele had with him a third volume[198] of Anne Steele's poetry and writings, but was unable to find a bookseller who would have them published. He also had a long poem of Polly's entitled 'Danebury Hill',[199] [a prehistoric camp just outside Broughton], but again he could get no one to publish it. He visited Vauxhall on the Thames, just upstream from the House of Commons and records that it was much changed since he was last there. On 20th August very early in the morning the family left London by stagecoach and travelled on the first day via Oxford, Chipping Norton and Moreton-in-Marsh about an hundred miles, stopping at Broadway Hill near Worcester for a night, before going on via Evesham to Pershore. They stayed at Pershore with Dr Ash and his family and appreciated the peaceful solitude having left behind the din of Newgate, going for walks over the River Avon, visiting a newly built mansion and having dinner in a moated castle with the owners. They returned to Bristol on 5th September, Bradford on 12th, Bratton on 14th and reached Broughton on 15th, staying with the Evans, the Heads and the Whitakers. William gave instructions to Polly to send their own chariot from Broughton to Bratton, to bring them home on the last stage of their journey. They must have travelled at least two hundred and fifty miles in six weeks, mostly, it would appear, by stagecoach. All the while Anne was lying at home in Broughton ill. In a

[198] Published in Bristol in 1780 by Caleb Evans.

[199] *Danebury* also published in Bristol at a later date.

letter from Pershore dated 27th August William Steele comments on what Polly must have told him about his sister that 'her lucid moments were very short and he hopes her pain is not so great.'

Anne Steele's Works Unpublished in her Lifetime

The third volume of Anne's poetry, which her brother failed to have published in London in 1777, was to appear three years later as a third volume added to a reprint of the two volumes published in 1760. It would appear, having regard to the state of her health, after her serious illness in June 1771, that most of the contents of the third volume were written and composed prior to 1770, during the years from 1760 to 1769. The volume consists of poems on nature, the spring, flowers, butterflies, poems written to bereaved friends, reflections on the New Year's bells of Broughton Church, poems on public events such as the fifth of November, as well as poems to specific friends such as Polly [Silvia], Molly [Amira] her half-sister, William Steele [Philander], and Mary Scott [Myra] from Milbourne Port. It also contained about twenty-five additional hymns and verses on spiritual subjects and about twenty pieces in prose written in the form of prayers and meditations on scriptural subjects. It followed very much the pattern of volumes one and two. Volume

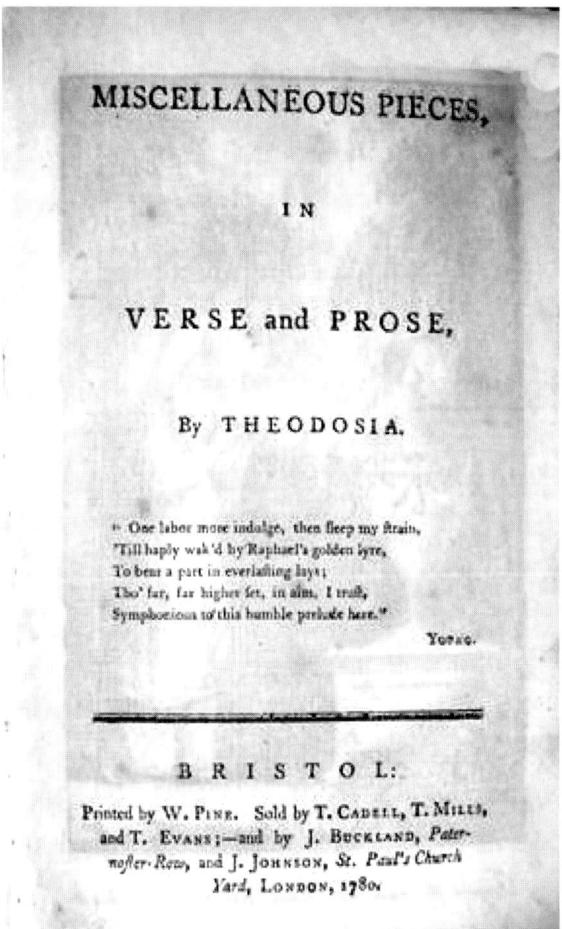
MISCELLANEOUS PIECES,

IN

VERSE and PROSE,

By THEODOSIA.

"One labor more indulge, then sleep my strain,
'Till haply wak'd by Raphael's golden lyre,
To bear a part in everlasting lays;
Tho' far, far higher set, in aim, I trust,
Symphonious to this humble prelude here."

YOUNG.

BRISTOL:

Printed by W. Pine. Sold by T. Cadell, T. Mills, and T. Evans;—and by J. Buckland, Pater-noster-Row, and J. Johnson, St. Paul's Church Yard, London, 1780.

Figure 37: Title Page of 'Miscellaneous Pieces', published 1780

one had contained hymns and occasional poems, volume two occasional poems and paraphrases of the Psalms, volume three, miscellaneous poems and miscellaneous pieces in prose. When in 1863 John Sheppard produced his single volume reprint of her works, he divided it into three sections: Hymns, Psalms and Poems. In the section on Hymns he included her hymns and some of her occasional verses on spiritual subjects making a total of one hundred and forty-four hymns.[200] He reprinted all her paraphrases of the Psalms[201] but in the third section of Poems he included only a brief selection of her miscellaneous verses and omitted all her prose writings.

But beside these published works there remains a substantial body of unpublished works. A selection of these was published in 1997 in a book entitled *Pursuing the Muses* by the late Dr Marjorie Reeves, herself a direct descendant of Caroline Whitaker of Bratton, who was a daughter of Anna Attwater of Bodenham, who descended from the Gay family of Haycombe, Bath. Much of this poetry is contained in manuscript books belonging to members of the family such as Anne Steele [Nancy], William Steele's eldest daughter by his second marriage, who later married a Tomkins of Abingdon. She copied these verses into her personal book for her own benefit, but though the authorship of the verse might appear to be either that of Anne Steele the hymnwriter, or her half-sister, Mary Wakeford, or her niece Polly, it is impossible to attribute this poetry with absolute certainty to any one of them. As this verse is copied, and that over a long period, it is impossible to identify the authoress by her own handwriting.

Anne Steele and Her Literary Circle

What is clear is that, as Dr Reeves shows, Anne Steele, when well, was at the centre of a small literary circle that exchanged letters on a regular basis and in them included verse on secular subjects. It is also clear that in the eighteenth century there was a definite movement in favour of women's education. Their talents had been undervalued, especially in the literary and scientific world which had been dominated by men. Anne Steele did not initiate this movement, but certainly she was surrounded by people involved in it. Her own brother was undoubtedly favourable to it and his wife's brother-in-law, Dr John Ash of Pershore, published a book in 1777 entitled *Sentiments on Education* which contained an essay on 'Female Accomplishments'. Polly, Anne's niece, was friendly with Mary Scott of Milbourne Port who published a substantial poem in 1774 entitled

[200] Included in this book.

[201] Also included.

The Female Advocate.[202] Polly was herself an accomplished poet, an interest developed by her aunt in her youth. The ideas contained in these publications must have been discussed at length in the family circle long before they were published.

The poetic correspondence, conducted under a series of classical pen names, contained both male and female writers. Largely the writers were within the Steele family circle. They included Caroline Attwater – Dorinda; Jane Attwater – Myrtilla; Marianne Attwater – Maria; Mary Steele (Bullock) – Delia; Polly Steele – Silvia; Anne herself – Silviana or Theodosia; Gay Thomas Attwater – Florio; William Steele – Philander; Joseph Wakeford – Portius. Outside the family were a small group of writers which included Philip Furneaux – Lucius; John Lavington – Lysander and Mary Scott – Myra. Other names appear, sometimes in the published poetry of Anne Steele, which cannot as yet be identified. This group of writers centred around Anne in her rural home at Broughton and copied a pattern of letter writing common in eighteenth-century literary circles, while being outside the Metropolis and centres of culture such as Bath. What is interesting is that it is possible that when Anne Steele rejected the hand of Benjamin Beddome in marriage in 1742, she put her interest in poetry before marriage and a family. Both Polly Steele, who also rejected a proposal in marriage, and Jane Attwater, who did not marry till late in life, were very involved in the ideas of this literary circle regarding women's education and their freedom to choose a single life and follow the pursuit of literary interests rather than marry and bring up a family. It is not at all clear why Anne rejected Benjamin Beddome, who was himself a poet and had similar interests, beliefs and background to herself, if it were not that she wished to pursue a literary career. It would appear that in this respect she had a profound influence on Polly Steele and Jane Attwater, young people very close to her.

Steele Family Culture

William Steele and his family would appear to be in the vanguard of liberal thinking among Particular Baptists in the eighteenth century, and that in the isolated rural setting of Broughton. The Steeles were close friends of Caleb Evans of Bristol, often staying with him on their journeys. Caleb Evans was a great supporter of 'liberty', defending the cause of the Americans in their War of Independence in 1775 and supporting the anti-slavery movement. The more educated members of the Particular Baptist congregations were clearly people who were forward thinking, and Anne Steele's abilities, which brought the family into prominence in the eighteenth century through her published works,

[202] STE 14/3.

and recognition as the only woman hymnwriter to rank with names such as John Newton, William Cowper, John Berridge, Augustus Toplady and Joseph Hart in spirituality, if not in poetic accomplishment, gave credence to the view that there was much latent ability among women that could be developed with better education. There is no doubt that, in the Nonconformist academies there was a much broader range of subjects studied, not limited as at Oxford and Cambridge to a strong emphasis on classical studies and mathematics, but embracing literature, history, modern and classical languages, geography, natural philosophy, logic, elocution and astronomy. It would seem highly likely that William Steele's outlook was shaped in such an academy and that contact with this influence affected the whole of Anne Steele's life. Anne herself had attended a Particular Baptist school at Trowbridge. Her stepsister Molly and her three nieces had all been given some education. But one wonders whether at Broughton there was any education provided by the Particular Baptist Church for the children of the Steele farm workers and estate employees who attended the Meeting, such as a Sunday school, where they could be taught to read and write.

It is interesting to know something about the library of books in the Steele household. Old William Steele's will bequeathed his books to Anne. There is no doubt that she was a great reader for most of her life. Mrs Steele's diary mentions a range of books on spiritual subjects which included *Navigation Spiritualized* by John Flavel, *Come and Welcome to Jesus Christ* by John Bunyan, *Alarm* to *the Unconverted* by Joseph Alleine, the Works of Joseph Stennett, *The Ecclesiastical History of New England* by Cotton Mather, the Works and Hymns of Isaac Watts, *The History of the Waldenses, The History of the Puritans* by Daniel Neal, the Works of James Hervey, *The Divine Attributes* by Stephen Charnock, sermons by ministers such as Wilson, Notcutt and Pearsal and various secular histories such as *The Life of William III [1703]*. Among the list of subscribers to John Gill's three volume *Body of Divinity* published in 1769 is 'Rev. William Steele, Broughton'. [Other subscribers included John Ash, Abraham Booth, Caleb and Hugh Evans, Andrew Gifford, John Lacey, Josiah Lewis, John Ryland, Augustus Toplady, Henry Venn, Daniel Turner, Benjamin Francis and Benjamin Wallin.] This would appear to be only a selection of a much larger library at *Grandfathers* built up by her father in his lifetime and added to by her brother and herself. Her brother in various commonplace books shows a classical background. One is inscribed 'Ex Libris Gul(ielmi) Steele jun,'[203] two poems are prefaced by quotations from Virgil, items by Alexander Pope include

[203] STE 4/2.

Messiah; A Sacred Eclogue in Imitation of Virgil's Pollio; The Temple of Fame; Eloisa to Abelard. We know from a letter he wrote when on a visit to Lewes in Sussex that William spent an afternoon sitting in the garden of the house in which he stayed, reading the letters of Pope and looking down the valley to Lewes Castle. It would appear also that William Steele had an interest in music, and a better ear for it than his stepmother who did not appreciate the organ of Salisbury Cathedral. At the end of this commonplace book William copied out the first verse of the hymn of Joseph Addison [1672-1719], which begins, 'The spacious firmament on high,' together with hymn tunes. A manuscript book of tunes for psalms and hymns[204] used at the Broughton Meeting has survived in the Steele collection and it includes the tune written by John Sheeles, a contemporary of Addison, especially for this hymn. The tunes are in four part settings. Like Beddome,Anne Steele regularly composed hymns for services at the chapel, which must have been read, verse by verse, probably by her father from the pulpit, and led by a group of singers with their manuscript tune books. How interesting it would have been to listen to this local Hampshire congregation with its undoubtedly broad dialect, a dialect now largely lost.

Josiah Lewis - A New Pastor

As already mentioned, Nathaniel Rawlings resigned his pastorate and left Broughton for Trowbridge on 21st November 1777. The church was now dependent on the ministry of their preaching elder, John Kent, and any other supply minister they could get. The Church Book records that on 21st December Josiah Lewis, from Marden in Kent, preached at Broughton and it would seem that his ministry was acceptable to the Broughton Church, because the entry is followed with one on 31st May 1778 revealing that he and his wife were received into membership and another showing that he was officially ordained as pastor on 14th October. He was described as 'a man of great learning, an able divine and a good preacher. In these respects he was, to all human appearance, calculated to build the church; but he was marred by an unhappy temper, which hindered his usefulness.'[205] Within four weeks of his taking his new pastorate, Anne Steele died.

Anne Steele's Death

As the year 1778 opened, Anne Steele's life had been gradually drawing to its close. In April or May she was sixty-one, and since her serious illness in 1771, when she appeared close to her end, her health had constantly been a cause of concern to her family. What lay behind her

---

[204] STE 14/1.

[205] HBBCH p.17.

brother's reference to her 'lucid moments' is not entirely clear, but it suggests either some type of dementia or a semi-conscious condition. The details of the weeks before her death are recorded in the diary of Jane Attwater, which survived at Bratton among the collection of material that came into the possession of Dr Marjorie Reeves. [Jane Attwater (1753-

Figure 38: Anne Steele's Gravestone

1844) married Joseph G. Blatch of Bratton in 1790 and spent the last fifty years of her life in Bratton, and lies buried with her sister Caroline Whitaker in the graveyard of the Particular Baptist Church, built there in 1734. She would have been the archivist of the Attwater material that found its way to Bratton and which formed the basis of Dr Marjorie Reeves' book *Sheep Bell & Ploughshare* published in 1978.] Writing on 4th November 1778, she records that she had gone the previous Monday [2nd] to Broughton to see Anne, who was nearing her end. She writes,

> 'I went to Broughton and found my beloved friend much indisposed. The amiable Theodosia nears the borders of the eternal world. She was extremely weak; could say but little. She told me she

> much wished for me a little time past, meaning when Dr Stennett and Mr [Caleb] Evans were there; not for her sake only but for my own sake. When I came away, going to take my leave of her, she took me by the hand and with affectionate tenderness said, "Farewell till we meet in a happier world." With tears I left her thinking I should never more see her this side of the grave. O that I may be prepared to meet her where pain and sorrow shall never enter. When I came home [to Bodenham] through Sarum [Salisbury] in the evening there was a boy accidentally let off a serpent [a wind instrument] before my horse's head. He frighted, jumped, the motion broke both the girths so that I was thrown on my knees. Very providentially I received very little hurt.'

This entry reveals that both Dr Samuel Stennett and Caleb Evans had travelled long distances from London and Bristol to come to Broughton to visit Anne on her death bed. It tells how highly she was regarded and how much she was respected by the leading ministers among the Particular Baptists. The Steele family, Henry, William senior and William junior, had placed the Broughton Church in a significant position among the Particular Baptist Churches through the blessing that had rested on their ministry and on Anne's hymns. Writing in her diary on Thursday 12th November, Jane says,

> 'Mr Steele sent a messenger with a letter to acquaint us of the death of the good and valuable Theodosia. He tells me in it, my good friend resigned her soul into the hands of her Great Creator without a murmur and almost without a sigh. She retained her senses to the last though she was capable of speaking but little. Her pains were very great, but her future prospect administered consolation to her soul. She is gone from this world of pain and sorrow and now in the full fruition of perfect bliss she is now in participation of those joys which eye hath not seen nor is it possible for us to conceive... Let the thought of her being released from heavy affliction... mitigate our sorrow.'

Jane goes on to express her anxiety about her mother, Anna Attwater, who had been a widow now for eleven years and with whom she was living, her two sisters, Caroline and Marianne having married and left Bodenham. She says, 'O bless my dear parent... dispel those gloomy doubts which have so long depressed her mind... I fear such a dejection will injure her health... a sense of her own sin and the sin of the nation quite weighs her down... lift up the light of thy reconciled countenance on her, O God, and grant her a continual sense of thy atoning love to her soul and enable her to go on her way rejoicing. I am much grieved to see her so low.' Anna Attwater was sixty-eight at the time of the death of Anne Steele and no doubt had many happy memories of times in their youth when Anne and William had come to her home at Haycombe and she had visited Broughton. Anne had often stayed at Bodenham with the Attwater family. Her death was a great blow to Anna.

In an entry dated 18th November [Wednesday] Jane says,

> 'Yesterday I came hither to this day attend the funeral solemnities of my dear departed friend Theodosia. Awful indeed is death. I went in to see her clay cold corpse. My heart shuddered at first, but when I beheld her placid serenity that dwelt on her countenance, I was not at all shocked. Deep anguish and sorrow filled my heart for the loss of such a faithful, such a valued friend on viewing her much loved form… the thought of the little kindnesses rushed into my mind and tender regret that now no more would that voice which used to soften the heart, that tongue that used to direct and caution every friend, perform its office. Silent and cold lie those hands that used to be employed in each kindness and benevolence... I followed my honoured friend to the grave [the family tomb in Broughton Parish Churchyard] after which we went to the Meeting. Mr Lewis preached from John the 14th chapter, 2nd and 3rd verses, "In my Father's house are many mansions; if it were not so I would have told you. I go to prepare a place for you. And if I go and prepare a place for you, I will come again and receive you unto myself; that where I am, there ye may be also." This text was chosen by Theodosia several years past. This was an excellent sermon. What Mr Lewis said to the relations of the deceased was very affecting and suitable, particularly when he addressed my dear Silvia [Polly Steele]; he did it in a most affectionate manner... Two of the dear deceased's hymns were sung which greatly affected me.'

During the course of this sermon[206] Josiah Lewis said,

> 'And why should I hesitate a moment in supposing that our dear friend, whose departure we this evening mourn, has a bright and happy mansion provided for her?... Give me leave... the sorrowing relatives of the deceased to recommend the text to your consideration, more particularly of each of you, the text which, you know, was chosen by her several years ago for the subject of her funeral discourse. 'Let not your heart be troubled.' [John 14. 1] I mean to excess. Sorrow not as those who are without hope, for her who now sleeps in Jesus... it will not be my business now, to raise the panegyric over the ashes of the dead. Our friend herself, I am informed, warmly requested that nothing of the kind might be spoken upon this occasion... You can look back with pleasure upon those many hours of free conversation you formerly had with her, (and I mean particularly on religious matters) for which some of you have told me she had a distinguished talent, and you are willing, I persuade myself, to acknowledge the benefit you received thereby. She was a person of real good sense... Her imagination, which

[206] STE 3/15.

was naturally vigorous, she had taken care to improve by an attention to books, of which through an uncommon fondness for them, she had read a great number... Upwards of six years she was confined to her room; through almost the whole of which time she was exercised with great bodily pain... Frequently did she acknowledge the righteousness of the divine procedure and that it was her duty and her wish to submit to whatever God was pleased to lay upon her...

The few last hours our friend had on earth, so far as spectators could judge, appeared to be more than ordinarily painful. At one time she said, "It is hard work," and at another, that "she endured unspeakable pain," that "She knew that her Redeemer lived," and at another to a friend that stood by, "She entreated her to pray that her faith might not fail." And there is all the reason we can wish for to conclude that her desire was granted. Being several hours in dying circumstances, at length she sunk gradually under the decays of nature, and at the instant she expired [which was without a sigh or groan], she raised up her hand to a considerable height, in the full enjoyment of reason, and gently waved it, an expression it was supposed by those who were near that all was well and that she was done with time, that angels were at hand and she was going to one of those mansions prepared for her in the world above... Thus lived and died our dear friend... What an honour does such a death as hers, reflect upon the religion of Jesus. What a striking evidence is it of the truth of that religion... Such a comfortable frame is methinks one of the noblest sights our eyes can behold. Now she has put off her sackcloth and is girded with gladness; and long before now, it has been echoed throughout the heavenly plains, here is one who is come out of great tribulation, who has washed her robes and made them white in the blood of the Lamb.'

The Memorial Services – Sunday 22nd November

On Sunday 22nd November following the funeral Jane was still at Broughton staying with Polly at *Broughton House*. Both were twenty-five, both had been greatly influenced in their lives by Anne, both had lost a parent, Polly her mother in 1762 and Jane her father in 1767. Neither was to marry until later in their lives, Jane in 1790 and Polly in 1797. As their loved ones were taken one by one, they were more and more drawn together. On this Sunday they went to the meeting and heard Mr Lewis preach in the morning from Genesis 46 verses 3, 4, 'Fear not to go down into Egypt etc.,' in which he likened Egypt to death and the grave. Jane says, 'He made a very good and ingenious discourse.' Of this discourse Jane has no more to say. Then she comes on to the afternoon sermon of which she has much to say.

'In the afternoon, Mr Kent preached from the last text of Scripture our dear Theodosia ever repeated, namely Job 19 verse 25, "I know that my Redeemer liveth." [He also preached from verses 26, and 27.]

He first spoke of the glorious Redeemer. This Redeemer is the Lord Jesus Christ. Isaiah says, 'Fear not, for thy Redeemer is the holy one of Israel.' A Redeemer supposes there is 1] something to be redeemed. The Church and the people of God are those whom Christ redeemed by His precious blood. 2] It implies that they were to be redeemed from something. They are redeemed from sin and the power of it and brought out of the state they were all in by nature into a state of grace, into a state of honour and happiness. 3] What was the price paid for the redemption of the people of God? Jesus gave Himself a ransom. "Thou art worthy... Thou hast redeemed us by Thy blood." "The ransomed of the Lord shall return and come."...

In the second place Job appropriates the Redeemer to himself. My Redeemer. Religion, my friends, is a personal thing. My religion will be of no use to you, or yours to me. We shall not answer for one another. Here is a higher act of faith, believing that the Redeemer lived... Paul says, "The life which I now live is by faith in the Son of God who loved me and gave Himself for me." Unbelief will often prevent our saying that, but when we are really convinced of our state by nature and have a sense of His pardoning love to our soul, we can say, "My Lord, My God." "Whom have I in heaven but Thee and there is none on earth that I desire beside Thee." You doubt all things. To whom else shall I go?

In the third place there is a still higher act of faith. "I know that my Redeemer liveth." An assurance of it. Philippians 3 verse 10, "That I may know..." When the people of God make a profession of their faith, they profess to have a knowledge of thirst, of a Redeemer, an appropriating faith in Him; that the Holy Spirit has witnessed with their spirit; they profess to be in measure dead to sin; to commit the keeping of their body and soul to God as Timothy expresses it, "I know in whom I have believed."

Fourthly, so see in what state we are in; we are all corrupted by sin. In us, that is in our flesh, dwelleth no good thing; there is none that doeth good. God beheld the children of men and saw that the imagination of their heart was evil continually. We see the necessity that there is of there being a change wrought in our hearts before we can be admitted to a world where nothing that defiles can ever enter. See the necessity of being born again, of being created anew in Christ Jesus, of having all the powers sanctified and reminded of the necessity for eternal life. You see here is twofold righteousness in Christ for Christians; to be made partakers of justification and sanctification as well as redemption which He has wrought out. The one hundred and forty-four thousand were sanctified as well as justified. Here is the completion of the Christian's happiness hinted at. He shall stand at the

> latter day. The dead in Christ shall rise first. But now is Christ risen... Wherefore comfort one another. Job saw by faith the glorious day in which he should be raised. This should support all believers under afflictive providences. The Christ who is their life shall appear. Then shall you also appear with Him in glory. Every eye shall see Him. One shall come and will not tarry. Jesus has said, "Father, I will that those thou hast given me..." Beloved, now are ye the sons of God. You will have an assimilating sight of Him. Jesus has said, "I am the resurrection." This will be a glorious resurrection indeed. We hope it will be turned into vision and faith into fruition. When the saints shall have a perfect enjoyment of those divine pleasures to which they aspired while on earth. Now your life is hid with Christ in God. God will change your vile body and make you like to Christ's glorious body. Those that sleep in Jesus God will bring with Him. Thy Redeemer, the Holy One of Israel. The Lord Jehovah is His Name. The ransomed of the Lord shall return to Zion with songs.
>
> Fifthly, learn from hence, you, the people of God, have supports far superior to those that the vain world experience in time of affliction. The people of the world are supported by a common providence. The people of God by the peculiar assistance, support and influence of the Holy Spirit. God overrules all for their good. 'Tis in very faithfulness they are afflicted. God corrects you like a father chastises his child for their good. They will find that it is for their gain in the end. The people of God shall not suffer any loss by death. They are freed from every evil of which sin was the procuring cause and are put in the possession of those inestimable blessings procured by the Glorious Redeemer. It is our indispensable duty to examine our own heart. Examine yourselves, seeing how much depends on it. Let us come to God and say, "Search me, O God, try me and know my thoughts, lead me in the way everlasting." We should be very careful not to deceive ourselves for the hope of the hypocrite shall perish. To such it shall be said, "Depart, ye cursed," but to the humble sincere Christian, "Come, ye blessed of my Father."'

Having copied the sermon in her diary, Jane adds a footnote, 'This was a very good plain discourse, but as it is some time since I heard, I cannot so well remember it.' It would appear that she must have made some notes at the time it was preached.

John Kent was closely connected to the Steele family. The Kent family had lived at Over Wallop since the days of the persecution. One of their number, John Kent, had taken out a Dissenter's Licence for his house and one for himself as a Teacher [Anabaptist] under the 1672 Declaration of Indulgence. He is mentioned in the Porton /Broughton Church Book in 1675/6. Stephen Kent was elected an elder in the Porton Church in 1683 and he and Richard Kent became pastors at the Whitchurch Meeting in

1690, Richard later going to be pastor at Southampton. In his will [1739] Henry Steele refers to Sarah Kent, daughter of my kinsman, Stephen Kent, of Over Wallop, 'Maltster'. This Stephen Kent was a ruling elder and deacon of the Broughton Church for many years. He kept the Church Book and had been treasurer until his death in 1751. It was his son, John, who preached the memorial service of Anne Steele on Sunday 22nd November 1778. John had been baptised by Henry Steele on 7th February 1727/8 and was called to the work of the ministry in the summer of 1732. He became assistant to Henry Steele and his successors till 1787 when old age forced him to give up preaching. As a young man he had worked in the timber business for Henry Steele and married Henry Steele's granddaughter, Sarah Etheredge, in 1734. He had been born in 1707 and was eight years older than William Steele, Anne's brother, and ten years older than Anne. Unlike Josiah Lewis he would have known Anne all her life in the church at Broughton and in the family timber business. He had a large family [ten children] and owned a farm. He died on 12th December 1796 at the age of eighty-nine, having been a member of the church for sixty-nine years and a minister for sixty-four years. He had seen the good days of prosperity at Broughton and also the decline at the end of the century. His ministry was experimental as well as expository, which was identical to that of Henry Steele and William Steele.

Among the congregation listening to his preaching on that Sunday in November 1778 were several generations of relatives of the Steele/Cator family. The oldest would have been Anna Attwater [the niece of the second wife of old William Steele], aged sixty-eight. William, Anne's brother, was sixty-three, though his second wife Martha was only forty-four. George Head, Philip Gibbs and Joseph Wakeford were in their fifties. Gay Thomas Attwater, his sisters Caroline Whitaker, and Marianne Head were all in their forties, as was Caroline's husband, Thomas Whitaker. Those in their twenties included Polly Steele, Jane Attwater, William Wakeford, James and Elizabeth Gibbs. Mary Wakeford was eighteen, Philip Whitaker thirteen, Anne Whitaker ten, William Steele's two girls, Anne nine and Martha eight. Besides these there could have been some of the Froude cousins from East Knoyle. As well as the family there would have been the whole Broughton congregation, many of whom had known Anne all her life and enjoyed singing her hymns in the Sunday services. Anne had lived just long enough to see the conclusion of the first pastorate at Broughton after her father's death, and see the beginning of the second pastorate. Mercifully she was spared from witnessing the doctrinal divisions which occurred in the pastorate of Josiah Lewis [1778-1788] and the decline in the Broughton Church from the days of prosperity in the years of persecution and the pastorates of

Henry and William Steele. Polly Steele suffered most in the death of Anne, as she had always been very close to her aunt and had nursed her in the six years at the end of her life in which Anne was confined to her bed. Polly, whom Anne had nurtured in her poetic ability, composed the verse which the village mason inscribed on the side of the family tomb in Broughton Parish Churchyard.

> 'Silent the lyre and dumb the tuneful tongue,
> That sung on earth her great Redeemer's praise,
> But now in heaven she joins the angelic song,
> In more harmonious, more exalted lays.'

Chapter 9

A Brother Beloved [1778-85]

After Anne's Death

William Steele survived his sister Anne by seven years, dying in 1785 at the age of seventy. Little contemporary evidence has survived for this period barring a few family letters and references in the Broughton Baptist Church Book. The family at *Broughton House* in these years consisted of William's second wife Martha, with his three daughters Mary [Polly], Anne and Martha. Also living with them was his wife's niece, Clarissa Goddard, and Lucy Kent, a cousin and companion of Polly. There would also have been various maids and men with jobs about the house or connected with the business, such as William Morant and John Dewy. Visitors included Myra Scott, Jane and Marianne Attwater, Amanda Froude, Patty Ash and others. Joseph Wakeford's family from Andover, including his son William and daughters Hannah and Mary were frequently at Broughton. The Steeles circle of friends, with whom they exchanged visits, included the Tomkins of Abingdon, the Evans of Bristol and the Ashes of Pershore.

Letters[207] from Dr. Caleb Evans to Polly are mainly concerned to offer help in Polly's downcast condition following the death of her aunt, to whom she had been so greatly attached. A letter[208] from Dr Turner of Abingdon was written with a similar intention and includes an invitation from the Tomkins family for the Steele family to visit them. Caleb Evans told her in a letter dated 12th December 1778 that he had preached on the Sunday after the death of Anne Steele from Anne's dying words, 'I know that my Redeemer liveth.' The Broughton Church Book records that in 1781 Clarissa Goddard [daughter of Samuel Goddard, Martha Steele's brother], was baptised and admitted as a member to the Broughton Baptist Church. Baptised with her at the same time was Mary Brice, one of John Kent's daughters and William Morant who worked for the Steeles. One of Polly's poems reveals that she had stayed with the Evans family at Bristol in 1782. A letter from Dr Evans written in the early years of the 1780s suggests that Polly should write another poem like *Danebury* and

---

[207] STE 5/16.

[208] ibid.

not leave her talents to 'waste their sweetness on the desert air.' The same letter shows that Polly had recently been staying with the Tomkins at Abingdon. It also reports that Thomas Whitaker, the husband of Caroline Whitaker had died at Bratton as had also Mrs Anna Attwater who had passed away on 8th April 1784. In a letter of Dr Evans written in 1785 he writes about the trouble Polly was having with her eyesight and two undated poems of Polly speak of this trouble, *The Increasing Defect of my Sight,*[209] and *Stanzas written when in Danger of Blindness.* This trouble, however, appears to have been only temporary as there is no further indication that Polly had any permanent eye condition.

The Steele Family Businesses

While the daily life went on in the home, William Steele would have been managing his twin businesses of the timber trade and farming, businesses which he had inherited from his father and in which he had worked all his life. Anne Steele had lived her life surrounded by a hive of activity. She and her stepmother had both at times complained about the constant activities and travels of William and his father. Old Mrs Steele disliked the constant absence of her husband and her stepson and worried about the dangers associated with their travels. Anne had felt that her father and her brother were too deeply involved in their business activities to the detriment of their family life. But the Puritan ethic of work was deeply engrained in the Steele family and from the days of old Henry Steele, who had founded the timber business and established contracts with the Admiralty and later invested his profits in farming, the family had prospered. Anne's brother William was the third generation of Steeles in the business. No doubt the village of Broughton had benefited, many of the villagers being employed in the family businesses. Also the Broughton Baptist Church had been liberally provided with funds by the family as well as with two very able pastors. William Steele, though never a minister himself, used to read sermons on a Sunday in the church when no minister was available. He also acted as secretary for the church and kept the Church Book and wrote up the minutes of the church meetings. While business was important in the family, the church and spiritual things were their primary concern. Old Mrs Steele's diary makes this quite clear, though it is a wonder how Henry Steele and William Steele senior managed their businesses and pastorates at the same time. It is evident that they led highly organized lives and made excellent use of their time.

---

[209] STE 5/5-5/7.

William Steele 1715-1785 in his youth

[Oil painting reproduced by permission of the owner]

Mary Steele (Polly) 1753-1813
daughter of William Steele IV and
Mary Steele [née Bullock] aged twenty-seven

[Oil painting 1780 reproduced by permission of the owner]

William Steele 1715-1785
(Oil painting 1780 reproduced by permission of the owner)

Martha Steele (née Goddard) 1734-1791
Second wife of William Steele IV
(Oil painting 1780 reproduced by permission of the owner)

Anne Steele 1769-1859
daughter of William Steele IV and Martha Steele
[née Goddard] aged eleven
[Oil painting reproduced by permission of the owner]

Martha Steele 1771-1834
daughter of William Steele IV and Martha Steele
[née Goddard] aged nine
[Oil painting reproduced by permission of the owner]

Broughton House and Farm [known as Pigeon Farm]
Painted about 1820, probably by Emma Tomkins [1796-1857] grand-daughter of William Steele IV.
The farm buildings will not have changed much between the death of Anne Steele in 1778 and 1820. The last surviving farm building, a Dutch barn, is visible in this oil painting [see also fig. 39]. Broughton House itself has, since 1778, been through several alterations.
[Reproduced by permission of the owner]

Broughton Village as seen from the Downs.
The larger part of the land, immediately beyond the village, was owned by the Steele Family.

The Timber Trade

In the last seven years of William's life the Steele businesses were at the height of their prosperity. Both William's great-great-grandfather [William I who built the family home *Grandfathers* and died in 1663] and his great-grandfather [William II who died in 1680] were carpenters and small farmers. His grandfather [Thomas I who died in 1708] was a house carpenter and small farmer and his grandfather's brother Henry [pastor of Broughton Baptist Church, who died in 1739] was a timber merchant and at the time of his death owned three farms. William's father [William III the next pastor, who died in 1769] was a timber merchant and owned several farms. As William Steele had worked in the timber trade with his Uncle Henry, so William, his son, had worked in the same business with him. It is clear that Henry Steele founded the timber business and started the Steele trade with the Admiralty in supplying timber for the building of warships. A letter[210] which William Steele III wrote to his first wife on 30th November 1714, about the time of her father's [Edward Froude] death spoke of Uncle Henry having gone to Portsmouth to contract. Letters[211] written by William III to his second wife at the time of their courtship in the spring of 1723 speak of his inability to come to Trowbridge to see her since he was in the process of purchasing timber to the total value of £1,900. William was working in conjunction with his uncle and purchasing large quantities of timber for which they had a ready market with the Navy Board. How or when Henry Steele established this contract is unknown.

The Navy Board had been constituted by Charles II in 1662 and handled the civil administration of the Navy until 1832. An early member of the Board was the diarist Samuel Pepys. It built and repaired ships, procured all necessary stores and equipment, kept reserve stocks and managed the Royal Dockyards at Chatham, Portsmouth and Plymouth. It was the largest commercial and industrial organisation of its time. It was under the Admiralty which was concerned with naval operations at sea. Since 1677 the Navy Board had used a system of public tender, advertising for supplies in the *London Gazette,* inviting bids, which were followed by negotiations in which the Navy Board tried to obtain the best supplies at the cheapest rate. This was followed by a contract between the supplier and the Navy Board which could extend for anything up to three or more years.[212] But up until 1720 the Navy Board had been notoriously behind with their payments and suppliers had often a hard time with their

---

[210] STE 1/2/x.

[211] STE 1/3.

[212] *Navy Contracts 1660-1832*, Bernard Pool (1966).

cash flow. Henry Steele had entered this market when things were difficult, but after 1720 the situation improved markedly and the Steeles were able to buy large quantities of oaks, knowing that they would get their money on time when they sold them to the Navy Board. Henry Steele died in 1739 and William Steele, his nephew, and young William, who was twenty-four at the time, took over the business.

Mrs Steele's surviving diaries record the sums that were spent on the purchase of oak trees in the years from 1736 to 1757. In total they amounted to £27,100.[213] The largest amount was £10,000 spent on timber in the Forest of Dean, just to the north of Portsmouth, bought from the Duke of Beaufort [the contract signed in Bath] and the smallest £100 spent on timber at Fordingbridge, a few miles away from Broughton. Another substantial amount of £6000 was purchased in 1749 at Petworth in Sussex. The principal sources of supply were the Royal Forests, the Forest of Dean, the New Forest, and the Alice Holt Forest[214], just north of Petworth. Also purchases were made from gentlemen with private estates. Sussex timber was markedly better than New Forest timber on account of the type of soil in which the trees grew. Most of the timber that the Steeles bought and sold had been planted at the time of the Restoration in 1660. The timber was sold in loads, which was usually one wagon containing one substantial tree [about 50 cubic feet of timber]. The Steeles sold principally to the Royal Dockyard at Portsmouth, though from various visits by William Steele IV to Plymouth, it might appear that they also traded with the Royal Dockyard there. The cost of transport was almost as much as the cost of the timber, but this cost was borne by the Navy Board, which also provided the labourers for felling the trees. The price paid by the Navy Board for one load varied from £3 to £4 depending on whether the wood was straight or curved. It took between two and three thousand loads to construct an average size warship of seventy to eighty guns. The timber could either be transported by road which was very slow and depended entirely on weather conditions, the maximum mileage being about twenty miles, or by sea if that were possible. If weather conditions were bad and the roads impassable it might take up to a year for a wagon [called a tugg] to reach its destination. Several teams of horse or oxen accompanied each tugg and worked in relays.[215]

The Steeles often visited Redbridge, a small port at the head of Southampton Water and it would appear that much of the timber they purchased around the Broughton area in such places as Whiteparish

---

[213] There is not a diary from 1736-49 so the figure could be much larger.

[214] *Forests and Sea Power1652-1862*, R. G. Albion, Harvard U. P. (1926), p.108.

[215] ibid. pp.103-5.

[£3,200], Redlynch [£4000], Fordingbridge [£100] and Langford [£900], as well as the New Forest, was ultimately shipped to Portsmouth via Redbridge. Timber felled in the New Forest was at such places as Bolder Wood, Castle Mal Wood, Eyeworth, Gad's Hill and Lady Cross. In fact in 1753 William IV had a ship built for himself at Redbridge, which was launched on the 31st August. It was obviously a merchant ship and was used to transport his own timber to Portsmouth, or other ship building yards such as Bursledon, Cowes or Buckler's Hard on the Beaulieu River. The ship, called 'The Willing Mind', disappeared in the English Channel in January 1758 during the Seven Years' War, and was almost certainly captured by the French when it was taking supplies to the English Fleet blockading the French coast.

Mrs Steele frequently records in her diary that William and his father had gone out to value timber, sometimes for two weeks at a time. Judging a standing tree was a fine art. Oak trees were slow growers and were not mature until about an hundred years old, when they would measure between fifteen and eighteen inches in diameter. John Evelyn, the English diarist, who died in 1706, wrote, 'A tree is a merchant adventurer; you shall never know what he is worth until he is dead.' Assessment would take into consideration dead branches, knot holes, the soil in which it had grown; tapping would be used for any hollow sound, but the whole assessment was not easy. A felled tree could be assessed much more easily. Smell, sight and sound were all employed in judging. It was unusual for a whole wood to be felled. Trees were selected individually and felled so as to do the least damage to those standing nearby.[216] The Steeles, judging by the successful nature of their business and its extent, would appear to have been experts in the field. In Mrs Steele's diary we read of several contracts which were not concluded. We read of visits to Wales across the Bristol Channel and other places but no timber was purchased. It was obviously not good enough. When the timber reached the dockyard it was assessed by inspectors and only the very best was used in the construction of the hulls of the warships. There were differences of opinion as to when it was best to fell the oaks, but generally they were felled in the spring. Timber merchants were essentially middlemen who bought and sold timber, buying the best and selling the best, contracting to buy and contracting to sell in an open competitive market, dictating to both sides and taking the principal profits. The Navy Board was not the only purchaser of timber. The East India Company regularly rebuilt ninety of their merchant ships every twelve years so there

[216] ibid. p.100.

was competition for the best timber and the price was kept up.[217] While the diary speaks of a timber yard at Broughton, it is clear that most of the timber went straight from the woods to the dockyard. It is possible that when the warships were repaired or scrapped the old timber might have come back to Broughton and been sold for house building. An uncle of William Steele III lived at Portsmouth and died there in 1751. His sister was William III's mother and it seems that he managed the Portsmouth end of the Steele timber business with the aid of a foreman, Frank Wade mentioned in Mrs Steele's diary. Frank Wade was the son-in-law of one of the deacons at the Broughton Church. He lived at Horndean and died there in 1758. William Steele IV went down to Portsmouth in December that year and brought his widow Betty Wade back to Broughton.

The building programmes of the Navy Board were largely dictated by the occurrence of wars or the threat of them. The end of the seventeenth century saw three Dutch Wars and the rise of Louis XIV in France and the development of a substantial French navy. This led in 1677 to a grant by Parliament of £600,000 and a building programme of thirty warships. When war broke out with France in 1689, Parliament voted £750,000 for the building of thirty warships. Twelve were built in the Royal Dockyards, but because of the urgency, eighteen were built by contract in merchant yards at Bursledon, Southampton and Shoreham. When the war of the Spanish Succession [1701-1713] broke out in 1708, five more warships were built for the Fleet. Between 1715 and 1750 the Navy Board largely concentrated on repairs, refits and replacement of old ships. When the Seven Years' War broke out in 1756 a large programme of building took place, with upward of fifty warships of sixty guns being built.[218] When the Steeles bought £15,900 of timber between 1751 and 1757 they knew there was a ready market for it and it is no surprise, as previously mentioned, that they took a great interest in the battles and events of that war. HMS *Victory* [with eleven sister ships] was in fact commissioned on 13th December 1758 and launched at Chatham in May 1765. She had one hundred and four guns and was a ship of over twenty thousand tons. The Navy Board usually kept a three-year stock of timber in the dockyards and reckoned that the proper time for seasoning was three and a half years. But in the hasty building that accompanied the Seven Years' War, unseasoned timber was used, which resulted in heavy costs and repairs during the American War of Independence between 1775 and 1783. The Navy found themselves with a large number of rotting ships and this resulted in a further eight warships being built in merchant

[217] *Royal Dockyards*, Roger Morriss (1983), p.88.
[218] *Navy Contracts (1660-1832)*, Bernard Pool (1966).

shipyards in 1779.[219] Thus there was a constant market for the Steele timber and as a result they became exceptionally prosperous as a family. As already mentioned, William Steele lost a little son when only three weeks old in 1772 and had no heir to take over the timber business. His daughter Polly eventually inherited most of his estate in 1785 and there is no indication that she tried to carry on the timber business. It would seem that some time in his lifetime William Steele ceased trading in timber and closed the business down, a business which had been in the family for at least seventy years, since his great-uncle Henry started it prior to 1714.

Land and Farming

The origins of the farming business and the beginnings of the landed estate are not so easy to trace. When William Steele I died in 1663 his estate was valued at twenty-seven pounds, and when his son William Steele II died in 1680 his estate was valued at fifty-five pounds. But when William II's son Thomas died in 1708, his estate was valued at one

Figure 39: Dutch Barn beside 'Broughton House'

thousand pounds of which five hundred and ninety pounds was in cash legacies. Thomas was the brother of Henry Steele and grandfather of Anne Steele. It would seem that he was working in the timber trade in

[219] ibid.

conjunction with his brother as well as having some landed estate. When Henry died in 1739 he left a substantial estate, which included five hundred and eighty pounds in cash legacies, plus three farms in Broughton, Over Wallop and Freefolk Priors near Whitchurch. The indications are that both Henry and Thomas were prospering in the timber trade and their contracts with the Navy Board and that they were investing their profits in land. Anne Steele's father and her brother William both followed in this line and successfully ran two separate businesses. When Henry Steele died he had no male heir and while his farms went to his three grandsons, it would appear that his part in the timber trade passed directly to his nephew William Steele III.

The money accruing from the timber trade was invested in land and property and when William Steele III died in 1769, he left cash legacies of two thousand two hundred and twenty pounds as well a substantial amount of land in Broughton, which included the Manor of Roake, and other land at Trowle Common, Trowbridge, which had been the property of his second wife, and land at Sedgehill which he had purchased from the brothers of his first wife. Some of the land he farmed himself, but some was let to tenant farmers. The bulk of his estate went to his son William IV but some of it went to Anne and some to his grandson William Steele Wakeford, who worked with his father in the Wakeford's Bank in Andover, which their family owned. *Grandfathers* was left to Anne but then passed to William Steele Wakeford [the son of her half-sister, Molly] in 1778 when she died. At a later date William bought it back from William Steele Wakeford. After his father's death William owned Pigeon House Farm, Godfreys Farm [with land in Broughton, East Tytherley and Lockerley], Goddards Farm, land in the Manor of Roake and the local mill, all in Broughton. He also had a farm at Nether Wallop, an estate at Halstock in Dorset, [which had come to him through his first wife], an estate at Roydon near Brockenhurst [which he owned from 1758-1771], and land at Sedgehill. In 1758, when he acquired Pigeon House Farm [having rented it since his marriage about 1749], he converted the farmhouse into a gentleman's Georgian residence and renamed it *Broughton House*. Like his father he farmed some of the land himself but let some of it to tenant farmers. When he died in 1785 he bequeathed the bulk of his estate to Polly, the daughter of his first wife. He left *Grandfathers* to his widow, Martha Steele. Polly married Thomas Dunscombe about 1790 at the time of the enclosure of the common land of Broughton. Being a substantial owner of land in Broughton, the Steele estate was awarded four hundred and seventy-nine acres of common land. At the time of Polly's death in 1813 the estate passed to her half-sister Anne who had married Joseph Tomkins of Abingdon in 1792. A map of the field system prior to the Enclosure Award of 1790[220], and the Broughton Tithe map of 1837[221] in the time of Joseph Tomkins, give an idea of the acreage of the Steele estate. The 1837 Tithe Award shows the Steele estate in Broughton to be about eight hundred and fifty acres. This would suggest that the original estate in Broughton owned by William at the time of his death in 1785 was about three hundred and seventy acres, but this did not include land at East Tytherley, Lockerley, Nether Wallop, Halstock, Roydon and Sedgehill. William was a substantial landowner and minor country gentleman.

Mrs Steele's diary[222] from 1730-1736 and 1749-1760 gives a detailed account of farming and weather conditions in the period. The Steeles were mostly arable farmers, while keeping a substantial flock of sheep on the down common land around Broughton. They also had some cows and many working and riding horses. Annually they attended [often the whole family, including Anne] the sheep fair at Weyhill, near Andover. This fair took place yearly on 29th September and witnessed the sale of up to one hundred and forty thousand sheep in a single day. It would appear that the lambs of the current year were sold at this time, while ewes and rams were bought for the flock at Broughton. On 14th July 1730 Mrs Steele wrote in her diary, 'A distemper is come into this place amongst the cattle, namely the murain, there being a great many pigs dead in it and about seven cows, one of them being ours.' It is not clear what 'the murain' was. Since the Steeles lost only one cow it seems unlikely to have been foot and mouth disease, but it may have been swine fever among the pigs and some other infection among the cattle, such as New Forest cattle disease [which caused kidney failure] and could have been brought in by an animal coming from the Forest to the village. The sheep were generally sheared in June and Mrs Steele mentions that in March 1751 nine of their sheep were killed by dogs, presumably at the time of the lambing season. The crops that were grown on their land included wheat, barley, oats and hay. The ground was manured and sown in April, depending on weather conditions. Hay came in at the end of June and beginning of July, though in the years 1751, 1752 and 1756 there was very wet weather and much of the hay lay ruined in the fields. In 1735 and 1751 hayricks were struck by lightening and set alight. Wheat harvest usually began in the last week of July, and in August 1756 Mrs Steele records that fifty acres were mown in a single day. This would have been by scythe [there were no mechanical mowing machines until the mid-

220 HRO. LA076651/97/06.

221 HRO. 2/M65/f7/36/1.

222 ALRPC STE 2/1/1-3.

nineteenth century] with the women and boys following the men as they mowed, binding the corn into sheaves and stacking them. It indicates that the Steeles must have had a considerable labour force at their disposal. Mrs Steele records that the family, including Anne, often rode out to the fields on their horses at harvest time. Sometimes when the weather was very bad, which it was in 1756, Mrs Steele records that the wheat had grown out in the stooks. The barley and oats came in at the end of August and beginning of September. On 10th September 1756 Mrs Steele records, 'Mr Steele is very busy in directing the work-folk in getting in the oats and barley, of which there is a plentiful crop, blessed be God.' All barns were built across the prevailing winds, which were south-west, and had two doors opposite each other in the centre. The doors were opened in the threshing season, the corn was beaten with flails and the wind was allowed to separate the grain and the chaff. As the Steeles owned the mill on the River Wallop, just downstream from *Grandfathers,* it would seem that they milled their own wheat and sold their flour locally.

Broughton Weather – Mid -Eighteenth Century

Mrs Steele refers to two great tempests at Broughton in January 1735 and September 1752. In the first some of their barns were badly damaged and in the second most of the fruit in the orchards was blown down, with extensive damage on land and sea. She records a huge storm in June 1753 with thunder and lightening, and at Downton a spectacular hailstorm which broke windows and destroyed whole fields of wheat and peas. Unusually fine years for harvest occurred in 1730, 1749, 1754, and 1757-1759. Exceptionally wet years occurred only in 1751, 1753 and 1756. Otherwise the weather was mixed, with alternate wet and fine spells. Mrs Steele mentions severe winters, when her husband and his son often rode out on business in deep snow. On occasions she refers to snow as late as March and April at Broughton. Equally she mentions exceptionally hot summers. She refers to extreme heat in the summer of 1757, and says the heat was burdensome in 1759. All in all, in the period of her diary, which runs for seventeen years, between 1730 and 1760, the weather appears to have been little different from the present day, and the Steeles must have found that their losses and gains spread themselves out over the years, so that what they lost on one crop they gained on another. Their twin roles as timber merchant and farmer brought them considerable prosperity, and shows Anne Steele writing her poetry, and enduring her ill health at the home at *Grandfathers,* while surrounded by the beauties of the countryside about her and watching the businesses of her father and her brother prosper.

The Death of William Steele Junior 1785

One of the great sadnesses of William Steele must have been the death of his son in 1772 when only a few weeks old. As he approached the end of his working life he had no heir to take over his businesses. His immediate heir was his oldest daughter Polly [born in 1753], the child of his first wife, Mary, née Bullock. Thereafter followed the daughters of his second marriage, children of Martha, née Goddard, Anne [born in 1769] and Martha [born in 1770]. His second wife was about twenty years younger than himself. William wrote out a draft will on 6th October 1785, but did not sign it nor have it witnessed. He felt it was wise to settle his estate, though obviously he did not have any sense of urgency. He had been a strong and active man all his life and excepting for attacks of gout, had had little ill-health. But as he grew older, and reached the allotted span of life, he was still carrying the burdens of two substantial businesses, including estate and property, not only locally in Broughton, but also in Wiltshire and Dorset, and he had no one to help him, or take over from him. Added to which he had responsibilities in the Broughton Baptist Church and was a trustee of Brown Street Baptist Church, Salisbury, as well as following in the steps of his father and watching over Bere Street Baptist Church, Whitchurch, and the daughter churches of Broughton at Downton, Lockerley, Winterslow and Ben Street, Nether Wallop. While he was busy and active, he had little apprehension in 1785 that his strength was giving way. The pastor of Broughton Baptist Church, Josiah Lewis, said at his funeral that while 'he appeared to those about him to be in decline, his dissolution was not apprehended to be so near... death made his advances upon him with great speed... and in a few days pulled down his constitution, which had the appearance of health and vigour.' Sometime during the second week of December 1785 he suffered a stroke and went unconscious. Josiah Lewis said at his funeral that 'the first day or two after his seizure... a veil appeared to be drawn over his mind, but he soon regained lucidity which he kept to the end.' He went on to say that 'the Saturday before he died... he prayed with great earnestness and fervour and with much propriety.' Gradually 'sinking under the decays of nature, he fell gently asleep in Jesus, the twenty-first instant, in the seventy-first year of his age'. His daughter Polly, writing to her friend Myra Scott of Milbourne Port confirmed the details of her father's last days and that he died on 21st December 1785.

His Will

His sudden death must have been a great shock to his wife and children. His widow was only fifty-one at the time, Polly was thirty-two, and his two younger daughters Anne and Martha were sixteen and fifteen respectively. Now upon the shoulders of his widow and Polly fell the responsibility for the management of his extensive estate. After his funeral his will, unsigned and not witnessed, had to be attested before a lawyer by his nephew William Steele Wakeford and by Thomas Warner of Romsey, as being 'all of the proper handwriting of the said William Steele deceased'. It demonstrates the unexpected nature of his death, both for himself and his family, and shows that the will was more of a draft than a completed document. In his will William Steele fails to mention his youngest daughter Martha except in a reference to his 'said wife and three daughters,' nothing is said about the residue of his estate or of any 'household goods', and there is no mention of any cash legacies. In fact he had only outlived his sister Anne [who was two years younger than he] by seven years and had not reached anywhere near the age of his father and great-uncle Henry, who both lived to be eighty. His will was proved in London on 9th March 1786 in the Prerogative Court of Canterbury [Prob. 11/1140], his widow and eldest daughter being declared his executrixes.

He left *Grandfathers* to his widow Martha for the term of her life. [After Anne's death in 1778 it had reverted according to her father's will to the Wakeford family, but William Steele had bought it back from them.] He also left her, for the term of her widowhood, his freehold and copyhold land in Nether Wallop in the occupation of Abraham Tanner. He left her an annuity of sixty pounds, to be paid half-yearly during her natural life issuing out of his real estate in Broughton [called Godfreys and Goddards Farms, and the Manor and Farm of Roake] and also his estate at Sedgehill, Wilts. To his eldest daughter Polly, he left *Broughton House* with its office buildings, gardens and land [called Pigeon House Farm], also his farm and lands called Godfreys Farm, situated in the parishes of Broughton, Tytherley and Lockerley, also his farm and lands called Goddards Farm, all of which were in the occupation of himself, Thomas Chandler, Solomon Sutherill and Josiah Kent. [This shows that he was still farming at the time of his death, though most of his estate was let to tenant farmers.] Also he gave to Polly the house and garden adjoining the Broughton Parish Churchyard [a lovely Georgian residence, obviously tenanted]. Further Polly inherited his estate at Halstock in Dorset, which had come to him through her mother. All the rest of his property, which included his Manor of Roak, with farm lands, and rents; a property adjoining *Grandfathers* including stables, and all his estate called Broughton Mill with land and buildings, he left in trust to his widow and Polly 'to apply the same in the maintenance, clothing and education of his beloved daughter Anne Steele until she attain the age of twenty-one years, or until she be married with the approbation of her mother'.

Josiah Lewis in his funeral address said of him, 'Our dear and honoured friend deceased was greatly indebted by providence and grace for many advantages which enabled him to fill up the character he sustained among us with reputation, comfort and usefulness. He was a man of good natural parts, of great humility of mind, and of so affable and cheerful a temper, as while it made him accessible to all sorts of persons, rendered his usefulness the more extensive, and could not but engage the esteem and affection of those that knew him.' Selina Anne Bompas, his great-granddaughter, who died at Cambridge in 1921 at the age of ninety, and who knew her grandmother [William's daughter Anne] well, spoke of him 'as a fine person in his upright and Christian character and superior mind'. Like his forebears, his life centred around the Baptist Church at Broughton, and none really knew the extent of his generosity. Selina Anne Bompas copied the inscription of his grave at a time when it was legible. Composed by Polly, it read;

'How lov'd ! how honour'd ! words can ne'er impart
Nor speak the loss of many a bleeding heart;
All, all that life ennobles and endears,
In memory's weeping eye in him appears,
Tenderest of fathers, husbands! Every name
Duty can dictate or affection frame;
The guide, the refuge still of the distressed,
Whose bliss arose from making others blest.
In life in death may thy example be
Our guide to heaven and happiness and Thee.'

Nearby on the grave of his little son William, born on 16th July and dying on 18th August 1772 was the verse:

'So fades the lovely blooming flower,
Frail smiling solace of an hour;
So soon our transient comforts fly,
And pleasure only blooms to die."

Had he lived, the boy would have been thirteen when his father died. No doubt the verse was the composition of his sorrowing father. Martha Steele only survived her husband by six years, dying on 31st May 1791 aged fifty-seven. On her grave was the Scripture, 'And God shall wipe away all tears from their eyes; and there shall be no more death, neither sorrow, nor crying, neither shall there be any more pain: for the former things are passed away.' [Revelation 21. 4].

Epilogue

When their mother died in 1791, the three daughters were left to run the family estate and live together at *Broughton House.* It was a big responsibility for Polly, who was thirty-eight at the time, while Anne was twenty-two and Martha twenty-one, hardly old enough to share much of the responsibility. Within eighteen months of her mother's death, on 19th December 1792 Anne married Joseph Tomkins and went to live at Oakley House near Abingdon and so left Polly and Martha alone. [Anne Tomkins' first child Mary Steele Tomkins was born in 1793. She married Charles Carpenter Bompas in 1822, and it is down this line that the Steele family traces its descent to the present day.] In 1795 Polly was baptised and joined the Broughton Church. Her aunt's prayers had finally been answered for her. She was forty-two at the time and was baptised by William Steadman the pastor of Broughton Church at the time. Writing in his journal[223] for 29th March 1795 he says, 'Miss Steele came before the Church; her narrative was read as she could not express herself verbally to her own satisfaction. We were all much affected and received her very cordially. Her sentiments on the divine decrees and the freedom of the human will are not so clear as those of some; she has thought much and very painfully about them, but is nearly in a state of equilibrium respecting both sides of the question. She discovered a mind greatly open to conviction and deeply impressed with the fear of God; her hope is wholly founded upon the mercy of God through Christ but her comfort is very little; I feel fully satisfied we did right in receiving her.' In the following year 1796, John Kent, the long-lived servant of Broughton Church, whose service reached back to the days of the first pastor, Henry Steele, died at the age of eighty-nine. Born ten years before Anne Steele, in 1707 he had watched her whole life and that of her brother William.

In January 1797 Polly married Thomas Dunscombe [1749-1810], a Baptist minister.[224] He had come from Tiverton in Devon, from the same church as John Rippon [1750-1836]. He was a student of Bristol Baptist College. He was ordained at Cote, Oxon, on 4th August 1773. Hugh Evans [1713-81] preached and Caleb Evans [1737-91], his son, gave the charge. Present at the service were Benjamin Francis of Shortwood, Nailsworth, Daniel Turner of Abingdon and his old college friend John Rippon. On this day he began a pastorate of twenty-five years. At the time he was twenty-four. During the years that followed he established new churches at Buckland and Bampton close to Cote, where chapels were built. He also restored the church at Faringdon and assisted a new

[223] Memoir of Rev. William Steadman DD p. 127.
[224] Baptist Quarterly Vol. XVI No. 7 July 1956 p.328.

struggling church at Oxford. As a single man he devoted his whole life to the work of the ministry. In 1792 he received the M.A. degree from Rhode Island College, America. When he married Mary Steele [Polly], he was nearly fifty years old and was coming to the end of his pastorate. It appears that both Anne and Martha, Polly's two half-sisters, were very much against the marriage, though the reason is not clear. Polly was forty-four at the time and it is clear from a letter to her half-sister Anne that the early years of her marriage were far from happy. She and her husband had gone to live at Yeovil the home town of her mother. His health does not appear to have been good, which may have been the reason why he gave up his pastorate at Cote. Anne, her half-sister, writing to her at Yeovil in January 1799 said, 'I read with tender regret that sentence of your letter, which related to your union with Mr D—. It is a melancholy picture to behold life wearing away in toilsome care and vain regrets.' The later years of their married life appear to have been happier, though they never had any children. They appear to have returned to live at *Broughton House* at least by 1802. He died at Faringdon on 4th October 1811 aged sixty-three. Polly died at Broughton on 14th November 1813 at the age of sixty and lies buried in the parish churchyard there.

The Broughton estate now came into the possession of Anne and Martha. Anne had initially lived with her family at Oakley House, near Abingdon, but a letter from Polly[225] to her dated 24th October 1805, shows that she had moved to Malpas, near Newport in Wales. A letter[226] which Anne wrote to Polly on 8th January 1808 shows that the Tomkins family were again on the move, looking for a house in Bath, possibly to rent. A letter from Polly to Anne dated 13th September shows them living at 9 Grosvenor Place, Bath. There a boy, William Steele Tomkins, was born in 1808, two previous boys having died in infancy. The Tomkins family then left Bath and lived at Southampton for a time before they returned to Broughton. The Broughton Tithe Award for 1837 shows Joseph Tomkins paying tithes on 836 acres of land. He died in 1847 at the age of eighty-four and Anne lived on another twelve years at Broughton in her widowhood, dying at the great age of ninety in 1859. She was the last of the Steele family to be born a Steele. Her sister Martha had predeceased her, dying in 1834 at the age of sixty. So by 1834 Anne and her husband were in sole possession of the Steele estate in Broughton. When Joseph Tomkins died in 1847 the Broughton estate passed to his son William Steele Tomkins I. At the time of his death in 1855

---

[225] STE 5/11/v.

[226] STE 5/11/xiii.

Broughton House was sold. But William Steele Tomkins' son William Steele Tomkins II bought it back in 1898 and lived there until his death in 1930 at the age of ninety-three. *Grandfathers* had come into the possession of the Bompas family, the last surviving member being Nita Bompas who died in 1970, when it was sold. At that time the family oil paintings and Anne Steele's writing desk were still to be seen in the house. Thus there remained a connection with the Steeles in Broughton as recently as 1970.

Figure 40: Anne Tomkins in her Old Age

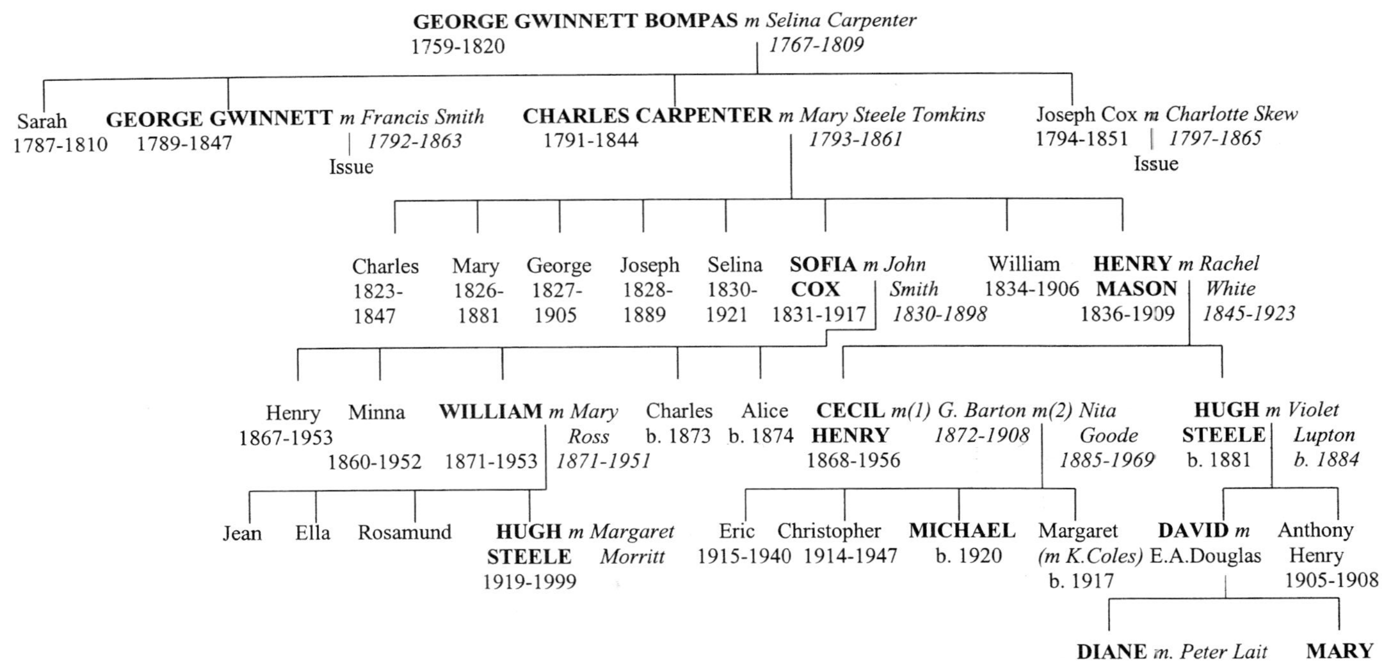

Figure 41: The Bompas Family Tree

Index

Bibliography

Primary Sources

Steele, Anne, *Poems on Subjects Chiefly Devotional* by Theodosia, 2 vols., 1st Edition, 1760.

Steele, Anne, *Poems on Subjects Chiefly Devotional* by Theodosia, 2 vols., 2nd Edition, 1780.

Steele, Anne, *Miscellaneous Pieces in Verse and Prose* by Theodosia, 1780, including a brief biography by Rev. Caleb Evans [1737-1791] of Bristol Baptist Academy.

Steele, Anne, The Works of Miss Anne Steele complete in Two Volumes comprehending Poems on Subjects Chiefly Devotional and Miscellaneous Pieces in Prose and Verse, heretofore published under the title of Theodosia, Boston, U.S.A, 1808.

Steele, Anne, *Hymns, Psalms & Poems* with Memoir by John Sheppard, published by Daniel Sedgwick, 1863.

Steele, Anne, *Hymns by Anne Steele* with Memoir by J.R.Broome, Gospel Standard Baptist Trust, 1967.

Angus Library, Regent's Park College, Oxford.

Diaries: *Diaries of Anne [Cator] Steele,* vol. 2 [13 July 1730 - 8 Feb. 1736]; vol. 4 [Jan. 1749-Dec 1752]; vol. 5 [Jan 1753 - 23 June 1760].

Letters: *Anne Steele, William Steele III, Anne [Froude] Steele, Anne [Cator] Steele, Mary Steele [Polly], Mary Wakeford, William Steele IV.*

Sermons: William Steele III 1710-1769.

Church Books: *Broughton Particular Baptist Church Books* 1655 onwards.

Late Dr Marjorie Reeves' Collection, Angus Library, Regent's Park College, Oxford.

Sermons of Richard Gay.

Diary of Jane Attwater.

Letters of Caroline Whitaker, John Gay, Richard Gay junior, and Anne Steele.

Family Records of the Whitakers.

Wiltshire & Swindon Record Office, Trowbridge, Wilts.
Wills, Presentments, Quarter Session Records, Parish Registers, Church Books.
Wiltshire Meeting House Certificates 1689-1852, Edited by J.H. Chandler, Wiltshire Record Society, Vol. XL, 1984.
Andrew's & Dury's Map of Wiltshire 1773, Wiltshire Record Society, Vol. VIII, 1952.

Hampshire Record Office, Winchester, Hants
Wills, Parish Registers, Wakeford Family Records, Enclosure Records, Broughton Tithe Award 1837.

Confessions of Faith
1596 English Separatist Confession.
1646 First Particular Baptist London Confession [2nd Edition] with Appendix by Benjamin Cox.
1647 The Westminster Confession of Faith.
1658 The Savoy Declaration.
1689 Particular Baptist Confession of Faith.

Secondary Sources

Albion, R.G., *Forests and Sea Power – The Timber Problem of the Royal Navy 1652-1862,* Harvard University Press, Cambridge, Mass. 1926.
Ashley, Maurice, *England in the Seventeenth Century,* Penguin Books, 1952.
Ashley Smith, J.W., *The Birth of Modern Education, The Contribution of the Dissenting Academies 1660-1800,* Independent Press Ltd. 1966.
Baptist Historical Society, vol. 1, No. 1, pp. 56-61, 1908, *Porton Baptist Church 1655-1685*, by Arthur Tucker.
Baptist Magazine, 1810, *Obituary of Nathaniel Rawlings.*
Baptist Quarterly, vol. I, No. 5, Jan. 1923, *Early Baptists in Hampshire,* by W.T.Whitley.
Baptist Quarterly, vol. XVI, No.7, pp.328, July 1956, *Ordination of Rev. Thomas Dunscombe at Cote, Oxon, 1773.*
Baptist Quarterly, vol. XXIV, No. 4, October 1971, *Caleb Evans, Minister of Broadmead Baptist Church, Bristol 1781-1791*, by Norman S. Moon.
Baptist Quarterly, vol. XXXII, No. 7, July 1988, *Anne Steele's Health, a Modern Diagnosis,* Dr M.F. Dixon and Hugh F. Steele-Smith.

Baptist Quarterly, vol. XXXVII, 1998, pp. 367-385, *Richard Gay of Haycombe,* by Kerry J. Birch.
Baugh, David, Edited by, *Naval Administration 1715- 1750,* 1977.
Benson, Louis, *The English Hymn*, 1915.
Bogue, David & Bennett, James, History of Dissenters from the Revolution to the year 1838, 3 vols., London, 1833-1839.
Bradby, Edward, *The Book of Devizes, Barracuda Books Ltd,* 1985.
Brown, Raymond, *The English Baptists of the 18th Century,* Baptist Historical Society, 1986.
Cawley, Richard J., *The History, Life and Theology of the Old Baptist Church, Devizes 1645-1963.* Unpublished Doctoral Thesis, 1999.
Chandler, John, *Salisbury, History and Guide,* Alan Sutton, 1992.
Cook, Faith, *Selina, Countess of Huntingdon*, Banner of Truth Trust, 2001.
Compton, Edward, *A History of the Baptist Church, Broughton, Hampshire,* Leicester, 1878.
Crosby, Thomas, *The History of the English Baptists,* 4 vols., London, 1788-1790.
Dictionary of National Biography.
Downes, Kerry, *The Georgian Cities of Britain,* Phaidon, Oxford, 1979.
Doel, William, *Twenty Golden Candlesticks*, London, 1890.
Dallimore, Arnold, A., *George Whitefield*, 2 vols., Banner of Truth Trust, 1970, 1980.
Davis, Arthur Paul, *Isaac Watts*, Independent Press Ltd., 1948.
Ella, George A., *James Hervey, Preacher of Righteousness,* Go Publications, 1997.
Gadd, David, *Georgian Summer, The Rise and Development of Bath*, Moonraker Press, 1987.
Green, John Richard, *A Short History of the English People*, Macmillan & Co. Ltd., 1902.
Hayden, Roger, Edited by, *The Records of a Church of Christ in Bristol, 1640-1687*, Bristol Record Society, 1974.
Hall, C. Sidney & Harry Mowvley, *Tradition and Challenge, The Story of Broadmead Baptist Church Bristol from 1685-1991,* publ., Broadmead Baptist Church, Bristol, 1991.
Haykin, Michael A.G., *The British Particular Baptists 1638-1910,* 3 vols., Particular Paptist Press, Missouri, U.S.A., 1998-2003
Ivimey, Joseph, *History of the English Baptists*, 4 vols., 1811.
Julian, John, *A Dictionary of Hymnology*, John Murray, London, 1908.
Lyon Turner, G., *The Early Hampshire Baptists*, 1911.
Macmillan, Donald D., *Great Furniture Styles 1660-1830*, Paul Hamlyn, London, 1965.

Manning, Bernard, L., *The Hymns of Wesley and Watts*, The Epworth Press, London, 1954.
Neal, Daniel, *The History of the Puritans*, 4 vols., London, 1732-1738.
Oliver, Robert, *Baptist Confession Making 1644-1689*, Lecture to Strict Baptist Historical Society, 1989.
Parr, Robert & Baron, Sewter, *Broughton in Hampshire*, publ., Broughton Local History Group, 1990.
Plumb, J.H., *England in the Eighteenth Century*, Penguin Books, 1950.
Pool, Bernard, *Navy Contracts 1660-1832*, 1966.
Ramsbottom, Benjamin A., *Stranger Than Fiction, The Life of William Kiffin,* Gospel Standard Trust Publications, 1989.
Reeves , Marjorie, *Sheep Bell and Ploughshare, the Story of Two Village Families*, Moonraker Press, 1978.
Reeves, Marjorie, *Pursuing the Muses, Female Education and Nonconformist Culture 1700-1900,* Leicester University Press, 1997.
Reeves, Marjorie, *History of Bratton Baptist Church 1662-1692,* 1962.
Rippon, John, *The Baptist Annual Register 1790-1793.*
Rogers, Kenneth H., *Wiltshire and Somerset Woollen Mills*, Pasold Research Fund Ltd., 1976.
Rogers, Kenneth H., *The Book of Trowbridge*, Barracuda Books Ltd., 1984.
Rogers, Kenneth H., *Warp and Weft, The Somerset and Wiltshire Woollen Industry,* Barracuda Books Ltd., 1986.
Sparkes, Ivan, *English Domestic Furniture 1100-1837*, Spurbooks Ltd., 1980.
Steadman, Thomas, *Memoir of The Rev. William Steadman, D.D.*, 1838.
Trevelyan, George Macaulay, *History of England*, Longmans, Green & Co., 1926.
Trevelyan, George Macaulay, *English Social History*, Longmans, Green & Co., 1945.
Victoria County History of Wiltshire, vol. III, 1956, pp. 99-149, *Protestant Nonconformity* by Dr Marjorie Reeves.
Watson, J. Steven, *The Reign of George III 1760-1815,* Oxford, 1960.
White, B.R., *The English Baptists of the Seventeenth Century*, The Baptist Historical Society, 1996.
Whitley, W.T., *A History of British Baptists,* London, 1923.
Young, Robert H., *The History of Baptist Hymnody in England 1612-1800,* part of unpublished Doctoral Dissertation, University of South Carolina, U.S.A., June 1959.

PART II

Hymns of Anne Steele[1]

1 Hymns, Poems & Psalms by Anne Steele, London 1863. pp. 1-156.

HYMN 1

Desiring to praise God.

1 ALMIGHTY Author of my frame,
To thee my vital powers belong;
Thy praise (delightful, glorious theme!)
Demands my heart, my life, my tongue.

2 My heart, my life, my tongue are thine;
Oh be thy praise their blest employ!
But may my song with angels' join?
Nor sacred awe forbid the joy?

3 Thy glories, the seraphic lyre
On all its strings attempts in vain;
Then how shall mortals dare aspire
In thought, to try th' unequal strain?

4 Yet the great Sovereign of the skies
To mortals bends a gracious ear;
Nor the mean tribute will despise,
If offer'd with a heart sincere.

5 Great God, accept the humble praise,
And guide my heart, and guide my tongue,
While to thy name I trembling raise
The grateful, though unworthy song.

HYMN 2

Imploring Divine Influence.

1 MY God, whene'er my longing heart
The praiseful tribute would impart,
In vain my tongue with feeble aim,
Attempts the glories of thy name.

2 In vain my boldest thoughts arise,
I sink to earth and lose the skies;
Yet I may still thy grace implore,
And low in dust thy name adore.

3 O let thy grace my heart inspire,
And raise each languid, weak desire;
Thy grace, which condescends to meet
The sinner prostrate at thy feet.

4 With humble fear let love unite,
And mix devotion with delight;
Then shall thy name be all my joy,
Thy praise my constant, blest employ.

5 Thy name inspires the harps above
With harmony, and praise, and love;
That grace which tunes th' immortal strings,
Looks kindly down on mortal things.

6 O let thy grace guide every song,
And fill my heart and tune my tongue;
Then shall the strain harmonious flow,
And heaven's sweet work begin below.

HYMN 3

Meditating on Creation and Providence.

1 LORD, when my raptur'd thought surveys
Creation's beauties o'er,
All nature joins to teach thy praise,
And bid my soul adore.

2 Where'er I turn my gazing eyes,
Thy radiant footsteps shine;
Ten thousand pleasing wonders rise,
And speak their source divine.

3 The living tribes of countless forms,
In earth, and sea, and air;
The meanest flies, the smallest worms,
Almighty power declare.

4 All rose to life at thy command,
And wait their daily food
From thy paternal, bounteous hand,
Exhaustless spring of good!

5 The meads, array'd in smiling green,
With wholesome herbage crown'd;
The fields with corn, a richer scene,
Spread thy full bounties round.

6 The fruitful tree, the blooming flower,
In varied charms appear;
Their varied charms display thy power,
Thy goodness all declare.

7 The sun's productive, quickening beams,
The growing verdure spread;
Refreshing rains and cooling streams
His gentle influence aid.

8 The moon and stars his absent light
Supply with borrowed rays,
And deck the sable veil of night,
And speak their Maker's praise.

9 Thy wisdom, power, and goodness, Lord,
In all thy works appear;
And O, let man thy praise record;
Man, thy distinguish'd care.

10 From thee the breath of life he drew;
That breath thy power maintains;
Thy tender mercy ever new,
His brittle frame sustains.

11 Yet nobler favours claim his praise,
Of reason's light possest;
By revelation's brighter rays
Still more divinely blest.

12 Thy providence, his constant guard
When threatening woes impend,
Or will th' impending dangers ward,
Or timely succours lend.

13 On me that providence has shone
With gentle, smiling rays;
O let my lips and life make known
Thy goodness and thy praise.

14 All bounteous Lord, thy grace impart;
O teach me to improve
Thy gifts with ever grateful heart,
And crown them with thy love.

HYMN 4

Redeeming Love.

1 COME, heavenly love, inspire my song
With thy immortal flame,
And teach my heart, and teach my tongue
The Saviour's lovely name.

2 The Saviour! O what endless charms
Dwell in the blissful sound!
Its influence every fear disarms,
And spreads sweet comfort round.

3 Here pardon, life, and joys divine
In rich effusion flow,
For guilty rebels lost in sin,
And doomed to endless woe.

4 In our first parent's crime we fell;
Our blood, our vital breath,
Deep ting'd with all the seeds of ill,
Sad heirs to sin and death.

5 Black o'er our wrath-devoted heads
Avenging justice frown'd;
While hell disclos'd her deepest shades
And horrors rose around.

6 Wrapt in the gloom of dark despair,
We helpless, hopeless lay:
But sovereign mercy reached us there,
And smil'd despair away.

7 God's only Son (stupendous grace!)
Forsook his throne above;
And swift to save our wretched race,
He flew on wings of love.

8 Th' Almighty former of the skies
Stoop'd to our vile abode;
While angels view'd with wondering eyes,
And hailed th' incarnate God.

9 The God in heavenly strains they sung,
Array'd in human clay;
Mysterious love! what angel tongue
Thy wonders can display?

10 Mysterious love, in every scene,
Through all his life appears:
His spotless life expos'd to pain
And miseries and tears.

11 What blessings on a thankless race
His bounteous hand bestow'd!
And from his tongue what wondrous grace,
What rich instruction flow'd!

12 The dumb, the deaf, the lame, the blind
Confess'd his healing power;
Disease and death their prey resign'd,
And grief complain'd no more.

13 Infernal legions trembling fled,
Aw'd by his powerful word;
And winds and seas his voice obey'd,
And own'd their sovereign Lord.

14 But man, vile man, his love abus'd,
Blind to the noblest good,
Blasphem'd his power, his word refus'd,
And sought his sacred blood.

15 Still his unwearied love pursu'd
Salvation's glorious plan;
And firm th' approaching horrors view'd,
Deserv'd by guilty man.

16 What pain, what soul-oppressing pain,
The great Redeemer bore;
While bloody sweat, like drops of rain,
Distill'd from every pore!

17 And ere the dreadful storm descends
Full on his guiltless head,
See him by his familiar friends
Deserted and betray'd!

18 While ruffian bands the Lord surround,
Relentless, murderous foes,
Meek as a lamb for slaughter bound,
The patient sufferer goes.

19 Arraign'd at Pilate's impious bar,
(Unparallel'd disgrace!)

See spotless innocence appear
In guilt's detested place!

20 When, perjury fails to stain his name,
The mob's envenom'd breath
Extorts his sentence, "Public shame
And painful lingering death."

21 Patient, the cruel scourge, he bore;
The innocent, the kind!
Then to the rabble's lawless power
And rudest taunts consign'd.

22 With thorns they crown that awful brow,
Whose frown can shake the globe;
And on their king in scorn bestow
The reed and purple robe.

23 Ah! see the fatal cross appears,
Heart-wounding, dreadful scene!
His sacred flesh rude iron tears,
With agonising pain.

24 Expos'd with thieves, to public view –
Could nature bear the sight?
The blushing sun his beams withdrew,
And wrapt the globe in night!

25 Then, Oh! what loads of wrath unknown
The glorious sufferer felt;
For crimes unnumber'd to atone,
To expiate mortal guilt!

26 The Father's blissful smile withdrawn,
In that tremendous hour;
Yet still the God sustain'd the man
With his almighty power.

27 "'Tis finished," now aloud he cries,
"No more the law requires;"
And now, (amazing sacrifice!)
The Lord of life expires.

28 Earth's firm foundation felt the shock,
With universal dread;
Trembled the mountain, rent the rock,
And wak'd the sleeping dead!

29 Now breathless in the silent tomb
His sacred body lies:
Thither his lov'd disciples come,
With sorrow-streaming eyes.

30 But see the promis'd morn appear!
Their joy revives again;
The Saviour lives; adieu to fear,
To every anxious pain.

31 His kindest words their doubts remove,
Confirm their wavering faith;
He bids them teach the world his love,
Salvation by his death.

32 Triumphant he ascends on high,
The glorious work complete;
Sin, death, and hell, low vanquish'd lie
Beneath his awful feet.

33 There, with eternal glory crown'd,
The Lord, the conqueror, reigns;
His praise the heavenly choirs resound
In their immortal strains.

34 Amid the splendours of his throne,
Unchanging love appears;
The names he purchas'd for his own,
Still on his heart he bears.

35 Still with prevailing power he pleads
Their cause for whom he died;
His Spirit's sacred influence sheds,
Their comforter and guide.

36 For them, reserves a radiant crown
Bought with his dying blood;
And worlds of light and joys unknown,
For ever near their God.

37 O the rich depths of love divine!
Of bliss, a boundless store;
Dear Saviour, let me call thee mine;
I cannot wish for more.

38 I yield to thy dear conquering arms,
I yield my captive soul;
O let thy all-subduing charms
My inmost powers control!

39 On thee alone my hope relies;
Beneath thy cross I fall,
My Lord, my life, my sacrifice,
My Saviour, and my all.

HYMN 5

The Great Physician. Luke 6. 19.

1 YE mourning sinners, here disclose
Your deep complaints, your various woes;
Approach, 'tis Jesus, he can heal
The pains which mourning sinners feel.

2 To eyes long clos'd in mental night,
Strangers to all the joys of light,
His word imparts a blissful ray,
Sweet morning of celestial day!

3 Ye helpless lame, lift up your eyes,
The Lord, the Saviour bids you rise;
New life and strength his voice conveys,
And plaintive groans are chang'd for praise.

4 Nor shall the leper hopeless lie
Beneath the Great Physician's eye;
Sin's deepest power his word controls,
That fatal leprosy of souls.

5 That hand divine, which can assuage
The burning fever's restless rage;
That hand, omnipotent and kind,
Can cool the fever of the mind.

6 When freezing palsy chills the veins,
And pale, cold death already reigns,
He speaks; the vital powers revive;
He speaks, and dying sinners live.

7 Dear Lord, we wait thy healing hand;
Diseases fly at thy command;
O let thy sovereign touch impart
Life, strength, and health to every heart!

8 Then shall the sick, the blind, the lame,
Adore their Great Physician's name;
Then dying souls shall bless their God,
And spread thy wondrous praise abroad.

HYMN 6

Longing Souls invited to the Gospel Feast.
Luke 14. 22.

1 YE wretched, hungry, starving poor,
Behold a royal feast!
Where mercy spreads her bounteous store
For every humble guest.

2 See, Jesus stands with open arms;
He calls, he bids you come;
Guilt holds you back, and fear alarms;
But see, there yet is room.

3 Room in the Saviour's bleeding heart:
There love and pity meet;
Nor will he bid the soul depart,
That trembles at his feet.

4 In him, the Father reconcil'd
Invites your souls to come;
The rebel shall be call'd a child,
And kindly welcom'd home.

5 O come, and with his children taste
The blessings of his love;
While hope attends the sweet repast
Of nobler joys above.

6 There, with united heart and voice,
Before th' eternal throne,
Ten thousand thousand souls rejoice
In ecstasies unknown.

7 And yet ten thousand thousand more
Are welcome still to come:
Ye longing souls, the grace adore;
Approach, there yet is room.

HYMN 7

Light and Deliverance.

1 THE weary traveller, lost in night,
Breathes many a longing sigh,
And marks the welcome dawn of light,
With rapture in his eye.

2 Thus sweet the dawn of heavenly day
Lost weary sinners find;
When mercy with reviving ray,
Beams o'er the fainting mind.

3 To slaves oppress'd with cruel chains,
How kind, how dear the friend,
Whose generous hand relieves their pains,
And bids their sorrows end!

4 Thus kind, thus dear, that friend divine,
Who ransoms captive souls,
Unbinds the cruel chains of sin,
And all its power controls.

5 Jesus, to thy soul-cheering light
My dawn of hope I owe;
Once wandering in the shades of night,
And lost in hopeless woe.

6 'Twas thy dear hand redeem'd the slave,
And set the prisoner free;
Be all I am, and all I have,
Devoted, Lord, to thee!

7 But stronger ties than nature knows,
My grateful love confine;
And ev'n that love thy hand bestows,
Which wishes to be thine.

8 Here, at thy feet, I wait thy will,
And live upon thy word;
O give me warmer love and zeal,
To serve my dearest Lord.

HYMN 8

A Morning Hymn.

1 LORD of my life, O may thy praise
Employ my noblest powers,
Whose goodness lengthens out my days,
And fills the circling hours.

2 Preserv'd by thy almighty arm,
I pass'd the shades of night,
Serene, and safe from every harm,
And see returning light.

3 While many spent the night in sighs,
And restless pains, and woes;
In gentle sleep I clos'd my eyes,
And undisturb'd repose.

4 When sleep, death's semblance, o'er me spread,
And I unconscious lay,
Thy watchful care was round my bed,
To guard my feeble clay.

5 O let the same almighty care
My waking hours attend;
From every danger, every snare,
My heedless steps defend.

6 Smile on my minutes as they roll,
And guide my future days;
And let thy goodness fill my soul
With gratitude and praise.

HYMN 9

An Evening Hymn.

1 GREAT God, to thee my evening song
With humble gratitude I raise;
O let thy mercy tune my tongue,
And fill my heart with lively praise.

2 Mercy, that rich unbounded store,
Does my unnumbered wants relieve;
Among thy daily craving poor,
On thy all-bounteous hand I live.

3 My days unclouded as they pass,
And every gently rolling hour,
Are monuments of wondrous grace,
And witness to thy love and power.

4 Thy love and power (celestial guard)
Preserve me from surrounding harms;
Can danger reach me, while the Lord
Extends his kind protecting arms?

5 My numerous wants are known to thee,
Ere my slow wishes can arise;
Thy goodness, measureless and free,
Is ready still with full supplies.

6 And yet this thoughtless, wretched heart,
Too oft regardless of thy love,
Ungrateful, can from thee depart,
And, fond of trifles, vainly rove.

7 When calm reflection finds a place,
How vile this wretched heart appears!
O let thy all-subduing grace
Melt it in penitential tears.

8 Seal my forgiveness in the blood
Of Jesus; his dear name alone
I plead for pardon, gracious God,
And kind acceptance at thy throne.

9 Let this blest hope my eyelids close,
With sleep refresh my feeble frame;
Safe in thy care may I repose,
And wake with praises to thy name.

HYMN 10

On a Stormy Night.

1 LORD of the earth, and seas, and skies,
All nature owns thy sovereign power;
At thy command the tempests rise,
At thy command the thunders roar.

2 We hear, with trembling and affright,
The voice of heaven (tremendous sound!)
Keen lightnings pierce the shades of night,
And spread bright horrors all around.

3 What mortal could sustain the stroke,
Should wrath divine in vengeful storms,
(Which our repeated crimes provoke,)
Descend to crush rebellious worms?

4 These dreadful glories of thy name
With terror would o'erwhelm our souls;
But mercy dawns with kinder beam,
And guilt and rising fear controls.

5 O let thy mercy on my heart
With cheering, healing radiance shine;

Bid every anxious fear depart,
And gently whisper, Thou art mine.

6 Then safe beneath thy guardian care,
In hope serene my soul shall rest;
Nor storms nor dangers reach me there,
In thee, my God, my refuge, blest.

HYMN 11

Searching after Happiness.

1 O HAPPINESS, thou pleasing dream,
Where is thy substance found?
Sought through the varying scenes in vain,
Of earth's capacious round.

2 The charms of grandeur, pomp, and show,
Are nought but gilded snares;
Ambition's painful steep ascent,
Thick set with thorny cares.

3 The busy town, the crowded street,
Where noise and discord reign,
We gladly leave, and tir'd, retreat
To breathe and think again.

4 Yet if retirement's pleasing charms
Detain the captive mind,
The soft enchantment soon dissolves;
'Tis empty all as wind.

5 Religion's sacred lamp alone,
Unerring points the way,
Where happiness for ever shines
With unpolluted ray:

6 To regions of eternal peace,
Beyond the starry skies;
Where pure, sublime and perfect joys
In endless prospect rise.

7 There Jesus, source of bliss divine,
Our glorious leader reigns;
He gives us strength to hold our way,
And crowns the traveller's pains.

8 Dear Saviour, let thy cheering smile
My fainting soul renew;
Then shall the heavenly Canaan yield
A sweet, though distant view.

9 Be thy almighty arm my stay,
My guide through all the road,
'Till safe I reach my journey's end,
My Saviour, and my God.

HYMN 12

Weary Souls invited to Rest. Matt. 11. 58.

1 COME, weary souls with sin distress'd,
The Saviour says, I'll give you rest;
The kind, the gracious call obey,
And cast your gloomy fears away.

2 Oppress'd with guilt, a painful load,
O come, and spread your woes abroad;
Divine compassion, mighty love,
Will all the painful load remove.

3 Here mercy's boundless ocean flows,
To cleanse your guilt and heal your woes;
Pardon, and life, and endless peace –
How rich the gift! how free the grace!

4 Lord, we accept with thankful heart,
The hope thy gracious words impart;
We come with trembling, yet rejoice,
And bless the kind inviting voice.

5 Dear Saviour, let thy powerful love
Confirm our faith, our fears remove,
And sweetly influence every breast,
And guide us to eternal rest.

HYMN 13

Thirsting after God. Isaiah 41. 17.

1 WHEN fainting in the sultry waste,
And parch'd with thirst extreme,
The weary pilgrim longs to taste
The cool, refreshing stream.

2 Should, sudden, to his hopeless eye
A crystal spring appear,
How would th' enlivening, sweet supply
His drooping spirits cheer!

3 So longs the weary, fainting mind,
Oppress'd with sins and woes,
Some soul-reviving spring to find,
Whence heavenly comfort flows.

4 Thus sweet the consolations are,
The promises impart,
Here flowing streams of life appear,
To ease the panting heart.

5 O may I thirst for thee, my God,
With ardent, strong desire;
And still through all this desert road,
To taste thy grace aspire.

6 Then shall my prayer to thee ascend,
A grateful sacrifice;

My plaintive voice thou wilt attend,
  And grant me full supplies.

HYMN 14

The Favour of God the only satisfying good. Psalm 4. 6, 7.

1 IN vain the erring world enquires
  For true substantial good;
While earth confines their low desires,
  They live on airy food.

2 Illusive dreams of happiness
  Their eager thoughts employ;
They wake, convinc'd their boasted bliss
  Was visionary joy.

3 Begone, ye gilded vanities;
  I seek some solid good;
To real bliss my wishes rise,
  The favour of my God.

4 My God, to thee my soul aspires;
  Dispel the shades of night,
Enlarge and fill these vast desires
  With infinite delight.

5 Immortal joy thy smiles impart,
  Heaven dawns in every ray;
One glimpse of thee will glad my heart,
  And turn my night to day.

6 Not all the good which earth bestows,
  Can fill the craving mind;
Its highest joys have mingled woes,
  And leave a sting behind.

7 Should boundless wealth increase my store,
  Can wealth my cares beguile?
I should be wretched still, and poor
  Without thy blissful smile.

8 Grant, O my God, this one request;
  Oh, be thy love alone
My ample portion; here I rest,
  For heaven is in the boon.

HYMN 15

The transforming Vision of God. Psalm 17. 15.

1 MY God, the visits of thy face
  Afford superior joy,
To all the flattering world can give,
  Or mortal hopes employ.

2 But clouds and darkness intervene,
  My brightest joys decline,
And earth's gay trifles oft ensnare
  This wandering heart of mine.

3 Lord, guide this wandering heart to thee;
  Unsatisfied I stray;
Break through the shades of sense and sin,
  With thine enlivening ray.

4 O let thy beams resplendent shine,
  And every cloud remove;
Transform my powers, and fit my soul
  For happier scenes above.

5 There Jesus reigns! may I be cloth'd
  With his divine array;
And when I close these eyes in death,
  Awake to endless day:

6 To endless day! to perfect life!
  To bliss without alloy!
Where not the least faint cloud shall rise,
  To intercept the joy:

7 To view, unveil'd, thy radiant face,
  Thou everlasting fair!
And chang'd to spotless purity,
  Thy glorious likeness wear:

8 To feast, with ever new delight,
  On uncreated good;
And drink full satisfying draughts
  Of pleasure's sacred flood.

9 O bliss too high for mortal thought!
  It awes, and yet inspires;
Fain would my soul, unfetter'd, rise
  In more intense desires.

10 Lord, raise my faith, my hope, my heart,
  To those transporting joys;
Then shall I scorn each little snare,
  Which this vain world employs.

11 Then, though I sink in death's cold sleep,
  I shall awake to bliss,
And in the likeness of my God,
  Find endless happiness.

HYMN 16

The Joys of Heaven.

1 COME, Lord, and warm each languid heart,
  Inspire each lifeless tongue;
And let the joys of heaven impart
  Their influence to our song.

2 Then to the shining seats of bliss
The wings of faith shall soar,
And all the charms of Paradise
Our raptur'd thoughts explore.

3 Pleasures, unsullied, flourish there,
Beyond the reach of time:
Not blooming Eden smil'd so fair,
In all her flowery prime.

4 No sun shall gild the blest abode
With his meridian ray,
But the more radiant throne of God
Diffuse eternal day.

5 Sorrow, and pain, and every care,
And discord there shall cease,
And perfect joy and love sincere
Adorn the realms of peace.

6 The soul, from sin for ever free,
Shall mourn its power no more,
But cloth'd in spotless purity,
Redeeming love adore.

7 There on a throne (how dazzling bright!)
Th' exalted Saviour shines;
And beams ineffable delight
On all the heavenly minds.

8 There shall the followers of the Lamb
Join in immortal songs;
And endless honours to his name
Employ their tuneful tongues.

9 While sweet reflection calls to mind
The scenes of mortal care,
When God, their God, for ever kind,
Was present to their prayer.

10 How will the wonders of his grace
In their full lustre shine?
His wisdom, power, and faithfulness,
All glorious! all divine!

11 The Saviour, dying, rising, crown'd,
Shall swell the lofty strains,
Seraph and saint his praise resound,
Through all the ethereal plains,

12 But oh! their transports, oh! their songs,
What mortal thought can paint?
Transcendent glory awes our tongues,
And all our notes are faint.

13 Lord, tune our hearts to praise and love,
Our feeble notes inspire;
Till in thy blissful courts above
We join the heavenly choir.

HYMN 17

Humble Worship

1 GREAT King of kings, eternal God,
Shall mortal creatures dare to raise
Their songs to thy supreme abode,
And join with angels in thy praise?

2 The brightest Seraph veils his face;
And low before thy dazzling throne,
With prostrate homage all confess
Thou art the infinite unknown.

3 Man, ah how far remov'd below,
Wrapt in the shades of gloomy night;
His brightest day can only show
A few faint streaks of distant light.

4 But see, the bright, the morning star!
His beams shall chase the shades away;
His beams, resplendent from afar,
Sweet promise of immortal day!

5 To him our longing eyes we raise,
Our guide to thee, the great unknown,
Through him, O may our humble praise
Accepted rise before thy throne.

HYMN 18

Praise for National Peace. Psalm 46. 9.

1 GREAT Ruler of the earth and skies,
A word of thy almighty breath
Can sink the world, or bid it rise;
Thy smile is life, thy frown is death.

2 When angry nations rush to arms,
And rage, and noise, and tumult reign;
And war resounds its dire alarms,
And slaughter spreads the hostile plains,

3 Thy sovereign eye looks calmly down,
And marks their course, and bounds their power;
Thy word the angry nations own,
And noise and war are heard no more.

4 Then peace returns with balmy wing;
(Sweet peace! with her what blessings fled!)
Glad plenty laughs, the valleys sing,
Reviving commerce lifts her head.

5 Thou good, and wise, and righteous Lord,
All move subservient to thy will;
And peace and war await thy word,
And thy sublime decrees fulfil.

6 To thee we pay our grateful songs,
Thy kind protection still implore;
O may our hearts, and lives, and tongues
Confess thy goodness and adore.

HYMN 19

The Voice of the Creatures.

1 THERE is a God; all nature speaks,
Through earth, and air, and seas, and skies;
See, from the clouds his glory breaks,
When the first beams of morning rise.

2 The rising sun, serenely bright,
O'er the wide world's extended frame,
Inscribes, in characters of light,
His mighty Maker's glorious name.

3 Diffusing life, his influence spreads,
And health and plenty smile around,
And fruitful fields and verdant meads;
Are with a thousand blessings crown'd.

4 Almighty goodness, power divine,
The fields and verdant meads display;
And bless the hand which made them shine,
With various charms profusely gay.

5 For man and beast, here daily food
In wide diffusive plenty grows;
And there, for drink, the crystal flood
In streams sweet winding, gently flows.

6 By cooling streams, and softening showers,
The vegetable race are fed,
And trees, and plants, and herbs, and flowers,
Their Maker's bounty smiling spread.

7 The flowery tribes, all blooming, rise
Above the faint attempts of art;
Their bright, inimitable dyes
Speak sweet conviction to the heart.

8 Ye curious minds, who roam abroad,
And trace creation's wonders o'er,
Confess the footsteps of the God,
And bow before him, and adore.

HYMN 20

A Rural Hymn.

1 TO your creator, God,
Your great preserver, raise,
Ye creatures of his hand,
Your highest notes of praise;
Let every voice
Proclaim his power,
His name adore,
And loud rejoice.

2 Let all creation join
To pay the tribute due;
Ye meaner ranks begin,
And man shall learn of you;
Let nature raise
From every tongue,
A general song
Of grateful praise.

3 Ye numerous fleecy flocks,
Far spreading o'er the plain,
With gentle artless voice
Assist the humble strain;
To give you food,
He bids the field
Its verdure yield
Extensive good.

4 Ye herds of larger size,
Who feed in meads below,
Resound your Maker's praise
In each responsive low;
You wait his hand;
The herbage grows,
The rivulet flows
At his command.

5 Ye feathered warblers, come
And bring your sweetest lays,
And tune the sprightly song
To your Creator's praise;
His work you are;
He tun'd your voice,
And you rejoice
Beneath his care.

6 Ye trees, which form the shade,
Or bend the loaded bough
With fruits of various kinds,
Your Maker's bounty shew;
From him you rose;
Your vernal suits,
And autumn fruits,
His hand bestows.

7 Ye lovely, verdant fields,
In all your green array,
Though silent, speak his praise,
Who makes you bright and gay;
While we in you,
With future bread
Profusely spread,
His goodness view.

8 Ye flowers, which blooming shew
A thousand beauteous dyes,
Your sweetest odours breathe,
A fragrant sacrifice
To him, whose word
Gave all your bloom,
And sweet perfume;
All-bounteous Lord.

9 Ye rivers, as you flow,
Convey your Maker's name,
(Where'er you winding rove)
On every silver stream;
Your cooling flood
His hand ordains
To bless the plains;
Great spring of good!

10 Ye winds, that shake the world,
With tempests on your wing,
Or breathe in gentler gales,
To waft the smiling spring;
Proclaim abroad
(As you fulfil
His sovereign will)
The powerful God.

11 Ye clouds, or fraught with showers,
Or ting'd with beauteous dyes,
That pour your blessings down,
Or charm our gazing eyes;
His goodness speak,
His praise declare,
As through the air
You shine or break.

12 Thou source of light and heat,
Bright sovereign of the day,
Dispensing blessings round,
With all-diffusive ray;
From morn to night,
With every beam,
Record his name,
Who made thee bright.

13 Fair regent of the night,
With all thy starry train,
Which rise in shining hosts,
To gild the azure plain;
With countless rays
Declare his name,
Prolong the theme,
Reflect his praise.

14 Let every creature join
To celebrate his name,
And all the various powers
Assist th' exalted theme.
Let nature raise
From every tongue
A general song
Of grateful praise.

15 But oh! from human tongues
Should nobler praises flow;
And every thankful heart
With warm devotion glow;
Your voices raise,
Ye highly blest
Above the rest;
Declare his praise.

16 Assist me, gracious God,
My heart, my voice inspire;
Then shall I grateful join
The universal choir;
Thy grace can raise
My heart, my tongue,
And tune my song
To lively praise.

HYMN 21

God my Creator and Benefactor.

1 MY Maker and my King,
To thee my all I owe;
Thy sovereign bounty is the spring
From whence my blessings flow.

2 Thou ever good and kind,
A thousand reasons move,
A thousand obligations bind
My heart to grateful love.

3 The creature of thy hand,
On thee alone I live;
My God, thy benefits demand
More praise than life can give.

4 Oh! what can I impart,
When all is thine before?
Thy love demands a thankful heart;
The gift, alas, how poor!

5 Shall I withhold thy due?
And shall my passions rove?
Lord, form this wretched heart anew,
And fill it with thy love.

6 O let thy grace inspire
My soul with strength divine;
Let all my powers to thee aspire,
And all my days be thine.

HYMN 22

Praise to God for the Blessings of Providence and Grace.

1 ALMIGHTY Father, gracious Lord,
Kind guardian of my days,
Thy mercies let my heart record
In songs of grateful praise.

2 In life's first dawn, my tender frame
Was thy indulgent care,
Long ere I could pronounce thy name,
Or breathe the infant prayer.

3 When reason with my stature grew,
How weak her brightest ray!
How little of my God I knew!
How apt from thee to stray!

4 Around my path what dangers rose!
What snares spread all the road!
No power could guard me from my foes,
But my preserver, God.

5 When life hung trembling on a breath,
'Twas thy almighty love
That sav'd me from impending death,
And bade my fears remove.

6 How many blessings round me shone
Where'er I turn'd my eye!
How many pass'd almost unknown,
Or unregarded, by.

7 Each rolling year new favours brought
From thy exhaustless store;
But ah! in vain my labouring thought
Would count thy mercies o'er.

8 While sweet reflection through my days
Thy bounteous hand would trace,
Still dearer blessings claim my praise,
The blessings of thy grace.

9 Yes, I adore thee, gracious Lord,
For favours more divine:
That I have known thy sacred word,
Where all thy glories shine.

10 'Tis here I view with pleasing pain,
How Jesus left the sky,
(Almighty love! surprising scene!)
For man, lost man, to die.

11 When blest with some transporting view,
That Jesus died for me,
For this sweet hope what praise is due,
O God of grace, to thee!

12 And may I hope that Christ is mine?
That source of every bliss,
That noblest gift of love divine –
What wondrous grace is this!

13 My highest praise, alas, how poor!
How cold my warmest love!
Dear Saviour, teach me to adore
As angels do above.

14 But frail mortality in vain
Attempts the blissful song;
The high, the vast, the boundless strain,
Claims an immortal tongue.

15 Lord, when this mortal frame decays,
And every weakness dies,
Complete the wonders of thy grace,
And raise me to the skies.

16 Then shall my joyful powers unite,
In more exalted lays,
And join the happy sons of light
In everlasting praise.

HYMN 23

Christ the Way to Heaven.

1 JESUS, the spring of joys divine,
Whence all my hopes and comforts flow;
Jesus, no other name but thine,
Can save me from eternal woe.

2 In vain would boasting reason find
The way to happiness and God;
Her weak directions leave the mind
Bewildered in a dubious road.

3 No other name will heaven approve;
Thou art the true, the living way
(Ordain'd by everlasting love)
To the bright realms of endless day.

4 Here let my constant feet abide,
Nor from the heavenly path depart;

O let thy Spirit, gracious guide,
Direct my steps, and cheer my heart.

5 Safe lead me through this world of night,
And bring me to the blissful plains,
The regions of unclouded light,
Where perfect joy for ever reigns.

HYMN 24

Life and Safety in Christ alone. John 6. 68.

1 THOU only sovereign of my heart,
My refuge, my almighty friend,
And can my soul from thee depart,
On whom alone my hopes depend?

2 Whither, ah! whither shall I go,
A wretched wanderer from my Lord?
Can this dark world of sin and woe,
One glimpse of happiness afford?

3 Eternal life thy words impart;
On these my fainting spirit lives;
Here sweeter comforts cheer my heart
Than all the round of nature gives.

4 Let earth's alluring joys combine;
While thou art near, in vain they call;
One smile, one blissful smile of thine,
My dearest Lord, outweighs them all.

5 Thy name my inmost powers adore,
Thou art my life, my joy, my care:
Depart from thee – 'tis death, 'tis more,
'Tis endless ruin, deep despair.

6 Low at thy feet my soul would lie,
Here safety dwells, and peace divine;
Still let me live beneath thine eye,
For life, eternal life, is thine.

HYMN 25

An Evening Reflection.

1 ANOTHER day is past,
The hours for ever fled,
And time is bearing me in haste,
To mingle with the dead.

2 Perhaps my closing eyes
No more may hail the light,
Seal'd up, before the morning rise,
In everlasting night.

3 But I've a part to live,
A never dying ray,
The soul, immortal, will survive
The ruins of her clay.

4 This mortal frame must lie
Unconscious in the tomb,
But oh! where will my spirit fly,
And what will be her doom?

5 On the tremendous brink
Of vast eternity,
Where souls with strange amazement shrink,
What will my prospect be?

6 When the dark gulph below,
With death and horror fraught,
Reveals its scenes of endless woe –
Oh dreadful, dreadful thought!

7 But lo! yon shining skies
Beam down a cheerful ray,
And bid my drooping hopes arise
To glorious realms of day.

8 'Tis there my Saviour lives,
My Lord, my life, my light;
His blissful name my soul revives –
Adieu to death and night

9 He conquered death and hell,
And his victorious love
Shall bear his ransom'd friends to dwell
In his bright courts above.

10 Jesus! And art thou mine?
O let thy heavenly voice
Confirm my hope with power divine,
And bid my soul rejoice.

11 Then shall my closing eyes,
Contented, sink to rest;
For if to night this body dies,
My spirit shall be blest.

HYMN 26

The Excellency of the Holy Scriptures.

1 FATHER of mercies, in thy word
What endless glory shines!
For ever be thy name ador'd
For these celestial lines.

2 Here mines of heavenly wealth disclose
Their bright, unbounded store;
The glittering gem no longer glows,
And India boasts no more.

3 Here may the wretched sons of want
Exhaustless riches find:

Riches, above what earth can grant,
And lasting as the mind.

4 Here, the fair tree of knowledge grows,
And yields a free repast,
Sublimer sweets than nature knows
Invite the longing taste.

5 Here may the blind and hungry come,
And light, and food receive,
Here shall the meanest guest have room,
And taste, and see, and live.

6 Amidst these gloomy wilds below,
When dark and sad we stray;
Here beams of heaven relieve our woe,
And guide to endless day.

7 Here springs of consolation rise,
To cheer the fainting mind;
And thirsty souls receive supplies,
And sweet refreshment find.

8 When guilt and terror, pain and grief,
United rend the heart,
Here sinners meet divine relief,
And cool the raging smart.

9 Here the Redeemer's welcome voice
Spreads heavenly peace around;
And life and everlasting joys
Attend the blissful sound.

10 But when his painful sufferings rise,
(Delightful, dreadful scene!)
Angels may read with wondering eyes
That Jesus died for men.

11 O may these heavenly pages be
My ever dear delight,
And still new beauties may I see,
And still increasing light.

12 Divine instructor, gracious Lord,
Be thou for ever near;
Teach me to love thy sacred word,
And view my Saviour there.

HYMN 27

The Influences of the Spirit of God in the Heart. John 14. 16, 17.

1 DEAR Lord, and shall thy Spirit rest
In such a wretched heart as mine?
Unworthy dwelling! glorious guest!
Favour astonishing, divine!

2 When sin prevails, and gloomy fear,
And hope almost expires in night,
Lord, can thy Spirit then be here,
Great spring of comfort, life, and light?

3 Sure the blest Comforter is nigh,
'Tis he sustains my fainting heart;
Else would my hopes for ever die,
And every cheering ray depart.

4 When some kind promise glads my soul,
Do I not find his healing voice
The tempest of my fears control,
And bid my drooping powers rejoice?

5 Whene'er to call the Saviour mine,
With ardent wish my heart aspires,
Can it be less than power divine,
Which animates these strong desires?

6 What less than thy almighty word
Can raise my heart from earth and dust,
And bid me cleave to thee, my Lord,
My life, my treasure, and my trust?

7 And when my cheerful hope can say
I love my God, and taste his grace,
Lord, is it not thy blissful ray,
Which brings this dawn of sacred peace?

8 Let thy kind Spirit in my heart
For ever dwell, O God of love,
And light and heavenly peace impart,
Sweet earnest of the joys above.

HYMN 28

Christ the Physician of Souls. Jerem. 8. 22.

1 DEEP are the wounds which sin hath made;
Where shall the sinner find a cure?
In vain, alas, is nature's aid;
The work exceeds all nature's power.

2 Sin, like a raging fever, reigns
With fatal strength in every part;
The dire contagion fills the veins,
And spreads its poison to the heart.

3 And can no sovereign balm be found,
And is no kind physician nigh,
To ease the pain, and heal the wound,
Ere life and hope for ever fly?

4 There is a great physician near;
Look up, O fainting soul, and live;
See, in his heavenly smiles appear
Such ease as nature cannot give.

5 See, in the Saviour's dying blood,
Life, health, and bliss, abundant flow;
'Tis only this dear, sacred flood
Can ease thy pain, and heal thy woe.

6 Sin throws in vain its pointed dart,
For here a sovereign cure is found;
A cordial for the fainting heart,
A balm for every painful wound.

HYMN 29

The Intercession of Christ. Heb. 7. 25.

1 HE lives, the great Redeemer lives,
(What joy the blest assurance gives!)
And now before his Father, God,
Pleads the full merits of his blood.

2 Repeated crimes awake our fears,
And justice arm'd with frowns appears;
But in the Saviour's lovely face
Sweet mercy smiles, and all is peace.

3 Hence then, ye black, despairing thoughts;
Above our fears, above our faults,
His powerful intercessions rise,
And guilt recedes, and terror dies.

4 In every dark, distressful hour,
When sin and Satan join their power;
Let this dear hope repel the dart,
That Jesus bears us on his heart.

5 Great advocate, almighty friend –
On him our humble hopes depend;
Our cause can never, never fail,
For Jesus pleads, and must prevail.

HYMN 30

The Condescension of God. 1 Kings 8. 27.

1 ETERNAL Power, almighty God,
Who can approach thy throne?
Accessless light is thy abode,
To angel-eyes unknown.

2 Before the radiance of thine eye
The heavens no longer shine,
And all the glories of the sky
Are but the shade of thine.

3 Great God, and wilt thou condescend
To cast a look below,
To this vile world thy notice bend,
These seats of sin and woe?

4 But oh! to shew thy smiling face,
To bring thy glories near--
Amazing and transporting grace
To dwell with mortals here!

5 How strange! how awful is thy love!
With trembling we adore;
Not all the exalted minds above
Its wonders can explore.

6 While golden harps and angel tongues
Resound immortal lays,
Great God! permit our humble songs
To rise and sound thy praise.

HYMN 31

The Heavenly Guest. Rev. 3. 20.

1 AND will the Lord thus condescend
To visit sinful worms?
Thus at the door shall Mercy stand
In all her winning forms?

2 Surprising grace! – and shall my heart
Unmov'd and cold remain?
Has this hard rock no tender part?
Must mercy plead in vain?

3 Shall Jesus for admission sue,
His charming voice unheard?
And this vile heart, his rightful due,
Remain for ever barr'd?

4 'Tis sin, alas, with tyrant power
The lodging has possest;
And crowds of traitors bar the door
Against the heavenly guest.

5 Lord, rise in thy all-conquering grace,
Thy mighty power display;
One beam of glory from thy face
Can drive my foes away.

6 Ye dangerous inmates, hence depart;
Dear Saviour, enter in,
And guard the passage to my heart,
And keep out every sin.

HYMN 32

God the Soul's only Portion. Lam. 3. 24.

1 IN vain the world's alluring smile
Would my unwary heart beguile;
Deluding world! its brightest day,
Dream of a moment, fleets away!

2 Earth's highest pleasures, could they last,
Would pall and languish on the taste;
Such airy chaff was ne'er design'd
To feed th' immortal, craving mind.

3 To nobler bliss my soul aspires,
Come, Lord, and fill these vast desires;
Be thou my portion; here I rest,
Since of my utmost wish possest.

4 O let thy sacred word impart
Its healing influence to my heart;
With power, and light, and love divine,
Assure my soul that thou art mine.

5 The blissful word, with joy replete,
Shall bid my gloomy fears retreat,
And heaven-born hope, serenely bright,
Shine cheerful through this mortal night.

6 Then shall my joyful spirit rise
On wings of faith above the skies;
And when these transient scenes are o'er,
And this vain world shall tempt no more.

7 O may I reach the blissful plains,
Where thy unclouded glory reigns,
And dwell for ever near thy throne,
In joys to mortal thought unknown.

HYMN 33

Faith in the Joys of Heaven. 2 Cor. 5. 7.

1 FAITH leads to joys beyond the sky;
Why then is this weak mind
Afraid to raise a cheerful eye
To more than sense can find?

2 Sense can but furnish scenes of woe,
In this low vale of tears;
No groves of heavenly pleasures grow,
No paradise appears.

3 Ah! why should this mistaken mind
Still rove with restless pain?
Delight on earth expect to find,
Yet still expect in vain?

4 Faith, rising upward, points her view
To regions in the skies;
There lovelier scenes than Eden knew
In bright perspective rise.

5 Oh! if this heaven-born grace were mine,
Would not my spirit soar,
Transported gaze on joys divine,
And cleave to earth no more?

6 If in my heart true faith appears,
How weak the sacred ray!
Feebly aspiring, press'd with fears,
Almost it dies away.

7 O thou, from whose almighty breath
It first began to rise,
Purge off these mists, these dregs of earth,
And bid it reach the skies.

8 Let this weak, erring mind no more
On earth bewildered rove,
But with celestial ardour soar
To endless joys above.

HYMN 34

Strength and Safety in God alone. Psalm 105. 4.

1 PERMIT me, Lord, to seek thy face,
Obedient to thy call,
To seek the presence of thy grace,
My strength, my life, my all.

2 All I can wish is thine to give;
My God, I ask thy love,
That greatest bliss I can receive,
That bliss of heaven above.

3 In these dark scenes of pain and woe,
What can my spirit find?
No happiness can dwell below,
To fill th' immortal mind.

4 To heaven my restless heart aspires;
O for a quickening ray
To invigorate my faint desires,
And cheer the tiresome way.

5 The path to thy divine abode
Through a wild desert lies;
A thousand snares beset the road,
A thousand terrors rise.

6 Satan and sin unite their art,
To keep me from my Lord;
Dear Saviour, guard my trembling heart,
And guide me by thy word.

7 Whene'er the tempting foe alarms,
Or spreads the fatal snare,
I'll fly to my Redeemer's arms,
For safety must be there.

8 My guardian, my almighty friend,
On thee my soul would rest;
On thee alone my hopes depend;
Be near, and I am blest.

HYMN 35

A Funeral Hymn.

1 WHILE to the grave our friends are borne,
Around their cold remains,

How all the tender passions mourn,
And each fond heart complains!

2 But down to earth, alas, in vain
We bend our weeping eyes;
Ah! let us leave these seats of pain,
And upward learn to rise.

3 Hope cheerful smiles amid the gloom,
And beams a healing ray,
And guides us from the darksome tomb,
To realms of endless day.

4 Jesus, who left his blest abode
(Amazing grace!) to die,
Mark'd when he rose the shining road
To his bright courts on high.

5 To those bright courts, when hope ascends,
The tears forget to flow;
Hope views our absent happy friends,
And calms the swelling woe.

6 Then let our hearts repine no more
That earthly comfort dies,
But lasting happiness explore,
And ask it from the skies.

HYMN 36

Sin the Cause of Sorrow.

1 THE pains that wait our fleeting breath
Too oft my mournful thoughts employ;
Amid the gloomy shades of death,
The hope of heaven is life, is joy.

2 But ah! how soon the blissful ray,
With guilt o'ershaded, disappears;
'Tis sin alone that clouds my day,
'Tis sin alone deserves my tears.

3 Yes, I have cause indeed to mourn,
When God conceals his radiant face;
And pray and long till he return,
With smiles of sweet forgiving grace.

4 Then weep, my eyes, complain, my heart,
But mourn not, hopeless of relief;
For sovereign mercy will impart
Its healing beams to ease my grief.

5 The Saviour pleads his dying blood,
Awake, my hope, away, my fears;
Through him I'll seek my absent God,
Till his returning smile appears.

HYMN 37

Entreating the Presence of Christ in his Churches. Hag. 2. 7.

1 COME, thou desire of all thy saints,
Our humble strains attend,
While with our praises and complaints,
Low at thy feet we bend.

2 When we thy wondrous glories hear,
And all thy sufferings trace,
What sweetly awful scenes appear!
What rich unbounded grace!

3 How should our songs, like those above,
With warm devotion rise!
How should our souls, on wings of love,
Mount upward to the skies!

4 But ah! the song, how cold it flows!
How languid our desire!
How faint the sacred passion glows,
Till thou the heart inspire!

5 Come, Lord, thy love alone can raise
In us the heavenly flame;
Then shall our lips resound thy praise,
Our hearts adore thy name.

6 Dear Saviour, let thy glory shine,
And fill thy dwellings here,
Till life, and love, and joy divine,
A heaven on earth appear.

7 Then shall our hearts enraptured say,
Come, great Redeemer, come,
And bring the bright, the glorious day,
That calls thy children home.

HYMN 38

Desiring to trust in God. Isaiah 26. 4.

1 GREAT source of boundless power and grace,
Attend my mournful cry;
In the dark hour of deep distress,
To thee, to thee I fly.

2 Thou art my strength, my life, my stay;
Assist my feeble trust;
Drive these distressing fears away,
And raise me from the dust.

3 O let me call thy grace to mind,
And trust thy glorious name;
Jehovah, powerful, wise, and kind,
For ever is the same.

4 Here let me rest, on thee depend,
My God, my hope, my all;
Be thou my everlasting friend,
And I can never fall.

HYMN 39

Watchfulness and Prayer. Matt. 26. 41.

1 ALAS, what hourly dangers rise!
What snares beset my way!
To heaven O let me lift my eyes,
And hourly watch and pray.

2 How oft my mournful thoughts complain,
And melt in flowing tears!
My weak resistance, ah, how vain!
How strong my foes and fears!

3 O gracious God, in whom I live,
My feeble efforts aid,
Help me to watch, and pray, and strive,
Though trembling and afraid.

4 Increase my faith, increase my hope,
When foes and fears prevail;
And bear my fainting spirit up,
Or soon my strength will fail.

5 Whene'er temptations fright my heart,
Or lure my feet aside,
My God, thy powerful aid impart,
My guardian and my guide.

6 O keep me in thy heavenly way,
And bid the tempter flee;
And let me never, never stray
From happiness and thee.

HYMN 40

Divine Compassion. Isai. 49. 14, 15, 16.

1 THE Lord forgets his wonted grace,
Afflicted Zion said;
My God withdraws his smiling face,
Withdraws his heavenly aid.

2 Shall the kind mother's gentle breast
No soft emotion share;
But, every tender thought suppress,
Forget her infant care?

3 The helpless child, that oft her eyes
Have watch'd with anxious thought,
While her fond breast appeas'd his cries –
And can he be forgot?

4 Strange as it is, yet this may be,
For creature-love is frail;
But thy Creator's love to thee,
O Zion, cannot fail.

5 No, thy dear name engraven stands,
In characters of love,
On thy almighty Father's hands,
And never shall remove.

6 Before his ever-watchful eye
Thy mournful state appears,
And every groan and every sigh
Divine compassion hears.

7 These anxious doubts indulge no more,
Be every fear suppressed;
Unchanging truth, and love, and power,
Command thy cares to rest.

HYMN 41

Desiring Assurance of the Favour of God.

1 ETERNAL source of joys divine,
To thee my soul aspires;
O could I say, "The Lord is mine,"
'Tis all my soul desires.

2 Thy smile can give me real joy,
Unmingled and refin'd,
Substantial bliss, without alloy,
And lasting as the mind.

3 Thy smile can gild the shades of woe,
Bid stormy trouble cease,
Spread the fair dawn of heaven below,
And sweeten pain to peace.

4 My hope, my trust, my life, my Lord,
Assure me of thy love;
O speak the kind transporting word,
And bid my fears remove.

5 Then shall my thankful powers rejoice,
And triumph in my God,
Till heavenly rapture tune my voice
To spread thy praise abroad.

HYMN 42

Hope encouraged in the Contemplation of the Divine Perfections.

1 WHY sinks my weak, desponding mind?
Why heaves my heart the anxious sigh?
Can sovereign goodness be unkind?
Am I not safe, if God is nigh?

2 He holds all nature in his hand;
That gracious hand on which I live

Does life, and time, and death command,
And has immortal joys to give.

3 'Tis he supports this fainting frame,
On him alone my hopes recline;
The wondrous glories of his name;
How wide they spread! how bright they shine!

4 Infinite wisdom! boundless power!
Unchanging faithfulness and love!
Here let me trust, while I adore,
Nor from my refuge e'er remove.

5 My God, if thou art mine indeed,
Then I have all my heart can crave;
A present help in times of need,
Still kind to hear, and strong to save.

6 Forgive my doubts, O gracious Lord,
And ease the sorrows of my breast;
Speak to my heart the healing word
That thou art mine – and I am blest.

HYMN 43

The Incarnate Saviour. John 1. 14.

1 AWAKE, awake the sacred song,
To our incarnate Lord;
Let every heart and every tongue
Adore th' eternal Word.

2 That awful Word, that sovereign power,
By whom the worlds were made
(O happy morn! illustrious hour!)
Was once in flesh array'd.

3 Then shone almighty power and love,
In all their glorious forms,
When Jesus left his throne above
To dwell with sinful worms.

4 To dwell with misery below
The Saviour left the skies;
And sunk to wretchedness and woe,
That worthless man might rise.

5 Adoring angels tun'd their songs
To hail the joyful day;
With rapture then let mortal tongues
Their grateful worship pay!

6 What glory, Lord, to thee is due!
With wonder we adore;
But could we sing as angels do,
Our highest praise were poor.

HYMN 44

Faith in God in Time of Distress. Hab. 3. 17, 18

1 SHOULD famine o'er the mourning field
Extend her desolating reign,
Nor spring her blooming beauties yield,
Nor autumn swell the foodful grain;

2 Should lowing herds and bleating sheep
Around their famish'd master die;
And hope itself despairing weep,
While life deplores its last supply:

3 Amid the dark, the deathful scene,
If I can say, the Lord is mine,
The joy shall triumph o'er the pain,
And glory dawn, though life decline.

4 The God of my salvation lives;
My nobler life he will sustain;
His word immortal vigour gives,
Nor shall my glorious hopes be vain.

5 Thy presence, Lord, can cheer my heart,
Though every earthly comfort die;
Thy smile can bid my pains depart,
And raise my sacred pleasures high.

6 O let me hear thy blissful voice,
Inspiring life and joys divine!
The barren desert shall rejoice;
'Tis paradise if thou art mine.

HYMN 45

Pardoning Love. Jer. 3. 22. Hos. 14. 4.

1 HOW oft, alas, this wretched heart
Has wandered from the Lord!
How oft my roving thoughts depart,
Forgetful of his word!

2 Yet sovereign mercy calls, Return;
Dear Lord, and may I come?
My vile ingratitude I mourn;
Oh take the wanderer home.

3 And canst thou, wilt thou yet forgive,
And bid my crimes remove?
And shall a pardon'd rebel live
To speak thy wondrous love?

4 Almighty grace, thy healing power
How glorious, how divine!
That can to life and bliss restore
So vile a heart as mine.

5 Thy pardoning love, so free, so sweet,
Dear Saviour, I adore;

O keep me at thy sacred feet,
And let me rove no more.

HYMN 46

The Goodness of God. Nahum 1. 7.

1 YE humble souls, approach your God
With songs of sacred praise;
For he is good, immensely good,
And kind are all his ways.

2 All nature owns his guardian care;
In Him we live and move;
But nobler benefits declare
The wonders of his love.

3 He gave his Son, his only Son,
To ransom rebel worms;
'Tis here he makes his goodness known
In its divinest forms.

4 To this dear refuge, Lord, we come;
'Tis here our hope relies;
A safe defence, a peaceful home,
When storms of trouble rise.

5 Thy eye beholds, with kind regard,
The souls who trust in thee;
Their humble hope thou wilt reward,
With bliss divinely free.

6 Great God, to thy almighty love,
What honours shall we raise?
Not all the raptur'd songs above
Can render equal praise.

HYMN 47

True Honour. Dan. 12. 3.

1 THERE is a glorious world on high,
Resplendent with eternal day;
Faith views the blissful prospect nigh,
While God's own word reveals the way.

2 There shall the favourites of the Lord
With never fading lustre shine;
Surprising honour! vast reward
Conferr'd on man, by love divine!

3 How blest are those, how truly wise,
Who learn and keep the sacred road!
Happy the men, whom heaven employs
To turn rebellious hearts to God.

4 To win them from the fatal way,
Where erring folly thoughtless roves;
And that blest righteousness display,
Which Jesus wrought, and God approves.

5 The shining firmament shall fade,
And sparkling stars resign their light;
But these shall know nor change, nor shade,
For ever fair, for ever bright.

6 No fancied joy beyond the sky,
No fair delusion is reveal'd;
'Tis God that speaks, who cannot lie,
And all his word must be fulfill'd.

7 And shall not these cold hearts of ours
Be kindled at the glorious view?
Come, Lord, awake our active powers,
Our feeble, dying strength renew.

8 On wings of faith and strong desire,
O may our spirits daily rise;
And reach at last the shining choir,
In the bright mansions of the skies.

HYMN 48

Divine Bounty. Col. 1. 19.

1 LORD, we adore thy boundless grace,
The heights and depths unknown,
Of pardon, life, and joy, and peace,
In thy beloved Son.

2 O wondrous gift of love divine,
Dear source of every good!
Jesus, in thee what glories shine!
How rich thy flowing blood!

3 Come, all ye pining, hungry poor,
The Saviour's bounty taste;
Behold a never failing store,
For every willing guest.

4 Here shall your numerous wants receive
A free, a full supply;
He has unmeasur'd bliss to give,
And joys that never die.

5 Can those, who hear the Saviour's voice,
Prefer earth's empty toys
(Ah, wretched souls! ah, fatal choice!)
To everlasting joys?

6 Lord, bring unwilling souls to thee,
With sweet, resistless power;
Thy boundless grace let rebels see,
And at thy feet adore.

HYMN 49

The heavenly Conqueror. Rev. 3. 21.

1 TO Jesus, our victorious Lord,
The praises of our lives belong;

For ever be his name ador'd,
Sweet theme of every thankful song.

2 Lost in despair, beset with foes,
Undone and perishing we lay;
His pity melted o'er our woes,
And sav'd the trembling, dying prey.

3 He fought, he conquer'd, though he fell;
While with his last expiring breath
He triumph'd o'er the powers of hell,
And, by his dying, vanquish'd death.

4 Now on his Father's throne he reigns,
And all the tuneful choir above
Resound in high immortal strains
The praises of victorious love.

5 Though still reviving foes arise,
Temptations, sins, and doubts appear,
And pain our hearts, and fill our eyes
With many a groan, and many a tear:

6 Still shall we fight, and still prevail,
In our almighty leader's name;
His strength, whene'er our spirits fail,
Shall all our active powers inflame,

7 Immortal honours wait above,
To crown the dying conqueror's brow,
And endless peace, and joy, and love,
For the short war sustain'd below.

8 Exalted near their Saviour's seat,
His saints shall dwell, their dangers o'er,
And cast their crowns beneath his feet,
And love and wonder and adore.

HYMN 50

Longing after unseen Pleasures. 2 Cor. 4. 18.

1 HOW long shall earth's alluring toys
Detain our hearts and eyes,
Regardless of immortal joys,
And strangers to the skies?

2 These transient scenes will soon decay;
They fade upon the sight;
And quickly will their brightest day
Be lost in endless night.

3 Their brightest day, alas, how vain!
With conscious sighs we own;
While clouds of sorrow, care, and pain,
O'ershade the smiling noon.

4 O could our thoughts and wishes fly
Above these gloomy shades,
To those bright worlds beyond the sky
Which sorrow ne'er invades!

5 There joys unseen by mortal eyes,
Or reason's feeble ray,
In ever-blooming prospect rise,
Unconscious of decay.

6 Lord, send a beam of light divine,
To guide our upward aim;
With one reviving touch of thine
Our languid hearts inflame.

7 Then shall on faith's sublimest wing
Our ardent wishes rise
To those bright scenes, where pleasures spring
Immortal in the skies.

HYMN 51

The Christian's Prospect.

1 HAPPY the soul, whose wishes climb
To mansions in the skies!
He looks on all the joys of time,
With undesiring eyes.

2 In vain soft pleasure spreads her charms,
And throws her silken chain;
And wealth and fame invite his arms,
And tempt his ear in vain.

3 He knows that all these glittering things
Must yield to sure decay;
And sees on time's extended wings,
How swift they flee away!

4 Nor low to earth in sorrow bends,
When pains and cares invade;
With cheerful wing his faith ascends
Above the gloomy shade.

5 To things unseen by mortal eyes,
A beam of sacred light
Directs his view, his prospects rise,
All permanent and bright.

6 His hopes are fix'd on joys to come;
Those blissful scenes on high
Shall flourish in immortal bloom,
When time and nature die.

7 O were these heavenly prospects mine,
These pleasures could I prove,

Earth's fleeting views I would resign,
  And raise my hopes above.

HYMN 52

Life a Journey.

1 LIFE is a journey, heaven my home,
  And shall I negligently stray?
In paths of danger heedless roam,
  Forget my guide, forget my way?

2 Think, O my soul, each flying hour
  Thy folly chides, thy speed alarms;
And shall an insect or a flower
  Amuse thee with their painted charms?

3 Such are the objects earth displays
  To tempt my stay, and gain my heart!
And shall I fondly, vainly gaze?
  Ye shining trifles, hence depart.

4 O think what glorious scenes above
  In bright unbounded prospect rise!
Nor let one vagrant passion rove,
  Nor leave a wish below the skies.

5 But ah! how weak my best desires,
  My warmest ardours soon decay;
My fainting soul, till grace inspires,
  Can ne'er pursue the heavenly way.

6 On thee I lean, all-gracious God;
  O breathe new life through all my
    powers,
Teach me to keep thy sacred road,
  And well improve my remnant hours.

HYMN 53

True Happiness to be found only in God.

1 WHEN fancy spreads her boldest wings
  And wanders unconfin'd,
Amid the unbounded scene of things
  Which entertain the mind;

2 In vain I trace creation o'er,
  In search of sacred rest;
The whole creation is too poor,
  Too mean, to make me blest.

3 In vain would this low world employ,
  Each flatt'ring specious wile;
There's nought can yield a real joy
  But my Creator's smile.

4 Let earth and all her charms depart,
  Unworthy of the mind;
In God alone this restless heart
  An equal bliss can find.

5 Great spring of all felicity,
  To whom my wishes tend,
Do not these wishes rise from thee,
  And in thy favour end?

6 Thy favour, Lord, is all I want;
  Here would my spirit rest;
O seal the rich, the boundless grant,
  And make me fully blest.

HYMN 54

Lasting Happiness.

1 IN vain my roving thoughts would find
A portion worthy of the mind;
On earth my soul can never rest,
For earth can never make me blest.

2 Can lasting happiness be found
Where seasons roll their hasty round,
And days and hours, with rapid flight,
Sweep cares and pleasures out of sight?

3 Arise, my thoughts, my heart, arise;
Leave this low world, and seek the skies;
There joys for ever, ever last,
When seasons, days, and hours are past.

4 Come, Lord, thy powerful grace impart,
Thy grace can raise my wandering heart
To pleasure perfect and sublime,
Unmeasur'd by the wings of time.

5 Let those bright worlds of endless joy,
My thoughts, my hopes, my cares employ,
No more, ye restless passions, roam;
God is my bliss, and heaven my home.

HYMN 55

Bidding adieu to Earthly Pleasures.

1 YE gay deceivers of the mind,
  Ye dreams of happiness, adieu;
No more your soft enchantments bind;
  This heart was never made for you.

2 The brightest joy your smile can boast
  Is but a moment's glittering light;
It sparkles now, and now 'tis lost,
  Extinguish'd in the shades of night.

3 Begone, with all your soothing charms;
  Pleasure on earth! – O empty name!
Superior joy my bosom warms,
  And heaven approves the sacred flame.

4 To perfect bliss my soul aspires,
That shines with never fading ray!
No less can satiate my desires
Than full delight and endless day.

5 Blest be the kind, the gracious power,
That gently call'd and bade me rise;
And taught my nobler thoughts to soar
To happiness beyond the skies.

HYMN 56

Longing for Immortality. 2 Cor. 5. 4.

1 SAD prisoners in a house of clay,
With sins, and griefs, and pains oppress'd,
We groan the lingering hours away,
And wish, and long to be releas'd.

2 Nor is it liberty alone,
Which prompts our restless, ardent sighs;
For immortality we groan,
For robes and mansions in the skies.

3 Eternal mansions! bright array!
O blest exchange! transporting thought!
Free from th' approaches of decay,
Or the least shadow of a spot!

4 There shall mortality no more
Its wide extended empire boast,
Forgotten all its dreadful power,
In life's unbounded ocean lost.

5 Bright world of bliss! O could I see
One shining glimpse, one cheerful ray
(Fair dawn of immortality!)
Break through these tottering walls of clay.

6 Jesus, in thy dear name I trust,
My light, my life, my Saviour God;
When this frail house dissolves in dust,
O raise me to thy bright abode.

HYMN 57

At the Funeral of a Young Person.

1 WHEN blooming youth is snatch'd away
By death's resistless hand,
Our hearts the mournful tribute pay,
Which pity must demand.

2 While pity prompts the rising sigh,
O may this truth, impress'd
With awful power – I too must die –
Sink deep in every breast.

3 Let this vain world engage no more;
Behold the gaping tomb!
It bids us seize the present hour,
Tomorrow death may come.

4 The voice of this alarming scene
May every heart obey,
Nor be the heavenly warning vain,
Which calls to watch and pray.

5 O let us fly, to Jesus fly,
Whose powerful arm can save;
Then shall our hopes ascend on high,
And triumph o'er the grave.

6 Great God, thy sovereign grace impart,
With cleansing, healing power;
This only can prepare the heart
For death's surprising hour.

HYMN 58

Sin the Sting of Death.

1 DEATH! 'tis a name with terror fraught;
It rends the guilty heart,
When conscience wakes remorseful thought
With agonizing smart.

2 'Tis guilt alone provokes that frown
Which all the soul alarms;
Gives terror to the monarch's crown,
And conquest to his arms!

3 Dear Saviour, thy victorious love
Can all his force control,
Can bid the pangs of guilt remove,
And cheer the trembling soul.

4 Victorious love! thy wondrous power
From sin and death can raise;
Can gild the dark departing hour,
And tune its groans to praise.

5 Then shall the joyful spirit soar
To life beyond the skies,
Where gloomy death can frown no more,
And guilt and terror dies.

6 No more, O pale destroyer, boast
Thy universal sway;
To heaven-born souls thy sting is lost,
Thy night, the gates of day.

HYMN 59

The Presence of Christ the Joy of his People.

1 THE wondering nations have beheld
The sacred prophecy fulfill'd
And angels hail'd the glorious morn
That saw the great Messiah born.

2 The prince! the Saviour, long desir'd,
Whom prophets taught, by heaven inspir'd,
And shewed far off the blissful day,
Rise o'er the world with healing ray.

3 Oft in the temples of his grace
His saints behold his smiling face,
And oft have seen his glory shine,
With power and majesty divine.

4 But soon alas, his absence mourn,
And pray and wish his kind return;
Without his life-inspiring light,
'Tis all a scene of gloomy night.

5 Come, dearest Lord, thy children cry,
Our graces droop, our comforts die;
Return, and let thy glories rise
Again to our admiring eyes:

6 Till fill'd with light, and joy, and love,
Thy courts below, like those above,
Triumphant hallelujahs raise,
And heaven and earth resound thy praise.

HYMN 60

Absence from God.

1 O thou, whose tender mercy hears
Contrition's humble sigh;
Whose hand, indulgent, wipes the tears
From sorrow's weeping eye:

2 See! low before thy throne of grace
A wretched wanderer mourn;
Hast thou not bid me seek thy face?
Hast thou not said, Return?

3 And shall my guilty fears prevail
To drive me from thy feet?
O let not this dear refuge fail,
This only safe retreat.

4 Absent from thee, my guide, my light,
Without one cheering ray,
Through dangers, fears, and gloomy night,
How desolate my way!

5 O shine on this benighted heart,
With beams of mercy shine;
And let thy healing voice impart
A taste of joys divine.

6 Thy presence only can bestow
Delights which never cloy:
Be this my solace here below
And my eternal joy.

HYMN 61

Desiring a Taste of Real Joy.

1 WHY should my spirit cleave to earth,
This nest of worms, this vile abode?
Why thus forget her nobler birth,
Nor wish to trace the heavenly road?

2 How barren of sincere delight,
Are all the fairest scenes below!
Though beauteous colours charm the sight,
They only varnish real woe.

3 Were I to mount the flying wind,
And search the wide creation round,
There's nothing here to suit the mind;
On earth no solid joy is found.

4 Oh! could my weary spirit rise,
And panting with intense desire,
Reach the bright mansions in the skies,
And mix among the blissful choir.

5 How should I look, with pitying eye,
On this low world of gloomy care,
And wonder, how my soul could lie
Wrapt up in shades and darkness there!

6 Say, happy natives of the sky,
What is it makes your heaven above?
You dwell beneath your Father's eye,
And feast for ever on his love.

7 My God, thy presence can impart
A glimpse of heaven to earth and night;
O smile, and bless my mournful heart,
Sweet foretaste of sincere delight.

8 Then shall my soul contented stay
Till my Redeemer calls me home;
Yet let me oft with transport say,
"Come, O my Lord, my Saviour, come."

HYMN 62

Humble Reliance.

1 MY God, my Father, blissful name!
O may I call thee mine;
May I with sweet assurance claim
A portion so divine!

2 This only can my fears control,
And bid my sorrows fly;
What harm can ever reach my soul
Beneath my Father's eye?

3 Whate'er thy providence denies,
I calmly would resign,

For thou art just, and good, and wise;
O bend my will to thine.

4 Whate'er thy sacred will ordains,
O give me strength to bear,
And let me know my Father reigns,
And trust his tender care.

5 If pain and sickness rend this frame,
And life almost depart,
Is not thy mercy still the same,
To cheer my drooping heart?

6 If cares and sorrows me surround,
Their power why should I fear?
My inward peace they cannot wound,
If thou, my God, art near.

7 Thy sovereign ways are all unknown
To my weak, erring sight;
Yet let my soul, adoring, own
That all thy ways are right.

8 My God, my Father, be thy name
My solace and my stay;
O wilt thou seal my humble claim,
And drive my fears away.

HYMN 63

The Presence of God the Life and Light of the Soul.

1 MY God, my hope, if thou art mine,
Why should my soul with sorrow pine?
On thee alone I cast my care;
O leave me not in dark despair.

2 Though every comfort should depart,
And life forsake this drooping heart;
One smile from thee, one blissful ray,
Can chase the shades of death away.

3 My God, my life, if thou appear,
Not death itself can make me fear;
Thy presence cheers the sable gloom,
And gilds the horrors of the tomb.

4 Not all its horrors can affright,
If thou appear, my God, my light;
Thy love shall all my fears control,
And glory dawn around my soul.

5 Should all created blessings fade,
And mourning nature disarray'd
Deplore her every charm withdrawn,
Light, hope, and joy, for ever gone.

6 Though nought remain below the sky,
To please my taste, my ear, my eye,
Be thou my hope, my life, my light,
Amid the universal night.

7 My God, be thou for ever nigh;
Beneath the radiance of thine eye,
My hope, my joy, shall ever rise,
Nor terminate below the skies.

HYMN 64

Resigning the Heart to God. Psalm 119. 94

1 THEE, dearest Lord, my soul adores,
I would be thine, and only thine;
To thee, my heart and all its powers,
With full consent, I would resign.

2 But ah! this weak inconstant mind,
How frail, how apt from thee to stray;
Trifles, as empty as the wind,
Can tempt my roving thoughts away.

3 Sure I am thine, or why this load
When earthly vanities beguile?
Why do I mourn my absent God,
And languish for thy cheering smile?

4 If thou return, how sweet the joy,
Though mix'd with penitential smart!
Then I despise each tempting toy,
And long to give thee all my heart.

5 Come, Lord, thy saving power display,
(Resistless power of love divine!)
And drive thy hated foes away,
And make me thine, and only thine.

HYMN 65

The Inconstant Heart

1 AH! wretched, vile, ungrateful heart,
That can from Jesus thus depart,
Thus fond of trifles vainly rove,
Forgetful of a Saviour's love!

2 In vain I charge my thoughts to stay,
And chide each vanity away;
In vain, alas! resolve to bind
This rebel heart, this wandering mind.

3 Through all resolves, how soon it flies
And mocks the weak, the slender ties!
There's nought beneath a power divine,
That can this roving heart confine.

4 Jesus, to thee I would return,
At thy dear feet repentant mourn;
There let me view thy pardoning love,
And never from thy sight remove.

5 O let thy love with sweet control
Bind all the passions of my soul,
Bid every vanity depart,
And dwell for ever in my heart.

HYMN 66

Cold Affections.

1 SURE I must love the Saviour's name,
Or is the heaven-born passion dead,
Extinguish'd the celestial flame,
And all my joys for ever fled?

2 At the sweet mention of his love,
How should the sacred ardour rise!
And every thought transported move
In grateful joy, and glad surprise.

3 Jesus demands this heart of mine,
Demands my wish, my joy, my care;
But ah! how dead to things divine,
How cold my best affections are!

4 What death-like lethargy detains
My captive powers with fatal art,
And spreads its unrelenting chains
Heavy and cold, around my heart!

5 'Tis sin, alas! with dreadful power
Divides my Saviour from my sight;
O for one happy, shining hour
Of sacred freedom, sweet delight.

6 See, dearest Lord, my wretched state,
And thy almighty power employ;
To thee I seek, on thee I wait,
For life, and liberty, and joy.

7 O let thy love shine forth, and raise
My captive powers from sin and death;
And fill my heart and life with praise,
And tune my last expiring breath.

8 Then bear me to the blissful seats
Of perfect freedom, life, and light,
Where thy redeem'd assembly meets,
To love and praise with full delight.

9 There shall my thoughts transported trace,
And all my soul for ever prove,
The boundless riches of thy grace,
The endless wonders of thy love.

HYMN 67

The Example of Christ.

1 AND is the gospel peace and love?
Such let our conversation be;
The serpent blended with the dove,
Wisdom and meek simplicity.

2 Whene'er the angry passions rise,
And tempt our thoughts or tongues to strife,
To Jesus let us lift our eyes,
Bright pattern of the Christian life!

3 O how benevolent and kind!
How mild! how ready to forgive!
Be this the temper of our mind,
And these the rules by which we live.

4 To do his heavenly Father's will,
Was his employment and delight;
Humility and holy zeal
Shone through his life, divinely bright!

5 Dispensing good where'er he came,
The labours of his life were love;
O! if we love the Saviour's name,
Let his divine example move.

6 But ah, how blind! how weak we are!
How frail! how apt to turn aside!
Lord, we depend upon thy care,
And ask thy Spirit for our guide.

7 Thy fair example may we trace,
To teach us what we ought to be;
Make us, by thy transforming grace,
Dear Saviour, daily more like thee.

HYMN 68

Retirement and Reflection.

1 HENCE, vain, intruding world, depart,
No more allure or vex my heart;
Let every vanity be gone;
I would be peaceful and alone.

2 Here let me search my inmost mind,
And try its real state to find,
The secret springs of thought explore,
And call my words and actions o'er.

3 Reflect how soon my life will end,
And think on what my hopes depend,
What aim my busy thoughts pursue,
What work is done, and what to do.

4 Eternity is just at hand;
And shall I waste my ebbing sand,
And careless view departing day,
And throw my inch of time away?

5 Eternity, tremendous sound!
To guilty souls, a dreadful wound;
But Oh! if Christ and heaven be mine,
How sweet the accents! how divine!

6 Be this my chief, my only care,
My high pursuit, my ardent prayer,
An interest in the Saviour's blood,
My pardon seal'd, and peace with God.

7 But should my brightest hopes be vain,
The rising doubt, how sharp its pain!
My fears, O gracious God, remove;
Confirm my title to thy love.

8 Search, Lord, O search my inmost heart,
And light, and hope, and joy impart;
From guilt and error set me free,
And guide me safe to heaven and thee.

HYMN 69

Hope in Darkness.

1 GOD is my sun; his blissful rays
Irradiate, warm, and guide my heart!
How dark, how mournful, are my days,
If his enlivening beams depart!

2 Scarce through the shades, a glimpse of day
Appears to these desiring eyes;
But shall my drooping spirit say,
The cheerful morn will never rise?

3 O let me not despairing mourn,
Though gloomy darkness spreads the sky;
My glorious sun will yet return,
And night with all its horrors fly.

4 Hope, in the absence of my Lord,
Shall be my taper; sacred light,
Kindled at his celestial word,
To cheer the melancholy night.

5 O for the bright, the joyful day,
When hope shall in assurance die!
So tapers lose their feeble ray,
Beneath the sun's refulgent eye.

HYMN 70

Death and Heaven.

1 OFT have I said, with inward sighs,
I find no solid good below;
Earth's fairest scenes but cheat my eyes,
Her pleasure is but painted woe.

2 Then why, my soul, so loath to leave
These seats of vanity and care?
Why do I thus to trifles cleave,
And feed on chaff, and grasp the air?

3 There is a world all fair and bright;
But clouds and darkness dwell between;
The sable veil obstructs my sight,
And hides the lovely, distant scene.

4 Whene'er I look with frighted eyes
On death's impenetrable shade,
Alas! what gloomy horrors rise,
And all my trembling frame invade!

5 O death, frail nature's dreaded foe,
Thy frown with terror fills my heart;
How shall I bear the fatal blow,
Which must my soul and body part?

6 'Tis sin which arms his dreadful frown,
This only points his deadly sting;
My sins which throw this gloom around,
And all these shocking terrors bring.

7 O could I know my sins forgiven,
Soon would these terrors disappear;
Then should I see a glimpse of heaven,
And look on death without a fear.

8 Jesus, my Saviour, and my God,
To thee my trembling spirit flies;
Thy merits, thy atoning blood,
On this alone my soul relies.

9 O let thy love's all-powerful ray
With pleasing force, divine control,
Arise, and chase these clouds away,
And shine around my doubting soul.

10 Then shall I change the mournful strain,
And bid my thoughts and hopes arise,
Above these gloomy seats of pain,
To glorious worlds beyond the skies.

11 With cheerful heart I then shall sing,
And triumph o'er my vanquish'd foe,
O death, where is thy pointed sting?
My Saviour wards the fatal blow.

12 O when will that illustrious day,
When will that blissful moment come,
That shall my weary soul convey
Safe to her everlasting home?

13 Then shall I leave these fetters here,
And upward rise to joys unknown;
And call, without an anxious fear,
The fair inheritance my own.

14 Adieu to all terrestrial things;
Come, bear me through the starry road,
Bright Seraphs, on your soaring wings,
To see my Saviour and my God.

HYMN 71

Redemption by Christ alone. 1 Peter 1. 18, 19.

1 ENSLAV'D by sin and bound in chains
Beneath its dreadful tyrant sway,
And doom'd to everlasting pains,
We wretched, guilty captives lay.

2 Nor gold, nor gems, could buy our peace,
Nor the whole world's collected store
Suffice to purchase our release;
A thousand worlds were all too poor.

3 Jesus the Lord, the mighty God,
An all-sufficient ransom paid;
Invalued price, his precious blood
For vile rebellious traitors shed.

4 Jesus the sacrifice became,
To rescue guilty souls from hell;
The spotless, bleeding, dying Lamb
Beneath avenging justice fell.

5 Amazing goodness! love divine!
O may our grateful hearts adore
The matchless grace, nor yield to sin,
Nor wear its cruel fetters more!

6 Dear Saviour, let thy love pursue
The glorious work it has begun,
Each secret lurking foe subdue,
And let our hearts be thine alone.

HYMN 72

The Mysteries of Providence.

1 LORD, how mysterious are thy ways!
How blind are we! how mean our praise!
Thy steps can mortal eyes explore?
'Tis ours to wonder and adore.

2 Thy deep decrees from creature-sight
Are hid in shades of awful night;
Amid the lines, with curious eye,
Not angel minds presume to pry.

5 Great God, I would not ask to see
What in futurity shall be;
If light and bliss attend my days,
Then let my future hours be praise.

4 Is darkness and distress my share?
Then let me trust thy guardian care;
Enough for me, if love divine
At length through every cloud shall shine.

5 Yet this my soul desires to know,
Be this my only wish below,
"That Christ is mine!" – this great request
Grant, bounteous God, and I am blest.

HYMN 73.

Refuge and Strength in the Mercy of God.

1 MY God, 'tis to thy mercy-seat
My soul for shelter flies;
'Tis here I find a safe retreat,
When storms and tempests rise.

2 'Tis here my faith resolves to dwell,
Nor shall I be afraid
Of all the powers of earth or hell,
If thou vouchsafe thy aid.

3 My cheerful hope can never die,
If thou my God art near;
Thy grace can raise my comforts high,
And banish every fear.

4 Against thy all-supporting grace
My foes can ne'er prevail;
But oh! if frowns becloud thy face,
Faith, hope, and life will fail

5 My great protector and my Lord,
Thy constant aid impart,
And let thy kind, thy gracious word,
Sustain my trembling heart.

6 O never let my soul remove
From this divine retreat;
Still let me trust thy power and love,
And dwell beneath thy feet.

HYMN 74

Desiring Resignation and Thankfulness.

1 WHEN I survey life's varied scene,
Amid the darkest hours,
Sweet rays of comfort shine between,
And thorns are mix'd with flowers.

2 Lord, teach me to adore thy hand,
From whence my comforts flow;
And let me in this desert land
A glimpse of Canaan know.

3 Is health and ease my happy share?
O may I bless my God;
Thy kindness let my songs declare,
And spread thy praise abroad.

4 While such delightful gifts as these
Are kindly dealt to me,
Be all my hours of health and ease
Devoted, Lord, to thee.

5 In griefs and pains thy sacred word
(Dear solace of my soul!)
Celestial comforts can afford,
And all their power control.

6 When present sufferings pain my heart,
Or future terrors rise,
And light and hope almost depart
From these dejected eyes,

7 Thy powerful word supports my hope,
Sweet cordial of the mind!
And bears my fainting spirit up,
And bids me wait resign'd.

8 And O, whate'er of earthly bliss
Thy sovereign hand denies,
Accepted at thy throne of grace,
Let this petition rise:

9 "Give me a calm, a thankful heart,
From every murmur free;
The blessings of thy grace impart,
And let me live to thee.

10 "Let the sweet hope that thou art mine,
My path of life attend;
Thy presence through my journey shine,
And bless its happy end."

HYMN 75

Desiring the Presence of God. Isaiah 50. 10.

1 HEAR, gracious God, my humble moan;
To thee I breathe my sighs;
When will the mournful night be gone?
And when my joys arise?

2 My God – O could I make the claim –
My Father and my friend,
And call thee mine, by every name,
On which thy saints depend!

3 By every name of power and love
I would thy grace entreat;
Nor should my humble hopes remove,
Nor leave thy sacred feet.

4 Yet though my soul in darkness mourns,
Thy word is all my stay;
Here I would rest till light returns
Thy presence makes my day

5 Speak, Lord, and bid celestial peace
Relieve my aching heart;
O smile, and bid my sorrows cease,
And all the gloom depart.

6 Then shall my drooping spirit rise,
And bless thy healing rays,
And change these deep complaining sighs,
For songs of sacred praise.

HYMN 76

Christ the Life of the Soul. John 14. 19.

1 WHEN sins and fears prevailing rise,
And fainting hope almost expires,
Jesus, to thee I lift my eyes;
To thee I breathe my soul's desires.

2 Art thou not mine, my living Lord?
And can my hope, my comfort die,
Fix'd on thy everlasting word,
That word which built the earth and sky?

3 If my immortal Saviour lives,
Then my immortal life is sure;
His word a firm foundation gives;
Here let me build, and rest secure.

4 Here let my faith unshaken dwell,
Immovable the promise stands;
Nor all the powers of earth or hell
Can e'er dissolve the sacred bands.

5 Here, O my soul, thy trust repose;
If Jesus is for ever mine,
Not death itself, that last of foes,
Shall break a union so divine.

HYMN 77

Aspiring towards Heaven.

1 VAIN world, be gone, nor vex my heart
With thy deluding wiles;
Hence, empty promiser, depart,
With all thy soothing smiles.

2 Superior bliss invites my eyes,
Delight unmix'd with woe;
Now let my nobler thoughts arise
To joys unknown below.

3 Yon starry plains, how bright they shine,
With radiant specks of light;
Fair pavement of the courts divine,
That sparkles on the sight!

4 'Tis distance lessens every star;
Could I behold them nigh,

Bright worlds of wonder would appear
To my astonish'd eye!

5 Thus heavenly joys attract my eyes,
My heart the lustre warms;
But could I reach those upper skies,
How infinite their charms!

6 Come, heaven-born faith, and aid my flight,
And guide my rising thought,
Till earth, still lessening to my sight,
Shall vanish, quite forgot.

7 But when to reach those blissful plains
Her utmost ardour tries,
And almost hears the charming strains
Of hymning angels rise,

8 Mortality, with painful load,
Forbids the raptur'd flight;
In vain she seeks heaven's bright abode
And sinks to earth and night.

9 O let thy love, my God, my King,
My hope, my heart, inspire;
And teach my faith with stronger wing
To rise, and warm desire.

10 Oft let thy shining visits cheer
This dark abode of clay,
Till I shall leave these fetters here,
And rise to endless day.

HYMN 78

God my only Happiness.

1 WHEN fill'd with grief, my anxious heart
To thee, my God, complains;
Sweet pleasure mingles with the smart,
And softens all my pains.

2 Earth flies with all her soothing charms,
Nor I the loss deplore;
No more, ye phantoms, mock my arms,
Nor tease my spirit more.

3 I languish for superior joy
To all that earth bestows;
For pleasure which can never cloy,
Nor change, nor period knows.

4 Still, must the scenes of bliss remain
Conceal'd from mortal eyes?
And must my wishes rise in vain,
And never reach the skies?

5 My God, O could I call thee mine
Without a wavering fear,
This would be happiness divine,
A heaven of pleasure here!

6 This joy my wishes long to find,
To this my heart aspires,
A bliss, immortal as the mind,
And vast as its desires!

HYMN 79

Mourning the Absence of God, and longing for his Gracious Presence.

1 MY God, to thee I call –
Must I for ever mourn?
So far from thee, my life, my all
O when wilt thou return?

2 Dark as the shades of night
My gloomy sorrows rise,
And hide thy soul-reviving light
From these desiring eyes.

3 My comforts all decay,
My inward foes prevail;
If thou withhold thy healing ray,
Expiring hope will fail.

4 Away, distressing fears;
My gracious God is nigh,
And heavenly pity sees my tears,
And marks each rising sigh.

5 Dear source of all my joys,
And solace of my care,
O wilt thou hear my plaintive voice
And grant my humble prayer?

6 These envious clouds remove;
Thy cheering light restore;
Confirm my interest in thy love
Till I can doubt no more.

7 Then if my troubles rise,
To thee, my God, I'll flee,
And raise my hopes above the skies,
And cast my cares on thee.

HYMN 80

God the only Refuge of the Troubled Mind.

1 DEAR refuge of my weary soul,
On thee, when sorrows rise,
On thee, when waves of trouble roll,
My fainting hope relies.

2 While hope revives, though press'd with fears,
And I can say, my God,

Beneath thy feet I spread my cares,
  And pour my woes abroad.

3 To thee I tell each rising grief,
  For thou alone canst heal;
Thy word can bring a sweet relief
  For every pain I feel.

4 But oh! when gloomy doubts prevail,
  I fear to call thee mine!
The springs of comfort seem to fail,
  And all my hopes decline.

5 Yet, gracious God, where shall I flee?
  Thou art my only trust,
And still my soul would cleave to thee,
  Though prostrate in the dust.

6 Hast thou not bid me seek thy face?
  And shall I seek in vain?
And can the ear of sovereign grace
  Be deaf when I complain?

7 No, still the ear of sovereign grace
  Attends the mourner's prayer;
O may I ever find access,
  To breathe my sorrows there.

8 Thy mercy-seat is open still;
  Here let my soul retreat,
With humble hope attend thy will,
  And wait beneath thy feet.

HYMN 81

Complaining at the Throne of Grace.

1 O'ERWHELM'D with restless griefs and fears,
  Lord, I approach thy mercy-seat,
With aching heart and flowing tears,
  To pour my sorrows at thy feet.

2 Can mournful penitence and prayer
  Address thy mercy-seat in vain?
Unnotic'd by thy gracious ear,
  Can sorrow and distress complain?

3 Thy promises are large and free,
  To humble souls who seek thy face;
O where for refuge can I flee,
  My God! but to the throne of grace?

4 My God! for yet my trembling heart
  Would fain rely upon thy word;
Fain would I bid my fears depart,
  And cast my burden on the Lord.

5 Thou see'st the tempest of my soul,
  These restless waves of fear and sin;
Thy voice can all their rage control,
  And make a sacred calm within.

6 Amid the gloomy shades of night,
  To thee I lift my longing eyes;
My Saviour God, my life, my light,
  When will thy cheering beams arise?

7 My thoughts recall thy favours past,
  In many a dark distressing hour,
Thy kind support my heart confess'd,
  And own'd thy wisdom, love, and power.

8 And still these bright perfections shine,
  Eternal their unclouded rays;
Unchanging faithfulness is thine,
  And just and right are all thy ways.

9 And can my vile ungrateful heart
  Still harbour black distrust and fear?
O bid these heavy clouds depart,
  Bright sun of righteousness, appear.

10 Let thy enlivening, healing voice,
  The kind assurance of thy love
Relieve my heart, revive my joys,
  And all my sins and fears remove.

HYMN 82

Submission to God under Affliction.

1 PEACE, my complaining, doubting heart,
  Ye busy cares, be still;
Adore the just, the sovereign Lord,
  Nor murmur at his will.

2 Unerring wisdom guides his hand;
  Nor dares my guilty fear,
Amid the sharpest pains I feel,
  Pronounce his hand severe.

3 To soften every painful stroke,
  Indulgent mercy bends,
And unrepining when I plead,
  His gracious ear attends.

4 Let me reflect with humble awe
  Whene'er my heart complains,
Compar'd with what my sins deserve,
  How easy are my pains!

5 Yes, Lord, I own thy sovereign hand,
  Thou just, and wise, and kind;
Be every anxious thought suppress'd,
  And all my soul resign'd.

6 But oh! indulge this only wish,
  This boon I must implore!

Assure my soul that thou art mine;
My God, I ask no more.

HYMN 83

Trusting in the Divine Veracity.

1 WHEN sin and sorrow, fear and pain,
My trembling heart dismay,
My feeble strength, alas, how vain!
It sinks and dies away.

2 My spirit asks a firmer prop;
I lean upon the Lord;
My God, the pillar of my hope
Is thy unchanging word.

8 On this are built the brightest joys,
Celestial beings know,
And 'tis the same almighty voice
Supports the saints below.

4 'Tis this upholds the rolling spheres,
And heaven's immortal frame;
Then, O my soul, suppress thy fears,
Thy basis is the same.

5 The sacred word, the solemn oath,
For ever must remain;
I trust in everlasting truth,
Nor can my trust be vain.

HYMN 84

Time flying and Death approaching,

1 AWAKE, my soul, nor slumbering lie
Amid the gloomy haunts of death;
Perhaps the awful hour is nigh,
Commission'd for my parting breath.

2 That awful hour will soon appear,
Swift on the wings of time it flies,
When all that pains or pleases here,
Will vanish from my closing eyes.

3 Death calls my friends, my neighbours hence,
And none resist the fatal dart;
Continual warnings strike my sense,
And shall they fail to reach my heart?

4 Shall gay amusements rise between,
When scenes of horror spread around?
Death's pointed arrows fly unseen,
But ah, how sure, how deep they wound!

5 Think, O my soul, how much depends
On the short period of a day;
Shall time, which heaven in mercy lends,
Be negligently thrown away!

6 Thy remnant minutes strive to use;
Awake! rouse every active power!
And not in dreams and trifles lose
This little now! this precious hour!

7 Lord of my life, inspire my heart
With heavenly ardour, grace divine;
Nor let thy presence e'er depart,
For strength, and life, and death are thine.

8 O teach me the celestial skill,
Each awful warning to improve!
And while my days are shortening still,
Prepare me for the joys above.

9 Ensure my nobler life on high,
Life, from a dying Saviour's blood!
Then, though my minutes swiftly fly,
They bear me nearer to my God.

HYMN 85

Victory over Death through Christ. 1 Cor. 15. 57

1 WHEN death appears before my sight
In all his dire array,
Unequal to the dreadful fight,
My courage dies away.

2 How shall I meet this potent foe,
Whose frown my soul alarms?
Dark horror sits upon his brow,
And victory waits his arms.

3 But see my glorious Leader nigh!
My Lord, my Saviour lives;
Before him death's pale terrors fly,
And my faint heart revives.

4 Jesus, be thou my sure defence,
My guard for ever near;
And faith shall triumph over sense,
And never yield to fear.

5 O may I meet the dreadful hour,
With fortitude divine;
Sustain'd by thy almighty power,
The conquest must be mine.

6 What though subdu'd this body lies,
Slain in the mortal strife,
My spirit shall unconquer'd rise
To a diviner life.

7 Lord, I commit my soul to thee;
Accept the sacred trust;

Receive this nobler part of me,
And watch my sleeping dust,

8 Till that illustrious morning come,
When all thy saints shall rise,
And cloth'd in full, immortal bloom,
Attend thee to the skies.

9 When thy triumphant armies sing
The honours of thy name,
And heaven's eternal arches ring,
With glory to the Lamb,

10 O let me join the raptur'd lays,
And with the blissful throng,
Resound salvation, power, and praise,
In everlasting song.

HYMN 86

Christ the Supreme Beauty. Isaiah 33. 17.

1 SHOULD nature's charms to please the eye
In sweet assemblage join,
All nature's charms would droop and die,
Jesus, compar'd with thine.

2 Vain were her fairest beams display'd,
And vain her blooming store;
E'en brightness languishes to shade,
And beauty is no more.

3 But ah! how far from mortal sight
The Lord of glory dwells!
A veil of interposing night
His radiant face conceals.

4 O could my longing spirit rise
On strong immortal wing,
And reach thy palace in the skies,
My Saviour and my King!

5 There myriads worship at thy feet,
And there (divine employ!)
The triumphs of thy love repeat,
In songs of endless joy.

6 Thy presence beams eternal day,
O'er all the blissful place!
Who would not drop this load of clay,
And die to see thy face?

HYMN 87

The Promised Land. Isaiah 33. 17.

1 FAR from these narrow scenes of night
Unbounded glories rise,
And realms of infinite delight,
Unknown to mortal eyes.

2 Fair distant land! – could mortal eyes
But half its joys explore,
How would our spirits long to rise,
And dwell on earth no more!

3 There pain and sickness never come,
And grief no more complains!
Health triumphs in immortal bloom,
And endless pleasure reigns!

4 From discord free and war's alarms,
And want, and pining care;
Plenty and peace unite their charms,
And smile unchanging there.

5 There rich varieties of joy,
Continual feast the mind;
Pleasures which fill, but never cloy,
Immortal and refin'd!

6 No factious strife, no envy there,
The sons of peace molest;
But harmony and love sincere
Fill every happy breast.

7 No cloud those blissful regions know,
For ever bright and fair!
For sin, the source of mortal woe,
Can never enter there.

8 There no alternate night is known,
Nor sun's faint sickly ray;
But glory from the sacred throne
Spreads everlasting day.

9 The glorious monarch there displays
His beams of wondrous grace;
His happy subjects sing his praise,
And bow before his face.

10 O may the heavenly prospect fire
Our hearts with ardent love,
Till wings of faith and strong desire
Bear every thought above.

11 Prepare us, Lord, by grace divine,
For thy bright courts on high;
Then bid our spirits rise and join
The chorus of the sky.

HYMN 88

The Heavenly Shepherd. Psalm 23. 1, 2, 3.

1 WHILE my Redeemer's near,
My shepherd and my guide,
I bid farewell to anxious fear;
My wants are all supplied.

2 To ever-fragrant meads,
Where rich abundance grows,
His gracious hand indulgent leads,
And guards my sweet repose.

3 Along the lovely scene,
Cool waters gently roll,
And kind refreshment smiles serene,
To cheer my fainting soul.

4 Here let my spirit rest;
How sweet a lot is mine!
With pleasure, food, and safety blest;
Beneficence divine.

5 Dear Shepherd, if I stray,
My wandering feet restore,
To thy fair pastures guide my way
And let me rove no more.

6 Unworthy as I am
Of thy protecting care,
Jesus, I plead thy gracious name,
For all my hopes are there.

HYMN 89

The Christian's Noblest Resolution. Joshua 24. 15.

1 AH, wretched souls, who strive in vain,
Slaves to the world, and slaves to sin!
A nobler toil may I sustain,
A nobler satisfaction win.

2 May I resolve with all my heart,
With all my powers to serve the Lord,
Nor from his precepts e'er depart,
Whose service is a rich reward.

3 O be his service all my joy;
Around let my example shine,
Till others love the blest employ,
And join in labours so divine.

4 Be this the purpose of my soul,
My solemn, my determin'd choice,
To yield to his supreme control,
And in his kind commands rejoice.

5 O may I never faint nor tire,
Nor wandering leave his sacred ways;
Great God, accept my soul's desire,
And give me strength to live thy praise.

HYMN 90

The Saviour's Invitation. John 9. 37.

1 THE Saviour calls; let every ear
Attend the heavenly sound;
Ye doubting souls dismiss your fear;
Hope smiles reviving round.

2 For every thirsty, longing heart,
Here streams of bounty flow,
And life, and health, and bliss impart,
To banish mortal woe.

3 Here springs of sacred pleasure rise,
To ease your every pain,
(Immortal fountain! full supplies!)
Nor shall you thirst in vain.

4 Ye sinners, come, 'tis mercy's voice;
The gracious call obey;
Mercy invites to heavenly joys –
And can you yet delay?

5 Dear Saviour, draw reluctant hearts;
To thee let sinners fly,
And take the bliss thy love imparts,
And drink and never die.

HYMN 91

Jesus the Best Beloved.

1 DEAR centre of my best desires
And sovereign of my heart;
What sweet delight thy name inspires!
What bliss thy smiles impart!

2 Jesus! O loveliest, dearest name!
And wilt thou condescend
To own the bold, yet humble claim,
My everlasting friend?

3 Too oft, alas, my passions rove
In search of meaner charms;
Trifles unworthy of my love
Divide me from thy arms.

4 Ye teasing vanities depart;
I seek my absent Lord;
No balm to ease my aching heart
Can all your joys afford.

5 Come, dearest Lord, with power divine,
And drive thy foes away;
O be my heart, my passions, thine,
And never, never stray.

HYMN 92

Desiring to know and love Him more.

1 THOU lovely source of true delight,
Whom I unseen adore,
Unveil thy beauties to my sight,
That I may love thee more.

2 Thy glory o'er creation shines;
But in thy sacred word
I read, in fairer, brighter lines,
My bleeding, dying Lord.

3 'Tis here, whene'er my comforts droop,
And sins and sorrows rise,
Thy love, with cheerful beams of hope,
My fainting heart supplies.

4 But ah, too soon the pleasing scene
Is clouded o'er with pain;
My gloomy fears rise dark between,
And I again complain.

5 Jesus, my Lord, my life, my light,
O come with blissful ray;
Break radiant through the shades of night,
And chase my fears away.

6 Then shall my soul with rapture trace
The wonders of thy love;
But the full glories of thy face
Are only known above.

HYMN 93

The Glorious Presence of Christ in Heaven. John 17. 24.

1 O for a sweet inspiring ray,
To animate our feeble strains,
From the bright realms of endless day,
The blissful realms, where Jesus reigns!

2 There low before his glorious throne
Adoring saints and angels fall,
And with delightful worship own
His smile their bliss, their heaven, their all.

3 Immortal glories crown his head,
While tuneful hallelujahs rise,
And love, and joy, and triumph spread
Through all th' assemblies of the skies.

4 He smiles, and seraphs tune their songs
To boundless rapture while they gaze;
Ten thousand thousand joyful tongues
Resound his everlasting praise.

5 There all the favourites of the Lamb
Shall join at last the heavenly choir;
O may the joy-inspiring theme
Awake our faith and warm desire.

6 Dear Saviour, let thy Spirit seal
Our interest in that blissful place;
Till death remove this mortal veil,
And we behold thy lovely face.

HYMN 94

The Happiness of the Saints above. John 17. 24.

1 O could we read our interest here,
Jesus, in these dear words of thine,
A heaven of pleasure would appear,
A blissful view of joys divine.

2 Dear Saviour, let thy boundless grace
Remove our guilt, our fears remove;
Then shall our thoughts with rapture trace
The radiant mansions of thy love.

3 There shall our hearts no more complain,
Nor sin prevail, nor grace decay;
But perfect joy for ever reign,
One glorious, undeclining day.

4 No darkness there shall cloud our sight;
These now dejected, feeble eyes
Shall gaze with infinite delight
On the full glories of the skies.

5 There shall we see thy lovely face,
And chang'd to purity divine
Partake the splendours of the place,
And in thy glorious likeness shine.

6 Yes, dearest Lord, to dwell with thee,
Thy praise our endless, sweet employ,
Must be immense felicity,
A full infinitude of joy!

7 O let thy Spirit now impart,
The kind assurance of thy love,
With sealing power to every heart,
Sweet earnest of the joys above.

HYMN 95

Hymn to Jesus.

1 JESUS, in thy transporting name
What blissful glories rise!
Jesus, the angels' sweetest theme!
The wonder of the skies!

2 Well might the skies with wonder view
A love so strange as thine!
No thought of angels ever knew
Compassion so divine!

3 Didst thou forsake thy radiant crown
And boundless realms of day,
(Aside thy robes of glory thrown)
To dwell in feeble clay?

4 Jesus, and didst thou leave the sky
For miseries and woes?
And didst thou bleed, and groan, and die,
For vile, rebellious foes?

5 Through the deep horrors of thy pain
Then love triumphant smil'd;
Earth trembled at the dreadful scene,
And heaven was reconcil'd.

6 Victorious love! can language tell
The wonders of thy power,
Which conquer'd all the force of hell
In that tremendous hour?

7 Is there a heart that will not bend
To thy divine control?
Descend, O sovereign love, descend,
And melt the stubborn soul.

8 O may our willing hearts confess
Thy sweet, thy gentle sway;
Glad captives of resistless grace
Thy pleasing rule obey.

9 Come, dearest Lord, extend thy reign,
Till rebels rise no more;
Thy praise all nature then shall join,
And heaven and earth adore.

HYMN 96

Praise to the Redeemer.

1 TO our Redeemer's glorious name,
Awake the sacred song!
O may his love (immortal flame!)
Tune every heart and tongue.

2 His love, what mortal thought can reach?
What mortal tongue display?
Imagination's utmost stretch
In wonder dies away.

3 Let wonder still with love unite,
And gratitude and joy;
Be Jesus our supreme delight,
His praise, our best employ.

4 Jesus who left his throne on high,
Left the bright realms of bliss,
And came on earth to bleed and die –
Was ever love like this?

5 Dear Lord, while we adoring pay
Our humble thanks to thee,
May every heart with rapture say,
The Saviour died for me.

6 O may the sweet, the blissful theme,
Fill every heart and tongue,
Till strangers love thy charming name,
And join the sacred song.

HYMN 97

Desiring to love Christ without wandering.

1 YE earthly vanities, depart,
For ever hence remove;
Jesus alone deserves my heart,
And every thought of love.

2 His heart, where love and pity dwelt
In all their softest forms,
Sustain'd the heavy load of guilt,
For lost, rebellious worms:

3 His heart, whence love abundant flow'd
To wash the stains of sin,
In precious streams of vital blood –
Here, all my hopes begin.

4 Can I my bleeding Saviour view,
And yet ungrateful prove,
And pierce his wounded heart anew,
And grieve his injur'd love?

5 Forbid it, Lord; O bind this heart,
This rebel heart of mine,
So firm, that it may ne'er depart,
In chains of love divine.

HYMN 98

The Exalted Saviour.

1 NOW let us raise our cheerful strains,
And join the blissful choir above;
There our exalted Saviour reigns,
And there they sing his wondrous love.

2 While seraphs tune th' immortal song,
O may we feel the sacred flame;
And every heart and every tongue
Adore the Saviour's glorious name.

3 Jesus, who once upon the tree
In agonizing pains expir'd,
Who died for rebels – yes, 'tis he!
How bright! how lovely! how admir'd!

4 Jesus, who died that we might live,
Died in the wretched traitor's place –
O what returns can mortals give,
For such immeasurable grace?

5 Were universal nature ours,
And art with all her boasted store,

Nature and art with all their powers,
Would still confess the offerer poor!

6 Yet though for bounty so divine,
We ne'er can equal honours raise,
Jesus, may all our hearts be thine,
And all our tongues proclaim thy praise.

HYMN 99

The Wonders of Redemption. 1 Pet. 3. 18.

1 AND did the holy and the just,
The Sovereign of the skies,
Stoop down to wretchedness and dust,
That guilty worms might rise?

2 Yes, the Redeemer left his throne,
His radiant throne on high,
(Surprising mercy! love unknown!)
To suffer, bleed, and die.

3 He took the dying traitor's place,
And suffered in his stead;
For man (O miracle of grace!)
For man the Saviour bled!

4 Dear Lord, what heavenly wonders dwell
In thy atoning blood!
By this are sinners snatch'd from hell,
And rebels brought to God.

5 Jesus, my soul, adoring, bends
To love so full, so free;
And may I hope that love extends
Its sacred power to me?

6 What glad return can I impart,
For favours so divine?
O take my all, this worthless heart,
And make it only thine.

HYMN 100

Communion with Christ at his Table.

1 TO Jesus, our exalted Lord,
(Dear name, by heaven and earth ador'd!)
Fain would our hearts and voices raise
A cheerful song of sacred praise.

2 But all the notes which mortals know,
Are weak and languishing and low;
Far, far above our humble songs,
The theme demands immortal tongues.

3 Yet while around his board we meet,
And worship at his glorious feet;
O let our warm affections move
In glad returns of grateful love.

4 Yes, Lord, we love and we adore,
But long to know and love thee more;
And while we taste the bread and wine,
Desire to feed on joys divine.

5 Let faith our feeble senses aid,
To see thy wondrous love display'd,
Thy broken flesh, thy bleeding veins,
Thy dreadful, agonizing pains.

6 Let humble, penitential woe,
With painful, pleasing anguish flow,
And thy forgiving smiles impart
Life, hope, and joy, to every heart.

HYMN 101

Faith in a Redeemer's Sufferings.

1 LORD, when my thoughts delighted rove
Amid the wonders of thy love,
Sweet hope revives my drooping heart,
And bids intruding fears depart.

2 But while thy sufferings I survey,
And faith enjoys a heavenly ray,
These dear memorials of thy pain,
Present anew the dreadful scene.

3 I hear thy groans with deep surprise,
And view thy wounds with weeping eyes,
Each bleeding wound, each dying groan,
With anguish fraught, and pains unknown.

4 For mortal crimes a sacrifice,
The Lord of life, the Saviour dies;
What love, what mercy, how divine!
Jesus, and can I call thee mine?

5 Repentant sorrow fills my heart,
But mingling joy allays the smart;
O may my future life declare
The sorrow and the joy sincere.

6 Be all my heart and all my days
Devoted to my Saviour's praise;
And let my glad obedience prove
How much I owe, how much I love.

HYMN 102

A Dying Saviour.

1 STRETCH'D on the cross the Saviour dies;
Hark! his expiring groans arise!
See, from his hands, his feet, his side,
Runs down the sacred crimson tide!

2 But life attends the deathful sound,
And flows from every bleeding wound;

The vital stream, how free it flows,
To save and cleanse his rebel foes!

3 To suffer in the traitor's place,
To die for man, surprising grace!
Yet pass rebellious angels by –
O why for man, dear Saviour, why?

4 And didst thou bleed, for sinners bleed?
And could the sun behold the deed?
No, he withdrew his sickening ray,
And darkness veil'd the mourning day.

5 Can I survey this scene of woe,
Where mingling grief and wonder flow;
And yet my heart unmov'd remain,
Insensible to love or pain?

6 Come, dearest Lord, thy power impart,
To warm this cold, this stupid heart;
Till all its powers and passions move,
In melting grief and ardent love.

HYMN 103

Meditating on the Redeemer's Sufferings.

1 RECALL, my heart, that dreadful hour,
When Jesus on the cursed tree
Infinite pains and sorrows bore –
Think, O my soul, was this for thee?

2 See, crown'd with thorns that sacred head,
With beams of glory once adorn'd!
That voice, which heaven and earth obey'd,
Is now by traitors mock'd and scorn'd.

3 And see those lovely, melting eyes,
Whence kind compassion often flow'd,
Now rais'd imploring to the skies,
For harden'd souls athirst for blood!

4 Those healing hands with blessings fraught,
Nail'd to the cross with pungent smart!
Inhuman deed! could no kind thought
To pity move the ruthless heart?

5 But oh! what agonies unknown,
His soul sustained beneath the load
Of mortal crimes! how deep the groan
Which calm'd the vengeance of a God!

6 He groan'd! he died! the awful scene
Of wonder, grief, surprising love
For ever let my heart retain,
Nor from my Saviour's feet remove.

7 Jesus, accept this wretched heart,
Which trembling, mourning, comes to thee;
The blessing of thy death impart,
And tell my soul, 'tis all for me.

HYMN 104

Sin the Cause of Christ's Death.

1 WAS it for sin, for mortal guilt,
The Saviour gave his vital blood?
For sin amazing anguish felt,
The wrath of an offended God?

2 When bleeding, groaning on the tree,
He breath'd such agonizing cries,
When nature suffer'd, Lord, with thee,
And darkness cloth'd the mourning skies.

3 And shall I harbour in my breast
(Tremble, my soul, at such a deed)
This dreadful foe, this fatal guest?
'Twas sin that made my Saviour bleed.

4 'Tis sin that would my ruin prove,
And sink me down to endless woe;
But O forbid it, heavenly love,
And save me from the cursed foe.

5 Ye sins, ye cruel sins, depart,
Your tyrant sway I cannot bear;
My rightful sovereign claims my heart;
Jesus alone shall govern here.

6 Come, glorious conqueror, gracious Lord,
Thy all prevailing power employ;
O come, with thy resistless word,
These hateful enemies destroy.

7 Guilty and weak to thee I fly,
My Lord, my Saviour, and my friend,
On thy almighty arm rely,
On thy atoning blood depend.

8 My all of hope is fix'd on thee,
For thou alone hast power divine;
O come, and conquer, Lord, for me,
And all the glory shall be thine.

HYMN 105

Christ dying and rising.

1 COME tune, ye saints, your noblest strains,
Your dying, rising Lord to sing,
And echo to the heavenly plains
The triumphs of your Saviour-King.

2 In songs of grateful rapture tell
How he subdu'd your potent foes,
Subdu'd the powers of death and hell,
And, dying, finish'd all your woes.

3 Then to his glorious throne on high
Return'd, while hymning angels round,
Through the bright arches of the sky,
The God, the conquering God, resound.

4 Almighty love! victorious power!
Not angel-tongues can e'er display
The wonders of that dreadful hour,
The joys of that illustrious day.

5 Then well may mortals try in vain,
In vain their feeble voices raise;
Yet Jesus hears the humble strain,
And kindly owns our wish to praise.

6 Dear Saviour, let thy wondrous grace
Fill every heart and every tongue,
Till the full glories of thy face
Inspire a sweeter, nobler song.

HYMN 106

On the Public Fast. Feb. 6, 1756.

1 SEE, gracious God, before thy throne
Thy mourning people bend!
'Tis on thy sovereign grace alone
Our humble hopes depend.

2 Tremendous judgments from thy hand,[2]
Thy dreadful power display;
Yet mercy spares this guilty land,
And yet we live to pray.

3 Great God, and why is Britain spar'd,
Ungrateful as we are?
O be these awful warnings heard,
While mercy cries forbear.

4 What numerous crimes increasing rise,
O'er all this wretched isle!
What land so favour'd of the skies,
And yet what land so vile?

5 How chang'd, alas! are truths divine,
For error, guilt, and shame!
What impious numbers, bold in sin,
Disgrace the Christian name!

6 O bid us turn, almighty Lord,
By thy resistless grace;
Then shall our hearts obey thy word,
And humbly seek thy face.

7 Then should insulting foes invade,
We shall not sink in fear;
Secure of never failing aid,
If God, our God, is near.

HYMN 107

National Judgments deprecated.
On the Fast. Feb. 11, 1757.

1 WHILE justice waves her vengeful hand
Tremendous o'er a guilty land,
Almighty God, thy awful power,
With fear and trembling, we adore.

2 Where shall we fly, but to thy feet?
Our only refuge is thy seat;
Thy seat, where potent mercy pleads,
And holds thy thunder from our heads.

3 While peace and plenty bless'd our days,
Where was the tribute of thy praise!
Ungrateful race! how have we spent
The blessings which thy goodness lent.

4 Pale famine now, and wasting war,
With threatening frown thy wrath declare;
But war and famine are thy slaves,
Nor can destroy when mercy saves.

5 Look down, O Lord, with pitying eye;
Though loud our crimes for vengeance cry,
Let mercy's louder voice prevail,
Nor thy longsuffering patience fail.

6 Encourag'd by thy sacred word,
May we not plead the blest record,
That when a humble nation mourns,
Thy rising wrath to pity turns.

7 O let thy sovereign grace impart
Contrition to each rocky heart,
And bid sincere repentance flow,
A general, undissembled woe.

8 Our arms, O God of armies, bless,
(Thy hand alone can give success)
And make our haughty neighbours own
That heaven protects the British throne.

9 Fair smiling peace again restore;
With plenty bless the pining poor,
And may a happy, thankful land
Obedient own thy guardian hand.

2 Earthquake at Lisbon, &c

HYMN 108

On the same. Pleading for Mercy.

1 COME, let our souls adore the Lord,
Whose judgments yet delay,
Who yet suspends the lifted sword,
And gives us leave to pray.

2 In armies, fleets, or strong allies,
No more we place our trust;
On God alone our hope relies,
Kind, potent, wise, and just.

3 Great is our guilt, our fears are great,
But let us not despair;
Still open is the mercy-seat
To penitence and prayer.

4 Kind Intercessor, to thy love
This blessed hope we owe;
O let thy merits plead above,
While we implore below.

5 O gracious God, for Jesus' sake,
Attend thy Britain's cry;
Nor let the kindling vengeance break
Destructive from thine eye.

6 Though justice near thy awful throne,
Attends thy dread command,
Lord, hear thy servants, hear thy Son,
And save a guilty land.

HYMN 109

National Judgments and Mercies a Call to Repentance. Nov. 1757.

1 LONG has divine compassion strove
With this rebellious land;
O justice, long has pleading love
Withheld thy dreadful hand.

2 At length, ye Britons, lift your eyes,
Your crimes no more pursue;
Behold the gathering tempest rise,
And tremble at the view.

3 See, fraught with vengeance how it spreads!
To mercy instant fly;
Ere yet it burst upon your heads,
Repent, repent or die.

4 Late raging storm, 'twas mercy stay'd;[3]
Her voice destruction heard;
The impetuous winds her voice obey'd,
And awful justice spar'd.

5 Shall every warning be in vain
Your ruin to prevent?
Indulgent mercy calls again,
Return, repent! repent!

6 The voice, ye Britons, hear with awe,
O hear, and turn to God;
Lest mercy, long abus'd, withdraw,
And leave you to the rod.

7 Amighty God, thy powerful grace
Can change us, and forgive;
Can save a guilty rebel race,
And say, Repent, and live.

8 O let thy powerful grace appear,
And justice sheath her sword;
Then shall a rescued nation fear,
And love, and praise the Lord.

HYMN 110

Resignation.

1 WEARY of these low scenes of night,
My fainting heart grows sick of time,
Sighs for the dawn of sweet delight,
Sighs for a distant, happier clime!

2 Ah, why that sigh? – peace, coward heart,
And learn to bear thy lot of woe;
Look round – how easy is thy part,
To what thy fellow-sufferers know.

3 Are not the sorrows of the mind
Entail'd on every mortal birth?
Convinc'd, hast thou not long resign'd
The flattering hope of bliss on earth?

4 'Tis just, 'tis right; thus he ordains,
Who form'd this animated clod;
That needful cares, instructive pains,
May bring the restless heart to God.

5 In him, my soul, behold thy rest,
Nor hope for bliss below the sky:
Come, Resignation, to my breast,
And silence every plaintive sigh.

6 Come, Faith and Hope, celestial pair!
Calm Resignation waits on you;
Beyond these gloomy scenes of care,
Point out a soul-enlivening view.

7 Parent of good, 'tis thine to give
These cheerful graces to the mind;

3 Off Louisburgh.

Smile on my soul, and bid me live
Desiring, hoping, yet resign'd!

8 Thy smile, sweet dawn of endless day!
Can make my weary spirit blest;
While on my Father's hand I stay,
And in his love securely rest.

9 My Father, dear, delightful name!
Replete with life, and joy sincere!
O wilt thou gracious seal my claim,
And banish every anxious fear!

10 Then, cheerful shall my heart survey,
The toils and dangers of the road,
And patient keep the heavenly way,
Which leads me homewards to my God.

HYMN 111

The Faithfulness of God. Isaiah 54. 10.

1 ALMIGHTY Sovereign, gracious Lord,
How full, how firm, thy royal word!
Thy love, how condescending and how kind!
Nor can the power of language more,
With all its force, with all its store,
Confirm the sacred deed, or more securely bind.

2 Sooner the mountains shall depart,
And from their firm foundation start,
Than thy eternal kindness shall remove!
Or I be shaken from thy heart,
If ever there I had a part,
If ever I possess'd an interest in thy love.

3 Yes, Lord, thy promises are clear;
Thy power and faithfulness appear,
Nor can I doubt omnipotence and grace;
But ah! myself, my sins I fear,
These springs of doubt are ever near,
These gloomy clouds which rise and hide thy lovely face.

4 O let thy mercy's healing ray
Arise, and chase these clouds away;
Thy Spirit's witness (evidence divine!)
Beam o'er my soul with sacred light;
Then shall my joys, all pure and bright,
Unclouded and serene, with pleasing lustre shine.

HYMN 112

Divine Contemplation.

1 HOW blest the minds which daily rise
To worlds unseen beyond the skies,
And lose this vale of tears!
On heaven-taught pinions while they soar,
And joys unknown to sense explore,
How low the cares of mortal life! how mean its bliss appears!

2 O for the wings of faith and love,
To bear my thoughts and hopes above
These little scenes of care!
Above these gloomy mists which rise,
And pain my heart, and cloud my eyes,
To see the dawn of heavenly day, and breathe celestial air.

3 Yet higher would I stretch my flight,
And reach the sacred courts of light
Where my Redeemer reigns;
Far-beaming from his radiant throne,
Immortal splendours, joys unknown,
With never-fading lustre shine, o'er all the blissful plains.

4 Ten thousand times ten thousand tongues
There join in rapture-breathing songs,
And tune the golden lyre
To Jesus their exalted Lord;
Dear name, how lov'd! and how ador'd!
His charms awake the heavenly strain, and every note inspire.

5 No short-liv'd pleasure there beguiles,
But perfect bliss for ever smiles,
With undeclining ray;
Thither my thoughts would fain ascend,
But ah! to dust and earth they bend,
Fetter'd with empty vanities, and chain'd to lifeless clay.

6 Dear Lord, and shall I ever be
So far from bliss, so far from thee,
An exile from the sky?
O break these chains, my wishes fire,
And upward bid my heart aspire;
Without thy aid I cannot rise; O give me wings to fly.

HYMN 113

Christ the Christian's Life.

1 O for the animating fire
That tun'd harmonious Watts's lyre,
To sweet seraphic strains!
Celestial fire, that bore his mind
(Earth's vain allurements left behind)
To yonder blissful plains.

2 There Jesus lives, (transporting name!)
Jesus inspir'd the sacred flame,
And gave devotion wings;
With heaven-attracted flight she soar'd,
The realms of happiness explor'd,
And smil'd, and pitied kings,

3 Come, sacred flame, and warm my heart;
Thy animating power impart,
Sweet dawn of life divine!
Jesus, thy love alone can give
The power to rise, the power to live;
Eternal life is thine.

4 If in my heart thy heavenly day
Has e'er diffus'd its vital ray,
I bless the smiling dawn;
But oh, when gloomy clouds arise,
And veil thy glory from mine eyes,
I mourn my joys withdrawn.

5 Then faith, and hope, and love decay;
Without thy life-inspiring ray,
Each cheerful grace declines;
Yet I must live on thee, my Lord,
For still in thy unchanging word
A beam of comfort shines.

6 The vital principle within,
Though oft depress'd with fear and sin,
Can never cease to be;
Though doubt prevails, and grief complains,
Thy hand omnipotent sustains
The life deriv'd from thee.

7 O come, thou life of every grace,
Reveal, reveal thy lovely face;
These gloomy clouds remove!
And bid my fainting hope arise
To thy fair mansions in the skies,
On wings of faith and love.

8 There life divine no languor knows,
But with immortal vigour glows,
By joys immortal fed;
No cloud can spread a moment's night,
For there thy smiles immense delight
And boundless glory shed.

HYMN 114

Desiring to love Christ and obey him.

"If ye love me, keep my commandments."

1 JESUS, my Lord, in thy dear name unite
All things my heart calls great, or good, or sweet;
Divinest springs of wonder and delight
In thee, thou fairest of ten thousand, meet.

2 Do I not love thee? Ah, my conscious heart
Nor boldly dares affirm, nor can deny;
O bid these clouds of gloomy fear depart
With one bright ray from thy propitious eye!

3 Do I not love thee? can I then allow
Within my breast pretenders to thy throne?
O take my homage; at thy feet I bow!
No other Lord my heart desires to own.

4 Take, take my passions in thy sovereign hand;
Refine and mould them with almighty skill;
Then shall I love the voice of thy command,
And all my powers rejoice to do thy will.

5 Thy love inspires the active sons of light;
With swift-wing'd zeal they wait upon thy word;
O let that love, in these abodes of night,
Bid my heart glow to serve my dearest Lord!

6 Come, love divine, my languid wishes raise!
With heavenly zeal this faint cold heart inflame,
To join with angels in my Saviour's praise,
Like them, obey his will, adore his name.

7 But can the mind, with heavy clay oppress,
To emulate seraphic ardour rise?
While sin pollutes her joys, forbids her rest,
How can she join the worship of the skies?

8 Yet he commands to love and to obey,
Whose hand sustains those happy spirits there;
In him, my soul, who is thy guide, thy stay,
In him confide, to him commit thy care.

9 Jesus my Lord, O give me strength divine!
Then shall my powers in glad obedience move;
Receive the heart that wishes to be thine,
And teach, O teach me to obey and love!

HYMN 115

Waiting for Morning. Psalm 30. 5.

1 LONG and mournful is the night,
Mental night of gloomy fear;
Source of comfort, source of light,
When, O when wilt thou appear?
Thy beams alone can bid the gloom depart,
And spread celestial morning o'er my heart.

2 Morning of that glorious day
Which the blest enjoy above,
Where, with full unclouded ray,
Shines thy everlasting love;
Where joy triumphant fills the bright abode,
O happy world! fair paradise of God!

3 Thither if the heart aspire,
Shall it, Lord, aspire in vain?
Shall the breathings of desire
Rise with unavailing pain?
O thou my guide, my solace, and my rest,
In this sad desert shall I rove unblest?

4 Sure the Lord of life is near,
Though a cloud his face conceal;
Jesus, when wilt thou appear?
When thy cheering beams reveal?
When shall thy beams of soul-reviving light
Dispel this gloomy cloud, this mental night?

5 Not in vain aspires the heart
That depends on thee alone;
Light and joy thou wilt impart,
Radiant dawn of bliss unknown.
Here let me wait, beneath thy guardian wing,
Till from thy smile celestial morning spring.

HYMN 116

The Happy Man. From the 23d Psalm.

1 HAPPY the man of heavenly birth,
Beyond the proudest boast of earth,
Whom mercy thus sustains;
To scenes of living verdure led;
Plenty and peace their blessings spread,
And not a thought complains.

2 Conducted by his gracious guide
Where streams of sweet refreshment glide,
And fed with food divine;
God is the guardian of his rest;
Beneath his smile, serenely blest,
He bids his soul recline.

3 Yet, should his feet forgetful stray,
His guide restores, and points the way
To safety, life, and peace;
Still mindful of his glorious name,
A faithful God is still the same,
His paths are righteousness.

4 Should gloomy shades the path o'erspread,
Dark as the mansions of the dead,
His heart no terrors wound;
His heavenly guardian ever near,
Sustains his hope, forbids his fear,
And comfort smiles around.

5 The constant bounty of his Lord
With rich provision spreads his board,
Amid repining foes;
While peace and gladness on his head
Their sweetest odours hourly shed,
His cup with bliss o'erflows.

6 O happy portion! lot divine!
Thus shall indulgent goodness shine
On all his future days;
For ever near his guardian God
Shall mercy fix his blest abode,
And tune his soul to praise.

HYMN 117

The Presence of God the only Comfort in Affliction.

1 IN vain, while dark affliction spreads
Her melancholy gloom,
Kind providence its blessings sheds
And nature's beauties bloom.

2 For all that charms the taste or sight
My heart no wish respires;
O for a beam of heavenly light
When earthly hope expires.

3 Thou only centre of my rest,
Look down with pitying eye,
While with protracted pain opprest,
I breathe the plaintive sigh.

4 Thy gracious presence, O my God,
My every wish contains,
With this, beneath affliction's load,
My heart no more complains.

5 This can my every care control,
Gild each dark scene with light;
This is the sunshine of the soul;
Without it all is night.

6 My Lord, my life, O cheer my heart
With thy reviving ray,
And bid these mournful shades depart
And bring the dawn of day.

7 O happy scenes of pure delight!
Where thy full beams impart
Unclouded beauty to the sight,
And rapture to the heart.

8 Her part in those fair realms of bliss
My spirit longs to know;
My wishes terminate in this,
Nor can they rest below.

9 Lord, shall the breathings of my heart
Aspire in vain to thee?
Confirm my hope, that where thou art
I shall for ever be.

10 Then shall my cheerful spirit sing
The darksome hours away,
And rise on Faith's expanded wing
To everlasting day.

HYMN 118

Faith and Hope in Divine Goodness encouraged by Past Experience. Psalm 23. 6.

1 LORD, while my thoughts with wonder trace
Thy favours past through all my days,
My thankful heart adores thy grace;
I trust that goodness which I praise.

2 Still from the same eternal spring
Thy various, constant bounties flow;
Beneath the shelter of thy wing
I view serene the shades of woe.

3 E'en death's tremendous vale appears
No more in gloomy terrors dress'd;
Thy smile, my God, forbids my fears,
While on thy gracious hand I rest.

4 Through the dark scenes of mortal care,
To humble faith's enraptur'd eye
The distant prospect opens fair,
Of radiant mansions in the sky.

5 Yes, Lord, in thy divine abode
My soul desires and hopes a place,
To dwell for ever near my God,
And view unveil'd thy lovely face.

6 With all my powers renew'd, refin'd,
To join the blissful choir above;
In strains immortal, unconfin'd,
To celebrate my Saviour's love.

HYMN 119

A Thought of Life and Death.

1 THE cares of mortal life, how vain!
How empty every joy!
While grief, and weariness, and pain
The fainting mind employ.

2 But O, that nobler life on high,
To which my hopes aspire!
Does it not prompt the frequent sigh,
And wake the warm desire?

3 When now and then a heavenly ray
Attracts my upward view,
Almost I hail th' approach of day,
And bid the world adieu.

4 Those happy realms of joy and peace
Fain would my heart explore,
Where grief and pain for ever cease,
And I shall sin no more.

5 No darkness there shall cloud the eyes,
No langour seize the frame;
But ever active vigour rise
To feed the vital flame.

6 But ah! – a dreary vale between
Extends its awful gloom;
Fear spreads, to hide the distant scene,
The horrors of the tomb.

7 The thoughts of death's envenom'd dart,
The parting pangs I fear
Alarm this timorous, fainting heart,
And still it lingers here.

8 O for the eye of faith divine,
To pierce beyond the grave!
To see that friend, and call him mine,
Whose arm is strong to save!

9 That friend who left his throne above,
Who met the tyrant's dart,
And (O amazing power of love!)
Receiv'd it in his heart.

10 Here fix my soul, for life is here;
Light breaks amid the gloom;
Trust in the Saviour's love, nor fear
The horrors of the tomb.

11 Jesus, in thee alone I trust;
O tell me I am thine!
I yield this mortal frame to dust;
Eternal life is mine.

HYMN 120

Desiring a firmer affiance in God under afflictions.

1 WHY is my heart with grief opprest?
Can all the pains I feel or fear
Make thee, my soul, forget thy rest,
Forget that God, thy God, is near?

2 Hast thou not often call'd the Lord
Thy refuge, thy almighty friend?
And canst thou fear to trust that word
On which thy hopes of heaven depend?

3 Mortality's unnumber'd ills
Are all beneath his sovereign hand;
Each pain which this frail body feels
Attends, obedient, his command.

4 Lord, form my temper to thy will!
If thou my faith and patience prove,
May every painful stroke fulfill
Thy purposes of faithful love.

5 O may this weak, this fainting mind,
A father's hand adoring see;
Confess thee just, and wise, and kind,
And trust thy word and cleave to thee.

HYMN 121

Trusting in his Mercy with Humble Submission and Hope.

1 INDULGENT still to my request,
How free thy tender mercies are!
With full consent my thoughts attest,
My gracious God, thy faithful care.

2 The hand that holds the rod I see;
That gentle hand I must adore;
That goodness, how divinely free,
Which my expectant hopes implore!

3 Thy hand sustains me lest I faint,
Or at the needful stroke repine;
Thy ear attends to my complaint;
The tenderest pity, Lord, is thine.

4 And can my heart desire in vain,
When he who chastens bids me sue,
That every sorrow, every pain,
Be blest to teach, reclaim, renew?

5 O yet support thy feeble child,
Till thy correcting hand remove!
Be all thy purposes fulfill'd,
And bid me sing thy sparing love.

HYMN 122

Entreating the Presence of God in Affliction.

1 LOW at thy gracious feet I bend,
My God, my everlasting friend;
Permit the claim, O let thy ear
My humble suit indulgent hear!

2 No earthly good my wish inspires;
Great is the boon my soul desires,
But thou hast bid me seek thy face,
Hast bid me ask thy promis'd grace.

3 O may thy favour (bliss divine!)
With fuller, clearer radiance shine!
Brighten my hopes, dispel my fears,
Till not a cloud of grief appears!

4 But O my heart, reflect with shame,
Canst thou prefer so bold a claim?
Conscious how often thou hast stray'd,
By empty vanities betray'd.

5 How oft, ungrateful to thy God,
Have trifles call'd thy thoughts abroad;
Till heavenly pity saw thee roam,
And bade affliction bring thee home.

6 And when the snares of earth were broke
By kind affliction's needful stroke,
Hast thou not own'd, with humble praise,
That just and right are all his ways?

7 Yes, gracious God, before thy throne
My vileness, and thy love I own;
O let that love, with beams divine,
Forgiving, healing, round me shine!

8 Whene'er, ungrateful to my God,
This heedless heart requires the rod,
Thy arm, supporting, I implore;
The hand that chastens can restore.

9 O may the kind correction prove
A fruit of thy paternal love!
Wean me from earth, from sin refine,
And make my heart entirely thine!

10 Then shall my thankful powers rejoice,
And wake to praise this feeble voice;
While mercy, power, and truth employ
My love, my wonder, and my joy.

HYMN 123

Acknowledging his Goodness in supporting and restoring.

1 NOW to thy heavenly Father's praise,
My heart, thy tribute bring:

That goodness which prolongs my days
With grateful pleasure sing.

2 Ye humble souls, who love the Lord,
Come join the pleasing theme;
His mercy, power, and truth record,
And bless his glorious name.

3 Whene'er he sends afflicting pains,
His mercy holds the rod;
His powerful word the heart sustains,
And speaks a faithful God.

4 A faithful God is ever nigh
When humble grief implores;
His ear attends each plaintive sigh,
He pities and restores.

5 No more let diffidence prevail
Our comforts to destroy;
His tender mercies never fail;
Be these our sweet employ.

6 Ah! how unequal to the theme
Our feeble efforts prove!
Ye heavens resound his glorious name,
While we adore and love.

7 Yet fain my grateful soul would bring
Her tribute to thy throne;
Accept the wish, my God, my King,
To make thy goodness known!

8 O be the life thy hand restores
Devoted to thy praise!
To thee, be sacred all my powers,
To thee, my future days!

9 Thy soul-enlivening grace impart;
A warmer love inspire;
And teach the breathings of my heart
Dependence and desire.

HYMN 124

Desiring to praise God for the Experience of his Goodness. Psalm 36. 7.

1 THE loving kindness of the Lord
(Delightful theme!) demands my lays;
Thou, worthy to be lov'd, ador'd,
O teach my heart to sing thy praise!

2 In vain my heart with pleasure tries,
My God, to count thy mercies o'er;
So numerous and so bright they rise,
I gaze, I wonder, I adore!

3 Yet all the powers I have are thine;
For thee those powers I would employ,
And dedicate to love divine,
With humble gratitude and joy.

4 The sweet experience of thy grace,
Which animates my voice to sing,
Incites my soul to seek thy face,
And trust the shelter of thy wing.

5 Thy guardian wing alone can bless;
I find repose and safety there;
The kindest refuge of distress,
A sure relief in every care.

6 O let the wretched sons of woe
To thee apply, on thee depend;
And bid the drooping mourners know
In thee a never-failing friend.

7 Could e'er one soul in deep distress
That fled to thee for refuge say,
"Indulgent mercy would not bless,
And justice frown'd my hopes away"?

8 Ah no, a thousand, thousand tongues
Thy love and truth adoring own,
And offer their united songs
With grateful joy before thy throne.

9 Not e'en those happy minds can trace,
With all their powers renew'd, refin'd,
The boundless glories of thy grace,
O thou omnipotently kind!

10 Ah how shall these poor languid powers
With frail mortality oppress'd
Display the grace my soul adores?
How speak the transports of the blest?

11 Dear Lord, accept my heart's desire,
Till death shall close these mortal days!
Then bid me join the heavenly choir,
And sing thy everlasting praise!

HYMN 125

Penitence and Hope.

1 DEAR Saviour, when my thoughts recall
The wonders of thy grace,
Low at thy feet asham'd I fall,
And hide this wretched face.

2 Shall love like thine be thus repaid?
Ah vile, ungrateful heart!
By earth's low cares detain'd, betray'd,
From Jesus to depart.

3 From Jesus, who alone can give
True pleasure, peace, and rest,
When absent from my Lord, I live
Unsatisfied, unblest.

4 But he, for his own mercy's sake,
My wandering soul restores;
He bids the mourning heart partake
The pardon it implores.

5 O, while I breathe to thee, my Lord,
The penitential sigh,
Confirm the kind, forgiving word
With pity in thine eye!

6 Then shall the mourner at thy feet,
Rejoice to seek thy face;
And grateful own how kind, how sweet,
Thy condescending grace.

HYMN 126

Devoting the Heart to Jesus.

1 JESUS, what shall I do to show
How much I love thy glorious name?
Let my whole heart with rapture glow
Thy boundless goodness to proclaim.

2 Yes, dearest Lord, my heart is thine,
Sacred to thee be all its powers!
O bid me give to love divine
The little remnant of my hours!

3 Thou narrow heart, ye fleeting hours,
How mean the tribute you can raise!
The grace my thankful soul adores
Claims an eternity of praise!

4 Lord, if a distant glimpse of thee
Can give such sweet, such rich delight,
What must their joy, their transport be,
Who dwell for ever in thy sight?

5 To that bright world my heart aspires,
Where all the glories of thy face,
Unveil'd, shall fill the soul's desires,
And tune the song to boundless grace!

6 O teach my heart, my life, my voice
To celebrate thy wondrous love!
Fulfil my hopes, complete my joys,
And bid me join the songs above.

HYMN 127

The Love of Christ exciting Thankful Devotion.

1 O dearer to my thankful heart
Than all the circling sun surveys!
Thy presence only can impart
Light, peace, and gladness to my days.

2 Beneath thy soul-reviving ray
E'en cold affliction's wintry gloom
Shall brighten into vernal day,
And hopes and joys immortal bloom.

3 Vain world, be gone with all thy toys,
I have no room for trifles here;
My heart aspires to nobler joys;
Thy fairest glories disappear.

4 Bright realms of bliss, where Jesus reigns,
My wish, my care, my hope invite;
Where raptur'd seraphs tune their strains
To themes of infinite delight.

5 See, Lord, thy willing subject bows
Adoring low before thy throne;
To thee I gladly pay my vows;
Thou art my sovereign, thou alone.

6 Smile on my soul, and bid me sing,
In concert with the choir above,
The glories of my Saviour King,
The condescensions of his love.

7 Amazing love! that stoop'd so low,
To view with pity's melting eye
A wretch, deserving endless woe!
Amazing love! – did Jesus die?

8 He died, to raise to life and joy
The vile, the guilty, the undone,
O let his praise my hours employ,
Till hours no more their circles run!

9 He died! – ye seraphs, tune your songs;
Resound, resound the Saviour's name;
For nought below immortal tongues
Can ever reach the wondrous theme.

HYMN 128

The Blind Man's Petition.

"Jesus, thou Son of David, have mercy on me."

Luke 18. 38, &c.

1 GREAT Saviour, born of David's race,
O look, with pity look this way!
A helpless wretch implores thy grace,
Implores thy mercy's healing ray!

2 Jesus, thou Lord of life divine,
To whom the sons of woe complain,
Is not unbounded mercy thine?
And can I ask, and ask in vain?

3 Did ever supplicating sigh
In vain to thee its grief impart?
Or mournful object meet thine eye,
That did not move thy melting heart?

4 Around thee crowd a plaintive throng;
I hear their importuning cries;
And now from every thankful tongue
I hear the glad Hosannah rise.

5 O look, with pity look on me,
Wrapp'd in the mournful shades of night!
My hope depends alone on thee,
Speak, Lord; thy word shall give me light!

6 'Tis mercy, mercy I implore!
Speak, Lord; thy humble suppliant raise!
Then shall my heart thy grace adore;
Then shall my tongue resound thy praise.

HYMN 129

Rest and Comfort in Christ alone.

1 WHERE shall I fly but to thy feet,
My Saviour, my almighty friend?
Dear names, beyond expression sweet!
On these my hopes of bliss depend.

2 Where shall I rest but on thy grace,
Thy boundless grace divinely free?
On earth I find no resting place;
Dear Saviour, bid me come to thee!

3 Though sin detains me from my Lord,
I long, I languish to be blest;
O speak one soul-reviving word,
And bid me come to thee, my rest.

4 When I this wretched heart explore,
Here no kind source of hope appears;
But O my soul, that grace adore,
Free grace, which triumphs o'er my fears.

5 Jesus, from thy atoning blood
My only consolation flows;
Hope beams from thee, my Saviour God,
My soul no other refuge knows.

HYMN 130

On the Fifth of November.

1 TO thee, Almighty God, we bring
The humble tribute of our songs;
O teach our thankful hearts to sing!
Or praise will languish on our tongues.

2 While Britain (favour'd of the skies)
Recalls the wonders God hath wrought;
Let grateful joy adoring rise,
And warm to rapture every thought.

3 When hell and Rome combin'd their power,
And doom'd these isles their certain prey;
Thy hand forbade the fatal hour;
Their impious plots in ruin lay.

4 Again our restless cruel foes
Resum'd, avow'd, their black design;
Again to save us God arose,
And Britain own'd the hand divine.

5 Why, gracious God, is Britain sav'd?
Why blest with liberty and light?
Nor by fell tyranny enslav'd,
Nor lost in superstition's night?

6 Not for our sakes, we conscious own,
A wretched, vile, ungrateful race;
'Tis done to make thy glory known,
To shew the wonders of thy grace.

7 The wonders of thy grace complete;
Reform this wretched, guilty land!
Let thankful love, beneath thy feet,
Confess thy kind, thy guardian hand!

8 Let every age adore thy name,
While nature's circling wheels shall roll!
Thy mercies every tongue proclaim,
And sound thy praise from pole to pole.

HYMN 131

On a Day of Prayer for Success in War.

1 LORD, how shall wretched sinners dare
Look up to thy divine abode?
Or offer their imperfect prayer
Before a just, a holy God?

2 Bright terrors guard thy awful seat,
And dazzling glories veil thy face!
Yet mercy calls us to thy feet;
Thy throne is still a throne of grace.

3 O may our souls thy grace adore;
May Jesus plead our humble claim;
While thy protection we implore
In his prevailing, glorious name.

4 With all the boasted pomp of war
In vain we dare the hostile field;
In vain, unless the Lord be there;
Thy arm alone is Britain's shield.

5 Let past experience of thy care
Support our hope, our trust invite!

Again attend our humble prayer;
Again be mercy thy delight!

6 Our arms succeed, our councils guide;
Let thy right hand our cause maintain;
Till war's destructive rage subside,
And peace resume her gentle reign.

7 O when shall time the period bring
When raging war shall waste no more;
When peace shall stretch her balmy wing
From Europe's coast to India's shore?

8 When shall the gospel's healing ray
(Kind source of amity divine!)
Spread o'er the world celestial day?
When shall the nations, Lord, be thine?

HYMN 132

Hymn for a Day of Public Thanksgiving for Peace.

1 GREAT God, inspire each heart and tongue
Thy wondrous goodness to proclaim;
And bid the animating song
Glow with devotion's lively flame.
To thee let favour'd Britain raise
Her sweetest notes of thankful praise.

2 But where shall we begin to trace
The wonders of thy hand divine?
In every season, every place,
How numerous and how bright they shine.
To God, ye favour'd Britons, raise
Your sweetest notes of thankful praise.

3 Abroad, protection and success
Proclaim'd that Britain's God was there;
At home, he bade fair plenty bless;
The fruitful fields confess'd his care.
To God, ye favour'd Britons, raise
Your sweetest notes of thankful praise.

4 But yet beneath the hostile sword
Has many a worthy patriot bled,
And many a mourning heart deplor'd
A friend, a son, a brother dead!
The sword is sheath'd – ye Britons, raise
To God your sweetest notes of praise.

5 The horrors of the sanguine field,
Which sadden'd victory's fairest plume,
To scenes of pleasure now shall yield,
And peace her gentle reign resume.
To God, ye favour'd Britons, raise
Your sweetest notes of thankful praise.

6 Kind peace, from her propitious smiles,
What numerous, various blessings flow!
Great God, to thee these happy isles
Unnumber'd obligations owe.
To thee let favour'd Britain raise
Her sweetest notes of thankful praise.

7 Crown, gracious God, thy gift of peace,
With gifts yet nobler, more divine!
O let thy all-prevailing grace
Make Britain more entirely thine!
Devotion then to thee shall raise
Sublimer notes of thankful praise.

HYMN 133

Breathing after God.

1 WHERE is my God? does he retire
Beyond the reach of humble sighs?
Are these weak breathings of desire
Too languid to ascend the skies?

2 Where is my God? can he be mine,
And yet so long conceal his face?
And must I every joy resign,
Nor hope for his returning grace?

3 Hence, guilty diffidence, depart;
His goodness never can decline;
He sees this weak, this trembling heart,
That yet aspires to call him mine.

4 He hears the breathings of desire;
The weak petition, if sincere,
Is not forbidden to aspire,
And hope to reach his gracious ear.

5 Look up, my soul, with cheerful eye;
See where the great Redeemer stands,
The glorious advocate on high,
With precious incense in his hands.

6 He sweetens every humble groan;
He recommends each broken prayer;
Recline thy hope on him alone,
Whose power and love forbid despair.

7 Teach my weak heart, O gracious Lord,
With stronger faith to call thee mine;
Bid me pronounce the blissful word,
My Father God, with joy divine.

HYMN 134

Filial Submission. Heb. 12. 7.

1 AND can my heart aspire so high,
To say, my Father God!

Lord, at thy feet I fain would lie,
And learn to kiss the rod.

2 I would submit to all thy will,
For thou art good and wise;
Let every anxious thought be still,
Nor one faint murmur rise.

3 Thy love can cheer the darksome gloom,
And bid me wait serene;
Till hopes and joys immortal bloom,
And brighten all the scene.

4 My Father – O permit my heart
To plead her humble claim,
And ask the bliss those words impart
In my Redeemer's name.

HYMN 135

Humble Trust.

1 WHY should my pining spirit be
So long a stranger to my Lord,
When promises divinely free,
Invite me in his sacred word?

2 Does he not bid the weary come,
And call the wretched sons of grief,
To him their refuge and their home,
Their heavenly friend, their sure relief?

3 Yes, by the kindest, tenderest names
My Lord invites my humble trust;
My diffidence he gently blames;
How soft the censure, and how just.

4 This trembling frame, worn out with pains,
On thee my guardian God depends;
And while my fainting heart complains,
To thee the plaintive groan ascends.

5 Though all the powers of nature fail,
And life's pale trembling lamp decline,
Thy grace can bid my faith prevail,
Can give me fortitude divine.

6 That grace which bids my hope aspire
Can every anxious fear remove,
Can give me all my soul's desire,
The full assurance of thy love.

HYMN 136

Hymn to Jesus.

1 SHALL loyal nations hail the day,[4]
That crowns their king with loud acclaim?
And shall not saints their homage pay,
To their beloved Saviour's name?
Ye saints, resound in joyful strains,
Jesus, the King of glory, reigns!

2 Jesus, who vanquish'd all your foes,
Who came to save, who reigns to bless,
From him your every comfort flows,
Life, liberty, and joy, and peace.
Resound, resound in joyful strains,
Jesus, the King of glory, reigns!

3 Yes, thou art worthy, dearest Lord,
Of universal, endless praise;
With every power to be ador'd,
That men or angels e'er can raise.
Let heaven and earth unite their strains,
Jesus, the King of glory, reigns!

4 But earth, nor heaven can e'er proclaim
The boundless glories of their king;
Yet must our hearts adore his name,
Dear name, whence all our blessings spring;
Resound, resound in joyful strains,
Jesus, the King of glory, reigns!

5 How mean the tribute mortals pay,
How cold the heart, how faint the tongue;
But Lord, thy coronation day
Shall tune a more exalted song;
Resounding in immortal strains,
Jesus, the King of glory, reigns!

6 He comes, he comes, with triumph crown'd,
In dazzling robes of light array'd;
Faith views the splendour dawning round;
Earth's fairest lustre sinks in shade.
Resound, resound in joyful strains,
Jesus, the King of glory, reigns!

HYMN 137

Encouragement to Trust in God.

"Casting all your care upon him, for he careth for you." 1 Peter 5. 7.

1 ENGAGING argument! here let me rest
With humble confidence and faith entire;
What less than this can calm my troubled breast?
What more can my distrustful heart desire?

2 Encouraged by so full, so sweet a word,
Fain would my soul forbid intruding fears;
To thee, almighty Father, gracious Lord!
Fain would I bring my load of anxious cares.

4 The coronation of George III.

3 But can a vile, a guilty creature dare
Aspire to hope for favours so divine?
Aspire to claim an interest in thy care,
Or boldly call the glorious blessing mine?

4 O let thy spirit's sacred influence seal
The kind assurance to my doubting soul;
The pardoning love, thy tender care reveal;
The blissful view shall all my fears control.

HYMN 138

The King of Saints.

1 COME, ye that love the Saviour's name,
And joy to make it known;
The sovereign of your hearts proclaim,
And bow before his throne.

2 Behold your King, your Saviour, crown'd
With glories all divine;
And tell the wondering nations round
How bright those glories shine.

3 While majesty's effulgent blaze
Surrounds his awful brow;
E'en angels tremble as they gaze,
And veil'd adoring bow.

4 But love attempers every ray,
Love, how divinely sweet!
That stoops to view the sons of clay,
And calls them to his feet!

5 Infinite power and boundless grace
In him unite their rays;
You that have e'er beheld his face,
Can you forbear his praise?

6 When in his earthly courts we view
The glories of our King;
We long to love as angels do,
And wish like them to sing.

7 And shall we long and wish in vain?
Lord, teach our songs to rise!
Thy love can animate the strain,
And bid it reach the skies.

8 O happy period! glorious day!
When heaven and earth shall raise
With all their powers the raptur'd lay,
To celebrate thy praise.

HYMN 139

Hymn for the Lord's Day Morning.

1 GREAT God, this sacred day of thine
Demands our souls' collected powers;
May we employ in work divine
These solemn, these devoted hours!
O may our souls adoring own
The grace which calls us to thy throne!

2 Hence, ye vain cares and trifles, fly;
Where God resides appear no more;
Omniscient God, thy piercing eye
Can every secret thought explore.
O may thy grace our hearts refine,
And fix our thoughts on things divine.

3 The word of life dispens'd today
Invites us to a heavenly feast;
May every ear the call obey;
Be every heart a humble guest!
O bid the wretched sons of need
On soul-reviving dainties feed!

4 Thy Spirit's powerful aid impart;
O may thy word with life divine
Engage the ear, and warm the heart;
Then shall the day indeed be thine;
Then shall our souls adoring own
The grace which calls us to thy throne.

HYMN 140

Happy Poverty, or the Poor in Spirit blessed.
Matt. 5. 3.

1 YE humble souls, complain no more;
Let faith survey your future store;
How happy, how divinely blest,
The sacred words of truth attest.

2 When conscious grief laments sincere,
And pours the penitential tear;
Hope points to your dejected eyes
The bright reversion in the skies.

3 In vain the sons of wealth and pride
Despise your lot, your hopes deride;
In vain they boast their little stores;
Trifles are theirs, a kingdom yours.

4 A kingdom of immense delight,
Where health, and peace, and joy unite;
Where undeclining pleasures rise,
And every wish hath full supplies.

5 A kingdom which can ne'er decay,
While time sweeps earthly thrones away;

The state which power and truth sustain
Unmov'd for ever must remain.

6 There shall your eyes with rapture view
The glorious Friend that died for you,
That died to ransom, died to raise
To crowns of joy and songs of praise.

7 Jesus, to thee I breathe my prayer;
Reveal, confirm my interest there!
Whate'er my humble lot below,
This, this my soul desires to know!

8 O let me hear that voice divine,
Pronounce the glorious blessing mine!
Enroll'd among thy happy poor,
My largest wishes ask no more.

HYMN 141

The Necessity of Renewing Grace.

1 HOW helpless guilty nature lies,
Unconscious of its load!
The heart unchang'd can never rise,
To happiness and God.

2 The will perverse, the passions blind
In paths of ruin stray;
Reason debas'd can never find
The safe, the narrow way.

3 Can aught beneath a power divine
The stubborn will subdue?
'Tis thine, almighty Saviour, thine
To form the heart anew.

4 'Tis thine the passions to recall,
And upwards bid them rise;
And make the scales of error fall
From reason's darken'd eyes.

5 To chase the shades of death away,
And bid the sinner live!
A beam of heaven, a vital ray,
'Tis thine alone to give.

6 O change these wretched hearts of ours,
And give them life divine!
Then shall our passions and our powers,
Almighty Lord, be thine.

HYMN 142

The Pearl of Great Price. Matt. 13. 46.

1 YE glittering toys of earth, adieu,
A nobler choice be mine;
A real prize attracts my view,
A treasure all divine.

2 Be gone, unworthy of my cares,
Ye specious baits of sense;
Inestimable worth appears,
The pearl of price immense.

3 Jesus, to multitudes unknown,
O name divinely sweet!
Jesus, in thee, in thee alone,
Wealth, honour, pleasure meet.

4 Should both the Indies at my call,
Their boasted stores resign,
With joy I would renounce them all,
For leave to call thee mine.

5 Should earth's vain treasures all depart,
Of this dear gift possess'd,
I'd clasp it to my joyful heart,
And be for ever blest.

6 Dear sovereign of my soul's desires,
Thy love is bliss divine;
Accept the wish that love inspires,
And bid me call thee mine.

HYMN 143

God's Omnipresence.

1 TREMBLE, my soul, with awful conscious fear;
The Lord, the God of Holiness, is here!
Ye sins and empty vanities depart;
Too long, alas, you have possess'd my heart.
Hence to eternal distance fly,
Nor dare the lightnings of his eye;
Dreadfully keen they pierce the soul
And every thought descry.

2 In vain I bid my lurking foes be gone;
Lord, 'tis thy grace, thy mighty grace alone,
Can drive them hence, and all my guilt forgive;
O speak the powerful word, and bid me live!
Life flows amid the crimson tide,
Which issued from the wounded side
Of Jesus, when for guilty man,
He suffer'd, groan'd, and died!

3 O let it flow to my polluted heart,
And life, and health, and purity impart!
The sacred blood shall wash my sins away;
Thy glories then shall shine with kindest ray
(Unmix'd with terrors) round my trembling soul,
And sovereign mercy all my fears control.

Then shall the thought inspire delight,
That I am in my Father's sight,
And thy bright presence bless mine eyes
With beams of heavenly light.

HYMN 144

Human Frailty.

1 O God of mercy, thou that hearest prayer!
Let these poor breathings reach thy gracious ear,
Weak, impotent, and blind, to thee I fly,
O may thy grace my every want supply,
Thy powerful grace, which only can impart
Conviction, life, and vigour to my heart.
Illuminate my yet beclouded eyes!
These empty trifles teach me to despise!
Let nobler cares, my time, my thoughts employ,
And bid my spirit pant for real joy!
Be thy almighty arm my strength, my guide,
And never from thy precepts let me slide.
Let thy kind influence make my future days
A life of pleasure, and a life of praise.

Index to Hymns

PART III

Psalms attempted in Verse[5]

by

Anne Steele

5 Hymns Poems & Psalms by Anne Steele, London 1863. pp.157-210

PSALM 1

1 HAPPY the man, whose heaven-directed feet
Avoid the crowded path where sinners meet;
Who shuns the lofty seat of impious pride,
Of men, who dare Jehovah's law deride.

2 He in that sacred, venerable law,
(Inspiring holy thoughts and pious awe,)
Continual meditates with new delight;
Guide of his day, and solace of his night!

3 Beneath heaven's kindest influence he shall grow,
Like a fair tree where cheering waters flow,
Whose grateful boughs confess the happy soil,
And crown'd with autumn's richest bounty smile.

4 Unfading and secure his hope shall stand,
And prosperous be the labours of his hand;
Not so the sinner's hope; he soon shall find
It flies like chaff before the driving wind.

5 How will the guilty tribes their sentence bear,
When God in awful judgment shall appear?
Then shall no sinner stand before his face,
Or in the blest assembly find a place.

6 The Lord looks down, and guides his children's way,
Safe to the regions of eternal day;
But oh, the flowery paths which sinners tread,
To darkness and to sure perdition lead .

PSALM 2

1 WHY do the heathen nations rise
With unavailing rage?
Why thus to dare th' avenging skies,
In impious plots engage?

2 Proud monarchs meet, and breathing war,
Raise their vain threat'nings high
Against the Lord, and boldly dare
His chosen king defy.

3 "Shall we submit to his commands,
And bend the suppliant knee?
No, let us break the servile bands,
We are, and will be free."

4 Heaven's awful Sovereign, thron'd on high,
Surveys their airy dreams,
He smiles contempt; in ruin lie
Their vainly labour'd schemes.

5 His dreadful anger now awakes;
Their hearts what terrors wound!
Almighty power affronted speaks,
And wrath attends the sound!

6 "My chosen king exalted see,
On Zion's sacred hill!
Attend the solemn fix'd decree,
And learn Jehovah's will!

7 "Thou art my Son, thee I proclaim
Earth's universal Lord;
Of powers, and potentates supreme,
Thy name shall be ador'd.

8 "Ask, and I give to thee alone,
The heathen's wide domain;
And earth's remotest ends shall own
Thy uncontested reign.

9 "Who will not to thy sceptre bow,
Shall feel thy iron rod;
And crush'd in helpless ruin, show
The vengeance of a God."

10 Be wise, ye monarchs, learn to fear
The power, of powers supreme;
With awful, trembling joy revere
The Lord's exalted name.

11 While mercy, with inviting rays,
Shines radiant in his eyes,
Approach; for should his anger blaze,
The unpardoned rebel dies.

12 When fury kindling in his eye
Each guilty breast alarms;
Happy the souls who gladly fly
Tor refuge to his arms.

PSALM 3

1 LORD, how my numerous foes increase!
How fast my troubles rise!
To thee, the sacred spring of peace,
My wearied spirit flies.

2 My numerous foes awake my fears,
While they exulting boast,
"No heavenly aid for him appears,
And all his hopes are lost."

3 But thou, my glory and my shield,
Wilt all my fears control;

A strong defence thy arm shall yield,
And raise my drooping soul.

4 To God I breath'd my ardent cry,
He gracious heard my prayer;
It reached his sacred throne on high,
And he remov'd my care.

5 I laid me down and slept secure;
I wak'd, for God was nigh;
Sustained by his almighty power,
My guard his watchful eye.

6 What though ten thousand foes in arms
Against me should appear;
And war resound its dire alarms,
I will not yield to fear.

7 Arise, O Lord, with saving power,
In my defence engage;
As oft thy potent arm before
Has crush'd their impious rage.

8 Salvation, Lord, is thine alone,
And all thy saints shall find
The bliss my thankful heart has known,
A God for ever kind.

PSALM 4

1 O LORD, my strength, my righteousness,
Attend my humble prayer;
Oft thou hast heard me in distress,
Renew thy ancient care.

2 How long shall scoffers turn with lies
My glory into shame?
Ah, cease these envious vanities,
Nor wound my injur'd name.

3 For know, the man of upright heart,
As his peculiar care,
The Lord himself has set apart,
And when I call will hear.

4 With trembling awe your heart survey,
And every sin repent;
Let true contrition close the day,
And future guilt prevent.

5 The sacrifice the Lord will own,
If thus you seek his face;
Thus humbly bow before his throne,
And trust his pardoning grace.

6 Vain is the toilsome search of good
In all things here below;
Thy smile alone, my gracious God,
Can real bliss bestow.

7 Thy smile, whence all my comfort springs,
With gladness fills my heart;
No joy increasing affluence brings
Such pleasure can impart.

8 My days by thy kind presence blest,
From thee my safety flows;
Thy favour guards my nightly rest,
And gives me sweet repose.

PSALM 8

1 LORD, how glorious is thy name
Through the wide earth's extended frame!
Majestic glories form thy seat,
And heaven adores beneath thy feet.

2 Thy power from tender babes can raise
A monument of wondrous praise:
At thy command the infant song
Shall still the proud blasphemer's tongue.

3 When all thy shining works on high
I meditate with raptur'd eye –
The silver moon, the starry train
Which gild the fair ethereal plain;

4 Lord, what is man, that he should share
Thy notice, thy indulgent care?
That man, frail child of earth, should be
The favourite of the Deity?

5 His place thy forming hand assign'd
But just below the angelic kind;
With noblest favours circled round,
And with distinguish'd honours crown'd:

6 Invested him with power and sway,
And bid the subject brutes obey;
Sovereign of all thy works below,
To him the meaner creatures bow:

7 The bleating flocks, the lowing herds,
The gliding fish, the flying birds;
All that the earth's wide circuit yields,
Natives of air, or seas, or fields.

8 But still let man adoring own,
That thou, O Lord, art King alone;
And through the earth's extended frame,
Declare the glories of thy name.

PSALM 13

1 HOW long wilt thou, O God of grace,
Forget thy wonted love?

How long conceal thy shining face,
Nor bid the cloud remove?

2 How long shall my dejected soul
(Thus pondering o'er her woes,)
In vain endeavour to control
The power of inward foes?

3 Lord, hear my prayer, and heal my woes,
Arise with cheering light;
Or soon these wretched eyes will close
In everlasting night.

4 The powers of darkness will rejoice
To see my life decay,
And triumph with insulting voice
Around their trembling prey.

5 But, Lord, thy mercy hitherto
Has been my only trust;
Let mercy now my joys renew,
And raise me from the dust.

6 Then shall my heart and tongue proclaim
The bounties of my God;
My songs with grateful rapture flame
And spread thy praise abroad.

PSALM 23

1 THE Lord, my shepherd and my guide,
Will all my wants supply;
In safety I shall still abide
Beneath his watchful eye.

2 Amid the verdant flowery meads
He makes my sweet repose;
When pain'd with thirst he gently leads
Where living water flows.

3 If from his fold I thoughtless stray,
He leads the wanderer home,
And shews my erring feet the way
Where dangers cannot come.

4 Though hastening to the silent tomb,
And death's dark shades appear;
Thy presence, Lord, shall cheer the gloom,
And banish every fear.

5 No evil can my soul dismay,
While I am near my God;
My comfort, my support and stay,
Thy staff and guiding rod.

6 Thy constant bounties me surround,
Amid my envious foes;
My favour'd head with gladness crown'd,
My cup with blessings flows.

7 Thus shall thy goodness, love, and care,
Attend my future days;
And I shall dwell for ever near
My God, and sing his praise.

PSALM 27

1 The Lord, my Saviour, is my light;
What terrors can my soul affright?
While God, my strength, my life, is near,
What potent arm shall make me fear?

2 When cruel foes, the sons of strife,
Came furious to devour my life;
Their vile designs at once o'erthrown
Confess'd the power that cast them down.

3 Should numerous hosts besiege me round,
My stedfast heart no fear shall wound:
Though war should rise in dread array,
God is my strength, my hope, my stay.

4 This only boon my heart desires;
For this my ardent wish aspires;
This will I seek with restless care,
Till God attend my humble prayer:

5 In his own house to spend my days,
My life devoted to his praise;
There would my soul his beauties trace,
And learn the wonders of his grace.

6 When troubles rise, my guardian, God,
Will hide me safe in his abode!
Firm as a rock my hope shall stand,
Sustain'd by his almighty hand.

7 Now shall my head exalted rise
Above surrounding enemies;
While my glad offerings to the Lord,
With grateful songs, his praise record.

8 Thou sacred spring of all my joys,
Whene'er I raise my plaintive voice,
O let thy sovereign mercy hear,
And answer all my humble prayer.

9 When thou with condescending grace
Hast bid me seek thy smiling face,
My heart replied to thy kind word,
Thee will I seek, all gracious Lord.

10 Hide not from me thy blissful ray,
Nor angry frown my hopes away;

Thy saving help has still been near;
God of my life, renew thy care.

11 Should every earthly friend depart,
And nature leave a parent's heart,
My God, on whom my hopes depend,
Will be my father and my friend.

12 O teach me, Lord, thy sacred way;
Uphold my steps, nor let me stray;
While enemies and fears alarm,
Extend thy kind, thy guardian arm.

13 Leave not my life to impious foes,
Whose rage no sense of justice knows;
Against my innocence they rise,
And breathe out cruelty and lies.

14 My hope was ready to depart,
But faith sustain'd my fainting heart;
I trusted in a gracious God,
And live to spread his praise abroad.

15 Ye humble souls, in every strait
On God with sacred courage wait;
His hand shall life and strength afford;
O wait continual on the Lord.

PSALM 30

1 THEE, Lord, my thankful soul would bless,
Thee all my powers adore!
Thy hand has rais'd me from distress;
My foes rejoice no more.

2 O Lord, my God, oppress'd with grief,
To thee I breath'd my cry!
Thy mercy brought divine relief,
And wip'd my tearful eye.

3 Thy mercy chas'd the shades of death,
And snatch'd me from the grave;
O may thy praise employ that breath
Which mercy deigns to save.

4 Come, O ye saints, your voices raise
To God in grateful songs;
And let the memory of his grace
Inspire your hearts and tongues.

5 His frown, what mortal can sustain?
But soon his anger dies;
His life-restoring smile again
Returns, and sorrow flies.

6 Her deepest gloom when sorrow spreads,
And light and hope depart,
His smile celestial morning sheds,
And joy revives the heart.

7 Beneath thy kind protecting arm
How did my soul rejoice!
And fondly hop'd no future harm
Should ever shock my joys.

8 Lord, 'twas thy favour fix'd my rest;
Thy shining face withdrew,
And troubles fill'd my anxious breast,
And pain'd my soul anew.

9 Again to thee, O gracious God,
I rais'd my mournful eyes;
To thee I spread my woes abroad,
With supplicating cries.

10 What glory can my death afford
In the dark grave confin'd?
Shall senseless dust adore the Lord,
Or call thy truth to mind?

11 Hear, O my God, in mercy hear,
Attend my plaintive cry;
Be thou, my gracious helper, near,
And bid my sorrows fly.

12 Again I hear thy voice divine;
New joys exulting bound;
My robes of mourning I resign,
And gladness girds me round.

13 Then let my utmost glory be
To raise thy honours high;
Nor let my gratitude to thee
In guilty silence die.

14 To thee, my gracious God, I raise
My thankful heart and tongue;
O be thy goodness and thy praise
My everlasting song.

PSALM 31

1 LORD, in thy great, thy glorious name
I place my hope, my only trust;
Save me from sorrow, guilt, and shame,
Thou ever gracious, ever just.

2 Attentive bow thy pitying ear,
Let mercy fly to my relief;
Be thou my refuge, ever near,
A sure defence from all my grief.

3 Thou art my rock, thy name alone
The fortress where my hopes retreat;

O make thy power and mercy known;
To safety guide my trembling feet.

4 Preserve me from the fatal snare
Of secret foes, who plot my fall;
And make my life thy tender care,
My God, my strength, my hope, my all.

5 To thy kind hand, O gracious Lord,
My soul I cheerfully resign;
My Saviour God, I trust thy word,
For truth, immortal truth, is thine.

6 I hate their works, I hate their ways,
Who follow vanity and lies;
But to the Lord my hopes I raise,
And trust his power, who built the skies.

7 In thee, my God, I will rejoice,
While mercy makes my soul her care;
For thou hast heard my mournful voice,
In all my sorrows God was near.

8 Thou hast not left my life to groan,
Where chains and tyrant foes oppress;
Enlarg'd by thee, my feet have known
The sweets of liberty and peace.

9 Thy wonted mercy, Lord, renew,
See how my inward troubles rise;
My melting soul with pity view,
And these dejected weeping eyes.

10 My life is spent in grief and tears;
In sighs my hours roll slow away;
My strength decays, while sins and fears
Sink all my frame in deep decay.

11 While black reproaches blot my fame,
And neighbours join with cruel foes,
My friends, who now forget the name,
With horror fly, and shun my woes;

12 Till from their memory I slide,
And sink in dark oblivion's shade,
A broken vessel thrown aside,
And mix unheeded with the dead.

13 I heard the cruel slander rise,
While foes and fears beset me round;
I heard the murderous bands devise
To crush me helpless to the ground.

14 But I have trusted in thy name,
O Lord, my hope, my fix'd abode;
And still avow'd my humble claim,
(O sweet support!) thou art my God.

15 My life, my all, is in thy hand;
Let thy almighty power control
The rage of this remorseless band,
And save my persecuted soul.

16 O let thy favour, bliss divine!
Thy smile with heavenly radiance break,
And round thy fainting servant shine;
O save me for thy mercy's sake.

17 Leave not my hope to sink in shame,
God of my prayer, in whom I trust;
Let wicked men, who hate thy name,
Lose all their glory in the dust.

18 Deep in the grave be lying tongues
In everlasting silence laid,
Whose proud disdain, and slanderous
wrongs
The injur'd innocent invade.

19 What endless bliss, O bounteous Lord,
(Immensely great, divinely free!)
Hast thou reserv'd for their reward,
Who fear thy name, and trust in thee!

20 Thy gracious hand shall near thee hide
These happy favourites of thy care;
Safe at thy feet they shall abide,
Nor pride, nor slander reach them there.

21 Blest be the Lord, for ever blest,
Whose mercy bids my fears remove;
The sacred walls which guard my rest
Are his almighty power and love.

22 I rashly said, I sink, I die,
Cut off, abandon'd to despair;
Yet thou, my God, hast heard my cry,
And gracious answer'd all my prayer.

23 Ye saints, to whom his mercy flows,
O love, for ever love the Lord;
While on the proud his hand bestows
A dreadful and a just reward.

24 Ye humble souls, who seek his face,
Let sacred courage fill your heart;
Hope in the Lord, and trust his grace,
And he shall heavenly strength impart.

PSALM 39

1 WHEN I resolv'd to watch my thoughts,
To watch my words and all my ways,
Lest I should with unwary faults,
Offend the God my life should praise,

2 In mournful silence long restrain'd,
My thoughts were press'd with secret grief;
My heart with sad reflection, pain'd,
In silence found no kind relief.

3 While thus the inward anguish burn'd,
My straiten'd speech at length found way;
My tongue in broken accents mourn'd
Before my God, and tried to pray.

4 Almighty Maker of my frame,
Teach me the measure of my days,
Teach me to know how frail I am,
And spend the remnant to thy praise.

5 My days are shorter than a span,
A little point my life appears;
How frail at best is dying man!
How vain are all his hopes and fears!

6 Vain his ambition, noise, and show!
Vain are the cares which rack his mind!
He heaps up treasures mix'd with woe,
And dies, and leaves them all behind.

7 O be a nobler portion mine;
My God, I bow before thy throne;
Earth's fleeting treasures I resign,
And fix my hope on thee alone.

8 Save me, by thy almighty arm,
From all my sins, and cleanse my faults;
Then guilt nor folly shall alarm
My soul, or vex my peaceful thoughts.

9 Beneath the chastening of thy hand,
Let not my heart or tongue repine;
But silent and submissive bend,
And bear the stroke because 'tis thine,

10 But O let mercy soon prevail,
Thy awful anger to remove;
The stroke is just, but I am frail;
Thy sparing goodness let me prove.

11 Frail man, how soon his beauty flies!
He sins, and God afflicts with pain;
Crush'd like the feeble moth he dies;
His strength, how impotent and vain!

12 Lord, wilt thou gracious hear my cry,
Pity my tears, and heal my woe?
As were my fathers, so am I,
A wretched stranger here below.

13 O spare me, and my strength restore,
Ere my few hasty minutes flee;
And when my days on earth are o'er,
Let me for ever dwell with thee.

PSALM 42

1 AS the poor hart tir'd in the chase,
Pants for the cool refreshing flood,
So pants my soul for streams of grace,
Thy cheering visits, O my God.

2 For God my thirsty spirit longs,
The sacred spring of living joy;
When shall I come with thankful songs,
Before my God? divine employ!

3 Through the sad night and mournful day,
My flowing tears have been my food,
While taunting foes continual say,
"And where is now thy Saviour God?"

4 My melting soul in grief is spent,
When I revolve my happier days;
When with the joyful throng I went
To thy abode with songs of praise.

5 Why, O my soul, thus sunk in woe?
Why thus with restless sorrows torn?
Hope thou in God; my song shall flow,
For his bright presence will return.

6 My heart sinks down oppress'd with grief;
Yet, O my God, I'll call to mind
Those seasons past, for my relief,
When I was blest, and thou wast kind.

7 Thy terrors overwhelm my soul,
Wave after wave, with dreadful roar;
So stormy seas like mountains roll,
And swelling billows drown the shore.

8 Yet will the Lord command his care,
His love (sweet morn!) shall cheer mine eyes;
And mix'd with praise my nightly prayer,
God of my life, to thee shall rise.

9 To thee I'll cry, my God, my rock:
Ah, why hast thou forgot thy care?
Why mourn I thus beneath the stroke
Of foes, who drive me near despair?

10 Their sharp reproaches pierce my heart
With daily anguish, while they say
(The thought is like a pointed dart)
"Where is thy God, thy boasted stay?"

11 Why sinks my fainting spirit down?
Why do my restless passions mourn?
What though my God a moment frown,
His blissful smile will yet return.

12 Then shall I spread his power abroad,
His smile my drooping hope shall raise;
My light, my health, my Saviour God
Shall tune my sighs to songs of praise.

PSALM 51

1 LORD, let thy mercy, full and free,
Vile as I am, extend to me;
And bid my numerous crimes remove,
All cancell'd by thy sovereign love.

2 O wash this guilty heart of mine,
For cleansing grace is only thine;
I own my sins, and still they rise
With recent horror to my eyes.

3 Against the God I love and fear
My aggravated crimes appear;
'Tis this alone awakes my smart,
And fills with grief my fainting heart.

4 While humbly prostrate in the dust,
I own thy awful sentence just;
My soul adores thy sacred word;
For ever righteous is the Lord.

5 Soon as my infant life began,
And nature fram'd the future man,
So soon did sin its taint impart,
The dire contagion seiz'd my heart.

6 Since inward truth thy laws require,
That inward truth, O Lord, inspire;
Through all my soul let wisdom shine,
And give me purity divine.

7 O let the sacred hyssop prove
Blest emblem of thy cleansing love;
Thy sovereign mercy can bestow
A heart more pure than falling snow.

8 Let thy reviving word impart
Peace, joy, and pardon, to my heart;
Then shall this broken frame rejoice,
And bless thy kind, thy healing voice.

9 Let all my sins (though deep their dye)
For ever in oblivion lie;
For ever blot the dreadful score,
And view the long account no more.

10 Create my inmost powers anew,
Make all my heart sincere and true;
O cast me not in wrath away,
Nor hide thy soul-enlivening ray.

11 Restore thy favour, bliss divine!
Those heavenly joys that once were mine;
Let thy own Spirit, kind and free,
Uphold and guide my steps to thee.

12 Then will I teach thy sacred ways,
With holy zeal proclaim thy praise;
Till sinners leave the dangerous road,
Forsake their sins, and turn to God.

13 O cleanse my guilt, and heal my pain,
Remove the blood-polluted stain;
Then shall my heart adoring trace,
My Saviour God, thy boundless grace.

14 Then shall my joyful tongue proclaim,
In grateful strains, thy glorious name;
Inspir'd by thee, my song shall flow,
And all thy wondrous mercy show.

15 If sacrifice would please my God,
My offerings should thy altars load;
But vain were all my offer'd store,
For blazing altars please no more.

16 This is the gift I would impart,
A humble, broken, contrite heart;
A broken heart, repentant sighs,
O God, thou never wilt despise.

17 O let thy goodness, Lord, appear,
To Zion, once thy chosen care;
Sustain'd and built by power divine,
Let Salem's walls distinguish'd shine.

18 To thee, the pious sacrifice
Accepted then shall daily rise;
Again the grateful offerings flame,
And glad devotion bless thy name.

PSALM 65

1 BEFORE thy throne, O God of grace,
Thy Sion would her vows perform;
Her ardent vows in deep distress –
O be her grateful praise as warm.

2 O thou who hear'st our humble cry,
Our God, our refuge, and our stay;
To thee shall mourning sinners fly,
To thee shall every nation pray.

3 Though sin prevails with dreadful sway,
And hope almost expiring lies,

Thy grace shall purge our sins away,
And bid our dying hopes arise.

4 Happy the man approv'd by thee,
Near to his God, thy chosen care;
Thy constant goodness he shall see,
The bounties of thy table share.

5 Whene'er thy injur'd people's cries
Ascend before thy awful throne,
All dreadful bright thy terrors rise,
And make thy grace and justice known.

6 Thou art the confidence and stay
Of the wide earth's remotest ends;
And those who try the dangerous sea,
On thee their hope, their all depends.

7 Thy awful word, with potent sound,
Firm bade the solid mountains stand;
Thy power encircles nature round;
All nature rests upon thy hand.

8 That word which stills the raging seas,
When the loud waves tempestuous roar,
Commands the warring world to peace,
And noise and tumult are no more.

9 Thy dreadful signs display'd abroad
Fill trembling nations with surprise;
The trembling nations own the God,
And lift their supplicating eyes.

10 The rising morn, the closing day,
Repeat thy praise with grateful voice;
Both in their turns thy power display,
And laden with thy gifts rejoice.

11 Earth's wide-extended varying scenes,
All smiling round, thy bounty show;
From seas or clouds, full magazines,
Thy rich diffusive blessings flow.

12 Now earth receives the precious seed,
Which thy indulgent hand prepares!
And nourishes the future bread,
And answers all the sower's cares.

13 Thy sweet refreshing showers attend,
And through the ridges gently flow,
Soft on the springing corn descend,
And thy kind blessing makes it grow.

14 Thy goodness crowns the circling year,
Thy paths drop fatness all around;
Ev'n barren wilds thy praise declare,
And echoing hills return the sound.

15 Her spreading flocks adorn the plain;
There plenty every charm displays;
Thy bounty clothes each lovely scene,
And joyful nature shouts thy praise.

PSALM 77

1 To God I rais'd my earnest cries,
To God, who rules the earth and skies;
His sovereign mercy deign'd to hear
My loud complaints with pitying ear.

2 The tedious day was spent in grief,
In humble prayer I sought relief;
But day and night the restless smart
Denied sweet comfort to my heart.

3 I thought on God with terrors arm'd;
New troubles then my soul alarm'd!
Then overwhelming sorrows rose,
Nor could complaining ease my woes.

4 Thy terrors, Lord, forbid my rest,
And silent anguish fills my breast;
And now in sad reflection rise
Past days and years before my eyes.

5 My nightly songs I call to mind,
And try some gleam of joy to find;
But search this wretched heart in vain,
For all is darkness, grief and pain.

6 Will God for ever leave his care?
Must I no more his favour share?
Shall long-lost mercy ne'er prevail?
And can his word for ever fail?

7 Array'd in frowns his angry face,
Has God forgot his wonted grace?
And clos'd the full, the boundless store
Of mercy, ne'er to open more?

8 But I rebuke my drooping heart;
Far hence, ye guilty fears, depart:
Still will I call past comforts o'er,
And trust almighty love and power.

9 This drooping heart again shall trace
The ancient wonders of thy grace;
The mighty works my God has wrought
Shall still employ my voice, my thought.

10 Thy way, O God, thy wondrous way,
While in thy temple I survey,
Struck with astonishment, I cry,
Where is a power so great, so high?

11 Whoe'er surveys thy works must own
That thou art God, and thou alone;

Thy favours to thy chosen care
The wonders of thy power declare.

12 Thy potent arm, for ever near,
Control'd their foes, control'd their fear;
And Jacob's sons (distinguish'd race!)
Confess'd thy kind delivering grace.

13 The waters with thy presence aw'd,
Beheld, and own'd their Maker, God;
The ocean shook with all its waves,
And trembled through its deepest caves.

14 The full clouds pour'd their watery store;
Amid the storm's impetuous roar,
Thy dreadful arrows flew abroad,
And sounding skies proclaimed the God!

15 Thy awful voice in thunder broke,
Heaven listen'd while th' Almighty spoke;
While o'er the world keen lightnings spread,
Earth trembled with unusual dread!

16 Thy path, O Lord, thy trackless way,
Lies in the deep unfathom'd sea;
No mortal thought can ever trace
Thy steps of wisdom, power and grace.

17 Thy people found thy guardian care;
Where'er they wander'd, God was there;
Till guided by thy prophet's hand,
They reach'd secure the promis'd land.

PSALM 84

1 HOW lovely, how divinely sweet,
O Lord, thy sacred courts appear!
Fain would my longing passions meet
The glories of thy presence there.

2 With strong desire my spirit faints;
I languish for thy blest abode;
This throbbing heart, oh, how it pants!
And all my powers cry out for God.

3 The sparrows near thy altar live,
And swallows there a nest obtain;
My God, my king, and wilt thou give
To birds, what I desire in vain?

4 Oh, blest the men, blest their employ,
Whom thy indulgent favours raise
To dwell in these abodes of joy,
And sing thy never-ceasing praise.

5 Happy the men, whom strength divine
With ardent love and zeal inspires!
Whose steps to thy blest way incline,
With willing hearts and warm desires.

6 Through Baca's thirsty vale they go;
But God commands, and springs arise,
And showers descend with copious flow,
To yield the pilgrim full supplies.

7 Still they pursue the painful road,
Increasing strength surmounts their fear;
Till all at length before their God,
In Sion's glorious courts appear.

8 O Lord of hosts, attend my prayer,
Our fathers' God, thy ear incline;
Shield of our lives, reveal thy care,
And on thy own anointed shine.

9 One day within thy sacred gate,
Affords more real joy to me
Than thousands in the tents of state;
The meanest place is bliss with thee.

10 God is a sun; our brightest day
From his reviving presence flows;
God is a shield, through all the way,
To guard us from surrounding foes.

11 He pours his kindest blessings down,
Profusely down on souls sincere;
And grace shall guide and glory crown
The happy favourites of his care.

12 O Lord of hosts, thou God of grace,
How blest, divinely blest, is he,
Who trusts thy love and seeks thy face,
And fixes all his hopes on thee!

PSALM 88

1 O LORD, my life, my Saviour God,
Hear, while I spread my woes abroad;
While day and night my mournful cries
Before thy throne incessant rise.

2 Let thy indulgent pitying ear
Incline to my distressful prayer;
With sorrow my full heart o'erflows,
And o'er me soon the grave will close.

3 My strength is lost, my life resign'd,
Among the dead my place assign'd;
Cut off from life, from hope and thee,
Scarce are the slain more lost than me.

4 Low in the grave my hopes are laid,
And darkness spreads its deepest shade;

Thy dreadful wrath afflicts my soul,
Like whelming waves thy terrors roll.

5 Far from these wretched eyes remov'd,
Are all the friends whom once I lov'd;
They fly my sorrows, while I moan,
Confin'd, unpitied, and alone.

6 In vain to ease my hopeless woe,
The streaming tears incessant flow;
To thee, O Lord, I breathe my cries,
And stretch my hands, and lift my eyes.

7 Wilt thou from dust thy wonders raise?
And shall the dead awake to praise?
Thy kindness shall the grave record,
Or life destroy'd adore thy word?

8 Where ne'er one cheering ray of light
Breaks through the deep, the solid night,
Shall thy almighty power be known?
Thy truth, shall dark oblivion own?

9 Yet still to thee my cries ascend;
My earnest cries, O Lord, attend;
My nightly groans, my morning prayer,
Shall seek thee, still with restless care.

10 Why, Lord, wilt thou reject my soul?
Thy smile can all my cares control;
Why wilt thou hide thy blissful face,
While I in vain implore thy grace?

11 Afflicted long have I complain'd,
And long a dying life sustain'd;
Expressless pain thy frowns impart;
Distracting horrors wound my heart.

12 Thy fierce displeasure who can bear?
'Tis death array'd in black despair;
Like swelling floods thy terrors rise,
O'erwhelm my heart, and comfort dies.

13 My dearest friends who shar'd my heart,
Far from those mournful scenes depart;
While o'er my solitary head
Dark shades and dismal silence spread.

PSALM 90

1 LORD, thou hast been thy children's God,
All-powerful, wise, and good, and just,
In every age their safe abode,
Their hope, their refuge, and their trust.

2 Before thy word gave nature birth,
Or spread the starry heavens abroad,
Or form'd the varied face of earth,
From everlasting thou art God.

3 Destruction waits thy awful word,
While mortal hope expiring mourns;
Obedient nature owns her Lord,
And dying man to dust returns.

4 Great Father of eternity,
How short are ages in thy sight!
A thousand years, how swift they fly,
Like one short, silent watch of night!

5 Thy anger, like a swelling flood,
Comes o'er the world with dreadful sway;
The tempest speaks the offended God,
And sweeps the guilty race away.

6 Uncertain life, how soon it flies!
Dream of an hour, how short our bloom!
Like spring's gay verdure now we rise,
Cut down ere night to fill the tomb.

7 Consum'd by thy vindictive frown,
Our blessings and our lives decay;
Our spirits sink despairing down,
And every comfort dies away.

6 Full in thy view our crimes appear,
Thy eye beholds each secret fault,
And marks, in holiness severe,
The sins of every inmost thought.

9 Our days, alas, how short their bound!
Though slow and sad they seem to run,
Revolving years roll swiftly round,
A mournful tale, but quickly done.

10 Perhaps to threescore years and ten
Protracted; or if longer still,
Ah, what can more but lengthen'd pain
The last sad tedious period fill?

11 What mortal thought can comprehend
The awful glories of thy throne?
Not all the terrors fear can lend,
Can make thy dreadful vengeance known.

12 Teach us to count our shortening days,
And with true diligence apply
Our hearts to wisdom's sacred ways,
That we may learn to live and die.

13 O may thy favour, Lord, return,
Nor thy bright presence long delay;
Nor let thy servants vainly mourn,
And weep their wretched lives away.

14 Soon let thy mercy cheer our hearts,
And tune our grateful songs of praise;
And let the joy thy smile imparts
Enliven all our future days.

15 O make our sacred pleasures rise
In sweet proportion to our pains,
Till ev'n the sad remembrance dies,
Nor one uneasy thought complains.

16 Let thy almighty work appear,
With power and evidence divine;
And may the bliss thy servants share
Continued to their children shine.

17 Thy glorious image fair impress'd
Let all our hearts and lives declare;
Beneath thy kind protection blest,
May all our labours own thy care.

PSALM 93

1 THE Lord, the God of glory reigns,
In robes of majesty array'd;
His rule omnipotence sustains,
And guides the worlds his hands have made.

2 Ere rolling worlds began to move,
Or ere the heavens were stretch'd abroad,
Thy awful throne was fix'd above;
From everlasting thou art God.

3 The swelling floods tumultuous rise,
Aloud the angry tempests roar,
Lift their proud billows to the skies,
And foam and lash the trembling shore.

4 The Lord, the mighty God, on high
Controls the fiercely raging seas;
He speaks! and noise and tempest fly;
The waves sink down in gentle peace.

5 Thy sovereign laws are ever sure,
Eternal holiness is thine;
And, Lord, thy people should be pure,
And in thy blest resemblance shine.

PSALM 102

1 LORD, hear thy servant's humble prayer,
And let my mournful cry
Ascend, and reach thy gracious ear,
And move thy pitying eye.

2 O do not hide thy blissful face,
When fears and sorrows rise;
But hear, and let thy sovereign grace
Return with quick supplies.

8 My days like smoke consume away,
And this poor dying frame
Sinks down to ruin and decay,
Scorch'd with affliction's flame.

4 My spirit fails, my hopes decline,
Like withering grass they fade;
And while beneath thy stroke I pine,
How tasteless is my bread!

5 My strength, with oft-repeated groans,
Is wasting fast away,
And leaves this skin, these feeble bones,
To wrinkles, and decay.

6 Like a poor solitary fowl,
Which in the desert roves,
Or like the melancholy owl,
That nightly haunts the groves,

7 I spend the watchful night alone;
Slow moves the tiresome shade,
While, like the plaintive bird, I moan,
All desolate and sad.

8 While all the day my cruel foes
In sharp reproaches join,
And more to aggravate my woes
Against my life combine.

9 My taste no food with comfort cheers,
'Tis ashes mix'd with woe;
And mingling with my drink, my tears
In briny torrents flow.

10 What comfort e'er can cheer my taste,
Beneath thy angry frown?
Rais'd by thy smile, I once was blest,
But thou hast cast me down.

11 I sink with hope's departing ray,
And life expiring fails;
So the faint shadow dies away,
When gloomy night prevails.

12 But thou, O Lord, shalt still endure,
Thy truth shall ne'er decay;
Thy love unalterably sure,
While ages roll away.

13 In Sion's cause thou wilt arise,
Thy mercy dawns around;
The time is come, her sorrow flies,
And all her hopes are crown'd.

14 That Sion which thy servants love,
Each heart her memory wears;
Their passions o'er her ruins move,
In sadly pleasing tears.

15 So shall the heathen nations fear
The Lord's exalted name;
Earth's haughty monarchs low revere
Thy majesty supreme.

16 When Sion's God, with power array'd,
Shall build her frame anew,
Then shall his glory be display'd
To our admiring view.

17 O let the humble destitute
Ne'er sink in sad despair;
The Lord will hear their mournful suit,
And answer all their prayer.

18 His truth, his mercy and his power
Shall fill the blest record,
And future ages shall adore
And love and praise the Lord.

19 From heaven, his high eternal throne,
(O condescending grace!)
Th' Almighty looks with pity down
On earth's low worthless race.

20 He sees the groaning prisoner's pain,
And brings a kind reprieve;
His hand shall loose the fatal chain,
And bid the victim live:

21 Live to declare his glorious name,
And spread his praise abroad,
And in his sacred courts proclaim
The mercy of his God.

22 Assembled there his saints attend,
And songs of praise repeat;
And there united nations bend,
And worship at his feet.

23 In life's mid-way my strength declin'd,
But 'twas my Father's hand;
My shortening days flew swift as wind,
At his supreme command.

24 I said, to thee, my God, I pray,
Whose years for ever last;
O take me not so soon away,
Ere half my days are past.

25 Earth's old foundations thou hast laid;
The heavens (a glorious frame!)
By thy almighty hand were spread,
And speak their Maker's name.

26 Their shining wonders all shall fade
By thy controlling power,
Chang'd like a vesture quite decay'd;
But thou shalt still endure.

27 Thy bright perfections, all divine,
Eternal as thy days,
Through everlasting ages shine,
With undiminish'd rays.

28 Thy servants' children still thy care,
Shall own their fathers' God;
To latest times thy favour share,
And spread thy praise abroad.

PSALM 103

1 AWAKE, my soul, awake, my tongue,
My God demands the grateful song,
Let all my inmost powers record
The wondrous mercy of the Lord.

2 Divinely free, his mercy flows,
Forgives my crimes, allays my woes,
And bids approaching death remove,
And crowns me with indulgent love.

3 He fills my longing soul with good,
Substantial bliss! immortal food!
Youth smiles renew'd in active prime,
And triumphs o'er the power of time.

4 In him the poor oppress'd shall find
A friend almighty, just and kind;
His glorious acts, his wondrous ways,
By Moses taught, proclaim his praise.

5 How free his plenteous mercies flow!
But his reluctant wrath how slow!
He chides, but soon his smile returns,
Nor long his dreadful anger burns.

6 How far beyond our vile deserts
Is every gift his hand imparts!
High as the bright expanded skies,
His vast unbounded mercies rise.

7 As distant as creating power
Has fix'd the east and western shore;
So far our numerous crimes remove,
At the sweet voice of pardoning love.

8 The tenderest yearning nature knows,
A father's love, too faintly shows

The ever-kind indulgent care
Which God's own happy children share.

9 He knows our frame, surveys our birth,
Compos'd of dust, frail sons of earth;
Man like a fair but short-liv'd flower,
Springs up and blooms one smiling hour.

10 But if a noxious blast arise,
Sudden its transient glory flies:
Those charms which made the scene so gay
Steal from the sight and die away.

11 But mercy with unchanging rays
For ever shines, while time decays;
And children's children shall record
The truth and goodness of the Lord

12 To those, who with delightful awe,
Love and obey his sacred law,
Whose hearts with warm devotion glow,
Whose lives their grateful duty show.

13 The Lord is king, his hand alone
Has fix'd in heaven his radiant throne;
He sends his sovereign laws abroad,
And heaven and earth confess the God.

14 Immortal, form'd by power divine,
Attending angels round him shine,
Observant wait his sacred will,
And his commands with joy fulfil.

15 Ye heavenly hosts, adore the Lord,
Who form'd you to obey his word;
Let everlasting praises rise
Through the bright armies of the skies.

16 While all his works his praise proclaim,
And men and angels bless his name;
O let my heart, my life, my tongue,
Attend and join the blissful song.

PSALM 116

1 I LOVE the Lord; his gracious ear
Inclin'd to my distressful prayer;
He heard my supplicating voice,
And bade my fainting heart rejoice.

2 For this, when future sorrows rise,
To him I'll breathe my humble cries;
For this, through all my future days,
Adore his name and sing his praise.

3 Death spread around his fatal chains,
To drag me to infernal pains;
I felt the agonizing dart,
And horror seiz'd my trembling heart.

4 'Twas then in my extreme distress,
I call'd upon the God of grace,
Whose power can death and hell control;
Lord, I beseech thee, save my soul.

5 For ever gracious is the Lord,
For ever faithful to his word;
By sweet experience now I prove
His mercy, his unchanging love.

6 The Lord preserves with tender care
The weak, the humble, and sincere;
Low in the dust my hopes were laid,
But God appear'd with timely aid.

7 Return, my soul, and sweetly rest
On thy almighty Father's breast;
The bounties of his grace adore,
And count his wondrous mercies o'er.

8 Thy mercy, Lord, preserv'd my breath,
And snatch'd my fainting soul from death,
Remov'd my sorrows, dried my tears,
And sav'd me from surrounding snares.

9 Now will I walk before the Lord,
A living witness to his word;
With faith and prayer I sought his face;
My griefs were great, and great his grace.

10 No meaner help, no mortal art,
Could ease the anguish of my heart;
My hasty tongue, in rash replies,
Pronounc'd the words of men but lies.

11 What shall I render to the Lord,
Or how his wondrous grace record?
To him my grateful voice I'll raise
And pour libations to his praise.

12 His crowded courts shall see me pay,
The vows of my distressful day;
In life and death the saints shall find
Their guardian God for ever kind.

13 Thy servant, Lord, is wholly thine,
By nature's ties, and bonds divine;
From deep distress and sorrow free,
Anew I give myself to thee.

14 To thee, with sacrifice of praise,
My invocations I will raise;
To thee my vows shall warm ascend,
While crowds the solemn rites attend.

15 O Salem, in thy sacred courts,
Where glory dwells and joy resorts,
To notes divine I'll tune the song,
And praise shall flow from every tongue.

PSALM 130

1 FROM the dark borders of despair
To thee, my God, I cry;
O wilt thou pitying hear my prayer,
And every plaintive sigh.

2 Lord, who shall stand before thy face,
If thou shouldst mark our faults?
With eye severe what hope of grace
Could cheer my mournful thoughts?

3 But sovereign mercy dwells with thee;
Hope dawns amid my fears;
Divine forgiveness, large and free,
Shall stay my flowing tears.

4 On God alone my soul would wait,
His sacred word my stay;
His sacred word can light create,
And turn my night to day.

5 As those who wait with longing eyes
To see the cheerful morn,
So shall my ardent wishes rise,
Till thou, my God, return.

6 Let fainting Israel on the Lord
With cheerful hope recline,
For power and mercy in his word
With boundless glory shine.

7 Unnumber'd though their sins appear,
And fill their hearts with pain,
His saving love dispels their fear,
And cleanses every stain.

PSALM 133

1 HOW pleasing is the scene, how sweet!
When kindred souls in friendship join,
Whose joys and cares united meet,
In bands of amity divine.

2 Less fragrant was the ointment pour'd
On Aaron's consecrated head,
When balmy sweets profusely shower'd,
Down to his sacred vesture spread.

3 Not flowery Hermon e'er display'd
(Impearl'd with dew) a fairer sight;
Nor Sion's beauteous hills, array'd
In golden beams of morning light.

4 'Tis here the Lord indulgent sheds
His kindest gifts, a heavenly store;
With life immortal crowns their heads,
When earth's frail comforts please no
more.

PSALM 137

1 WHERE Babel's rivers winding stray,
A silent, cool retreat we chose;
There lost in thoughtful sadness lay,
And pondering o'er our mighty woes.

2 Our mighty woes increasing rise,
Revolving Sion's hapless fate;
And louder griefs, and streaming eyes,
Deplore her wretched, ruin'd state.

3 No more could music soothe our cares;
Our harps, neglected and unstrung,
(Vanish'd their once delightful airs)
All silent on the willows hung.

4 Our barbarous masters mock'd our pains,
While with insulting haughty tongues,
They bade us tune the charming strains,
And give them one of Sion's songs.

5 Ah, no; shall Sion's sacred airs,
Inspir'd by heaven, be thus profan'd?
Be sung to please such ears as theirs,
Whose impious arms destroy'd our land?

6 Far from our dear-lov'd native soil,
Shall we resume the pleasing lay?
Can rugged bondage wear a smile,
Or ever-wasting grief be gay?

7 If I forget thy ruin'd state,
Jerusalem, my heart's desire,
Then let my useless hand forget
Her skill to strike the sounding lyre.

8 If I indulge a mirthful song,
Or thy dear name my memory leave,
All silent let my faithless tongue
Fast to my mouth for ever cleave.

9 Jerusalem, lamented name!
Shall still my mournful voice employ!
And I the sadly pleasing theme
Prefer to every thought of joy.

10 Remember, Lord, proud Edom's sons,
Who cruel, urg'd the conquering foe
To raze her beauteous towers at once,
And lay her lofty structures low.

11 Such ruin, Babel, thou shalt share,
And sure reward awaits thy guilt;
Then shall thy heart untaught to spare,
Repay the blood thy hand has spilt.

12 Happy the man who then shall rise,
(While heaven the righteous vengeance owns,)
And dash with unrelenting eyes,
Thy bleeding babes against the stones.

PSALM 138

1 To thee, my God, my heart shall bring
The lively grateful song;
Attending kings shall hear me sing,
With rapture on my tongue.

2 Before thy throne with prostrate joy,
I will adore thy name;
Thy praise shall be my best employ,
Thy love and truth my theme.

3 Amid the glories of thy name,
Thy truth exalted shines!
A faithful God thy words proclaim
In everlasting lines.

4 When in the day of deep distress,
To thee, my God, I cried,
With strength divine thy powerful grace
My fainting soul supplied.

5 The monarchs of the earth shall hear,
And join my sacred lays;
Thy glorious name with joy revere,
And sing thy wondrous praise.

6 The eternal God looks kindly down,
And smiles on humble souls;
But from afar his piercing frown
The sons of pride controls.

7 What though around my painful way
Continual trouble grows;
Thy saving hand shall be my stay,
And crush my wrathful foes.

8 Thou, Lord, wilt all my hopes fulfil,
To thee the work belongs;
Let endless mercy guide me still,
And tune my grateful songs.

PSALM 142

1 TO God, the refuge of his saints,
I humbly breath'd my ardent prayer,
And pour'd out all my long complaints,
And spread before him every care.

2 My spirit overwhelm'd with grief,
Surrounding snares beset my way;
Of thee, O Lord, I sought relief,
Whose eyes my devious path survey.

3 All other helps I found were vain,
And hope, and friends, and comfort fail'd;
To thee alone I told my pain,
While yet my potent fears prevail'd.

4 To thee, my God, I breath'd my cries,
Dear refuge of my fainting heart;
Thou on whom all my hope relies,
I am undone if thou depart.

5 Thou see'st me wretched, weak, and low;
O Lord, attend my plaintive cry,
And save me from my every foe:
My foes how strong! how weak am I!

6 O free my soul, dissolve the chain,
Then shall I spread thy praise abroad;
Thy saints shall join the cheerful strain,
And speak the bounties of my God.

PSALM 143

1 HEAR, O my God, with pity hear
My humble supplicating moan;
In mercy answer all my prayer,
And make thy truth and goodness known.

2 And O let mercy still be nigh;
Should awful justice frown severe,
Before the terrors of thine eye,
What trembling mortal can appear?

3 My persecuting foes prevail;
Almost I yield my struggling breath;
The cheerful rays of comfort fail,
And sink me to the shades of death.

4 While thus oppressive sorrows flow,
Unintermitting o'er my head;
My inmost powers are whelm'd in woe,
And all my hopes and joys are fled.

5 I call to mind the former days;
Thy ancient works declare thy name,
Thy truth, thy goodness, and thy grace;
And these, O Lord, are still the same.

6 To thee I stretch my suppliant hands,
To thee my longing soul aspires;

As cheering showers to thirsty lands,
Come, Lord, and fill these strong desires.

7 Come, Lord, on wings of mercy fly;
My spirit fails at thy delay;
Hide not thy face; I faint, I die,
Without thy blissful healing ray.

8 Speak to my heart; the gloomy night
Shall vanish, and sweet morning break;
In thee I trust, my guide, my light;
Teach me the way my feet should take.

9 My soul's desires ascend to thee;
O save me from my numerous foes;
To thy kind guardian wing I flee,
For safe defence and sweet repose.

10 Teach me to do thy sacred will;
Thou art my God, my hope, my stay;
Let thy good Spirit lead me still,
And point the safe, the upright way.

11 Thy name, thy righteousness I plead;
O Lord, revive my drooping heart;
Let these distressing fears recede,
And bid my troubles all depart.

12 Those unrelenting foes destroy,
Which thus against my peace combine;
Then shall thy service be my joy,
And all my active powers be thine.

PSALM 144

1 BLEST be the Lord, my strength, my shield,
Amid the dangers of the field;
'Tis he instructs me for the fight,
And arms me with resistless might.

2 His constant love, his saving power,
Is my defence, my sacred tower;
Rebellion hears his potent word,
And my glad people own their Lord.

3 Lord, what is man, that he should share
Thy kind regard, thy constant care?
Can all the weak, the wretched race,
Deserve such condescending grace?

4 Man's short existence, frail at best,
Is empty vanity confess'd;
His life, a shadow, fleets away,
And leaves no traces of its stay.

5 Descend from heaven, almighty Lord,
And earth shall tremble at thy word;
The smoking hills with conscious fear,
Shall own their awful Maker near.

6 While thy keen pointed lightnings fly,
Like flaming arrows through the sky,
My foes dispers'd shall rise no more,
Nor dare the terrors of thy power.

7 O let thy potent arm control
These threatening waves that round me roll,
These sons of vanity that rise,
With fraudful hands and impious lies.

8 Then shall thy name new songs inspire,
And wake to joy the sounding lyre,
And every tuneful string shall raise
In various notes, my grateful praise.

9 'Tis power divine, 'tis God alone,
Whom kings preserv'd in dangers, own;
Who saves, in war's tumultuous strife,
From raging swords his servant's life.

10 O Lord, thy saving power oppose
To these invading, threatening foes,
These strangers to thy sacred laws,
Whose boast is vain, and false their cause.

11 Then shall our sons beneath thy care,
Grow up like plants erect and fair;
Our daughters shall like pillars rise,
Where royal buildings charm the eyes.

12 Then plenty shall our stores increase,
Plenty, the lovely child of peace;
The fold its fleecy wealth shall yield,
And pour its thousands o'er the field.

13 The well-fed ox shall then afford
His cheerful labours to his lord;
No more shall cruel plunder reign,
Nor want, nor misery complain.

14 O happy people! favoured state!
For whom peculiar blessings wait;
Happy! who on the Lord depend,
Their God, their guardian and their friend,

PSALM 145

1 MY God, my king, to thee I'll raise
My voice, and all my powers;
Unwearied songs of sacred praise
Shall fill the circling hours.

2 Thy name shall dwell upon my tongue,
While suns shall set and rise,

And tune my everlasting song,
When all creation dies.

3 Great is the Lord! our souls adore,
We wonder whilst we praise!
His power what creature can explore,
Or equal honours raise?

4 Yet shall thy works, almighty Lord,
Our noblest songs adorn;
Thy glorious acts we will record
For ages yet unborn.

5 Thy praise shall be my awful theme,
The wonders of thy power;
I'll speak the honours of thy name,
And bid the world adore.

6 The men that hear my sacred lyre,
Shall spread thy praise around;
While thy tremendous deeds inspire
To notes of solemn sound.

7 But sweetly flowing strains shall tell
The riches of thy grace;
And songs of grateful joy reveal
Thy spotless righteousness.

8 How full the Lord's compassions flow!
His wrath, how slow to rise!
Swift pardon smiles upon his brow,
And every terror dies.

9 How large his tender mercies are!
How wide his power extends!
On his beneficence and care
The universe depends.

10 Great God, whilst nature speaks thy praise,
With all her numerous tongues,
Thy saints shall tune diviner lays,
And love inspire their songs.

11 Thy power and grandeur they shall sing.
The glories of thy reign;
Thy wondrous deeds, Almighty King,
Shall fill the raptur'd strain.

12 Thy kingdom, Lord, for ever stands,
While earthly thrones decay;
And time submits to thy commands,
While ages roll away.

13 The falling saint, with powerful grace,
The God of love will raise;
The humble, bending with distress
Shall rise and speak his praise.

14 To thee, O Lord, for daily meat,
Thy creatures lift their eyes;
On thee, their common Father, wait,
From thee receive supplies.

15 Thy sovereign bounty freely gives
Its inexhausted store;
And universal nature lives
On thy sustaining power.

16 Holy and just in all its ways,
Is providence divine;
In all its works immortal rays
Of power and mercy shine.

17 Whoe'er invokes the God of grace,
Shall find him ever near;
To all that humbly seek his face
He lends a pitying ear.

18 His pitying ear attends the cry
Of those who fear his name;
Their every want he will supply,
And raise their sinking frame.

19 How blest in his protecting care,
The souls who love the Lord!
While impious men his vengeance dare,
And die beneath his sword.

20 The praise of God, delightful theme!
Shall fill my heart and tongue;
Let all creation bless his name,
In one eternal song.

PSALM 146

1 Ye sons of Zion, praise the Lord,
Come tune your songs in sweet accord,
Awake, my soul, awake and join
The sacred hymn, in notes divine.

2 The praises of my God, my king,
(While I have life or breath to sing,)
Shall fill my heart, and tune my tongue,
Till heaven improve the blissful song.

3 No more in princes vainly trust,
Frail sons of earth; man is but dust!
With all his pride, with all his power,
The helpless creature of an hour.

4 He breathes, he thinks, but ah, he dies
No more the potent, or the wise;
The scheme his morning thoughts begun,
Sinks down before the setting sun.

5 Happy the man, whose hopes divine
On Israel's guardian God recline!

Who can with sacred transport say,
This God is mine, my help, my stay.

6 Heaven, earth, and sea declare his name;
He built and fill'd their spacious frame:
But o'er creation's fairest lines
His steadfast truth unchanging shines.

7 His justice favours those who mourn
Beneath the proud oppressor's scorn;
The hungry poor his hand sustains,
And breaks the wretched captive's chains.

8 To sightless eyes, long clos'd in night,
His touch restores the joys of light;
Poor mourners rais'd confess his care;
He loves the humble and sincere.

9 If wandering strangers friendless roam,
Divine protection is their home;
The Lord relieves the widow's cares,
And dries the weeping orphan's tears.

10 But vengeance waits the impious race
Who hate his laws, and scorn his grace;
Their ways to sure destruction tend,
And all their hopes in ruin end.

11 The Lord shall reign for ever king,
And age to age his glory sing;
Thy God, O happy Zion, reigns,
Resound his praise in joyful strains.

PSALM 147

1 PRAISE ye the Lord: Oh, blissful theme,
To sing the honours of his name!
'Tis pleasure, 'tis divine delight,
And praise is lovely in his sight!

2 His Salem now the Lord restores;
No more her ruin she deplores;
Again the scatter'd tribes return,
And Israel's sons no longer mourn.

3 No more their breaking hearts despair;
He binds their wounds with tender care;
His healing hand removes their pain,
And cheerful comfort smiles again.

4 He counts the host of starry flames,
Knows all their natures and their names;
Great is our God! his wondrous power
And boundless wisdom we adore.

5 How gracious is the Lord! how kind!
To raise the meek dejected mind;
But awful terrors in his frown
Shall cast rebellious sinners down.

6 Sing to the Lord, let praise inspire
The grateful voice, the tuneful lyre;
In strains of joy, proclaim abroad
The endless glories of our God.

7 He veils the sky with treasur'd showers;
On earth the plenteous blessing pours;
The mountains smile in lively green,
And fairer blooms the flowery scene.

8 His bounteous hand (great spring of good!)
Provides the brute creation food;
He feeds the ravens when they cry;
All nature lives beneath his eye.

9 In nature what can him delight,
Most lovely in its Maker's sight?
Not active strength his favour moves,
Nor comely form he best approves.

10 Dear to the Lord, for ever dear,
The heart where he implants his fear;
The souls who on his grace rely,
These, these are lovely in his eye.

11 Jerusalem, his honours raise;
Thy God, O Zion, claims thy praise;
His mighty arm defends thy gates,
His blessing on thy children waits.

12 Sweet peace, to crown the happy scene,
O'er thy fair border smiles serene;
The finest wheat luxuriant grows,
And joyful plenty round thee flows.

13 He speaks! and swiftly from the skies
To earth the sovereign mandate flies;
Observant nature hears his word,
And bows obedient to her Lord.

14 Now thick descending flakes of snow
O'er earth a fleecy mantle throw;
Now glittering frost o'er all the plains
Extends its universal chains.

15 At his fierce storms of icy hail
The shivering powers of nature fail;
Before his cold what life can stand,
Unshelter'd by his guardian hand?

16 He speaks! the ice and snows obey,
And nature's fetters melt away;
Now vernal gales soft rising blow,
And murmuring waters gently flow.

17 But nobler works his grace record;
To Israel he reveals his word;
To Jacob's happy sons alone
He makes his sacred precepts known.

18 Such bliss no other nation shares;
The laws of heaven are only theirs;
Ye favour'd tribes your voices raise,
And bless your God in songs of praise.

PSALM 149

1 COME, praise the Lord, ye tuneful bands,
Ye saints assembled in his name;
New strains of joy your God demands,
New mercies all your praises claim.

2 Let Israel's tribes, with blessings crown'd,
Their God, their mighty Maker sing;
And Sion's sons with joy resound
The endless glories of their king.

3 His name the measur'd dance shall guide,
And joy and sacred mirth inspire;
His name shall o'er the song preside,
And tune the sweet, the charming lyre.

4 He bends complacent to your praise;
Your God approves the blest employ;
The thankful meek his love will raise
To crowns of everlasting joy.

5 O let the saints aloud rejoice,
And sounds of glory fill the song;
All day let rapture tune their voice,
And night the blissful strain prolong.

6 Let every mouth be fill'd with praise,
The God of heaven their awful theme;
Whilst his resistless sword displays,
In heaven-taught hands his dreadful name.

7 Bright terrors wait his high commands,
When justice waves the flaming sword,
Vindictive o'er the heathen lands,
Which hate his saints, and scorn his word.

8 While haughty princes bound in chains,
Confess the just, the powerful God;
Let awful joy in warlike strains,
Proclaim his glorious acts abroad.

9 His hand, thus righteously severe,
Fulfills the threatenings of his word;
Thus honour'd shall the saints appear,
Adore the great, the glorious Lord.

PSALM 150

1 PRAISE ye the Lord; let praise employ
In his own courts your songs of joy;
The spacious firmament around
Shall echo back the joyful sound.

2 Recount his works in strains divine;
His wondrous works how bright they shine;
Praise him for his almighty deeds,
Whose greatness all your praise exceeds.

3 Awake the trumpet's piercing sound,
To spread your sacred pleasures round;
While sweeter music tunes the lute,
The warbling harp and breathing flute.

4 Ye virgin train with joy advance,
To praise him in the graceful dance;
To praise awake each tuneful string,
And to the solemn organ sing.

5 Let the loud cymbal sounding high,
To softer deeper notes reply;
Harmonious let the concert rise,
And bear the rapture to the skies.

6 Let all whom life and breath inspire,
Attend, and join the blissful choir;
But chiefly you who know his word,
Adore, and love, and praise the Lord.

PART IV

Prose Works of Anne Steele[6]

6 Miscellaneous Pieces in Verse and Prose by Theodosia, Collected Works, Vol. III, 1780.

FRIENDSHIP

FRIENDSHIP has been oft my favourite theme and afforded many a pleasing thought; but hitherto my experience of this blessing answers not my ideas. Perhaps they are raised too high, or, it may be, this is too near akin to all other earthly pleasures which fly our wishes or disappoint our expectations.

Let me then raise my thoughts from earth and consider this amiable subject in its divine perfection. Let me meditate on the friendship of the blessed Jesus, who says, 'Henceforth I call you not servants but friends etc.' Wondrous condescension! delightful assurance! infinitely more engaging than the dearest ties on earth! an interest in his friendship how desirable, how extensive the blessing! it contains everything we need for time and eternity.

The dearest friend on earth, though his heart be ours and his will ever ready, may want the power to assist us. In necessities, dangers, and distresses we can have no more than his tenderest concern, his sincerest good wishes. We disclose our griefs with unavailing confidence, while friendship mourns but cannot help us. But Jesus is infinitely powerful; all power in heaven and in earth is his. He is able as well as willing to save to the uttermost; to him we may lay open all our hearts and pour out our souls without reserve; to him lament our frailties, for he alone can correct them; to him reveal our wants, he can supply them all; to him we may tell our sorrows; he can and will remove or give us strength to bear them; to him we may recount our comforts and our joys, for he is the spring from whence they flow; he only can continue and increase them.

Our friends may be so far distant in our greatest extremities that we may be deprived even of the benefit of their kind condolence and compassionate sympathy, because they cannot be acquainted with our distress, but Jesus is ever near, ever ready to assist his beloved friends. He hears every groan and pities every sorrow, he is touched with a feeling of their infirmities, and his divine compassion and sympathizing tenderness are far beyond all that mortal friendship ever knew! Are they exposed to want, affliction, and distress he shares in all their sufferings, and to express how intimately his affection is united to them, he even speaks of those sufferings as his own – I was sick, I was in prison etc. – and kind offices done to the least of those whom he graciously condescends to call his brethren he rewards as done to himself; and if he hide his blissful face, yet still they dwell upon his heart, and in his own best time he will relieve them. His sovereign hand can turn afflictions into blessings, and grief shall terminate in joy.

> His own soft hand shall wipe the tear
> From every weeping eye. (Watts)

In straits and difficulties, if we apply to earthly friends for counsel, and receive the best advice they are capable of giving, they are weak short-sighted creatures like ourselves, and by following their directions, we may be led into irretrievable errors and misfortunes, but Jesus the heavenly friend, is infinite in wisdom. He guides his favourites by his counsels, the unerring dictates of his sacred word, makes their way plain before them, by the constant care of his providence, and conducts them, through all the difficulties and embarrassments of life, to eternal safety and happiness.

Human nature is frail, and the warmest, sincerest friendship may cool and change to indifference; and though friendship is ever ready to put the most favourable construction on the behaviour, to place every action in its fairest light, and to pity and forgive the faults it cannot mend, yet as it cannot know the heart, and judges only by words and actions, these are liable to misunderstandings and false representations, which may interrupt its course, and perhaps entirely dissolve those ties, which seemed too firm for time and chance to loosen.

But if the love of Jesus is unchangeable, he that made the heart knows all its inmost recesses, and can never be misinformed, can never mistake; if there is a principle of sincere love to him, though buried amid a thousand imperfections, that love himself inspired he approves, and will reward. The soul once his is his for ever; not all the powers of earth or hell, not things present nor things to come, shall be able to separate from his everlasting love.

In mortal friendships, the satisfaction a generous mind enjoys in obliging, and the sentiments of a grateful heart in being obliged, are exceedingly agreeable; but this heavenly friend engages our warmest, our everlasting gratitude, and even gratitude is swallowed up in wonder, when we meditate on the immeasurable extent of his divine beneficence, in what he has done, is still doing, and will do for the objects of his love. Of enemies and traitors he has made friends and favourites! for guilty, lost, undone creatures, deserving nothing but never-ending misery and eternal death, he has purchased pardon, life and immortal happiness; and this with his own most precious blood! It would be a surprising effect of friendship for a man to lay down his life for his friend, but Jesus freely gave his life for such as were his inveterate enemies. Stupendous love! Astonishing goodness!

At death, earthly friendships are dissolved; with the friend our comforts die, and the satisfaction we enjoyed in their society leaves only a painful remembrance of the pleasures we have lost. But Jesus lives for ever, lives to make intercession for his friends above, to communicate constant supplies of grace to them below, to guide them through all the scenes of mortal life, to guard them from every danger, to strengthen them in encountering their last enemy, crown them with victory, and bring them safe to his glorious presence, to live with him for ever and ever. Happy, happy souls! who have an interest in this all-sufficient, this ever-lasting friend! O may I never rest satisfied till I can say with a humble, yet well-grounded confidence, 'This is my beloved, this is my friend!' Blessed Jesus! teach me to know thee and to love thee more; let me hear the voice of thy sacred Spirit whispering to my heart that thou art mine; assure me of my interest in thy almighty, thy unchangeable love; then shall I be blest indeed.

My Lord, my Saviour, my almighty Friend,
O wilt thou, gracious, own the humble claim!
And let thy Spirit, sacred evidence,
Confirm it to my soul with power divine!
Tell me, O tell me thou art mine indeed,
And fill my heart with gratitude and love!
But ah! how weak, how languishing and low
My strongest gratitude, my highest love.
How cold the warmest ardours of my soul,
For blessings so divine! how poor a gift
This vile, this wretched heart! and yet 'tis all
A worthless worm can offer, mean return!
Nor can I tender this without thy aid.
O help me to surrender all my heart,
Its powers and passions, to thy sovereign love!
Accept it, Lord, and make it thine entire!
Let thy abounding grace remove my guilt,
Forgive my wanderings, fix me thine for ever
In bands which time nor death have power to loose!

THE EVIL OF SIN

WHEN I reflect on the state of innocence, happiness and glory of man at his first creation, surrounded with earthly delights, and in the full enjoyment of his Maker's favour, on his fall from that blissful state, and the endless train of miseries in which all his wretched descendants were involved, sharers in the guilt, their blood tainted with the dire infection, by nature blind to their own felicity, and inclined to go astray from God, and pursue the road to destruction, I cannot but pronounce sin the greatest evil, the source of pain and sorrow, and the cause of temporal and eternal death. But never does my heart appear so vile as when it mourns at the foot of my Redeemer's cross; never does sin appear so hateful, so detestable, as when I meditate on his dreadful sufferings; 'tis here I see that infinite justice was offended, and infinite punishment incurred, since nothing but an infinite satisfaction could atone. Not all the glorious angels which surround the throne of God, though shining in the highest excellence of created purity, could have paid the dreadful debt; the work was impossible to any power below omnipotence. The eternal Son of God, O glorious triumph of almighty love! enthroned in all the glories of the deity, left his Father's bosom for these abodes of sin and misery, and became a man of sorrows and acquainted with grief; exposed to shame, contempt, and infamy, resigned himself to the most cruel agonizing tortures; and, O amazing thought! made his soul an offering for sin! Dreadful evil! which nothing less than the sufferings of the Son of God could expiate! And shall I allow it a place in my heart? Almighty grace forbid! But alas! so weak, so depraved is this wretched heart, as to give way to the destructive insinuations of this dangerous, this fatal enemy! The strongest efforts of my reasoning powers can make but a feeble, an unavailing resistance, and often may my soul complain, the evil which I would not that do I. Who shall deliver me from the body of this death? O that I could say with joyful assurance, 'I thank God through Jesus Christ my Lord!' Is there not, O blessed Saviour, infinite efficacy in thy precious blood, to cleanse as well as to atone for sin? And wilt thou not grant the powerful influences of thy Holy Spirit to purify the heart that desires to wear thy sacred image, and to strengthen a weak, a helpless creature that fain would be devoted to thy service? O let me hear thy gracious voice saying, 'I will, be thou clean,' and assuring my soul that thou wilt strengthen, and help and uphold me with the right hand of thy righteousness! Shew me my interest in these kind promises, and enable me to look up with humble hope and say, that though iniquities prevail against me, thou wilt purge my transgressions away! Nothing is too hard for omnipotence to effect, nor can the hope be lost which is fixed on infinite goodness and invariable truth.

WEARY SOULS INVITED TO REST

Come unto me all ye that labour and are heavy laden and I will give you rest. Matt. 11. 28.

REVIVING sound! Who is the kind friend that thus in the hour of distress cheers the poor fainting sinner with the healing voice of comfort? May his word be depended on? And is he able to make good the important promise? Listen again, O doubting soul, attend the compassionate Saviour's voice! 'Tis 'I that speak in righteousness, mighty to save.' Yes, his faithfulness and power are unquestionable; but is it possible that he should be willing to save a rebel who has rejected his authority, turned a deaf ear to his gracious calls, and strayed far from him in paths of sin and vanity? Hearken to his own words! 'The Son of Man came to seek and to save that which was lost.' Encouraging assurance to a heedless wanderer sensible of his folly! But can it extend to such vile wretches as have sinned with a high hand, and by a long course of rebellion declared, we will not have this man to reign over us? Yes, even such as these are invited to come, for Jesus Christ came into the world to save sinners, of whom (says a favoured servant of his) I am chief, and after enumerating his acts of treason and rebellion, yet, says he, I obtained mercy! How strange, how amazing is the compassion of this tender-hearted Saviour, when a poor deluded sinner has roamed through all the pleasures of sense, in the vain pursuit of satisfaction, tired and restless, panting beneath a heavy load of guilt, and surrounded with darkness and terrors, a beam sent from heaven breaks through the dismal gloom, and points him to Jesus Christ, as the only refuge, the only rest! May he not reasonably fear that if in this last extremity, he applies to that mercy which he has so long abused, he shall be rejected with indignation? No, for the blessed Redeemer says, 'him that cometh to me I will in no wise cast out.' Come then, weary, heavy laden sinner, come to Jesus and he will give thee rest. Methinks the words present the idea of a weary traveller who has gone a long journey over a sandy desert, bending beneath a heavy burden, scorched with the piercing heat of the sun, and just ready to faint. In this extremity, O how desirable a cool, refreshing shade! How would the sight of it, though at a distance, animate his spirits, and invigorate his feeble steps to reach it! Thus desirable, thus animating, is a sight of Jesus Christ to a poor sensible sinner, groaning beneath a heavy load of guilt, and scorched with terrible apprehensions of the wrath of an offended God! How refreshing then is this shadow of a great rock in a weary land! How suitable, how seasonable an all-powerful and merciful Saviour to them that are ready to perish. But the rest which the great

Redeemer gives is not only refreshment but satisfaction; this is what the flattering world with all the allurements it displays, cannot pretend to bestow. Say, ye deluded votaries of pleasure, riches or honour, have you ever found satisfaction? No, for whether in the pursuit, or in the attainment of their wishes, disappointment ever attends them.

And say, ye happy souls who have sat under your Redeemer's shadow with great delight, have you ever found any enjoyment in your former attachments equal to a moment's hope of an interest in his favour? No, says a sincere lover of Jesus,

> Let earth's alluring charms combine;
> While thou art near, in vain they call;
> One smile, one blissful smile of thine,
> My dearest Lord, outweighs them all!

Mr. Herbert represents the Creator as pouring a variety of blessings on man, but reserving rest, that at length finding no satisfaction in creature enjoyments, weariness might bring him home to God, the centre of his rest. 'Tis not in the nature of earthly good to yield satisfaction. The mind, whether desiring or possessing, is still restless and uneasy, till led by divine grace to Jesus, who only can give rest to the weary – so Dr. Young:

> Man's sickly soul, tho' turn'd and toss'd for ever
> From side to side, can rest on nought but thee;
> Here in full trust, hereafter in full joy.

This rest only can suit the nature and fill the desires of an immortal soul; it is not only present refreshment and true satisfaction, but eternal joy! How would it embitter the pleasure and destroy the repose of a weary traveller seated in a cool delightful shade, if at the end of his journey, he expected nothing but pain and misery! So when a poor sinner is brought to Jesus Christ and begins to enjoy refreshment and satisfaction, how would it alarm and terrify his soul, and embitter all his comfort, to know that there was a possibility that he might at last be shut out from that rest which remains for the people of God! But adored be everlasting love, the divine veracity is engaged for the endless happiness of all that come to Jesus Christ! He who is the way, the truth, and the life, has said, 'I give unto them eternal life, and they shall never perish.' Eternal life! and the hope and expectation of it confirmed to the believing soul, by the strongest, and most inviolable assurances! This is rest indeed! who would not come to the great Redeemer at his kind invitation to receive a blessing so desirable, so immense? Well may the happy Christian who has tasted that the Lord is gracious, say, 'Return unto thy rest O my soul, for the Lord has dealt bountifully with thee!' Blessed be that almighty grace which has convinced me of my wretched, my undone condition, and brought me to Jesus Christ, imparted to me some delightful tastes of that divine refreshment, that ineffable satisfaction, which he only can bestow, and encouraged my humble hope to look forward to that glorious rest, that state of perfect and invariable felicity which he has prepared for them that love him! O let every one who has been enabled to obey the blessed Redeemer's invitation, and found rest in him, pity the deplorable condition of those poor, deluded, wretched souls who are still roving, restless, in the vain pursuit of satisfaction where they can never find it! Convince them, O merciful Saviour, of their miserable state, display the almighty power of thy resistless grace, bring them weary and heavy laden to thee, and give them rest.

MOTIVES TO DIVINE MEDITATION

WHAT have I to do with this vain world? Have I not long since renounced it as incapable of making me happy, and therefore unworthy of my care? and yet it will intrude with its vexatious, teasing vanities to hinder, or at least to interrupt my attention to awful realities. Again I repeat, vain world be gone. O that I could shut my heart effectually against thy mischievous influences! The fashion of this world passeth away; its amusements fleet before me in quick succession on the wings of time, and soon these eyes will close upon the transient scene, to open on eternity. Eternity – amazing idea! – how shall these active, thinking, reasoning faculties which are now so often busied with trifles be employed through the endless duration? The sacred word assures me that everyone shall receive for the things done in the body according to that he hath done, whether it be good or bad. God is just, and everlasting misery must be the portion of every wretched soul who leaves this mortal stage unsanctified and unforgiven; then will the powers of thought and reflection be employed in bitter yet unavailing remorse and unutterable anguish, far from God and far from hope, in the dismal regions of despair, where the worm dieth not, and the fire is not quenched! Dreadful eternity! Tremble, O my soul, and fly for refuge to Jesus who delivereth from the wrath to come; in him is safety, life, and bliss for ever. Thanks be to God for his unspeakable gift! And can I, do I hope for an interest in this almighty Saviour? and through his all-sufficient merits for an entrance into the mansions of glory where love and praise and raptures inconceivable shall employ the active joyful powers of every happy spirit through the ever-circling ages of eternity! blissful eternity! And have I any hope of joining in that sweet employ, and shall I not begin it here? O blessed Redeemer, work in my heart by thy own Spirit a sincere contrition for all my vile offences and ungrateful wanderings! Increase my faith, my hope, my love and joy, and fix my thoughts in delightful meditation on the pains thou hast suffered, and the happiness thou hast prepared for them that love thee! And what heart, O adorable Saviour, but must love thee that has ever enjoyed a glimpse of thy infinite excellence with hope of an interest in thy .great salvation! Can I reflect unmoved on the state of never-ending misery my sins deserve, on the dreadful pains thou hast suffered to redeem lost, perishing sinners who come to thee as their only refuge, and on the heaven of everlasting joy thou hast ensured to them for their glorious inheritance? Can I meditate on these animating subjects which I hope have sometimes warmed my heart, and not wonder at my frequent coldness? Alas how frail is my heart! how foolish and ungrateful! frail and foolish indeed, to be tempted away from my true interest, my only happiness, by empty vanities! And O what vile ingratitude to be forgetful of such infinite obligations! Shall admiring angels search into the glorious wonders of redeeming love with all the ardour of intense desire? and shall I be cold to its surprising charms, and hardly raise a languid wish to reach the immortal theme? Yet angels cannot taste the sweets of pardon, nor feel the transporting joys of salvation from eternal woe, for those happy spirits have never sinned.

Ye sons of harmony who ardent tune
To boundless joy the heaven-resounding song,
O could I hear your rapture-breathing strains,
How would my kindling powers awake to praise
And join with ecstasy the blissful theme;
Earth's flattering trifles then should tempt in vain,
Nor interrupt my sweet, my blest employ.

But O my great Redeemer! thou only canst inspire the sacred flame, thou only canst teach me the celestial song; grant me the kind influences of that blessed Spirit which thy gracious promise encourages me to ask; display before me the amazing wonders of thy love, give me the assured hope of pardon and salvation through thy infinite merits; teach me to begin the work of heaven below, and bring me at last to the glorious assembly of the ransomed of the Lord, to join the celestial choir in strains of harmony and praise unknown below, and repeat with immortal ardour, 'Blessing, honour, glory, and power unto him that sitteth upon the throne, and unto the Lamb for ever and ever.'

THOUGHTS IN SICKNESS, AND ON RECOVERY

OF what a feeble texture is this mortal tabernacle! and how much is the tenant mind (though of an immortal nature) pained and depressed by its weakness, and hurt by the storms which shake the tottering frame! The first attacks of a fever have so weakened my nerves and spirits, that every sprightly faculty and almost every cheerful thought is sunk in a stupid languor; a listless inattention even to common things overspreads me, conversation is tasteless, and reading and thinking almost impracticable. But alas, this is not the worst! The bounties of providence and the blessings of grace hardly excite a grateful thought, or quicken a warm desire – wretched state! And can I know it, and yet not be affected with it? Am I enough awake to feel my chains, and yet not wish for liberty? Let me try to rouse myself from this lethargy of the mind, and if I cannot look forward through the gloom which hangs so heavy on my intellectual sight, let me look back and try to recover some little remembrance of past scenes. Shall the immortal spirit united to this frail disordered body be so much influenced by its weakness, as if it were to sink with it into the common earth? Think, O my soul, hadst thou not once nobler views and brighter hopes? Couldst thou not once, conscious of thy great original, look up to the glorious author of thy being with ardent desires after the enjoyment of his favour as the only good that could fill thy capacious wish? Couldst thou not at some happy seasons delight in the contemplation of his infinite perfections, and desire to know him more, to love him more, and to be more like him? How often hast thou mourned the unhappy influence of earthly vanities that have drawn thee aside from the centre of thy best desires, and longed to cast thyself at the feet of heavenly mercy, in deep abasement yet with humble penitential hope, and wished to dwell for ever beneath the attractive, the constraining influences of pardoning love! Surely there was something even in those painful sensibilities preferable, far preferable, to this death-like stupor.

The Lord liveth, and blessed be my rock, blessed be the Lord who hath not turned away my prayer, nor his mercy from me. Adored, for ever adored, be the riches of divine love manifested in the great Redeemer, who is able to save to the uttermost all that come unto God by him, through whom I hope I have found sweet access to the throne of grace, and been enabled to pour my humble breathings there.

Whence are these quickenings after so much deadness, this deep abasement in the sense of my exceeding vileness, my utter unworthiness, mingled with such admiring views of the infinite condescension of the great God, the almighty power of pardoning grace, and O, with the delightful hope of my interest in it! Can I ascribe the happy alteration to anything below the influences of his own Spirit? O for the continuance of those divine influences, quickening, cheering, strengthening, and purifying my heart! My heart, alas how frail, how apt to lose the relish of divine enjoyments, and grow cold, ungrateful and remiss. O blessed Redeemer, let the heavenly Comforter abide with me for ever, to preserve me in this state of trial and temptation, and guide me safe to the kingdom of thy glory. Infinite grace, that so vile a sinner should be favoured with the hope of a dwelling there! My Saviour God! and hast thou prepared a place for me in the mansions of light? And wilt thou come again and receive me to thyself? And shall I rejoice in thy blissful presence for ever? O confirm the glorious hope to my thankful, yet still desiring soul!

> Then faith shall triumph o'er the grave
> And trample on the tombs;
> My Jesus, my Redeemer lives;
> My God, my Saviour comes. (Watts)

Amid these delightful hopes, the terrors of death disappear, its pains are supportable, and the gloomy vale is brightened with some reviving beams from the regions of immortal day! What evil can I fear if thou art with me? Thy smile is celestial comfort. O let it cheer my fainting heart in the awful hour of dissolution, till mortality is swallowed up in life. But why, O my soul, these rising doubts? Shall they be suffered to cloud thy dawning happiness, and cast a shade on all thy comforts? Has not thy Redeemer said, 'Fear not little flock, for it is your Father's good pleasure to give you the kingdom'? Were anything in myself the motive, I were lost indeed; but 'tis his good pleasure, his sovereign grace, and what can be too great for infinite bounty? My vileness, my unworthiness can be no bar. Almighty grace, and utter unworthiness! Contemplate, O my soul with delightful wonder the astonishing contrast! and sink lower still in thy own eyes, while the glories of divine mercy are exalted above all thy wonder and thy praise! Whether life or death, all is yours, and ye are Christ's, and Christ is God's; what fulness, what immensity of bliss is contained in the glorious assurance! And am I (so vile, so wretched) permitted to hope an interest in it? O the heights, the depths, the unsearchable wonders of almighty grace! Forgive, O gracious God, forgive these guilty, unbelieving thoughts which would embitter my comforts, and rob thee of the humble tribute which my grateful heart would bring to the footstool of thy throne! Rebuke the tempter, and confirm the comforting hope which thy word now affords, that the God of peace shall bruise Satan under my feet shortly.

'Bless the Lord, O my soul, and all that is within me bless his holy name. Bless the Lord O my soul, and forget not all his benefits.' But O how shall my narrow thoughts and narrower words recount them? How am I surrounded with mercies! Indulgent goodness has blessed me with unnumbered favours, both temporal and spiritual, and even this affliction, may I not call it a blessing from the happy effects which I hope it has produced? May I not esteem it a paternal correction to reprove my ungrateful coldness, to awaken me to a state of sensibility, and renew the relish of those important blessings which have been almost neglected, or at best too faintly sought? How gentle, O my God, were the strokes of thy chastising hand; how kind the teachings of thy word, and how sweet the consolations of thy promises to my soul! O may thy goodness dwell upon my grateful heart, and animate all my powers and passions to a delightful activity in thy service! 'Return unto thy rest, O my soul, for the Lord hath dealt bountifully with thee'; he only is the proper centre of my rest, and all the enjoyments of nature without the kind influences of his grace are weariness and vanity. Vainly does the roving mind expect satisfaction among the pleasures of sense and time.

Creatures without a God
Can yield me no supply. (Watts)

But sweetened with the hope of his favour, and enjoyed as blessings from the hand of an indulgent Father, every comfort of life acquires a power to entertain and please. O how inexcusable the folly of my past wanderings! And yet, convinced as at present I hope I am of my true interest, so deceitful is this wretched heart that I fear to trust it, I fear I shall again relapse into cold indifference and vile ingratitude. Gracious God, maintain in my soul this necessary self-diffidence, inspire me with constant breathings for the aids of thy almighty grace and an entire dependence on thy strength in the sense of my own weakness. Let thy praise be my business and delight, thy favour my felicity here and my portion for ever!

What is there in this world of vanity that I should wish to stay for? how frail is the tenure of earthly bliss, how unsatisfying to the mind which with divine ambition looks forward to immortal happiness! The dearest comforts of life are painfully sweet. O that I could enjoy them with thankfulness unmingled with anxious apprehensions of the pangs of separation! O for a stronger faith, for brighter views of the invisible glories of the upper world! glories invisible to the eye of sense, but revealed in the sacred word to the believing soul O for a more assured hope of my interest there! then how sweet were the expectation of meeting the friends united to my heart by the ties of nature, friendship and piety, in the regions of immortal love and unprecarious felicity! then though I were left to pursue alone my painful pilgrimage, how comforting were the hope that in a little time I should follow them to my father's house. Perhaps I may go before them? Whenever I am called, O may the messenger be welcome to my soul! may the smiles of my Redeemer rising o'er the gloomy shades of death dispel all its horrors and open before me the transporting prospect of eternal joy! O may the blissful foretastes of heaven prevail over the agonies of nature, comfort my mourning friends, and sweeten the parting tear! But why these reflections? my business, my important business is to examine where my hope is fixed, to seek earnestly to the God of grace for the unerring influences of his Holy Spirit to guide me in the way to heaven, to strengthen my faith, my hope, and every grace, to make me fit for that state of spotless purity, and then receive me to himself. May my title to the inheritance of the saints in light be secured to my soul through the infinite merits of a crucified exalted Saviour, and let time and circumstance, O gracious God, be resigned to thy sovereign disposal. This is a state of probation; perhaps it may please God to exercise me with many trials before I leave this mortal stage. Hitherto my lot has been easy compared with that of many of my fellow Christians, and why should I expect to reach the haven and escape the storms of trouble which others meet with? I am indeed unable to sustain them, but everlasting strength can support me. O may the anchor of my soul be sure and steadfast! Father of mercy and God of all comfort, say to my soul, 'My grace is sufficient for thee', and I shall be safe.

Appendix I – Extract from the Diary of Mrs Steele[7]

(Mrs Steele's Diary, Volume II July 13, 1730 – 31st December 1730. The spelling and punctuation are as in the original.)

I use to think my very best Experience is in this book or the next.

July, 13 in 1730 I did not sleep well thro ye indisposition that attended me ye evening past, yet I had that on my mind ye are dead and your Life is hid with Christ in God and when Christ who is our light shall appear etc but I could not take much comfort from it being bad in in my head and enclin'd to melancholy all day breathing out my complaints to ye lord, lamenting before him my frailty and sinfulness, desiring I may be as ready as I seems willing to obey God when he sends his messenger Death to call me home for tho I have met with no worldly cross or disappointment yea I enjoy as much as heart can wish for yet knowing this is not my Eternal home these warnings makes me look for Death nor can I see anything worth desiring to stay longer here except God have any work for me to do to promote his interest in ye worly and if so then ye languige of my soul seems to be, lord here am I find me

14 I was better in health this morning but was tho'tfull about a distemper that is come into this place amongst ye cattle viz ye murain there being a great many pigs dead in it and about seven cows one of them being ours, I endevour'd to view ye hand of God in all these things thinking on that, is there evel in a citty and ye lord hath not done it (?) that was much in my tho'ts, Alas who shall live when God doth this.

15 I had something troubled me thro reading a lettere, yet it makes me see the uncertainty of Earthly comfortd, and makes me love and praise God who has (I hope in mercy) bestow'd so much of this worlds good things that I have no need to be beholding to any but him who has so freely given it to me and I beg I may be enabled to use it for his glory, I found wrath and anger to arise and disturb my mind and that came with power and ye kind one to another tender hearted foriving one another even as God for Christs sake has forgiven you this soon wrote a sweet serenaty in my breast and I was enabled to pray to God earnestly that he was subdue ye vanitys and follys of my relatives and work true conversion on ye souls of my young relations, I was in a praying agreeable frame in ye evening

---

7 STE 2/1/1.

16 I was ill most part of this day yet I read and convers'd about ye best things, that scripture was much on my mind ye evening past, but we have ye mind of Christ and it came very suitable, something I spoke to one vex'd my mind yet I can't see there was any sin in it, I would be more carefull and therefore desire of God that he would set a watch before my lips

17 I was very ill this morning yet it wore off and I walk'd out, and had agreeable chat with one and after had some discours with Ben. Who seems much better then he have done and I was enclin'd to thankfullness

18 Busied about worldly things this day yet I read and was stir'd up to lively earnest prayer that came to my mind and much affected me am I not better to thee then ten sons this made me think tho some relatives at a distance from me don't yeield that comfort I might hope for yet God in his makeing good his promises far far better then all that

Sab 19 I was not in so good a frame as in the evning past not did I I hear as I could desire in ye morning yet I heard much better in ye afternoon the last from but rather rejoice because your names are written in heaven and do hope I did truely experience what I heard, the question this evening was what Christ hath done for us as prophet priest and king, but I was very bad in my head which rendered ye opportunity burthensome

20 I was not well this day thro which I was stuppid and unprofitable.

21 Not mmch better this morning yet after I had discours with some about their souls concern which brot me in a better frame I walk'd out and that came to me that which we hath seen and heard declare we unto you &cc I had some suitable meditations, I was after griev'd to see that Ben. was again in that soul(?) ....tion

22 There being several people here my time was taken up in ... yet I was after enabled to unbosom myself sweetly to God I had ...suitable scriptures came to my mind on which I meditated I had thinking on a particular case that came to me (One line lost)....might be apply'd to a child of God says it is fixed and settled there as being born with him and rooted in his very nature and not plucked up without great difficulty and diligence, the smart of punishment makes him very wary of his sin and watchfull against it, I had that on my tho'ts as many as were ordained to Eternal life believ'd, and that, said I not if thou would believe thou shouldst see ye Glory of God

23 I am troubled with a pain in my tooth yet I am not so barren as some times I have some tho'ts on ye last sermon I heard from Luke 10;20 and tho there was several eveidences of our names being written in heaven laid down yet I took most comfort from two of them viz from the evidence which was true love to Christ and can hope my love do appear (as it was enquir'd) in mourning ye absence of Christ, in longing desires after Christ, in high admirations of his excelencys and a ready disposition to set forth his Glory, in a diligent seeking after Christ in ye use of means, in delight in ye ordinances of Christ, in a real love to his people, in a univer sal and cheerful obedience to ye will of Christ, and in a fervent zeal for his honour and glory in ye world, and those things are tr truely ye experience of my soul, tho ye eveidence was weaning from the world and actual forsaking of it with regard to trust and ye chiefest love this I tho't also I could experience, the other evidences tho I know I have experienced them did not seem so plain to me at this time, I had after a good deal of discors with one and another about ye best things and in perticular with a young kinswoman that I liked his (?) discours very well, I afterwards reflected upon myself to think what a changable creature I am I tho't twas well for us that God is not man that he should lye or ye son of man that he should repent

24 The weather being very hot and I haveing ye Ague and fevour every day I was unfit for anything yet in the evening the desires of my soul run out after God I walk'd out in ye evening and was delighted with sweet meditations haveing a great many scriptures came to my mind that vers of Wattses was much on my mind, my soul come meditate yet day and think how near it stands, When thou must leave this house of clay, and fly to unknown lands, this made mw endevour to see how I sfcands even upon ye brink of Eternaty and also to try to take a view by faith of the diettant unknown land that in Heb(?) 12;22 was much on my mind, But ye are come unto Zion ye city of ye living God; the whole three verses was very entertaining to my tho'ts yet me tho't that seem'd to crown ye rest viz and to Jesus the Mediator, had it not been for that the former words, God ye Judge of all must needs have sentenced and condemned me these tho'ts in a measure wore off at my comeing in

25 being very ill this morning I remark'd nothing, in the evening "Willy Steele was bro't home in safety, I beg'd of ye lord sincerely that he would make us a blessing and comfort to each other, he being to continue at home

Sab 26 I was very ill this morning yet I went to meeting and heard Uncle pretty well from truely God is good &cc I was better in ye afternoon and heard Mr Steele diligently from they that sow in tears shall reap in Joy, after which Sarah Beck and Martha gave in their experience to ye Church I had some convers with some, the last week1s question was finished, being ask'd something about one of those that spoke their experience what I know concerning it haveing had conversation with and good hope in her yet by speaking but little more that seem'd to surprize me and I find it allways twas so and hearing how well others could speak that came to my mind, every-man hath his proper gift from God one after this manner and another after that, diversity of gifts by ye same Spirit

27 I read great part of this day and was in a pretty good frame

28 Much ye same this day in ye evening I had discours with Ben who talk after his old doubting desponding manner this have always some influence upon me and stirs me up in prayer I had several suitable scriptures on this occassion came with powere as I will surely have mercy upon him saith ye lord, and for a small momemnt I hid my face &cc and O thou afflicted with tempest but not comforted &cc this made me firmly to think,...designs of mercy for him tho he argues so much against it....had convers with his sister who is in a great measure brot....dark condition and her faith fix'd I hope on the rock. ... would be except with the lord.

(29th) ???

30 I was drawn out in my moring duty perticularly for others I tho't on that, but mine own vineyard have I not kept and me thinks (?) I leaves in a great measure the concerns of my own soul and prays for and thinks on others more then on my own, I beg I may not neglect my own concerns to the dishonour of God but that I may duly enquire whether the peace I enjoy is that real peace of God that passeth all understanding mentioned in Phil. 4:7 after which I hoped it was that came to my mind peace I leave with you rny peace I give unto you not as ye world giveth

31 I continued in the same quiet peaceable frame reading a great deal of ye time in a large History of ye Monarchs of England, and by reading that about ye powder plot I found ray affections warm'd and drawn out to praise God in my evening duty

August 1 My time has been employ'd much as it was ye day past, I have been troubled with a pain in my teeth and have something of ye Ague and fevour every day yet I was in a humble praying frame in ye evening

Sab 2 Mr Steele is gon to Sarum for ye work of ye day I was in a sweet enlarg'd praying frame being stir'd up by reading Flavels Last

Chapeter of Navigation Spiritualized, I heard Uncle in ye morning from being justified freely by his grace, and had some agreeable discours between ye meetings and heard John Sutton from how much more shall ye ...if Christ, I heard both times indiferantly well but was often very bad in my head, yet I went to Uncle Steele with Mary Strong and saw cause to bless God who enabled her to talk to Uncle better then I expected

I am indispos'd in body this morning and seems to haee some uneasiness in my mind fearing whether I main't be tho't to put persons forward concerning their joyning with ye Church but I know and ye lord he knows that I never would put forward any but such whom I have good grounds to hope are believers in Christ for none but such I apprihend have a right to ye ordinances of Gods house and what I what I do of that kind is with an eye to ye honour and Glory of God always bringing such cases to ye lord by prayer and supplycation for direction both for myself and others that came to my mind even them will I bring to my high mountain and make them joyfull in my house of prayer & cc and that Him that confesseth me before men him will I confess before my father &cc

4 I was tho'tful this day thro ye ring out ye bell for a neighbour that fel from thatching a wheat rick ye day past then wel and now in etrnaty and both myself and Reiitions are liable to ye same sdden stroke I desire to be prepar'd for it, Mr Steele is gon toward Sedghil to be out some days I beg'd preservation for him I was in in a melancholy frame crying earnestly to the lord

5 It has pleas'd ye lord to bestow a very plentiful crop of corn He have been pleas'd also to give as fine a season for bringing in ye wheat as can be desir'd for which my heart is drawn out in thankfulness, it being Mr Britton's day at Wallop I have tho'ts of goung out but am afraid I am not able to perform ye walk I bring ye case to ye lord desireing to be directed strengthened and assissted and may in every thing be to ye praise and Glory of God I went with co-mpany we had suitable convers on ye way, I heard from Awake O North Wind &cc but thro ye heat and my indisposition I was a very bad hearer I got home but was very much tired

6 And this day I was in a very stuppid condition I went out there being three to be Baptiz'd but I had something of ye fevour and was in a very bad frame Mr Britton soke from Acts 10;47 but I don't know that I receiv'd any benifit thro my own negligence and stupidity, I after talk'd with Ben. who is now in a very bad obstinate condition at which I was greiv'd Mr Steele came home safe thro mercy, but I was not thankfull

7 I was ill this morning and in a sad stuppid frame, in ye evening I look'd back and lamented my sad barrenness for sometimes past together with my unthankfullness for mercys receiv'd and considering how near the time is that I am (God willing) to approach ye table of ye lord I found my heart drawn out in suitable and earnest desires and after in meditations haveing many sweet scriptures on my mind

8 I have had a great many tho'ts this day about ye things of God and have some cause to lament how many vain wicked Athiestical tho'ts have of late intruded themselves into my mind yet thro ye mercy of God I did not harbour them I have had some very suitable scriptmres on my mind and have read and considered and have been affected with my experience since my last sitting down at ye lords table and am this evening in a humble, praying, confessing, resiign'd frame O that I may be ac (cepted ?)

Sab 9 I hope I did earnestly desire ye spirit and preasence of ye lord this day Mr Eastman from what must I do to be sav'd &cc I heard pretty diligently.....in ye ordinance of ye lords supper I tho't on that lord whu dost thou (line lost)..... I seem'd to have some small views of ye happiness of ye saints above and that came to my mind eye hath not seen nor ear heard &cc heard in the afternoon from the Righteous is more excelent then his neighbour and great did ye advantage of ye Righteous seem to appear of which number I hope I am considered as cloath'd with ye robes of Christs righteousness, I renounce all dependence on anything els, we had a great deal of company in ye evening and ye question was, if Christ as pro-phey, priest, and king hath done so much for us what may we learn f from hence twas answer(d in many things and left fior ye improvement of another evening it being a profitable oppertunity

10 One came this day about his soul concerns which was a means to stir me up & also to quicken me in prayer & make me more thankfull, yet I was ruffled by another in ye evening

11 I had a good deal of lovely lively discours this day with one & another I do earnestly desire to be made usefull in my day and generation

12 My child is very ill thro a surfeit I desire ye lord to do his pleasure & teach me to submit, I have been reading Bunians Come & Welcome to Jesus, it has even rais'd my love into a flame to think how freely & willing Christ forgives poor comeing sinners & oh how thankfull would I be I had some discours with Ben. who seems better enquiring into ye nature & essence of Christ being willing (as I hope) to fix his faith on a right bottom I inform'd him as well as I was capable & after refflected upon myself to think how little of God I do know

13 I employ'd my tho'ts great part of this day about God ye father God ye Son, & God ye holy spirit yet but one God in essence equal in power & Glory, but alas ye more I view ye more I seem at a loss I tho't on that camst thou by searching find out God &cc ah what a poor short sighted creature am I in spiritual things oh that God would be pleas'd to reveal more spiritual knowledge to me if it me for his honour

14 I have been in a studious tho'tfull frame great part of this day I was affected by reading in Flavells Spiritual Husbandry & that was very pleasant to me viz they that are joyned to ye are one spirit, and I hope I am rely joyned & united to Christ, and what love & thankfulness I can here express

15 I was not in so lively a frame this morning yet I saw cause to be admiring ye goodness of God in removing ye Ague both from me & ye child & has given us a pretty good measure of health I desire I may use & improve it for ye Glory of God, in looking back on ye days of my youth on some of my follies & vanitys, & how ye lord preserv'd & deliver'd me my affections was sweetly drawn out after God desiring to be usefull to others that came powerfully to my mind O taste & see that ye lord is good blessed are all they that trust in him this I know I have experienced for God has been beyond measure good to me, that came after with power they that trust in ye lord shall be a Mount Zion that cannot be moved but abideth for ever on which I had some sweet meditations

Sab 16 I was not in so good a frame this morning heard Uncle from for consideration that endureth such contraction of sinners &cc but I was very sleeppy & stuppid and after had some conversation with one, the last weeks question was ended but I had a bad pain in my head & Mr Steele was not very well he haveing been troubled with ye Ague for aome time past it was a barren Sabbath to me or rather my heart was such

17 Busied about worldly things great part of ye day yet in ye evening I had good oppertunity of talking closely to one (under affliction thro the loss of a relation) about ye concerns of his soul begging ye lord to make it usefull there seemong some signs of providence, in my meditations on it I admir'd ye kindness of God to me on such occassions how my mouth is fill'd with argue-ments & how may suitable scripture (fill it ?) bro't to my mind I tho't on that , they spake as ye spirit gave them assisatnce

18 This day here was several Christian friends with whom in a suitable manner giveing the best advice I could to ones I was sweetly affected by hearing Mr Steele give advice..

19 I was disturbed in mind this morning by hearing Couzen Fezard (Tezard) was married to the afore names Lawer of Ringwood and also by hearing that something I lately spoke to a sick neighbour was misrepresented to ye Church minister, yet I know I had said nothing but what the word of God will bear me out in, as others heard also, the sick man had told me he Depended upon his prayers for salvation, and I told him that would leave him short of salvation for there is salvation to be had in none but Christ advizing him & directing him as wel as I could mentioning several agreeable scrip tures to show him he must believe in Christ in order to be saved I had some moments of comfort in prayer I had ye Ague again & was very bad in my head, Molly had it again to this morning

20 This morning Mr Steele & William with Brother Benham is set out for Bristol to be out a week I am in a poor dejected condition yet I beg'd earnestly for their preservation in journeying & that they may be kept from all sin & danger I had agreeable conversation with some

21 I wak'd with that on my mind the Eternal God is thy refuge yet in my morning duty I could not pray as I could desire nor be in a good frame all day

22 That which have very often of late come in my mind came very lively this morning viz Arise ye dead & come to judgement I at first tho't it had been a scripture & tho I can't find it is yet it has been usefull to make me tho't full I mourn'd out my complaints before ye lord I found some little crosness attending worldly concerns which made me fretfull & too much unfit for my evening duty

Sab 23 My desires was drawn out very much in my morning duty for Mr Steele who is as far as I know at Bristol there to preach t this day I beg'd he may be so assisted as maybe for ye Glory of God & ye good of Souls & in due time bro't home in safety I went out & heard Uncle from Heb. 12:3 but I could not be much affected I satid at home in ye afternoon with Molly who had ye Ague very bad I endevour'd & desirfd to improve my time, & looking for something I was directed soon to find that came to me very present in trouble how dp I daily experience God to be a very present help to me on all occassions oh that I could walk worthy as a child of such a God

24 My time have been taken up the great patt of this day about wordly things to ye neglecting of ehat is better

25 The last evening & this day I have discours with two mwn that have begin & talk'd very warmly of the concerns of souls & another world

pretending to know & also to do a great deal and also talketh of a new life and dependence on Christ and ye like when I know neither of their lives or conversations are agreeable to what they say (for they will both be drunk) I had a great many tho'ts about it & several suitable scriptiures which I saw cause to bless G God for because they came so suitable, that by their fruits shall ye know them, and that Rev. 3:9 that say they are jews & are not but do lye &cc I thoSt these must needs meet with a great disapointment, and if it should be thus with me to & that came, verily there is a word for ye righteous, but I tho't I do think they are mistaken and doubtless they think me so to and what if I should be mistaken and that came very powerfull Blessed is the man that heareth me walking daylp at my gate waiting at ye post of my doors &cc and this was very seasonable & comfortable for I do daily wait on God & hope I shall obtain favour of ye lord

26 I met with something ye last evening that reprov'd my to hasty speaking and I know I am conscious of guilt many times in that way in not well weighing what I am about to speak I was very much troubl ed in my evening duty crying to ye lord to set a watch before my lips, that came to my mind the tongue can no man tame it is an unruly member full of deadly guaxsK poison, yet I awak!d in ye morning in a thankfull loving frame adoring ye lord that I had sense of these things, that being on my mind and since I live yet Jesus wear ye crown, I have been earnest with ye lord on account of those that journey that they may be bro't home in safety with mercyfull tide-ings from my relations and as Nanny Steele is now to come home for to abide with us God would make us a blessing and comfort to each other they came all safe home thos very late bringing news my mother & relations are well

27 I should have been very thankfull for great mercys but I was...

Appendix II – A Sermon of William Steele[8]

(The spelling and punctuation have been preserved as in the original, though the layout has been clarified somewhat.)

Finished at Wallop & Bro July 22 1750
At Downton to ye mark July15 1750
At Whitchurch August 5 1750

John ye 19 and part of ye 5 vers

Behold the man

It may be proper to take notice of the occasion of the words in order the better to understand them in the forgoing chapter we have acount of the betraying of our Lord by Judas one of his professed deciples of his being taken and led to tryall where he was unjustly charged with being a malifactor as the reason of his being brought to judgment vers 30 and with being guilty of blasphemy in profsing to be the Son of God chap 19 e 7, at your leasure you may read and consider the history of our Lords tryall unjust condemnation and crucifiction and death recorded by the severall evangelest which was permited (tho most unjust with regard to those concerned in it) being the way designed to accomplish the great designs of grace in the great and glorious work of redemption and salvation but what I would take notice of at present as leading to my tex is Piliats conviction of the inocence of our Lord of his being rightfull king of the Jews and some awefull aprehentions of his being the Son of God the Masiah expected by the Jews and that therefore Piliat declared he found no falt in him and was willing to releas him tho at the clamer of the Jew who preferred Barrabas a rober before him he released the robber and took and scourged the blessed Jesus who tho he submited to suffer and die was king and Lord of all and when Pilate had unjustly delivered him to the soulders tis noted they plated a crown of thorns and put it on his head and put upon him a purpale robe and then mocked him sayeing haile King of the Jews vers 2 & 3 at ye 4 vers tis said Pilate therefore went forth and saith unto them behold I bring him forth to you that you may know that I find no falt in him which dos farther argue Piliates conviction of our Lords inocence and yet he consented to his crucifiction which argues the greatness of his sin at ye 5 vers which contains my tex tis said then came Jesus forth again wereing the crown of thorns and the purple robe and then Pilate saith unto

8 Original in the Angus Library, Regent's Park College, Oxford.

them behold the man but then the chief priest and officers insted of being moved with compasion at the indignity offerd to our Lord and the punishment inflicted on him cryed out saying crucify him crucify him which Pilate consented to tho he declared he found no falt in him to which the Jews replyed we have a law and by our law he ought to die, because he made himself the Son of God, when Pilate heard that saying he was the more afraid and sought to relase Christ till the Jews cryed out saying if thou let this man go thou art not Cesars frind and this prevaild shews that he feard the king more than he feard God and then Pilate brought forth Christ to judgmt and calls upon the Jews to behold thier king vers 14 but they disowned him as such said they had no king but Cesar tis the same person here called King that in our tex Pilate calls the man that he calls to behold in the circumstance or this state of humiliation and sufferings inflicted on him behold the man the word are a note of attention or call to behold which implyes that there is something remarkable respecting the object to be beheld something not common but uncommon or exterordenary and this might be considered both

1 with respect to Pilate and the persons then present and what he called them to

or else

2 as tis left upon record and may be applycable to us and are instructive to us and all that have the gospel

I shall only give some brief hints concern the first and consider and speake of it chiefly with regard to the latter

as to ye 1) and here when Pilate says behold the man here are two things to be considered

1 the object and the circumstances or state that he was in that they were called to behold

2 how they were to behold him and what is implyed they should have done in beholding of him

and as to the

1 tis the man and the circumstance or condition he was in and may intend the man whome ye have brought before me whome ye acuse and want to have tryed condemned and crucified and who is in part condemed whome ye have thus crown'd with thorns and arayd and whome you thus mock and deride as a king behold him in this curcumstance and see if he deserves it at your hands

2 when Pilat calls to behold him it is not barely to behold him with thier bodyly eyes under thes indignities in this persicuted condition but tis a call to consider him and what was needfull and proper to be considered concerning him which are such things as these perticulerly

1 they should have considered who and what he had and did profess himself to be, the doctrine that he taught and the great work he profesedly came to perform and what his deciples belived and taught of him as that he was not only the Son of man but also truely the Son of God, God and man in one person the true Masiah promised Son the spirituall king redemer and saviour and that he came to perform the great work of redemption and salvation as a prophet to teach them the divine will, as a prist to attone for transgresions and as a king to rule and save his people with a spirituall and eternal salvation and was posesed of all perfection to acomplish the great design so that tis no commen but an exterordenary person you have to behold, if his doctrine be true in fact all which should be duely weiged and considered before they proceed to areign and condem him

2 it may imply that they should have considered what they thought of him and charged him with a mear cheat a deciver and blasphemer quite the revers to what he profesed himself to be and to what his followers declared of him they should have considen that it was a matter of vast importance for if the former was true he was not only the best of men innocent holy harmless undefiled and separat from sinners as he was man but also more than man was truely the Son of God of the same esence perfection and glory as the Father tho it was vailed in the flesh and who therefore deserv'd the chiefest love and the highest prais (instead of the indignity put upon him) both for the sake of his divine perfections and the great things he did for man but on the other hand if they thought of him and charged against as a dicever was just then he must needs be the greatest deciever in matter of the greatest moment and the very worst of men to put so great a cheat on man so that you see there is a wide difference he must be either the best of men and infinitely more and better than all men or the worst of men and justly deserveing of the death inflicted on him

3 it therefore implys that they should have considered what Christ had done for the profe of what he professed to be and of the truth of the doctrine that he taught such as a whole life of goodness love and mercy such as the excelent doctrine that he taught which was every

way worthy of God and such as the many mericals which he wrought and that were the seals of heaven to his truth all which together with the exact fulfilling of Scripture prophises in him might and would have convinced of his being truely the Son of God had they not been blind in sin which hinderd them from knowing of him for had they known him they would not have crucifed the Lord of life and glory and tho Pilat might not have all thes things on his thoughts when he called them to behold the man yet the nature of the thing dos plainly imply that they should have but beheld and consider him that they might not have crucifed the Lord and then I ad

4 it implys that they should have behilded him so as to consider the grounds of thier charge and the proofs of what they aledged against him lest they should proceed wrongfully to judgment and condemnation for if thier charge against him as a dicever had been just thier act had been the same in putting of him to death but if all thier acusation was fals then the sin in crucifying of the Lord is exeeding great and from the history of his charg tryall condemnation and death tis plain that nothing but fals witness was brought against him and that if sin in ginerall and malice in particular had not blinded thier minds they must needs have seen the inocenc of the Lord and not have put him to death but they were wilfully blind and malitious against the Lord and in his crucifiction was guilty of heinous sin and the sin is charged against them Act 2:23 him being deliverd by the determinate counsel and foreknowledge of God ye by wicked hands have crucifed and slain these short hints may suffice concerning beholding of the man with regard to Pilat and the persons then present and what he called them too

I come

2 to consider the words as they are left upon record and may be applycable to us and instructive to us and all that have the gospel which is what I intend cheefly to be incisting on and I propose to proceed in a method to this porpos or would endevor

1 to shew who and what man this is that is the object we are called to behold

2 to shew wherein we may and should now behold him

3 to shew in what state or states and condition we should behold him

4 to shew where with we should behold him as he is thus represented to us in these states or circumstances

5 to shew what we may behold in and concerning him

6 to shew what may be intended by and implyed in a right beholding of him and of these things concerning him

7 to shew the use or improvement we should make thereof

and as I have proposed these severall gineral heads so that I may not be tedious I propose to be but short in speaking to them

to ye 1 the man we are called to behold is the same person that Pilate called the Jews to behold when in my tex he said behold the man and whom he also calls thier king and calls them to behold as such it was and in a spirituall sence is truely the King of his church and people tho called so in mockery by his enimies who crucifed him and notwithstanding all the raige of his enimies as mediator he is set up as King on the holy hill of Zion according to Ps 2 e 6 and his humiliation was the way to his exaltation and Glory hence it was foretold of him he shall drink of the brook in the way therefore shall he lift up the head Ps 110 e 7 and agreeable to this is what we have Philip 2 e 5 downward tis said let this mind be in you which was in Christ Jesus who being in the form of God thought it not robery to be equall with God but made himself of no reputation and took upon him the form of a servant and was made in the likeness of man and being found in fashion as a man he humbled himself and became obedient unto death even the death of the cross wherefore God hath highly exalted him and given him a name above every name tis this humbled this exalted man that we are called to behold and concerning him I note

1 that tho he is called the man and was truely man and as such more excelent than other men, yet he was more than a man and was and is truely the eternall Son of God as those who was concerned in his crucifying was made to acknowledge and confess when they saw the maricles that attended his death Math 27 e 54 and who was and is therefore truely God as well as man tho he was charged with blasphemy by his enimies for profesing and owneing of himself so to be this man therefore that we are called to behold is the great Immanuel God with us or God in our nature Matt 1 e 23 the true Mesiah the redeemer King and Saviour that was held forth in types and shadows in provisees and promises and who now accordingly is come and has performed his work in his state of humiliation and now is exalted and reigns above and tis with regard to his twofold nature we should now behold him as the glorious object of our faith and hope

2 I note concerning him that we are called to behold who is both God and man is also the prophit Priest and king of his church and people and who as such has all perfection and was perfectly capable of exicuting all his offices to the glory of God and the salvation and happyness of his people and as such we should behold and imbrace him

3 I note concerning him that he is the head and husband of his church and people he chose them for his bride entered into covenant engagement with his Father for them to redeem them and has redeemed them for himself by his blood courts them by his gospel captivates them by the almight power of his grace recieve's them into a married union and relation to him selves as the wife of his love and care and in that indesolveable relation will enjoy them for ever in the kingdom of his grace when he espouses belivers to himself and secondly in the kingdom of his glory where the marriage is solemnized above and where they will be everlastingly happy in his dear imbraces for all perfections meet in him and he is a husband that is infinitely better than any or all the sons of men and such a husband of his people we should behold with wonder love and joy and this may suffice for the first ginerall head which was to shew who and what man this is that we should behold

I come as proposed

2 to shew where or wherein we may and should behold him and this in a few particulars

1 we may and should behold him in his word the revelation we have concerning him which is the sacred scriptures for by this he is plainly reveled and made known in his natures his divine perfections his excelency and glory in his offices and the relation in which he stands to his church and people in the wonders of his love and grace and in whatever is needfull to be known concerning him and therefore this our Lord refers to for the knowledge of himself John 5 e 39 Search the Scriptures for in them ye think ye have eternal life and they are they which testify of me and the Scriptures are said to be able to make a man wise unto salvation thro faith in Christ Jesus 2 of Timothy 3 e 15 the Scriptures revele the knowledge of Christ and are as a glass to represent him in his sutableness his beauty his excelency and glory tis therefore in the reading and study of the Scriptures that we may and should behold the Lord not in the records of nature or

the light thereof abstracted from the Scripture but in the light of the records of the Scripture we may behold his glory for tho the works of creation and providence may in part make him known as God in the glory of his wisdom and his power yet these do not make him know as God and man as mediator redeemer and Saviour in his suteableness and fullness this depend purely upon divine revelation or the sacred Scriptures in this therefore we should seek the knowledge of him and in this as a glas we may behold his glory

2 we may and should behold him in his works both in his works of nature and his acts of grace for tho as I have hinted these abstractedly from the Scripture do not make him know as mediator and in his suteableness and fullness as such yet when the Scripture make know what his works of nature and acts of grace are as creation providence and redemption then in and by these we may behold his divine perfections his excellency and glory to fill our souls with holy admiration and captivate our hearts to love and this is the use and improvement we should make of the contemplation of them and here I would note that all his works and acts in generall and all the parts in perticular conspire to proclaim his excelency and glory these are therefore noble subjects of contemplation to delight the soul seeing that in them we may behold our Lord in his excellency and glory

3 we may and should behold him in his ordenances in all his gospel ordenances such as the ministry of the word baptism and the Lords Supper for these were designed to make him known and by these he is held forth and represented to us in his nature in his offices in his relations and in his beauty excelency and glory and in these belivers have beheld him with wonder love and joy and in these they have had the pleasing discoveries of his love and grace and in them they have had the sweet enjoyment of him on these therefore we should joyfull attend to behold the Lord in his beauty and glory to love adore and praise his name and this leads me to ad in the next place

4 that we may and should behold him in the asimblies of his saints or in his house his church and people where his worship and his ordenances are performed for there acording to divine declaretion his gracious presence is tis there he unvails his glory and revels his will and there he holds communion with his people and there he gives them the pledges of his love this made it so desireable to the psalmes that it made him say one thing have I desired of the Lord and that will I seek after that I may dwell in the house of the Lord all the days of my life that I may behold the beauty of the Lord and to enquire in

his temple Ps 27 e 4 and how aimable are thy tabernacles o Lord of host my soule longeth yea even fainteth for the courts of the Lord Ps 84 e 1:2 and vers 10 a day in thy courts is better than a thousand I had rather be a door keeper in the house of my God than to dwell in the tents of wickedness and in a gospel dispensation when in the house or church of God the worship is more spirituall and refined the delight and pleasure must when grace is high in excercise be proportionablely refined and encresed would any then have the experimentall knowledge and enjoyment of the Lord they must seek after it in the asimbles of his saints where his pure worship is performed where the Lords gracious presence is and ther thy may behold him in his beauty excelency and glory when the inquirery was made to the Lord tell me o thou whome loveth where thou feedest where thou makest thy flock to rest at noon etc the answer is if thou know not o thou fairest among women go thy way forth by the footsteps of the flock and feed thy keeds besides the shepherds tents Songs 1 e 7: 8 plainly intending that there the Lord was to be seen and enjoyed and this is the same with the asimbles of the saints the church and people of God and dos shew that tis in and with them that we may behold the Lord in his beauty and glory I may ad

5 that we may and shall behold him in heaven its self his glorious residence above where with the regard to the full desplay of his excelency and glory it may be said his honour dweleth his gracious presence as I have hinted is with his church below in the kingdom of his grace and there we may behold him but his glorious presence is with his church above in heaven the glorious house of God and there the saints shall behold his glory acording to the Lords mediatorial prayer for them as at John 17 e 24 Father I will that they also whome thou hast given me may be with me that they may behold my Glory and o how entertaining and satisfy will this be to the soule, to behold him in the glass of the gospel tends to transform the soule into his likeness and therefore thus to behold and enjoy him is the ernest and beginning of true happyness and to behold Christ in the fullness of his glory where the soules likeness to the Lord will be compleat and the enjoyment of him full and endness this must be ful satesfaction and perfect happyness and this is the sight of Christ that our soules should aspire after and seek to attaine and this may suffice for the 2d thing proposed which was to shew where we may and should behold the man who is our redeemer Lord and Saviour and this was proper and needfull to be shewen for to what purpose would be to be called to behold the Lord unless we know where he may be seen

I come now as proposed[9]

3 to shew in what state or states we should behold the Lord and this also in a few particulers

1 we may and should behold him in his eternal state of existence before his incarnation or the time of his asumeing our nature for in that state he is reveled unto us in his eternal designs of love and grace and in covenant transactions with the Father for the great work of redemption and salvation he engaiged to perform, and tho actual eternal exsistence is proper only to the divine nature that is unchangablely the same for ever and therefore from everlasting to everlasting he is God yet as the Son the second person in the Trinity acording to the eternall covenant was to asume the human nature that he might be both God and man in one person to be a fit mediator redeemer and Savior so in that sence with regard to his twofold nature and mediator he was set up from everlasting as the head of those he was to redeem and save according to Proverbs 8 e 23 & 30 I was set up from everlasting and then was I by him as one brought up with him rejoycing allways before him and his delight was with the sons of men now to behold the Lord in this eternal state as it soposeth the view of eternal transaction of love and grace which is the rise or spring of all acts of grace and salvation that in time we are partakers of this is both delightfull and profitable to the soule this is eternal love and grace that is the fountaine head of all our happyness and this therefore is the first state in which we may behold our Lord and to behold and consider him as he is reveld in his everlasting love to such sinners as we in the eternal purposes of his grace and in his covenant ingaigement for our redemption and salvation is exceeding delightfull and profitable to our souls

2 we may and should behold him in his state of incarnation and humiliation when he assumed our nature and vailed his glory in the flesh and in all the wonders of his life and death for in this state he is plainly reveld and made known to us and in which state he acompleshed the eternal designs of love and grace respecting the great and glorious work of redemption and here in we have the wonderfull and glorious desplays there of how wonderfull is it that the eternal Son of God who is the brightness of his Fathers glory and the exspres immage of his person should humble himself to take our nature and become man that he who is soverane Lord of all should take upon him the form of a servent live a poor and persecuted life

9 Note at side of page states 'May 20 1750 at Bro'

and died a shamefull and painfull death that he should stand in the law place of sinners suffer in thier steed from men and devels and from God his Father as a righteous judge and die a ransom to redeem and save from divine wrath and hell and save to eternall happyness and all this for the love he bore to such sinners as we, this shews he is full of wonder love and grace and this must need be the joyfull subject of eternal praise in this state of humiliation we may behold this wonderfull man our Lord redeemer with wonder love and joy and we may view him in all the parts of his life on earth which was nothing but goodness love and mercy most delighfull to behold and the noblest patern to imitate and follow in his doctern it was infinitely excelent and perfect and the manner of his teaching superior to all men hence tis noted he taught as one haveing authority and not as the scribes Math 7 e 29 and thos that was sent to take him said of him never man spake like this man John 7 e 46 and he taught not only outwardly and ministerally with superior excelency to all men but he also taught inwardly and efficasiously to cause the soule to understand and in this together with all the maricals he wrought he displayed the glory of his divinity tho he vailed it in the flesh & tis noted of him that he went about doing good and healing all manner of deseases and he healed not only the desorders of the body but the malodys of the soule o how wonder then is Christ the mediator who is God and man if we behold him in his state of humiliation the wonders of his life and death in the acomplishment of his vast designs of love and grace and to behold him in this state must needs be exceedingly entertaining and profitable to our soules tis profitable on a two fold acount first in its tendency to make us humble in a sight and sence of sin that cost our redeemer all the sufferings of his body and all the sorrows of his soule and secondly in yt it desplays both the lovelyness and love of Christ to atract our soules to love and adore the Lord and therefore in his state of incarnation and humiliation we should behold the man who died for us and who is our redeemer and our Lord

3 we may and should behold him in his resurection state or state of exaltation and glory for in this state he is reveld represented and made known to us in the sacred Scriptures and here in this state we may behold him, as haveing finished the great work of redemption and salvation (so far as it refers to his humiliation and sufferings) as haveing made full satisfaction for transgression compleat attonement for the sin of his people and paid the full price of redemption and brought in an everlasting righteous to cloath them, as haveing

obtained all the blessing of grace and glory for them, and as have conquered all the powers of hell and death and sin for his people here therefore we may behold him in the triumphs of his death in his resurection which is the demonstration the price was fully paid the great work of his humiliation fully done and this is the foundation of the believers hope and joy here we may behold him as giving direction to his people for the rule of thier conduct in the kingdom of his grace acording to his owne divine perfections and as is excently suted to the welfare of his church and people and here we may behold him in his asention to glory where he is gon to prepare mantions for his people in which he will have them to dwell with him for ever where he ever lives to interced for them and where he reigns as king of nations and king of saints in the bright desplay of his deity and from where he sheds the influences of his grace on his people here to prepare them for and bring them to himself above and o how etertaineing and joyfull must it be thus to behold our redeemer and our Lord when faith is in its lively exercise to behold the glory of it this is the state our Lord now is in and in this state he is represented to us and we are called to behold his glory and these short hints may suffice to shew in what state or states we may and should behold our Lord

but may any say these are unseen things to our bodily eyes how therefore can we behold them I therefore proceed to the next thing proposed

4 to shew where with we should behold the Lord in these states in all his excelency and glory and of this first

1 negatively not with our bodyly eyes for with these we cannot now behold him. Such beholding of him was proper to the time of his incarnation and to those who was then with him and many of these who then beheld him with thier bodyly eyes were yet strangers to a saveing knowledge of him in his natures his excelancy and glory not with stand all the evidences thereof some may posibly think how happy they should have been if they had lived in the time of our Lords being on earth to have seen his works the desplayes of his deaty but if they had only seen him with thier bodily eyes and no light of grace within they would not have seen his beauty so as to desire him nor have had any saveing benifit by beholding of him but remaining ignorant of Christ they might have joyned in crucifying the Lord of glory and so have been guilty of that dreadful sin so that as we cannot now see the Lord with our bodily eyes let us remember

such a sight do not nescesaryly imply the saving knowledge of Christ nor interest in him tis true the time is comeing when some shall see Christ with the eyes of thier bodys in the fullness of glory and which will be thier happyness for it sopposeth likeness to and the enjoyment of him henc holy Job said I know that my redeemer liveth and that after my skin worms destroy my body yet in my flesh shall I see God Job 19 e 25, 26 27 but such a sight is not attainable while we were bodies of mortality tho our eyes may behold the records of the Lord and our ear hear the joyfull sound of his love and graces and so be instremental to aright discerning of him but

2 to come to the posative part and then I note tis to be understood of a spiritual beholding of the Lord and it must be with our understanding and by faith

1 we must understand the revelation of this glorious man who is both God and man the great redeemer Lord and Saviour or else we cannot behold his beauty excelency and glory and unles the Lord openeth our understand by his Spirit and grace and giveth a capacity of discerning we cannot understand the revelation of the Lord so as to behold his glory but as it must be thus with our understanding so as I hinted

2 it must be by faith realising the truth of what is reveled concerning Christ without which there can be no beholding of it hence faith is called the substance of things hoped for the evidence of things not seen Heb 11 e 1 that is not seen by bodily eyes these cannot behold invisible things as, this is only the property of faith and therefore tis noted of Moses that by faith he forsook Egypt not fearing the wrath of the king for he endured as seeing him who is invisible Heb 11 e 27, Christ the redeemer and Saviour in his excelency and glory and the grace of the promises through him are invisable things, both to the bodily eye and to the carnel mind, or unbeliver for such can see no beauty in Christ so as to desire him, but this is clearly discerned by faith which is as the eye to the gracious soule by which to behold the redeemers glory and all that the gracious soul understands and beliveth concerning Christ the Lord apears as real to such as any thing of naturall objects beheld by bodily eyes tis therefore with the understanding and by faith that we should behold the object in my tex and these short hints may suffice as to ye 4 things which was to shew wherewith we should behold the Lord in the state of his eternal existance and

covenant transaction, in the state of his incarnation, and humiliation, in his resurection state, or state of exaltation and glory, as he is represented to us for all these states we cannot now behold him but by understand and by faith

I come

5 as proposed to shew what we may and should behold in and concerning Christ the object reveled and that we are called to behold or look upon in the states in which he is represented to us by his word and works the call to behold him implys that there is some thing wonderfully excelent to behold that is worthy of our attention and yt claims our due regard this therefore should ingaige our soules in the contemplation of this divine object of faith and of this I would note

1 we may and should behold the transendant beauty excelency and glory of his person for with respect to this he is infinitely fairer than the sons of men, as man he was perfect in beauty without blemish or spot as God he is the creater and therefor all the beauty of the cretures and infinitely more are found in him are his property and glory and therefor as God and man the beauty and glory of his person is infinitely beyond compare and therefor tho the spouse attempts a description of him and makes use of metaphors to set it forth Song 5 e 10 and downwards my beloved is white and ruddy the cheefest among ten thousand and so on yet to shew her utter incapacity to set it forth to the full shee says at v 16 his mouth is most sweet yea he is altogether lovely tis true we cannot now behold the beauty and glory of his person with our bodyly eyes as the deciples did at his transfigeration and the saints will when they shall be raised and their bodies glorified but with the eye of faith in the glass of the gospel we may behold the redeemers beauty and glory to delight and transform our soules

2 in shewing what we may and should behold in and concerning Christ the Lord I note that we may and should behold all his works and the acts of grace performed by him such as creation providence and redemption and all the acts of grace containd in them in these as I have already hinted we may behold the Lord but what I now take notice of is that we should behold and consider these his wonderfull works and acts and they are truely and wonderfully great henc the psalmist said at ye 111 e 2:3 the works of the Lord are great sought out by them that have pleasure therein his works are honourable and glorious, and as tis so with regard to all his works of creation and providence in gineral tis emmanently so with regard the more

wonderfull and glorious work of redemption in perticular and all his acts of grace contained therein what was spoaken concerning what our Lord performed in the days of his flesh may properly be applyd to all that he has done in the great and glorious work of redemption and salvation Mark 7 e 37 and they were beyond measure astonished saying he hath done all things well he maketh both the deaf to hear and the dumb to speak, and therefore his works of nature and acts of grace are the noblest subjects of contemplation and that which will aford the greatest delight and profit to the soule when sutablely engaiged in the contemplation of them and when we are called to behold the Lord it must imply a call to behold the works and wonders he has done and we should never be forgetfull of the works of the Lord nor be regardless of the operation of his hands and that because as I have hinted in these the Lord is seen and this leads me to ad in the

3 place that in beholding of the Lord we should behold and consider the esential and infinite perfections of his nature that his works and acts declare and that divine revelation declare concerning him and that in part shine forth in every state in which we should behold the Lord such as [10]

1 his infinite wisdom that laid the great designs and

2 his allmighty power by which his works were and are all performed

3 his infinite goodness love and mercy that is ye eternal spring of all and that shines forth and are gloriously desplayed in what ye Lord hath done for his church and people

4 his truth and faithfullness manifested and gloriously desplayed in fullfilling of his covenant engaigements and covenant promises for his church and people while he was on earth and which is the asuranc that he will perform them all as they refer to what he will yet do for them to compleat thier eternal happyness in glory

5 his unchangeableness which when aded to all his divine perfection is the unchangeable and sure foundation for his peoples hope and trust for all supplys of grace in the way and for glory in the end in short all the perfections of the deaty meet in him so that he is every way and completely capable of the government of his vast domions for his Fathers glory for his

10 Note at side of page states, 'Wallop July 8 1750'

own honour and glory and for the happyness of his church and people in short all divine perfections are his property and glory so that nothing can be wanting nothing can be aded to make him more comepleat and tis all these divine perfections that claim our attention our highest reverance and regard tis these that render him the supreme object of contemplation admireation adoration and the eternal object of his peoples love the unchangeable sure foundation of their hope and trust and ye eternal spring of thier everlasting joy and praise and as all these his divine perfections call for our cloasest and most delightfull attention shall not these ingaige our soule in love and praise I yeat ad

4 that as we are called to behold him it implys that we may and should behold the treasures of grace that are in him for his church and people and that freely flow from him to supply all thier needs whiles here and to make them compleatly happy hereafter for as all divine perfections meet in him and are his esential properties and glory so all fullness is him for his people henc tis said it pleased the Father that in him should all fullness dwell Colosions 1 e 19 and of his fullness have all we riceved and grace for grace John 1 e 16 tis sometimes exspresedley a fountain to denote the fullness of the grace that is in Christ and tis called and open fountain to denote the freeness of it as tis free for and freely springs up and flowes to supply the wants and satisfy his people that come unto him hince tis said with thee is the fountaine of life Ps 36 e 9 and in that day there shall be a fountaine opend to the house of Daved and to the inhabitants of Jerusalem for sin and for uncleanness Zec 13 e 1 and the grace that is in Christ is also sometimes exspresed or set forth by rivers of water to shew the abundance the fullness and freeness of his grace to supply the wants of all that come unto him Isaiah 32 e 2 and a man shall be as an hiding place from the wind a covet from the tempest as rivers of water in a dry place and as a shadow of a great rock in a wery land but all the nobelest metiphors come very far short of seting forth the infinite perfection and fullness of the grace that is in Christ for his people for tis infinitely beyond compare and this is what we are called to behold and may behold in our great redeemer Lord and Saviour

I come [11]

11 Note at side of page states, 'Bro July 8 1750'

6 as proposed to shew what may be implyed and intended in and by a right beholding of him and of these things concerning him and this in a few perticulers

1 it soposeth there must be a visive facelty or capacity of beholding of it and this none have till tis given by the Lord who eluminates the soul opens the understanding and gives a capacity of discerning to behold this glorious object reveled in the Gospel and the wonders of divine love & grace henc tis said ye eyes of your understing being enlightend that ye may know what is the hope of your calling etc Eph 1 e 18 plainly implying that without this there could be no beholding of spiritual objects and things among other parts of the deploreable circumstances that the Scripture represents man in by the fall blindness is one and from this as well as other callamities Christ the redeemer was to deliver and save according to Is 42 e 6:7 the Lord hath called thee in righteousness and will hold thine hand and will keep thee and give thee for a covenant of the people for a light of the Gentiles to open the blind eyes to bring out the prisoners from the prison and them that set in darkness from the prison house and the Lord performs the work by the allmighty power of his Spirit on the heart tis said then opened he the understanding that they might understand the Scriptures Luk 24 e 45 and tis said ye were sometimes darness but now are ye light in the Lord Eph 5 e 8 as persons that are blind by nature cannot behold naturall objects and things so persons in an unconverted state being blinded in thier understanding by sin can not behold spirituall objects and things in a spriritual manner till thier understandings are opened by the Lord this therefore is one thing necesaryly implied in a right beholding of the Lord and as it dos thus sopose there must be a understanding facelty given so I note that there must be also a power given to belive or the real principel of saveing faith wrought in the soule because tis by faith the object is seen and apears real to the soule and this men are destitute of being born in unbelief and sin and persons must be born again and have the grace of understanding and of faith in order to a right beholding of the Lord because as I have shewn tis thereby we behold his glory and then

2 in a right beholding of this divine object there must be the excercise of the understanding faculty that is given and the acts and excercise of that faith that is planted in the soule the sutable imployment of the restored facelty and of faith and other graces and in order to this we should use the means to improve the measure of our knowledge and understanding and to excite the excercise of faith and pray for a

blessing that by understanding and by faith we may behold the Lord in his glory as he is desplayed in his words and works and to behold him understanding and believeingly imply that we should so understand and belive as to recieve and imbrace the object (whome we understand and in whome we belive) with our whole hearts in his natures beauty excelency and glory in all his offices and relations in which he stands to his church and people or we can never be said rightly to behold the Lord we must so behold him as to place all our hope and trust in him and live upon him for all the blessings of the kingdom of grace and for everlasting glory in the end or else it cannot be said we rightly behold the Lord again

3 rightly to behold the Lord is to behold him with love desire and delight of soul that is so as to love him with the cheafest love because of the transendant beauty excelency and glory we behold in him and perticulerly becaus of the greatness of his love to us desplayed in the great things he hath done for us and becaus of the benifits that flow from him and this love to Christ will allways attend or follow the saveing knowledg of Christ and true faith in him and with out love there cannot be a right beholding of him the spous of Christ as true belivers in him are represented in the Song of Soloman as being ardent in love to Christ and without this none can be said rightly to behold the Lord and as it must be a beholding of Christ so as thus to love him so as I have hinted under this it must be so as to desire him that is so as to desire a evident intrest in him and so as to desire the enjoyment of him in his ordenances and providences in the kingdom of his grace whilst here as the ernist of thier happyness and in the fullness of it in the kingdom of his glory as the perfect of true happyness and this when enjoyed is as I have hinted under this is attended with sweet complacency and delight in him and therefore the spous said I sate down under his shadow with great delight and his frute was sweet unto my tast he brought me into his banquiting house and his banner over me was love stay me with flagens and comfort me with apples for I am sick of love Song 2 e 3-5[12]

4 rightly to behold the Lord is to behold him with admiration reverance and adoration from the beliving views of his infinite greatness his beauty excelency and glory and so as to be truely humbled before him and according to the discoveries we have of his infinite greatness his excelency and glory so our admiration will arise so will be our holy awe and reverance of the Lord so will our adoration be to

12 Note at side of page states, Downton July 15 1750

him and so our souls will be humble before the Lord like the psalmis what is man that thou art mindfull of him and the son of man that thou dost viset him Ps 8 e 4 I again ad

5 that to behold the Lord aright is to behold him so as to submit unto him and yeld up ourselves in a glad divotin to his service from the views of his divine excelency and from the powerfull constaints of his love and grace for as the beliveing and delightfull views of his divine perfection will allways constran to love the Lord so love will constrain to obedience that so it may prove the sincerity of love to ye Lord in the time of our Lords incarnation many that behild him with thier bodyly eyes were not captivated to love him and therefore turnd away from him and did not obey him but when any had thier understanding enlighted to the saveing knowledg of Christ and were wrought over to true faith in him these fill in love with Christ and didn't turn from him but were devoted to his service so now those that read of him in his word and here of him in the ministeration of it if they have nothing but some slight thought of Christ and head notions of him and have no true faith in him nor love to him such turn away from Christ to vanity and sin and are not constrained to obediean but thos who in the reading or his word understand and have the saveing knowledge of Christ and true faith in Christ and sincere love to him these are constained to obedience to Christ to a delightfull divotion to his service as the Lord as well as Saviour of thier soules and with out this there cannot be a right beholding of the Lord

6 rightly to behold the Lord is to behold him so as to be joyfull in him for he is both the foundation and fountain of his peoples joy and all that truely belive in him and view him in his excelencys and glory with an apropreateing act of the soule cannot but be joyfull in him tis true he may sometimes hide his face for a season from his own people and then they mourn but when faith prevailes in its lively excercis and Christ returns and makes his gracious visits, then the soule cannot but rejoyc in him with exceeding joy, hence tis said whome haveing not seen ye love in whome tho now you see him not yet beliveing ye rejoyce with joy unspeakable and full of glory 1 Peter 1 e 8 and allways according to the clearness of the belivers views of what Christ is to and of what he has done and will do for the soule so in proportion will the joy arise and acording to the measure of experance of his divine perfections and of the enjoyment of him so will the joy encrese and when faith shall be turned into

vision and hope into fruition then the joy will be full and the happiness compleat again I ad

7 rightly to behold the Lord is to behold him so as to be influenced to speak and live his praise and those who have the saveing knowledg of Christ in his excelency and glory that have aquaintanc with him and the experimentall enjoyment of him cannot but have a dispotion of soule to speak of the excelency of thier Lord and when grace prevails in its proper excercis they are ready when called unto it to say with the spous to the enquirer my beloved is white and ruddy the chiefest among ten thousand his head is as the most fine gould and so on till at last to shew her incapacity of seting of it forth unto the full she crys out yea he is alltogether lovely this is my beloved and this is my friend Song 5 from ye 9 to ye end what our Lord speaks Luke 19 e 40 may be fitly applyed to all that have the saveing and delightfull sight of Christ and experimentall communion with him; if thes should hold thier peace the stones would immediatly cry out plainly implying that to speak the praises of the Lord is in seperable from aright beholding of him again

8 to behold the Lord aright is to behold him so as to be led to a delightfull imitation of him so as to be transferd more and more into his likeness and be made meet to gloryfy the Lord here and to enjoy him forever and so as to seek after this as the satisfaction of the soule and as the highest happyness in this the psalmist placed it when he said as for me I will behold thy face in righteousness I shall be satisfied when I awake with thy likeness Ps 17 e 15 and all that rightly behold the Lord have these desires thereby kindled up in thier soules and when grace prevailes in its proper exercise they can be satisfied in nothing short of this and here I conclude the sixth gineral head proposed which was to shew what may be imply or intended in and by aright beholding of the Lord

I come now as proposed

7 and lastly to shew the use or improvement we should make of what have been spoaken

1 in a use of information and from what have been said we may learn

1 that the Lord Jesus Christ the Son of God the great redeemer and Saviour is the best of beings the most delightfull and profitable object to behold for his divine perfections renders him infinitely beyond compare and his sutables and fullness renders him also most worthy of our choic and aright behold of

him imploys a gracious propriaty and intrest in him and tends to transform the soule into his like ness and make us meet to glorify him here and enjoy him for ever and therefor tis both delightfull and profitable to the soule

2 from what have been said we may learn the greatness of the folly and sin of those who eagerly run to behold objects of vanity and sin and neglect seeking to behold the Lord who is infinitely more excelent and glorious than any and all the things of this world and yet tis matter of lammentation to consider that there are multidues of such fools and sinners among the sons of men instances of this kind have lately been, crouds have attend carnel excercises and envented lys to entertain the carnel mind to draw away from of the necesary sopports of life and wast the moments of precious time and had there been at the same time a providential call to attend the minestry of the word in which Christ is held forth in his excelency and glory tis to be feard the congeregation would have been exceeding thin this is a sad and malencoly truth and sheweth such folly and sin to be very great again we may learn

3 that mankind are dreadfull depraved and blinded by sin and therefore they have no desire after the knowledge of this charming object nor after an intrest in him have no capacity of beholding his excelency and glory till they are new formed and changed by the Lord

4 in the next place we may therefore learn the absolute need there is for men to be born again or changed by the allmighty power of divine grace to be raisd from a death in sin to a life of grace to be changed from darkness to light that so they may be made capable to behold the Lord in his beauty excelency and glory and to imbrace him with thier whole harts which none can unles they are born again and therefore our Lord said except a man be born again he cannot see the kingdom of God Jo 3 e 3 however the doctrine of the new birth is neglected and despised by many you may see tis absolutely necessary in order to true happyness

5 From what has been said we may learn the happyness of them that are right beholders of the Lord for 1 they are truely born again are blessed with a capcity of discerning to behold the beauty of the Lord 2 it affords thier soules truely rationall pleasure delight and joy 3 it sopoeseth thier gracious propriaty and intrest in the Lord 4 that they are and shall be like him and

shall enjoy him for ever and therefore they are truely and shall be everlastingly happy

6 from what has been said we may infer ye misery of those who remain strangers to Christ and never rightly look unto him to behold his excelency and glory and to imbrace him they as miserable at present being in a state of blindness sin and death and arc strangers to the need and worth of Christ and therefore reject and never look unto him for salvation and besides Christ there is no other Saviour and if they so live and die the guilt of sin will remain on them and they must endure the wrath of God and suffer the vengence of eternal fire I therefore ad

7 from what has been said we may learn that tis the duty and concern of all to examen if we are such as rightly behold the Lord for what will the transendant excelency of the object avail us or the happyness of the right beholders of him if we are strangers to him and have not behild his excelency and glory nor made choice of him as our portion our redeemer and our Lord if we thus remain as you have heard we shall be undon for ever tis therefore our great concern to examen how tis with our soules & therefore

2 we should come to a use of tryall and we may improve som thing that have been spoaken by way of tryall, if we are grosly ignorant of Christ and know nothing of his divine excelency so as to love and desire him we are not right beholders of him but if we have some knoledge of him and hope we have behild his glory then to try if tis of a right kind and if we have been rightly beholding of the Lord let us enqire

1 where have we behild him is it as under the 2 gineral head as first have we seen him

1 in his word the revelation we have of him

2 in his works of nature and his acts of grace

3 have we seen him in his gospel ordenances

4 in the asimblees of his saints if in these we have seen him in his beauty so as to desire him so as to imbrace and delight in him and if

5 we have seen him in heaven then we may have ground to hope we have had some saving views of him here and shall have the open vision and enjoyment of him above

2 for farther tryall let us enquire in what state or states we have beheld the Lord is it as under the third head as

1 in his state of eternal exsistance before his incarnation for in that state he is reveled in ye word

2 in his state of incarnation and humiliation when he asumed our nature and veild his glory in the flesh and in the wonders of his life his sufferings and death for redemption and salvation and

3 have we beheld him in his reserection state his state of exaltation and glory for in this state he is also reveled and made known,

if we hope we have seen him in this threefold state and in all these have beheld his excelency and glory then for farther tryall let us enquire

3 wherewith have we seen him is it as undar the 4 head not with our bodyly eyes but with our understanding and by faith do we understand and belive the revelations of him and do we realise divine reports concerning the redeem and Saviour and in that sence behold his glory if it be so in truth we have had our understandings enlighten by divine grace and are blessed with the grace of faith and rightly behold the Lord and if we thus hope then for further enquiry

4 what have we beheld in and concerning Christ the Lord is it as under ye 5 gineral head as

1 have we seen the transendant beauty and glory of his person and dos he apear to us infinitely fairer than the sons of men dos he apear to be the chiefest among ten thousand and is he altogether lovely to us

2 have we seen and considered the noble works and acts of grace performed by him in which his glory is desplayed and have this filld our soules with wonder adoration love and praise

3 have we seen the esentiall and glorious perfections of the Lord that his works and acts declare and that divine revelation confirm concerning him as 1 his infinite wisdom 2 his allmighty power 3 his infinite goodness love and mercy 4 his truth and faithfullness and 5 his unchangableness in all the glorious perfections of his natur as the sure foundation of our hope and joy and do these render him charming to our soules

4 have we behild the treasures of his love and grace yt are in him and freely flow from him do this make him apear very sutable and exceeding precious to our soules if we hope we have behild these things in and concerning the Lord

5 then for farther tryall enquire to know if our beholding of him is of aright kind is it as under the 6 gineral head

1 I noted it soposeth a visiv or understanding facelty given and the habit of faith in the soule and do find we have recd this grace and favor from the Lord

2 noted it sopposeth the excercis of the understanding faculty and of faith try then if thes are excercised about this divine object and is it pleasant to our soules then this proves the reception of this grace from God and we are right beholders of the Lord

3 do we so behold the Lord so as to love desire and delight in him that so as to love him with the chefest love becaus of the transendant beauty exelency and glory we behold in him and becaus of the bennifits flowing from and therefore do our soules desire him

4 do we behold him with admiration reverance and adoration

5 do we behold him so as to choos him for our Lord as well and Saviour and so as to submit unto him and yeld up our selves in a glad divotion to his service

6 is it so as to rejoyce in him with great and refined joy and

7 so as to speak and live his praise

8 is it so as to be thereby led to a delightfull imitation of him and be transforded in a measure to his likeness to be made meet to gloryfy and enjoy him and so as to seek after this

as that without which we can never be fully satisfied nor completely happy

if these things be the real experance of our soules we have ground to conclude that we are right beholders of the Lord have a gracious propriaty and intrest in him and shall be everlastingly happy in the enjoyment of him above but not so if we are strangers to all thes by thes and such like things we may try our souls and we must pray for asistance in this great and need full work that we may be preserved from deceiveing of our owne soules say with the psalmest search me O God and know my heart try me and know my thought see if there be any wicked way in me and lead me in the way everlasting Ps[13]

3 a use of exhortation first to those who have not yet beheld the Lord and do not behold him aright let such be exhortd without delay to seek after the saveing knowledg of Christ and sight of him so as to imbrace and trust in him and as motives to it consider

1 that the transendent excelency and glory of the Lord and the treasure of his love and grace that renders him the most charming object to behold and one infinitely most worthy of your choice all the beauty and glory of the whole creation are but sparks of his fullness but emanations and manifestations of the boundless perfection that he does poses and that are his esence and his glory o that your eyes were open to behold him that he might apear the cheafest among ten thousand and alltogether lovely to your souls

2 consid that all the objects of this world that may atract your minds are but emptyness and vanity in comparison of Christ they are unsatifying in thicr nature and uncertain in point of enjoyment and yet shall thes draw away to minds from Christ the chief good

3 consider the happiness of all them that look unto Jesus this divine object aright for it will be to the saving of thier soules hence tis said look unto me and be ye saved all ye ends of the earth

4 as a farther motive consider the dreadfull conequenc if you live and die rejecting of Christ and never savingly behold him such

13 Full Scripture reference not cited.

will be undon for ever for there is no other Saviour but Christ ye Lord Acts 4 e 12 neither is there salvation in any other for there is no other name under heaven given amongst men whereby we must be saved and if you dont behold him so as to belive in and imbrace him here you will behold him as your judge to condem you at the judgment day and sentance you to the torments of eternal fire remember now is the acepted time now is the day of salvation you that are grown in years and yet are strangers to Christ consider how near you are unto the grave and seek after a sight of Christ to the saving of your soul before your moments are fled away and you that are young and whose mind may turn to the vanitys of youth rember you are not sure of life you may have a few moment to the grave and then it will be to late to see after Christ tis the present time and day is yours and you have no asureanc of to morrow and should God spare your life for some time on earth yet delay not looking unto Jesus who is the most charming object in the univers and the sooner you behold him aright the greater and longer will be your refined delight and joy seek therefore a sight of Christ in his word and works and in his ordenances and pray that you may find him to the saveing of your soules

second to those who have seen the Lord and that do behold his beauty excellency and glory be exorted

1 to bless and prais the Lord who have brought you to a saveing sight of the redeemer and give him all the glory

2 rejoyce in the Lord whos divine perfections you behold and speak and live his prais

3 recommend him unto others in his excelencies his sutableness and fullness especially to enquireing soules say to them with the spous my beloved is white and rudy the cheefest among ten thousand that his mouth is most sweet and that he is alltogether lovely Song[14] that as humble instrument you may be usefull in the divine hand to persuad soules to look unto Christ for the saving of thier soule and pray that God would bless your endevers for thier good that multudes may joyn with you in magnifying your great redeem and your Lord

14 Full Scripture reference not cited.

Appendix III – A Hymn by James Fanch and Daniel Turner (1791)[15]

Beyond the glittering starry globe
Far as th' eternal hills,
There, in the boundless worlds of light,
Our great Redeemer dwells.

Immortal angels, bright and fair,
In countless armies shine,
At his right hand, with golden harps,
To offer songs divine.

"Hail! Prince," they cry, "for ever hail!
Whose unexampled love
Moved thee to quit these glorious realms
And royalties above!"

While thou didst condescend on earth
To suffer rude disdain,
They cast their honours at thy feet,
And waited on thy train.

Blest Angels, who adoring wait
Around the Saviour's Throne,
Oh! tell us, for your eyes have seen,
The wonders he has done.

Ye saw him, when the heavens and earth,
A chaos first, he made,
And night involved the formless deep
In her tremendous shade.

And when, amidst the darksome void,
He bade the light arise,
And kindled up those shining orbs
That now adorn the skies.

Ye saw – and in melodious song
Your powerful voices raise,
While all the new-born worlds resound
Their great Creator's praise.

And, when on earth he deign'd to dwell,
In mortal flesh array'd,
Ye wondering saw the holy child
In Bethlehem's stable laid.

While in the lowly crib reposed,
His mother's tender care,
Ye stood around his homely bed,
And watch'd his slumbers there.

When fasting in the desert long
His spotless soul was tried,
Ye saw him there the Tempter foil,
And soon his wants supplied.

Ye heard what gracious words he spoke,
The hearts of men to win;
And saw, well pleased, the listening crowd
Drink the sweet doctrine in;

Beheld diseases, tempests, death,
His sovereign word obey,
And how, on dark benighted minds,
He poured eternal day.

Saw him, from busy scenes retired
To spend the midnight hours,
While pure devotion fill'd his soul
With all her rapturous powers.

When on the sacred mount he shone,
In his own light array'd,
Ye saw, and own'd your Sovereign there,
And your just homage paid;

Saw, when o'er Salem's fearful doom
He shed the tender tear;
And how, to all his gracious calls,
She turned the deafened ear.

In all his toils, and dangers too,
Ye did his steps attend;
Oft paused, and wondered, how at last
This scene of love would end.

And when the powers of hell combined
To fill his cup of woe,
Your pitying eyes beheld his tears
In bloody anguish flow.

As on the torturing cross he hung,
And darkness veil'd the sky,
Ye saw, aghast, that awful sight,
The Lord of Glory die!

Astonish'd, here ye search and learn
High Heaven's mysterious ways,
That thus to guilty dying man
Immortal life conveys.

Anon he bursts the gates of death,
Subdues the tyrant's power:
Ye saw th' illustrious Conqueror rise,
And hailed the blissful hour,

Tended his chariot up the sky,
And bore him to his throne;
Then swept your golden harps, and cried
"The glorious work is done!"

My soul the joyful triumph feels,
And thinks the moments long,
Ere she her Saviour's glory sees,
And joins your rapturous song.

---

15 The Book of Praise, by Roundell Palmer, Macmillan, 1863 pp.79-82.

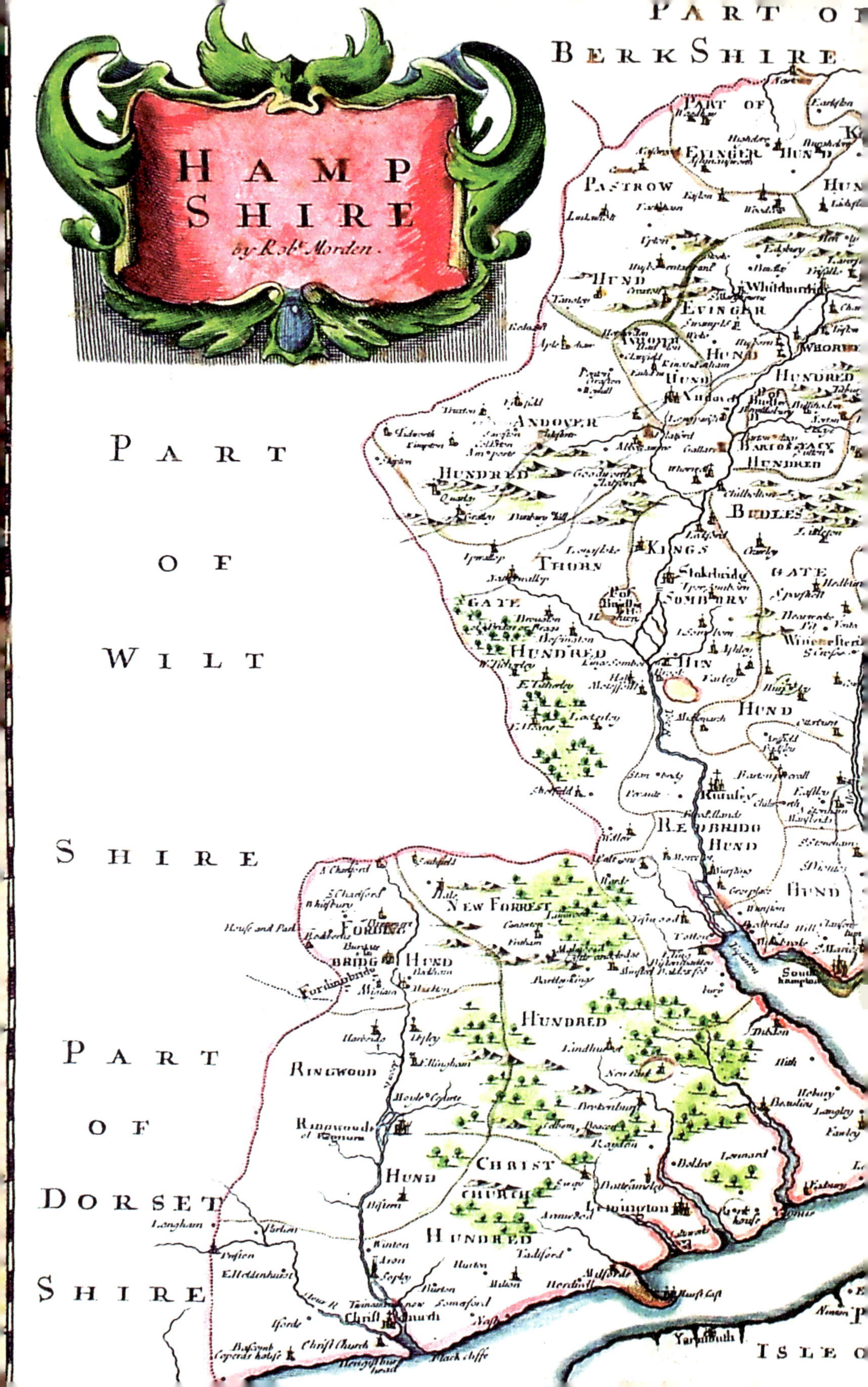

HAMP SHIRE
by Robt. Morden.
PART OF BERKSHIRE
PART OF WILT SHIRE
PART OF DORSET SHIRE
PASTROW
HUND
EVINGER
ANDOVER
HUNDRED
THORN
GATE
HUNDRED
KINGS
SOMBURY
REDBRIDG
HUND
NEW FORREST
HUNDRED
RINGWOOD
HUND
CHRIST
CHURCH
HUNDRED
Lymington
Christ Church
Yarmouth